McGraw-Hill

Dictionary of

Astronomy

Sybil P. Parker
Editor in Chief

McGraw-Hill

New York   San Francisco   Washington, D.C.   Auckland

Bogotá   Caracas   Lisbon   London   Madrid   Mexico City

Milan   Montreal   New Delhi   San Juan   Singapore

Sydney   Tokyo   Toronto

Library of Congress Cataloging in Publication Data

McGraw-Hill dictionary of astronomy / Sybil P. Parker, editor in chief.
    p.   cm.
    ISBN 0-07-052434-3 (alk. paper)
    1. Astronomy—Dictionaries.   2. Astrophysics—Dictionaries.
  3. Aerospace engineering—Dictionaries.   I. Parker, Sybil P.
  II. McGraw-Hill, Inc.
  QB14.M36   1997
  520'.3—dc21   97-5934

McGraw-Hill

A Division of The McGraw-Hill Companies

All text in this dictionary was published previously in the McGRAW-HILL DICTIONARY OF SCIENTIFIC AND TECHNICAL TERMS, Fifth Edition, copyright © 1994 by McGraw-Hill, Inc. All rights reserved.

2 3 4 5 6 7 8 9 0   DOC/DOC   9 0 2 1 0 9 8 7

ISBN 0-07-052434-3

This book is printed on recycled, acid-free paper containing a minimum of 50% recycled, de-inked fiber.

This book was set in Helvetica Bold and Novarese Book by Progressive Information Technologies, Emigsville, Pennsylvania. It was printed and bound by R. R. Donnelley & Sons Company, The Lakeside Press.

McGraw-Hill books are available at special quantity discounts to use as premiums and sales promotions, or for use in corporate training programs. For more information, please write to the Director of Special Sales, McGraw-Hill, 11 West 19th Street, New York, NY 10011. Or contact your local bookstore.

Preface

The *McGraw-Hill Dictionary of Astronomy* concentrates on the vocabulary of astronomy and related fields. With 3400 terms, it serves as a major compendium of the specialized language that is essential to understanding astronomy and related fields. The language of astronomy embraces many unique disciplines which are usually represented in specialized dictionaries and glossaries. Scientists, engineers, researchers, students, teachers, librarians, writers, and the general public will appreciate the convenience of a single comprehensive reference.

Terms and definitions in the Dictionary represent three fields: astronomy, astrophysics, and aerospace engineering. Astronomy is the science concerned with celestial bodies and with the observation and interpretation of radiation received in the vicinity of earth from the component parts of the universe. The branch of astronomy known as astrophysics treats the physical properties of celestial bodies, such as luminosity, size, mass, density, temperature, and chemical composition, as well as the origin and evolution of celestial bodies. Aerospace engineering is the branch of engineering that pertains to the design and construction of aircraft and space vehicles and of power units; this field also deals with the special problems of flight both in the earth's atmosphere and in space, such as the flight of air vehicles and the launching, guidance, and control of missiles, earth satellites, and space vehicles and probes.

The terms selected for this Dictionary are fundamental to understanding astronomy and related fields. All definitions were drawn from the *McGraw-Hill Dictionary of Scientific and Technical Terms* (5th ed., 1994). Along with definitions and pronunciations, defining terms include synonyms, acronyms, and abbreviations where appropriate. Such synonyms, acronyms, and abbreviations also appear in the alphabetical sequence as cross references to the defining terms.

The *McGraw-Hill Dictionary of Astronomy* is a reference that the editors hope will facilitate the communication of ideas and information, and thus serve the needs of readers with either professional or pedagogical interests in these disciplines.

Sybil P. Parker
Editor in Chief

Editorial Staff

How to Use the Dictionary

ALPHABETIZATION. The terms in the McGraw-Hill Dictionary of Astronomy are alphabetized on a letter-by-letter basis; word spacing, hyphen, comma, solidus, and apostrophe in a term are ignored in the sequencing. For example, an ordering of terms would be:

Agena	**airspace**
age of the moon	**Alioth**
air breakup	**all-burnt time**

FORMAT. The basic format for a defining entry provides the term in boldface and the single definition in lightface:

term Definition.

A term may be followed by multiple definitions, each introduced by a boldface number:

term **1.** Definition. **2.** Definition. **3.** Definition.

A simple cross-reference entry appears as:

term *See* another term.

A cross reference may also appear in combination with definitions:

term **1.** Definition. **2.** *See* another term.

CROSS REFERENCING. A cross-reference entry directs the user to the defining entry. For example, the user looking up "Acrux" finds:

Acrux *See* Crucis.

The user then turns to the "C" terms for the definition. Cross references are also made from variant spellings, acronyms, abbreviations, and symbols.

A/E ratio *See* absorptivity-emissivity ratio.
aestival *See* estival.
AGE *See* aerospace ground equipment.

ALSO KNOWN AS . . ., etc. A definition may conclude with a mention of a synonym of the term, a variant spelling, an abbreviation for the term, or other such information, introduced by "Also known as . . .," "Also spelled . . .," "Abbreviated . . .," "Symbolized . . .," "Derived from . . .." When a term has more than one definition, the positioning of any of these phrases conveys the extent of applicability. For example:

term **1.** Definition. Also known as synonym. **2.** Definition. Symbolized T.

In the above arrangement, "Also known as . . ." applies only to the first definition; "Symbolized . . ." applies only to the second definition.

term Also known as synonym. **1.** Definition. **2.** Definition.

In the above arrangement, "Also known as . . ." applies to both definitions.

Pronunciation Key

Vowels

a	as in bat, that
ā	as in bait, crate
ä	as in bother, father
e	as in bet, net
ē	as in beet, treat
i	as in bit, skit
ī	as in bite, light
ō	as in boat, note
ȯ	as in bought, taut
u̇	as in book, pull
ü	as in boot, pool
ə	as in but, sofa
au̇	as in crowd, power
ȯi	as in boil, spoil
yə	as in formula, spectacular
yü	as in fuel, mule

Semivowels/Semiconsonants

w	as in wind, twin
y	as in yet, onion

Stress (Accent)

ˈ   precedes syllable with primary stress

ˌ   precedes syllable with secondary stress

¦   precedes syllable with variable or indeterminate primary/secondary stress

Consonants

b	as in bib, dribble
ch	as in charge, stretch
d	as in dog, bad
f	as in fix, safe
g	as in good, signal
h	as in hand, behind
j	as in joint, digit
k	as in cast, brick
k̲	as in Bach (used rarely)
l	as in loud, bell
m	as in mild, summer
n	as in new, dent
n̲	indicates nasalization of preceding vowel
ŋ	as in ring, single
p	as in pier, slip
r	as in red, scar
s	as in sign, post
sh	as in sugar, shoe
t	as in timid, cat
th	as in thin, breath
t̲h̲	as in then, breathe
v	as in veil, weave
z	as in zoo, cruise
zh	as in beige, treasure

Syllabication

·   Indicates syllable boundary when following syllable is unstressed

Contents

A

Abell richness classes   A scale of six categories of richness into which clusters of galaxies are classified, based on the number of galaxies observed in the cluster that are not more than 2 magnitudes fainter than the third-brightest member. { 'ā· bəl 'rich·nəs ˌklas·əz }

aberration   The apparent angular displacement of the position of a celestial body in the direction of motion of the observer, caused by the combination of the velocity of the observer and the velocity of light. { ˌab·ə'rā·shən }

ablation   The intentional removal of material from a nose cone or spacecraft during high-speed movement through a planetary atmosphere to provide thermal protection to the underlying structure. { ə'blā·shən }

ablative cooling   The carrying away of heat, generated by aerodynamic heating, from a vital part by arranging for its absorption by a nonvital part. { 'a·blə·div 'kül·iŋ }

ablative shielding   A covering of material designed to reduce heat transfer to the internal structure through sublimation and loss of mass. { 'a·blə·div 'shēld·iŋ }

abort   **1.** To cut short or break off an action, operation, or procedure with an aircraft, space vehicle, or the like, especially because of equipment failure. **2.** An aircraft, space vehicle, or the like which aborts. **3.** An act or instance of aborting. { ə'bȯrt }

abort zone   The area surrounding the launch within which malperforming missiles will be contained with known and acceptable probability. { ə'bȯrt 'zōn }

absolute angle of attack   The acute angle between the chord of an airfoil at any instant in flight and the chord of that airfoil at zero lift. { 'ab·sə·lüt 'aŋ·gəl əv ə'tak }

absolute ceiling   The greatest altitude at which an aircraft can maintain level flight in a standard atmosphere and under specified conditions. { 'ab·sə·lüt 'sēl·iŋ }

absolute magnitude   **1.** A measure of the brightness of a star equal to the magnitude the star would have at a distance of 10 parsecs from the observer. **2.** The stellar magnitude any meteor would have if placed in the observer's zenith at a height of 100 kilometers. { 'ab·sə·lüt 'mag·nə·tüd }

absorptivity-emissivity ratio   In space applications, the ratio of absorptivity for solar radiation of a material to its infrared emissivity. Also known as A/E ratio. { əbˌsȯrp'tiv·əd·ē ˌē·mə'siv·ə·tē ˌrā·shō }

acceleration feedback   The use of accelerometers strategically located within the body of a missile so that they sense body accelerations during flight and interact with another device on board the missile or with a control center on the ground or in an airplane to keep the missile's speed within design limits. { ak⟨sel·ə'rā·shən 'fēd· bak }

acceleration mechanisms   The ways in which cosmic-ray and solar-flare particles may have acquired their high energies. { ak⟨sel·ə'rā·shən 'mek·ə·niz·əmz }

accretion   A process in which a star gathers molecules of interstellar gas to itself by gravitational attraction. { ə'krē·shən }

accretion disk   A viscous structure consisting of gas lost by a red giant or supergiant flowing around a companion main-sequence star or compact object (white dwarf, neutron star, or black hole). { ə'krē·shən ⟨disk }

accretion hypothesis   Any hypothesis which assumes that the earth originated by the gradual addition of solid bodies, such as meteorites, that were formerly revolving about the sun but were drawn by gravitation to the earth. { ə'krē·shən hī'päth·ə· səs }

accretion theory   A theory that the solar system originated from vortices in a disk-shaped mass. { ə'krē·shən 'thē·ə·rē }

accumulator   A device sometimes incorporated in the fuel system of a gas-turbine engine to store fuel and release it under pressure as an aid in starting. { ə'kyü· myə⟨lād·ər }

Achilles   An asteroid; member of the group known as the Trojan planets. { ə'kil·ēz }

Achilles group   See Greek group. { ə'kil·ēz ⟨grüp }

acoustic Mach meter   A device which registers data on sound propagation for the calculation of Mach number. { ə'küs·tik 'mäk ⟨mēd·ər }

acoustic theory   The linearized small-disturbance theory used to predict the approximate airflow past an airfoil when the disturbance velocities caused by the flow are small compared to the flight speed and to the speed of sound. { ə'küs·tik 'thē·ə· rē }

Acrux   See Crucis. { 'ā⟨crəks }

actinometry   The science of measurement of radiant energy, particularly that of the sun, in its thermal, chemical, and luminous aspects. { ⟨ak·tə'näm·ə·trē }

active center   A localized, transient region of the solar atmosphere in which sunspots, faculae, plages, prominences, solar flares, and so forth are observed. { 'ak·tiv 'sen· tər }

active communications satellite   Satellite which receives, regenerates, and retransmits signals between stations. { 'ak·tiv kə⟨myü·nə'kā·shənz 'sad·ə⟨līt }

active controls technology   The development of special forms of augmentation systems to stabilize airplane configurations and to limit, or tailor, the design loads that the airplane structure must support. { 'ak·tiv kən'trōlz ⟨tek'näl·ə·jē }

active galaxy   A galaxy whose central region exhibits strong emission activity, from radio to x-ray frequencies, probably as a result of gravitational collapse; this category includes M82 galaxies, Seyfert galaxies, N galaxies, and possibly quasars. { 'ak· tiv 'gal·ək·sē }

active prominence A classification of prominences of the sun; such a prominence is rapidly moving, and is the most frequent type. { 'ak·tiv 'präm·ə·nəns }

active prominence region Portions of the solar limb that display active prominences, characterized by down-flowing knots and streamers, sprays, frequent surges, and curved loops. Abbreviated APR. { 'ak·tiv 'präm·ə·nəns ˌrē·jən }

active region A localized, transient, nonuniform region on the sun's surface, penetrating well down into the lower chromosphere. { 'ak·tiv 'rē·jən }

active satellite A satellite which transmits a signal. { 'ak·tiv 'sad·ə,līt }

active Sun The Sun during the portion of its 11-year cycle in which sunspots, flares, prominences, and variations in radio-frequency emission reach their maximum. { 'ak·tiv 'sən }

actual exhaust velocity **1.** The real velocity of the exhaust gas leaving a nozzle as determined by accurately measuring at a specified point in the nozzle exit plane. **2.** The velocity obtained when the kinetic energy of the gas flow produces actual thrust. { 'ak·chə·wəl ig'zóst və,läs·əd·ē }

adapter skirt A flange or extension of a space vehicle that provides a ready means for fitting some object to a stage or section. { ə'dap·tər ˌskərt }

Adhara A star of spectral type B2II. Also known as ε Canis Majoris. { ə'där·ə }

adiabatic approximation The approximation that the pressure and density of gas in a star are related by the adiabatic law. { ¦ad·ē·ə¦bad·ik ə,präk·sə'mā·shən }

Adonis An asteroid with an orbital eccentricity of 0.779 and a perihelion well inside the orbit of Venus that passed about 1 × 10⁶ miles (1.6 × 10⁶ kilometers) from earth in 1936. { ə'dän·əs }

Adrastea A small satellite of Jupiter, having an orbital radius of 80,140 miles (128,980 kilometers) and radial dimensions of 7, 6, and 5 miles (12, 10, and 8 kilometers). Also known as Jupiter XV. { ə'dras·tē·ə }

advance of the perihelion The slow rotation of the major axis of a planet's orbit in the direction of the planet's revolution, due to gravitational interactions with other planets and other effects such as those of general relativity. { əd'vans əv thə ¦per·ə¦hēl·yən }

aeon A billion (10⁹) years. Also spelled eon. { 'ē,än }

A/E ratio See absorptivity-emissivity ratio. { ¦ā¦ē ˌrā·shō }

aerial sound ranging The process of locating an aircraft by means of the sounds it emits. { 'e·rē·əl 'saund ˌranj·iŋ }

aeroduct A ramjet type of engine designed to scoop up ions and electrons freely available in the outer reaches of the atmosphere or in the atmospheres of other spatial bodies and, by a metachemical process within the engine duct, to expel particles derived from the ions and electrons as a propulsive jetstream. { 'e·rō,dəkt }

aerodynamic center A point on a cross section of a wing or rotor blade through which the forces of drag and lift are acting and about which the pitching moment coefficient is practically constant. { ˌe·ro·dī'nam·ik 'sent·ər }

aerodynamic characteristics The performance of a given airfoil profile as related to

3

lift and drag, to angle of attack, and to velocity, density, viscosity, compressibility, and so on. { ˌe·ro·dī′nam·ik ˌkar·ik·tə′ris·tiks }

aerodynamic chord   A straight line intersecting or touching an airfoil profile at two points; specifically, that part of such a line between two points of intersection. { ˌe·ro·dī′nam·ik ′kȯrd }

aerodynamic configuration   The form of an aircraft, incorporating desirable aerodynamic qualities. { ˌe·rō·dī′nam·ik kən‚fig·yə′rā·shən }

aerodynamic control   A control surface whose use causes local aerodynamic forces. { ˌe·ro·dī′nam·ik kən′trōl }

aerodynamic instability   An unstable state caused by oscillations of a structure that are generated by spontaneous and more or less periodic fluctuations in the flow, particularly in the wake of the structure. { ˌe·ro·dī′nam·ik ‚in·stə′bil·əd·ē }

aerodynamic missile   A missile with surfaces which produce lift during flight. { ˌe·ro·dī′nam·ik ′mis·əl }

aerodynamic moment   The torque about the center of gravity of a missile or projectile moving through the atmosphere, produced by any aerodynamic force which does not act through the center of gravity. { ˌe·ro·dī′nam·ik ′mō·mənt }

aerodynamic stability   The property of a body in the air, such as an aircraft or rocket, to maintain its attitude, or to resist displacement, and if displaced, to develop aerodynamic forces and moments tending to restore the original condition. { ˌe·ro·dī′nam·ik stə′bil·əd·ē }

aerodynamic time   A characteristic time equal to the mass of an aircraft divided by the product of the gross wing area, the density of air, and the air speed. { ˌe·ro·dī′nam·ik ′tīm }

aerodynamic vehicle   A device, such as an airplane or glider, capable of flight only within a sensible atmosphere and relying on aerodynamic forces to maintain flight. { ˌe·ro·dī′nam·ik ′vē·ə·kəl }

aerodyne   Any heavier-than-air craft that derives its lift in flight chiefly from aerodynamic forces, such as the conventional airplane, glider, or helicopter. { ′e·rōˌdīn }

aerofoil   See airfoil. { ′e·rōˌfȯil }

aeromotor   An engine designed to provide motive power for an aircraft. { ′e·rōˌmōd·ər }

aeronaut   A person who operates or travels in an airship or balloon. { ′e·rōˌnȯt }

aeronautical engineering   The branch of engineering concerned primarily with the design and construction of aircraft structures and power units, and with the special problems of flight in the atmosphere. { e·rə′nȯd·ə·kəl en·jə′nir·iŋ }

aerophysics   The physics dealing with the design, construction, and operation of aerodynamic devices. { ¦e·rōⵏfiz·iks }

aeropulse engine   See pulsejet engine. { ′e·rōˌpəls ′en·jən }

aeroservoelasticity   The study of the interaction of automatic flight controls on aircraft and aeroelastic response and stability. { ¦e·rōˌsər·vōⵏi·las′tis·əd·ē }

aerospace ground equipment Support equipment for air and space vehicles. Abbreviated AGE. { ¦e·rō¦spās 'graùnd i,kwip·mənt }

aerospace vehicle A vehicle capable of flight both within and outside the sensible atmosphere. { ¦e·rō¦spās 'vē·ə·kəl }

aerostat Any aircraft that derives its buoyancy or lift from a lighter-than-air gas contained within its envelope or one of its compartments; for example, ships and balloons. { 'e·rō,stat }

aestival See estival. { 'es·tə·vəl }

afterbody 1. A companion body that trails a satellite. 2. A section or piece of a rocket or spacecraft that enters the atmosphere unprotected behind the nose cone or other body that is protected for entry. 3. The afterpart of a vehicle. { 'af·tər,bäd·ē }

afterburner A device for augmenting the thrust of a jet engine by burning additional fuel in the uncombined oxygen in the gases from the turbine. { 'af·tər,bər·nər }

afterburning The function of an afterburner. { 'af·tər,bərn·iŋ }

afterburnt Having completed transformation of the solid propellant to gaseous form. { 'af·tər,bərnt }

afterflaming With liquid- or solid-propellant rocket thrust chambers, a characteristic low-grade combustion that takes place in the thrust chamber assembly and around its nozzle exit after the main propellant flow has been stopped. { 'af·tər,flām·iŋ }

Agamemnon An asteroid, one of a group of Trojan planets whose periods of revolution are approximately equal to that of Jupiter, or about 12 years. { ,ag·ə'mem·nən }

AGE See aerospace ground equipment.

Agena See Centauri. { ə'jen·ə }

age of the moon The elapsed time, usually expressed in days, since the last new moon. { 'āj əv thə 'mün }

agricultural aircraft Aircraft adapted or designed for use in agriculture and forestry. { ¦ag·rə¦kəl·chə·rəl 'er,kraft }

aileron The hinged rear portion of an aircraft wing moved differentially on each side of the aircraft to obtain lateral or roll control moments. { 'āl·ə,rän }

air base 1. In the U.S. Air Force, an establishment, comprising an airfield, its installations, facilities, personnel, and activities, for the flight operation, maintenance, and supply of aircraft and air organizations. 2. A similar establishment belonging to any other air force. 3. In a restricted sense, only the physical installation. { 'er ,bās }

airboat See seaplane. { 'er,bōt }

airborne Of equipment and material, carried or transported by aircraft. { 'er,bòrn }

air breakup The breakup of a test reentry body within the atmosphere. { 'er 'brāk,əp }

aircraft Any structure, machine, or contrivance, especially a vehicle, designed to be supported by the air, either by the dynamic action of the air upon the surfaces of the structure or object or by its own buoyancy. Also known as air vehicle. { 'er,kraft }

aircraft axes   *See* axes of an aircraft. { 'er‚kraft 'ak‚sēz }

aircraft bonding   Electrically connecting together all of the metal structure of the aircraft, including the engine and metal covering on the wiring. { 'er‚kraft 'bänd·iŋ }

aircraft engine   A component of an aircraft that develops either shaft horsepower or thrust and incorporates design features advantageous for aircraft propulsion. { 'er‚kraft ‚en·jən }

aircraft instrumentation   Electronic, gyroscopic, and other instruments for detecting, measuring, recording, telemetering, processing, or analyzing different values or quantities in the flight of an aircraft. { 'er‚kraft ‚in·strə·mən'tā·shən }

aircraft instrument panel   A coordinated instrument display arranged to provide the pilot and flight crew with information about the aircraft's speed, altitude, attitude, heading, and condition; also advises the pilot of the aircraft's response to his control efforts. { 'er‚kraft 'in·strə‚mənt ‚pan·əl }

aircraft propeller   A hub-and-multiblade device for transforming the rotational power of an aircraft engine into thrust power for the purpose of moving an aircraft through the air. { 'er‚kraft prə‚pel·ər }

aircraft propulsion   The means, other than gliding, whereby an aircraft moves through the air; effected by the rearward acceleration of matter through the use of a jet engine or by the reactive thrust of air on a propeller. { 'er‚kraft prə‚pəl·shən }

aircraft pylon   A suspension device externally installed under the wing or fuselage of an aircraft; it is aerodynamically designed to fit the configuration of specific aircraft so as to create the least amount of drag; it provides a means of attaching fuel tanks, bombs, rockets, torpedoes, rocket motors, or machine-gun pods. { 'er‚kraft 'pī‚län }

aircraft testing   The subjecting of an aircraft or its components to simulated or actual flight conditions while measuring and recording pertinent physical phenomena that indicate operating characteristics. { 'er‚kraft ‚test·iŋ }

airfoil   A body of such shape that the force exerted on it by its motion through a fluid has a larger component normal to the direction of motion than along the direction of motion; examples are the wing of an airplane and the blade of a propeller. Also known as aerofoil. { 'er‚fóil }

airfoil profile   The closed curve defining the external shape of the cross section of an airfoil. Also known as airfoil section; airfoil shape; wing section. { 'er‚fóil 'prō‚fīl }

airfoil section   *See* airfoil profile. { 'er‚fóil ‚sek·shən }

airfoil shape   *See* airfoil profile. { 'er‚fóil ‚shāp }

airframe   The basic assembled structure of any aircraft or rocket vehicle, except lighter-than-air craft, necessary to support aerodynamic forces and inertia loads imposed by the weight of the vehicle and contents. { 'er‚frām }

air intake   An open end of an air duct or similar projecting structure so that the motion of the aircraft is utilized in capturing air to be conducted to an engine or ventilator. { 'er ¦in‚tāk }

air launch   Launching from an aircraft in the air. { 'er ‚lónch }

airlift   **1.** To transport passengers and cargo by the use of aircraft. **2.** The total weight of personnel or cargo carried by air. { 'er‚lift }

air log   A distance-measuring device used especially in certain guided missiles to control range. { 'er ˌläg }

airplane   A heavier-than-air vehicle designed to use the pressures created by its motion through the air to lift and transport useful loads. { 'erˌplān }

air propeller   A hub-and-multiblade device for changing rotational power of an aircraft engine into thrust power for the purpose of propelling an aircraft through the air. { 'er prəˌpel·ər }

Air Pump   See Antlia. { 'er ˌpəmp }

airship   A propelled and steered aerial vehicle, dependent on gases for flotation. { 'erˌship }

airspace   **1.** The space occupied by an aircraft formation or used in a maneuver. **2.** The area around an airplane in flight that is considered an integral part of the plane in order to prevent collision with another plane; the space depends on the speed of the plane. { 'erˌspās }

airspeed   The speed of an airborne object relative to the atmosphere; in a calm atmosphere, airspeed equals ground speed. { 'erˌspēd }

air stack   A group of planes flying at prescribed heights while waiting to land at an airport. { 'er ˌstak }

airstart   An act or instance of starting an aircraft's engine while in flight, especially a jet engine after flameout. { 'erˌstärt }

air strip   See landing strip. { 'er ˌstrip }

air taxi   A carrier of passengers and cargo engaged in charter flights, feeder air services to large airline facilities, or contract airmail transportation. { 'er ˌtak·sē }

air transportation   The use of aircraft, predominantly airplanes, to move passengers and cargo. { ˈer ˌtranz·pər'tā·shən }

air vane   A vane that acts in the air, as contrasted to a jet vane which acts within a jetstream. { 'er ˌvān }

air vehicle   See aircraft. { 'er ˈvē·ə·kəl }

Aitken's formula   The expression used to determine the separation limit for true binary stars: $\log p'' = 2.5 - 0.2m$, where p'' = limit, m = magnitude. { ˈāt·kənz ˈfórm·yə·lə }

Al Velorum stars   See dwarf Cepheids. { ˈāˈlī və'lór·əm ˌstärz }

Alcor   The star 80 Ursae Majoris. { 'alˌkór }

Aldebaran   A red giant star of visual magnitude 1.06, spectral classification K5-III, in the constellation Taurus; the star α Tauri. { al'deb·ə·rən }

Algenib   A star in the constellation Pegasus. { ˌal'jen·əb }

Algol   An eclipsing variable star of spectral classification B8 in the constellation Perseus; the star β Persei. Also known as Demon Star. { 'alˌgól }

Algol symbiotic   A symbiotic star consisting of a red giant, a main-sequence star, and

7

Alioth

an accretion disk of gas from the red giant that forms around the main-sequence star and is heated by it. { 'al͵gól ͵sim·bē'äd·ik }

Alioth   Traditional name for a second-magnitude star in the Big Dipper; the star ε Ursae Majoris. { 'al·ē͵äth }

all-burnt time   The point in time at which a rocket has consumed its propellants. { ¦ól ¦bərnt ͵tīm }

all-burnt velocity   See burnout velocity. { ¦ól ¦bərnt və'läs·əd·ē }

all-weather aircraft   Aircraft that are designed or equipped to perform by day or night under any weather conditions. { 'ól ¦weth·ər 'er͵kraft }

all-weather fighter   A fighter aircraft equipped with radar and other special devices which enable it to intercept its target in the dark, or in daylight weather conditions that do not permit visual interception; it is usually a multiplace (pilot plus navigator-observer) airplane. { 'ól ¦weth·ər 'fīd·ər }

almucantar   See parallel of altitude. { ¦al·myü¦kan·tər }

Alnilam   A star in the constellation Orion. { al'nil·əm }

α Aquilae   See Altair. { ¦al·fə 'ak·wə͵lē }

α Boötis   See Arcturus. { ¦al·fə bō'ō·təs }

α Canis Minoris   See Procyon. { ¦al·fə ͵kā·nəs 'mī·nər·is }

α Carinae   See Canopus. { ¦al·fə kə'rī͵nē }

α Centauri   A double star, the brightest in the constellation Centaurus; apart from the sun, it is the nearest bright star to earth, about 4.3 light-years away; spectral classification G2. Also known as Rigil Kent. { ¦al·fə sen'tó·rē }

α Crucis   A double star in the constellation Crux that is 220 light-years from the sun; spectral classification BO.5V. Also known as Acrux. { ¦al·fə 'krü·səs }

α Lyrae   See Vega. { ¦al·fə 'lī·rə }

α Piscis Australis   The brightest star in the southern constellation Piscis Australis. Also known as Fomalhaut. { ¦al·fə 'pis·kəs 'ós·trə·ləs }

Alphonsus   A moon crater. { al'fän·səs }

Altair   A star that is 16.5 light-years from the sun; spectral type A7IV-V. Also known as α Aquilae. { al'tīr or 'al͵ter }

Altar   See Ara. { 'al͵tär }

altitude circle   See parallel of altitude. { 'al·tə͵tüd ͵sər·kəl }

altitude valve   A valve that adjusts the composition of the air-fuel mixture admitted into an airplane carburetor as the air density varies with altitude. { 'al·tə͵tüd·͵valv }

altitude wind tunnel   A wind tunnel in which the air pressure, temperature, and humidity can be varied to simulate conditions at different altitudes. { 'al'tə ͵tüd 'wind ͵tən·əl }

Amalthea   The innermost known satellite of Jupiter, orbiting at a mean distance of 1.13 × 10⁵ miles (1.82 × 10⁵ kilometers); it has a diameter of about 150 miles (240 kilometers). Also known as Jupiter V. { ˌäm·äl′thē·ə }

American Ephemeris and Nautical Almanac   An annual publication of the U.S. Naval Observatory containing tables of the predicted positions of various celestial bodies and other data of use to astronomers and navigators. { ə′mer·ə·kən i′fem·ə·rəs an ′nȯd·i·kəl ′ȯl·məˌnak }

AM Herculis star   See polar. { ¦ā¦em ′hər·kyə·ləs ¦stär }

Amor   An asteroid with an orbital eccentricity of 0.448 that approached to about 1 × 10⁷ miles (1.6 × 10⁷ kilometers) from earth. { ′äˌmȯr }

Amor object   Any asteroid which crosses the orbit of Mars. { ′äˌmȯr ′äb·jekt }

Amphitrite   An asteroid with a diameter of about 120 miles (200 kilometers), mean distance from the sun of 2.554 astronomical units, and S-type surface composition. { ′am·fə′trīˌdē }

amplitude   The range in brightness of a variable star, usually expressed in magnitudes. { ′am·pləˌtüd }

analemma   A figure-eight-shaped diagram on a globe showing the declination of the sun throughout the year and also the equation of time. { ˌan·ə′lem·ə }

Ananke   A small satellite of Jupiter with a diameter of about 14 miles (23 kilometers), orbiting with retrograde motion at a mean distance of 1.3 × 10⁷ miles (2.1 × 10⁷ kilometers). Also known as Jupiter XII. { ə′naŋ·kē }

And   See Andromeda.

Andr   See Andromeda.

Andromeda   A constellation with a right ascension of 1 hour and a declination of 40°N. Abbreviated And; Andr. { ˌan′dräm·ə·də }

Andromeda Galaxy   The spiral galaxy of type Sb nearest to the Milky Way. Also known as Andromeda Nebula. { ˌan′dräm·ə·də ′gal·ək·sē }

Andromeda Nebula   See Andromeda Galaxy. { ˌan′dräm·ə·də ′ne·byə·lə }

Andromedids   A meteor shower whose radiant is located near the star γ Andromedae, and which reaches its peak about November 27; associated with the Biela comet. Also known as Bielids. { ˌan′dräm·əˌdidz }

angle of attack   The angle between a reference line which is fixed with respect to an airframe (usually the longitudinal axis) and the direction of movement of the body. { ′aŋ·gəl əv ə′tak }

angle of cant   In a spin-stabilized rocket, the angle formed by the axis of a venturi tube and the longitudinal axis of the rocket. { ′aŋ·gəl əv ′kant }

angle of climb   The angle between the flight path of a climbing vehicle and the local horizontal. { ′aŋ·gəl əv ′klīm }

angle of commutation   The difference between the celestial longitudes of the sun and a planet, as observed from the earth. { ′aŋ·gəl əv ˌkäm·yə′tā·shən }

9

angle of departure

angle of departure The vertical angle, at the origin, between the line of site and the line of departure. { 'aŋ·gəl əv di'pär·chər }

angle of descent The angle between the flight path of a descending vehicle and the local horizontal. { 'aŋ·gəl əv di'sent }

angle of glide Angle of descent for an airplane or missile in a glide. { 'aŋ·gəl əv 'glīd }

angle of pitch The angle, as seen from the side, between the longitudinal body axis of an aircraft or similar body and a chosen reference line or plane, usually the horizontal plane. { 'aŋ·gəl əv 'pich }

angle of roll The angle that the lateral body axis of an aircraft or similar body makes with a chosen reference plane in rolling; usually, the angle between the lateral axis and a horizontal plane. { 'aŋ·gəl əv 'rōl }

angle of stall The angle of attack at which the flow of air begins to break away from the airfoil, the lift begins to decrease, and the drag begins to increase. Also known as stalling angle. { 'aŋ·gəl əv 'stȯl }

angle of vertical The angle on the celestial sphere between a given vertical circle and the prime vertical circle. { 'aŋ·gəl əv 'vərd·ə·kəl }

angle of yaw The angle, as seen from above, between the longitudinal body axis of an aircraft, a rocket, or the like and a chosen reference direction. Also known as yaw angle. { 'aŋ·gəl əv 'yȯ }

angular diameter The angle subtended at the observer by a diameter of a distant spherical body which is perpendicular to the line between the observer and the center of the body. { 'an·gyə·lər ˌdī'am·əd·ər }

anisotropy The departure of the cosmic microwave radiation from equal intensity in all directions. { ¦aˌnī'sä·trə·pē }

annual aberration Aberration caused by the velocity of the earth's revolution about the sun. { 'an·yə·wəl ab·ə'rā·shən }

annual equation A variation in the moon's apparent motion caused by variations in the distance of the earth from the sun during the course of the year. { 'an·yə·wəl i'kwā·zhən }

annual parallax The apparent displacement of a celestial body viewed from two separated observation points whose base line is the radius of the earth's orbit. Also known as heliocentric parallax. { 'an·yə·wəl 'par·əˌlaks }

annual variation The change in the right ascension and declination of a star during one year, due to the combined effect of the star's proper motion and the precession of the equinoxes. { 'an·yə·wəl ver·ē'ā·shən }

annular eclipse An eclipse in which a thin ring of the source of light appears around the obscuring body. { 'an·yə·lər i'klips }

anomalistic month The average period of revolution of the moon from perigee to perigee, a period of 27 days 13 hours 18 minutes 33.2 seconds. { əˈnäm·əˈlis·tik 'mənth }

anomalistic period The interval between two successive perigee passages of a satellite

10

in orbit about a primary. Also known as perigee-to-perigee period. { əˌnäm·əˌlis·tik 'pir·ē·əd }

anomalistic year   The period of one revolution of the earth about the sun from perihelion to perhihelion; 365 days 6 hours 13 minutes 53.0 seconds in 1900 and increasing at the rate of 0.26 second per century. { əˌnäm·əˌlis·tik 'yēr }

anomaly   In celestial mechanics, the angle between the radius vector to an orbiting body from its primary (the focus of the orbital ellipse) and the line of apsides of the orbit, measured in the direction of travel, from the point of closest approach to the primary (perifocus). Also known as true anomaly. { ə'näm·ə·lē }

ansae   1. The ends of the rings of Saturn, as seen from the earth. 2. Opposing extension or knots of a celestial object, such as a planetary nebula or lenticular galaxy. { 'an·sē }

Ant   See Antlia.

Antares   A red supergiant variable binary star of stellar magnitude 0.9, 520 light-years from the sun, spectral classification M1-Ib, in the constellation Scorpius; the star α Scorpii. { an'tar·ēz }

ante meridian   1. A section of the celestial meridian; it lies below the horizon, and the nadir is included. 2. Before noon, or the period of time between midnight (0000) and noon (1200). { ˌan·tē məˌrid·ē·ən }

anthelic arc   A rare type of halo phenomenon appearing in an area 180° from the sun's azimuth and at the sun's elevation. { ant'hē·lik 'ärk }

anthelion   A luminous white spot which occasionally appears on the parhelic circle 180° in azimuth away from the sun. Also known as counter sun. { ant'hēl·yən }

anthropic principle   The assertion that the presence of intelligent life on earth places limits on the many ways the universe could have developed and could have caused the conditions of temperature that prevail today. { an'thräp·ik 'prin·sə·pəl }

anticenter   The direction in the sky opposite to that of the center of the Galaxy, located in the constellation Auriga. { ˌan·tē'sent·ər }

anticrepuscular rays   Extensions of crepuscular rays, converging toward a point 180° from the sun. { ˌan·tē·kri'pəs·kyə·lər 'rāz }

antidrag   1. Describing structural members in an aircraft or missile that are designed or built to resist the effects of drag. 2. Referring to a force acting against the force of drag. { ˌan·tē'drag }

anti-icing   The prevention of the formation of ice upon any object, especially aircraft, by means of windshield sprayer, addition of antifreeze materials to the carburetor, or heating the wings and tail. { ˌan·tē'īs·iŋ }

antinode   Either of the two points on an orbit where a line in the orbit plane, perpendicular to the line of nodes and passing through the focus, intersects the orbit. { 'an·təˌnōd }

antisolar point   The point on the celestial sphere which lies directly opposite the sun from the observer, that is, on the line from the sun through the observer. { ˌan·tēˌsō·lər ˌpóint }

11

antantail

antitail A structure occasionally observed in comets that appears to extend from the coma toward the sun, and usually has the appearance of a spike. { 'an·tē͵tāl }

Antlia A constellation with a right ascension of 10 hours and declination of 35°S. Abbreviated Ant. Also known as Air Pump. { 'ant·lē·ə }

Antonadi scale A scale for measuring seeing conditions, ranging from I for perfect conditions to V for very bad conditions. { ͵än·tō'näd·ē ͵skāl }

A-1 time A particular atomic time scale, established by the U.S. Naval Observatory, with the origin on January 1, 1958, at zero hours Universal Time and with the unit (second) equal to 9,192,631,770 cycles of cesium at zero field. { ͵ā ͵wən ͵tīm }

apareon The point on a Mars-centered orbit where a satellite is at its greatest distance from Mars. { ͵a'par·ē·ən }

apastron That point of the orbit of one member of a binary star system at which the stars are farthest apart. { ͵a'pas·trən }

aphelion The point on a planetary orbit farthest from the sun. { ə'fēl·yən }

aphesperian The farthest point of a satellite in its orbit about Venus. { ͵a·fə'spir·ē·ən }

apoapsis The point in an orbit farthest from the center of attraction. { ͵ap·ō͵ap·səs }

apocenter See apofocus. { 'ap·ə͵sen·tər }

apocronus The farthest point of a satellite in its orbit about Saturn. Also known as aposaturnium. { ͵ap·ə͵krō·nəs }

apofocus The point on an elliptic orbit at the greatest distance from the principal focus. Also known as apocenter. { ͵ap·ə͵fō·kəs }

apogalacteum The point at which a celestial body is farthest from the center of the Milky Way. { ͵ap·ə·gə'lak·tē·əm }

apogee That point in an orbit at which the moon or an artificial satellite is most distant from the earth; the term is sometimes loosely applied to positions of satellites of other planets. { 'ap·ə͵jē }

apojove The farthest point of a satellite in its orbit about Jupiter. { ͵ap·ə͵jōv }

Apollo 1. To the Greeks, the planet Mercury when it was a morning star. 2. An asteroid with a very eccentric orbit and perihelion inside the orbit of Venus that passed about 1.8 × 10⁶ miles (3 × 10⁶ kilometers) from earth in 1932. { ə'päl·ō }

Apollo object Any asteroid which crosses the earth's orbit. { ə'päl·ō 'äb·jikt }

Apollo program The scientific and technical program of the United States that involved placing men on the moon and returning them safely to earth. { ə'päl·ō ͵prō·grəm }

apolune Farthest point of a satellite in an elliptic orbit about the moon. Also known as aposelene. { ͵ap·ə͵lün }

apomercurian The farthest point of a satellite in its orbit about Mercury. { ͵ap·ə͵mər'kyür·ē·ən }

apoplutonian The farthest point of a satellite in its orbit about Pluto. { ͵ap·ə·plü'tōn·ē·ən }

12

apoposeidon   The farthest point of a satellite in its orbit about Neptune. { ˈap·ə· pə'sīd·ən }

aposaturnium   *See* apocronus. { ˈap·ə·sə'tər·nē·əm }

aposelene   *See* apolune. { ˈap·ə·sə'lēn }

apouranian   The farthest point of a satellite in its orbit about Uranus. { ˈap·ō'yü'rān· ē·ən }

apparent   A term used to designate certain measured or measurable astronomic quantities to refer them to real or visible objects, such as the sun or a star. { ə'pa·rənt }

apparent horizon   *See* horizon. { ə'pa·rənt hə'rīz·ən }

apparent libration in longitude   *See* lunar libration. { ə'pa·rənt lī'brā·shən in 'län· jə'tüd }

apparent magnitude   An index of a star's brightness relative to that of the other stars; it does not take into account the difference in distance between the stars and is not an indication of the star's true luminosity. { ə'pa·rənt 'mag·nə'tüd }

apparent noon   Twelve o'clock apparent time, or the instant the apparent sun is over the upper branch of the meridian. { ə'pa·rənt 'nün }

apparent place   *See* apparent position. { ə'pa·rənt 'plās }

apparent position   The position on the celestial sphere at which a heavenly body (or a space vehicle) would be seen from the center of the earth at a particular time. Also known as apparent place. { ə'pa·rənt pə'sish·ən }

apparent solar day   The duration of one rotation of the earth on its axis with respect to the apparent sun. Also known as true solar day. { ə'pa·rənt ˈsō·lər 'dā }

apparent solar time   Time measured by the apparent diurnal motion of the sun. Also known as apparent time; true solar time. { ə'pa·rənt ˈso·lər 'tīm }

apparent sun   The sun as it appears to an observer. Also known as true sun. { ə'pa· rənt 'sən }

apparition   A period during which a planet, asteroid, or comet is observable, generally between two successive conjunctions of the body with the sun. { ˌap·ə'rish·ən }

applications technology satellite   Any artificial satellite in the National Aeronautics and Space Administration program for the evaluation of advanced techniques and equipment for communications, meteorological, and navigation satellites. Abbreviated ATS. { ˌap·lə'kā·shənz ˈtek'näl·ə·jē ˈsad·ə,līt }

appulse   1. The near approach of one celestial body to another on the celestial sphere, as in occultation or conjunction. 2. A penumbral eclipse of the moon. { ə'pəls }

apron   A protective device specially designed to cover an area surrounding the fuel inlet on a rocket or spacecraft. { 'ā·prən }

Aps   *See* Apus.

apse   *See* apsis. { aps }

apsidal motion   The precession of the periastron of a binary system in the orbital plane of the two stars, resulting from tidal gravitational moments. { 'ap·sə·dəl 'mō·shən }

apsis   In celestial mechanics, either of the two orbital points nearest or farthest from the center of attraction. Also known as apse. { 'ap·səs }

APU   See auxiliary power unit.

Apus   A constellation with a right ascension of 16 hours and declination of 75°S. Abbreviated Aps. { 'ā·pəs }

Aqil   See Aquila.

Aql   See Aquila.

Aqr   See Aquarius.

Aquarius   A constellation with a right ascension of 23 hours and declination of 15°S. Abbreviated Aqr. Also known as Water Bearer. { ə'kwer·ē·əs }

Aquila   A constellation with a right ascension of 20 hours and declination of 5°N. Abbreviated Aqil; Aql. { 'ak·wə·lə }

Ara   A constellation with a right ascension of 17 hours and declination of 55°S. Also known as Altar. { 'ä·rə }

Arago distance   The angular distance from the antisolar point to the Arago point. { 'a·rə‚gō 'dis·təns }

Arc   A radio source consisting of two bundles of parallel filaments adjoining the source Sagittarius A near the center of the Milky Way Galaxy. { ärk }

archeoastronomy   The study which attempts to reconstruct the astronomical knowledge and activity of prehistoric people and its influence on their cultures and societies. { ¦är·kē·ō·ə'strän·ə·mē }

Archer   See Sagittarius. { 'är·chər }

arc jet engine   An electromagnetic propulsion engine used to supply motive power for flight; hydrogen and ammonia are used as the propellant, and some plasma is formed as the result of electric-arc heating. { ¦ärk ¦jet 'en·jən }

Arcturus   A star that is 36 light-years from the sun; spectral classification K2IIIp. Also known as α Boötes. { ‚ärk'tùr·əs }

areal velocity   In celestial mechanics, the area swept out by the radius vector per unit time. { 'er·ē·əl və'läs·əd·ē }

area rule   A prescribed method of design for obtaining minimum zero-lift drag for a given aerodynamic configuration, such as a wing-body configuration, at a given speed. { 'er·ē·ə ‚rül }

areocentric   With Mars as a center. { ‚ar·ē·ō'sen·trik }

areodesy   Determination, by observation and measurement, of the exact positions of points on, and the figures and areas of large portions of, the surface of the planet Mars, or the shape and size of the planet Mars. { 'ar·ē·ō‚des·ē }

areographic   Referring to positions on Mars measured in latitude from the planet's equator and in longitude from a reference meridian. { ‚ar·ē·ō'graf·ik }

14

areography   The study of the surface features of Mars, or its geography. { ˌarˈēˈägˈrəˈ fē }

areology   The scientific study related to the properties of Mars. { ˌarˈēˈälˈəˈjē }

Ares   The planet Mars. { ˈerˌēz }

Arethusa   An asteroid with a diameter of about 126 miles (210 kilometers), mean distance from the sun of 3.069 astronomical units, and C-type surface composition. { ˌarˈəˈthüˈzə }

Arg   See Argo.

Argelander method   A technique to estimate the brightness of variable stars; it involves estimating the difference in magnitude between the variable stars as compared to one or more stars that are invariable. { ˈärˈgəˌlandˈər ˌmethˈəd }

Argo   The large Ptolemy constellation; a southern constellation, now divided into four groups (Carina, Pupis, Vela, and Pyxis Nautica). Abbreviated Arg. Also known as Ship. { ˈärˈgō }

argument   An angle or arc, as in argument of perigee. { ˈärˈgyəˈmənt }

argument of latitude   The angular distance measured in the orbit plane from the ascending node to the orbiting object; the sum of the argument of perigee and the true anomaly. { ˈärˈgyəˈmənt əv ˈladˈəˌtüd }

argument of perigee   The angle or arc, as seen from a focus of an elliptical orbit, from the ascending node to the closest approach of the orbiting body to the focus; the angle is measured in the orbital plane in the direction of motion of the orbiting body. Also known as argument of perihelion. { ˈärˈgyəˈmənt əv ˈperˈəˈjē }

argument of perihelion   See argument of perigee. { ˈarˈgyəˈmənt əv ˈperˈəˈhēlˈyən }

Ari   See Aries.

Ariel   A satellite of the planet Uranus orbiting at a mean distance of 119,000 miles (192,000 kilometers). { ˈarˈēˈəl }

Aries   A constellation with a right ascension of 3 hours and declination of 20°N. Abbreviated Ari. Also known as Ram. { ˈerˌēz }

Aristarchus   A crater on the moon. { ˌarˈəˈstärˈkəs }

arm population   See population I. { ˈärm ˌpäpˈyəˌläˈshən }

arrester hook   A hook in the tail section of an airplane; used to engage the arrester wires on an aircraft carrier's deck. { əˈresˈtər ˌhuk }

Arrow   See Sagitta. { ˈarˈō }

arrow wing   An aircraft wing of V-shaped planform, either tapering or of constant chord, suggesting a stylized arrowhead. { ˈarˈōˌrüt ˌwiŋ }

artificial asteroid   An object made by humans and placed in orbit about the sun. { ˈärdˈəˈfishˈəl ˈasˈtəˌróid }

artificial feel   A type of force feedback incorporated in the control system of an aircraft or spacecraft whereby a portion of the forces acting on the control surfaces are transmitted to the cockpit controls. { ¦ärd·ə¦fish·əl 'fēl }

artificial gravity   A simulated gravity established within a space vehicle by rotation or acceleration. { ¦ärd·ə¦fish·əl 'grav·əd·ē }

artificial satellite   Any human-made object placed in a near-periodic orbit in which it moves mainly under the gravitational influence of one celestial body, such as the earth, sun, another planet, or a planet's moon. { ¦ärd·ə¦fish·əl 'sad·ə‚līt }

ascending node   Also known as northbound node. **1.** The point at which a planet, planetoid, or comet crosses to the north side of the ecliptic. **2.** The point at which a satellite crosses to the north side of the equatorial plane of its primary. { ə'send·iŋ ¦nōd }

ascent   Motion of a craft in which the path is inclined upward with respect to the horizontal. { ə'sent }

ashen light   A faint, luminous glow sometimes observed over the right side of Venus when it is close to inferior conjunction, probably due to electrical disturbances in the ionosphere of Venus. { 'ash·ən ¦līt }

aspect   The apparent position of a celestial body relative to another; particularly, the apparent position of the moon or a planet relative to the sun. { 'a‚spekt }

aspect ratio   The ratio of the square of the span of an airfoil to the total airfoil area, or the ratio of its span to its mean chord. { 'a‚spekt ‚rā·shō }

assault aircraft   Powered aircraft, including helicopters, which move assault troops and cargo into an objective area and which provide for their resupply. { ə'sȯlt 'er‚kraft }

assisted takeoff   A takeoff of an aircraft or a missile by using a supplementary source of power, usually rockets. { ə'sis·təd 'tāk‚ȯf }

association   A sparsely populated grouping of very young stars that appear to have had a common origin and have not yet had time to disperse. { ə‚sō·sē'ā·shən }

A star   See A-type star. { 'ā ‚stär }

asterism   A constellation or small group of stars. { 'as·tə‚riz·əm }

asteroid   One of the many small celestial bodies revolving around the sun, most of the orbits being between those of Mars and Jupiter. Also known as minor planet; planetoid. { 'as·tə‚rȯid }

asteroid belt   The region between 2.1 and 3.5 astronomical units from the sun where most of the asteroids are found. { 'as·tə‚rȯid ‚belt }

astral   Characteristic of a specific star or stars; stellar is the accepted term. { 'as·trəl }

astral dome   See astrodome. { 'as·trəl ‚dōm }

astre fictif   Any of several fictitious stars assumed to move along the celestial equator at uniform rates corresponding to the speeds of the several harmonic constituents of the tide-producing force. { 'as·tər 'fik‚tif }

astro-   A prefix meaning star or stars and, by extension, sometimes used as the equivalent of celestial, as in astronautics. { 'as·trō }

16

astrochemistry The science that applies the principles of chemistry to matter in space. { ˈas·trō′kem·ə·strē }

astrochronology The use of stellar phenomena in chronology. { ˈas·trō·krə′näl·ə·jē }

astrodome A transparent dome in the fuselage or body of an aircraft or spacecraft intended primarily to permit taking celestial observations in navigating. Also known as astral dome; navigation dome. { ′as·trō‚dōm }

astrodynamics 1. The practical application of celestial mechanics, astroballistics, propulsion theory, and allied fields to the problem of planning and directing the trajectories of space vehicles. 2. The dynamics of celestial objects. { ‚as·trō·dī′nam·iks }

astrogeology The science that applies the principles of geology, geochemistry, and geophysics to the moon and planets other than the earth. { ‚as·trō‚jē′äl·ə·jē }

astrograph A telescope designed to be used exclusively for astronomical photography. { ′as·trō‚graf }

astrographic position See astrometric position. { ˈas·trō‚graf·ik pə′zish·ən }

astrograph mean time A form of mean time, used in setting an astrograph; mean-time setting of 1200 occurs when the local hour angle of Aries is 0°. { ′as·trō‚graf ˈmēn ′tīm }

astrometric binary star A binary star that may be distinguished from a single star only from the variable proper motion of one of its components. { ˈas·trəˈme·trik ′bī‚ner·ē ′stär }

astrometric position The position of a heavenly body or space vehicle on the celestial sphere corrected for aberration but not for planetary aberration. Also known as astrographic position. { ˈas·trəˈme·trik pə′zish·ən }

astrometry The branch of astronomy dealing with the geometrical relations of the celestial bodies and their real and apparent motions. { ə′sträm·ə·trē }

astronaut In United States terminology, a person who rides in a space vehicle. { ′as·trə‚nȯt }

astronautical engineering The engineering aspects of flight in space. { ˈas·trəˈnȯd·ə·kəl ‚en·jə′nir·iŋ }

astronautics 1. The art, skill, or activity of operating spacecraft. 2. The science of space flight. { ‚as·trə′nȯd·iks }

astronomic See astronomical. { ‚as·trə′näm·ik }

astronomical Of or pertaining to astronomy or to observations of the celestial bodies. Also known as astronomic. { ‚as·trə′näm·ə·kəl }

astronomical almanac A publication giving the tables of coordinates of a number of celestial bodies at a number of specific times during a given period. { ‚as·trə′näm·ə·kəl ′ȯl·mə‚nak }

astronomical atlas A set of maps of celestial phenomena, often developed in conjunction with an astronomical catalog, and providing a clear picture of the spatial relations between the phenomena. { ‚as·trə′näm·ə·kəl ′at·ləs }

17

astronomical catalogue A list or enumeration of astronomical data, generally ordered by increasing right ascension of the objects listed. { 'as·trə'näm·ə·kəl 'kad·əl‚äg }

astronomical constants The elements of the orbits of the bodies of the solar system, their masses relative to the sun, their size, shape, orientation, rotation, and inner constitution, and the velocity of light. { ‚as·trə'näm·ə·kəl 'kän·stəns }

astronomical coordinate system Any system of spherical coordinates serving to locate astronomical objects on the celestial sphere. { ‚as·trə'näm·ə·kəl ‚kō'órd·ə·nət ‚sis·təm }

astronomical date Designation of epoch by year, month, day, and decimal fraction. { ‚as·trə'näm·ə·kəl 'dāt }

astronomical day A mean solar day beginning at mean noon, 12 hours later than the beginning of the civil day of the same date; astronomers now generally use the civil day. { ‚as·trə'näm·ə·kəl 'dā }

astronomical distance The distance of a celestial body expressed in units such as the light-year, astronomical unit, and parsec. { ‚as·trə'näm·ə·kəl 'dis·təns }

astronomical eclipse See eclipse. { ‚as·trə'näm·ə·kəl i'klips }

astronomical ephemeris See ephemeris. { ‚as·trə'näm·ə·kəl i'fem·ə·rəs }

astronomical nutation A small periodic motion of the celestial pole of celestial bodies, including the earth, with respect to the pole of the ecliptic. { ‚as·trə'näm·ə·kəl nü'tā·shən }

astronomical observatory A building designed and equipped for making observations of astronomical phenomena. { ‚as·trə'näm·ə·kəl əb'zər·və‚tór·ē }

astronomical scintillation Any scintillation phenomena, such as irregular oscillatory motion, variation of intensity, and color fluctuation, observed in the light emanating from an extraterrestrial source. Also known as stellar scintillation. { ‚as·trə'näm·ə·kəl sint·əl'ā·shən }

astronomical time Solar time in an astronomical day that begins at noon. { ‚as·trə'näm·ə·kəl 'tīm }

astronomical triangle A spherical triangle on the celestial sphere. { ‚as·trə'näm·ə·kəl 'trī‚aŋ·gəl }

astronomical twilight The period of incomplete darkness when the center of the sun is more than 6° but not more than 18° below the celestial horizon. { ‚as·trə'näm·ə·kəl 'twī‚līt }

astronomical unit Abbreviated AU. **1.** A measure for distance within the solar system equal to the mean distance between earth and sun, that is, about 92,956,000 miles (149,598,000 kilometers). **2.** The semimajor axis of the elliptical orbit of earth. { ‚as·trə'näm·ə·kəl 'yü·nət }

astronomical year See tropical year. { ‚as·trə'näm·ə·kəl 'yir }

astrophysics A branch of astronomy that treats of the physical properties of celestial bodies, such as luminosity, size, mass, density, temperature, and chemical composition, and with their origin and evaluation. { ‚as·trō'fiz·iks }

18

Aten The first asteroid found to have a period less than that of the earth, 346.93 days, with an orbital eccentricity of 0.19. { 'ä/ten }

Aten asteroid An asteroid whose period is less than that of the earth. { 'ä/ten 'as·tə/róid }

athodyd A type of jet engine, consisting essentially of a duct or tube of varying diameter and open at both ends, which admits air at one end, compresses it by the forward motion of the engine, adds heat to it by the combustion of fuel, and discharges the resulting gases at the other end to produce thrust. { 'ath·ə/did }

Atlantic standard time See Atlantic time. { ət'lan·tik ¦stan·dərd /tīm }

Atlantic time A time zone; the fourth zone west of Greenwich. Also known as Atlantic standard time. { ət'lan·tik 'tīm }

Atlas The innermost known satellite of Saturn, which orbits at a distance of 85 × 10³ miles (137 × 10³ kilometers), just outside the A ring, and has an irregular shape with an average diameter of 20 miles (30 kilometers). { 'at·ləs }

atmospheric braking 1. Slowing down an object entering the atmosphere of the earth or other planet from space by using the drag exerted by air or other gas particles in the atmosphere. 2. The action of the drag so exerted. { ¦at·mə¦sfir·ik 'brāk·iŋ }

atmospheric entry The penetration of any planetary atmosphere by any object from outer space; specifically, the penetration of the earth's atmosphere by a crewed or uncrewed capsule or spacecraft. { ¦at·mə¦sfir·ik 'en·trē }

atomic rocket A rocket propelled by an engine in which the energy for the jetstream is to be generated by nuclear fission or fusion. Also known as nuclear rocket. { ə'täm·ik 'räk·ət }

ATS See applications technology satellite.

attack plane A multiweapon carrier aircraft which can carry bombs, torpedoes, and rockets. { ə'tak /plān }

attitude The position or orientation of an aircraft, spacecraft, and so on, either in motion or at rest, as determined by the relationship between its axes and some reference line or plane or some fixed system of reference axes. { 'ad·ə/tüd }

attitude control 1. The regulation of the attitude of an aircraft, spacecraft, and so on. 2. A device or system that automatically regulates and corrects attitude, especially of a pilotless vehicle. { 'ad·ə/tüd kən/trōl }

attitude gyro Also known as attitude indicator. 1. A gyro-operated flight instrument that indicates the attitude of an aircraft or spacecraft with respect to a reference coordinate system. 2. Any gyro-operated instrument that indicates attitude. { 'ad·ə/tüd /jī·rō }

attitude indicator See attitude gyro. { 'ad·ə/tüd 'in·də/kād·ər }

attitude jet 1. A stream of gas from a jet used to correct or alter the attitude of a flying body either in the atmosphere or in space. 2. The nozzle that directs this jetstream. { 'ad·ə/tüd /jet }

A-type star In star classification based on spectral characteristics, the type of star in whose spectrum the hydrogen absorption lines are at a maximum. Also known as A star. { 'ā/tīp /stär }

AU   See astronomical unit.

Auger shower   A very large cosmic-ray shower. Also known as extensive air shower.
{ ō'zhā ¦shaù·ər }

augmentation   The apparent increase in the semidiameter of a celestial body, as observed from the earth, as the body's altitude (angular distance above the horizon) increases, due to the reduced distance from the observer. The term is used principally in reference to the moon. { ˌȯg·mən'tā·shən }

augmentation system   An electronic servomechanism or feedback control system which provides improvements in aircraft performance or pilot handling characteristics over that of the basic unaugmented aircraft. { ˌȯg·mən'tā·shən ˌsis·təm }

augmenter tube   A tube or pipe, usually one of several, through which the exhaust gases from an aircraft reciprocating engine are directed to provide additional thrust. { ȯg'men·tər ˌtüb }

Aur   See Auriga.

Auri   See Auriga.

Auriga   A constellation with a right ascension of 6 hours and declination of 40°N. Abbreviated Aur; Auri. { ȯ'rī·gə }

Aurora   An asteroid with a diameter of about 132 miles (220 kilometers), mean distance from the sun of 3.153 astronomical units, and C-type surface composition. { ə'rȯr·ə }

auroral   The period of dusk before sunrise. { ə'rȯr·əl }

autogiro   A type of aircraft which utilizes a rotating wing (rotor) to provide lift and a conventional engine-propeller combination to propel the vehicle through the air. { ˌȯd·ō'jī·rō }

automatic stability   Stability achieved with the controls operated by automatic devices, as by an automatic pilot. { ¦ȯd·ə¦mad·ik stə'bil·əd·ē }

automatic stabilization equipment   Apparatus which automatically operates control devices to maintain an aircraft in a stable condition. { ¦ȯd·ə¦mad·ik ˌstā·bə·lə'zā·shən i,kwip·mənt }

autumn   The season of the year which is the transition period from summer to winter, occurring as the sun approaches the winter solstice; beginning is marked by the autumnal equinox. Also known as fall. { 'ȯd·əm }

autumnal   Pertaining to the season autumn. { ȯ'təm·nəl }

autumnal equinox   The point on the celestial sphere at which the sun's rays at noon are 90° above the horizon at the Equator, or at an angle of 90° with the earth's axis, and neither North nor South Pole is inclined to the sun; occurs in the Northern Hemisphere on approximately September 23 and marks the beginning of autumn. Also known as first point of Libra. { ȯ'təm·nəl 'ē·kwə,näks }

auxiliary circle   In celestial mechanics, a circumscribing circle to an orbital ellipse with radius *a*, the semimajor axis. { ȯg'zil·yə·rē 'sər·kəl }

auxiliary fluid ignition   A method of ignition of a liquid-propellant rocket engine in which a liquid that is hypergolic with either the fuel or the oxidizer is injected into the combustion chamber to initiate combustion. { ȯg'zil·yə·rē 'flü·əd ig'nish·ən }

auxiliary landing gear   The part or parts of a landing gear, such as an outboard wheel, which is intended to stabilize the craft on the surface but which bears no significant part of the weight. { ȯg'zil·yə·rē 'land·iŋ ˌgir }

auxiliary power unit   A power unit carried on an aircraft or spacecraft which can be used in addition to the main sources of power. Abbreviated APU. { ȯg'zil·yə·rē 'paủ·ər ˌyü·nət }

aviation   **1.** The science and technology of flight through the air. **2.** The world of airplane business and its allied industries. { ˌā·vē'ā·shən }

axes of an aircraft   Three fixed lines of reference, usually centroidal and mutually perpendicular: the longitudinal axis, the normal or yaw axis, and the lateral or pitch axis. Also known as aircraft axes. { 'akˌsēz əv ən 'erˌkraft }

axial-flow jet engine   **1.** A jet engine in which the general flow of air is along the longitudinal axis of the engine. **2.** A turbojet engine that utilizes an axial-flow compressor and turbine. { 'ak·sē·əl 'flō ¦jet 'en·jən }

axis of thrust   *See* thrust axis. { 'ak·səs əv ˌthrəst }

azimuth   Horizontal direction of a celestial point from a terrestrial point, expressed as the angular distance from a reference direction, usually measured from 0° at the reference direction clockwise through 360°. { 'az·ə·məth }

azimuth error   The angle by which the east-west axis of a transit telescope deviates from being perpendicular to the plane of the meridian. { 'az·ə·məth ˌer·ər }

azimuth tables   Publications providing tabulated azimuths or azimuth angles of celestial bodies for various combinations of declination, altitude, and hour angle; great-circle course angles can also be obtained by substitution of values. { 'az·ə·məth ˌta·bəlz }

B

Baade's window An unusually transparent region about 4° from the galactic center. { 'bä·dəz ,win·dō }

Babcock magnetograph An instrument used to measure weak magnetic fields on the sun. { 'bab,käk mag'ned·ə,graf }

backout An undoing of previous steps during a countdown, usually in reverse order. { 'bak,aút }

bailout The exiting from a flying aircraft and descending by parachute in an emergency. { 'bāl,aút }

bailout bottle A personal supply of oxygen usually contained in a cylinder under pressure and utilized when the individual has left the central oxygen system, as in a parachute jump. { 'bāl,aút 'bäd·əl }

Baily's beads Bright points of sunlight appearing around the edge of the moon just before and after the central phase of a total solar eclipse. { 'bāl,ēz ˈbēdz }

balance **1.** The equilibrium attained by an aircraft, rocket, or the like when forces and moments are acting upon it so as to produce steady flight, especially without rotation about its axes. **2.** The equilibrium about any specified axis that counterbalances something, especially on an aircraft control surface, such as a weight installed forward of the hinge axis to counterbalance the surface aft of the hinge axis. { 'bal·əns }

Balance See Libra. { 'bal·əns }

balanced surface A control surface that extends on both sides of the axis of the hinge or pivot, or that has auxiliary devices or extensions connected with it, in such a manner as to effect a small or zero resultant moment of the air forces about the hinge axis. { 'bal·ənst 'sər·fəs }

ballast A relatively dense substance that is placed in the cab of a balloon and can be thrown out to reduce the load or can be shifted to change the center of gravity. { 'bal·əst }

ballonet One of the air cells in a blimp, fastened to the bottom or sides of the envelope, which are used to maintain the required pressure in the envelope without adding or valving gas as the ship ascends or descends. Also spelled ballonnet. { ˈbal·əˈnā }

ballonnet See ballonet. { ˈbal·əˈnā }

balloon A nonporous, flexible spherical bag, inflated with a gas such as helium that is lighter than air, so that it will rise and float in the atmosphere; a large-capacity balloon can be used to lift a payload suspended from it. { bə'lün }

balloon astronomy

balloon astronomy   The observation of celestial objects from instruments mounted on balloons and carried to altitudes up to 18 miles (30 kilometers), to detect electromagnetic radiation at wavelengths which do not penetrate to the earth's surface. { bə'lün ə'strän·ə·mē }

balloon cover   A cover which fits over a large, inflated balloon to facilitate handling in high or gusty winds. Also known as balloon shroud. { bə'lün ˌkəv·ər }

balloon shroud   See balloon cover. { bə'lün ˌshraud }

balloon-type rocket   A liquid-fuel rocket, such as the Atlas, that requires the pressure of its propellants (or other gases) within it to give it structural integrity. { bə'lün ˈtīp 'räk·ət }

ballute   A cross between a balloon and a parachute, used to brake the free fall of sounding rockets. { 'baˌlüt }

Bamberga   An asteroid with a diameter of about 129 miles (215 kilometers), mean distance from the sun of 2.686 astronomical units, and C-type surface composition. { 'bämˌbər·gə }

bank   The lateral inward inclination of an airplane when it rounds a curve. { baŋk }

bank-and-turn indicator   A device used to advise the pilot that the aircraft is turning at a certain rate, and that the wings are properly banked to preclude slipping or sliding of the aircraft as it continues in flight. Also known as bank indicator. { ˈbaŋk ən 'tərn 'in·dəˌkād·ər }

bank indicator   See bank-and-turn indicator. { 'baŋk 'in·dəˌkād·ər }

barium star   A peculiar, low-velocity, strong-lined red giant or subgiant star of spectral type G, K, or M, whose spectrum has anomalously strong lines of barium, sometimes with strong bands of methyldadyne (CH), molecular carbon (C₂), and cyanogen radical (CN). { 'bar·ē·əm ˌstär }

Barnard's loop   A large emission nebula, about 10° by 140° in size, around the central portion of Orion, that consists of an expanding shell of gas that probably originated in a supernova. { 'bär·nərdz ˌlüp }

Barnard's star   A star 6.1 light-years away from earth, of visual magnitude 9.5 and proper motion of 10.31 seconds of arc annually. { 'bär·nərdz ˈstär }

barometric fuel control   A device that maintains the correct flow of fuel to an engine by adjusting to atmospheric pressure at different altitudes, as well as to impact pressure. { bar·ə'met·rik 'fyül kənˌtrōl }

barred spiral galaxy   A spiral galaxy whose spiral arms originate at the ends of a bar-shaped structure centered at the nucleus of the galaxy. { ˈbärd ˈspī·rəl 'gal·ik·sē }

barycenter   The center of gravity of the earth-moon system. { 'bar·əˌsen·tər }

barycentric element   An orbital element referred to the center of mass of the solar system. { ˌbar·ə'sen·trik 'el·ə·mənt }

baryon-to-photon ratio   The estimated ratio of the number of baryons (mostly protons and neutrons) to photons (mostly in the cosmic microwave radiation) in the universe. { 'bar·ē·än tə 'fōˌtän 'rā·shō }

batten   Metal, wood, or plastic panels laced to the envelope of a blimp in the nose

24

cone to add rigidity to the nose and provide a good point of attachment for mooring. { 'bat · ən }

Bautz-Morgan classification   A classification of clusters of galaxies into three categories, ranging from type I in which the cluster contains a supergiant elliptical galaxy, to type II in which the cluster contains no member that is significantly brighter than the general bright population. { 'baúts 'mòr · gən ,klas · ə · fə,kā · shən }

bay   A space formed by structural partitions on an aircraft. { bā }

Bayer letter   The Greek (or Roman) letter used in a Bayer name. { 'bī · ər ,led · ər }

Bayer name   The Greek (or Roman) letter and the possessive form of the Latin name of a constellation, used as a star name; examples are α Cygni (Deneb), β Orionis (Rigel), and η Ursae Majoris (Alkaid). { 'bī · ər ,nām }

Bayer's constellations   Thirteen constellations in the southern hemisphere named by J. Bayer. { 'bī · ərz ,kan · stə'lā · shənz }

beam rider   A missile for which the guidance system consists of standard reference signals transmitted in a radar beam which enable the missile to sense its location relative to the beam, correct its course, and thereby stay on the beam. { 'bēm ,rīd · ər }

beam riding   The maneuver of a spacecraft or other vehicle as it follows a beam. { 'bēm ,rīd · iŋ }

Bear Driver   See Boötes. { 'ber ,drīv · ər }

beat Cepheid   A dwarf Cepheid that displays two or more nearly identical pulsation periods, resulting in periodic amplitude fluctuations in its light curve. { 'bēt 'sef · ē · əd }

Becklin-Neugebauer object   A compact source of infrared radiation in the Orion Nebula, probably a collapsing protostar of large mass. Abbreviated BN object. { 'bek · lin 'nòi · gə,baú · ər ,äb,jekt }

Beehive   See Praesepe. { 'bē,hīv }

Belinda   A satellite of Uranus orbiting at a mean distance of 46,760 miles (75,260 kilometers) with a period of 15 hours, and with a diameter of about 42 miles (68 kilometers). { bə'lin · də }

Bellatrix   A bluish-white star of stellar magnitude 1.7, spectral classification B2-III, in the constellation Orion; the star γ Orionis. { bə'lā · triks }

Berenice's Hair   See Coma Berenices. { ,ber · ə'nē · səz 'her }

Besselian elements   Data on a solar eclipse, giving, for selected times, the coordinates of the axis of the moon's shadow with respect to the fundamental plane, and the radii of umbra and penumbra in that plane; the data allow one to derive local circumstances of the eclipse at any point on the earth's surface. { bə'sel · yən ¦el · ə · mənts }

Besselian star numbers   Constants used in the reduction of a mean position of a star to an apparent position; used to account for short-term variations in precession, nutation, aberration, and parallax. { bə'sel · yən 'stär ,nəm · bərz }

Besselian year   See fictitious year. { bə'sel · yən ,yir }

Be star   A star of spectral type B in the Draper catalog that has emission lines indicating mass loss and a surrounding gaseous shell. { ¦bē¦ē ˌstär }

beta   For dust grains ejected from the nucleus of a comet, the ratio of the radiation pressure force to the solar gravitational force. { 'bād·ə }

β Canis Majoris stars   See beta Cephei stars. { 'bād·ə 'kan·əs mə'jȯr·əs ˌstärz }

β Centauri   A first-magnitude navigational star in the constellation Centaurus; 200 light-years from the sun; spectral classification B0. Also known as Agena; Hadar. { ¦bā·də sen'tȯ·rē }

β Cephei stars   A class of pulsating variables lying above the upper main sequence with short periods of 3$\frac{1}{2}$-6 hours, spectral classes B0 to B3, and doubly periodic light curves. Also known as β Canis Majoris stars. { 'bād·ə 'sef·ē,ī ˌstärz }

β Crucis   A star in the constellation Crux that is 370 light-years from the sun, with magnitude 1.3, spectral classification B0.5IV. Also known as Mimosa. { ¦bā·də 'krü·səs }

Betelgeuse   An orange-red giant star of stellar magnitude 0.1-1.2, 650 light-years from the sun, spectral classification M2-Iab, in the constellation Orion; the star α Orionis. { 'bed·əl,jüs }

Bianca   A satellite of Uranus orbiting at a mean distance of 36,760 miles (59,160 kilometers) with a period of 10 hours 27 minutes, and with a diameter of about 27 miles (44 kilometers). { bē'äŋk·ə }

Bianchi cosmology   A model of the universe which is homogeneous but not necessarily isotropic. { bē'aŋ·kē käz'mäl·ə·jē }

Biela Comet   A comet seen in 1852 at one perihelion passage; presumed to have separated into two bodies. { 'bē·lä ˌkäm·ət }

Bielids   See Andromedids. { 'bē,lidz }

big bang theory   A theory of the origin and evolution of the universe which holds that approximately 2×10^{10} years ago all the matter in the universe was packed into a small agglomeration of extremely high density and temperature which exploded, sending matter in all directions and giving rise to the expanding universe. Also known as superdense theory. { ¦big 'baŋ ˌthē·ə·rē }

big crunch   A singularity at the origin of a black hole into which all the matter and radiation in a closed universe would eventually collapse. { ¦big ¦krənch }

Big Dipper   A group of stars that is part of the constellation Ursa Major. Also known as Charles' Wain. { ¦big 'dip·ər }

Big Four   A group of large asteroids including Ceres, Pallas, Vesta, and Juno, the first four that were discovered. { ¦big ¦fȯr }

binary pulsar   A pulsar which forms one component of a binary star. { 'bīn·ə·rē 'pəl,sär }

binary star   A pair of stars located sufficiently near each other in space to be connected by the bond of mutual gravitational attraction, compelling them to describe an orbit around their common center of gravity. Also known as binary system. { 'bīn·ə·rē 'stär }

binary system   See binary star. { 'bīn·ə·rē 'sis·təm }

biosatellite   An artificial satellite designed to contain and support humans, animals, or other living material in a reasonably normal manner for a period of time and to return safely to earth. { ¦bī·o'sad·əl₁īt }

biplane   An aircraft with two wings fixed at different levels, especially one above and one below the fuselage. { 'bī₁plān }

bipolar nebula   A nebula consisting of two relatively symmetrical bright lobes with a star between them. { bī₁pōl·ər 'neb·yə·lə }

Blaauw mechanism   An explanation for the disruption of a binary system as being due to the decrease in the gravitational binding force when a shell of gas ejected by the primary component overtakes the secondary. { 'blō ₁mek·ə₁niz·əm }

black drop   As seen through a telescope, an apparent dark elongation of the image of Venus or Mercury when the planets' images are at the sun's limb. { ¦blak 'dräp }

black dwarf   A star that cannot generate thermonuclear energy. { ¦blak 'dwȯrf }

blade loading   A rotor's thrust in a rotary-wing aircraft divided by the total area of the rotor blades. { 'blād ₁lōd·iŋ }

Blasius theorem   A theorem that provides formulas for finding the force and moment on the airfoil profiler. { 'blä·zē·əs ₁thir·əm }

blast chamber   A combustion chamber, especially in a gas-turbine, jet, or rocket engine. { 'blast ₁chām·bər }

blast deflector   A device used to divert the exhaust of a rocket fired from a vertical position. { 'blast di'flek·tər }

blast-off   The takeoff of a rocket or missile. { 'blast₁ȯf }

blazar   A type of quasar whose light exhibits strong optical polarization and large variability. { 'blā₁zär }

BL Herculis stars   W Virginis stars of relatively low luminosity and mass. { ¦be¦el 'hər·kyə·ləs ₁stärz }

blimp   A name originally applied to nonrigid, pressure-type airships, usually of small size; now applied to airships with volumes of approximately 1,500,000 cubic feet (42,000 cubic meters). { blimp }

blind landing   Landing an aircraft solely by the use of instruments because of poor visibility. { ¦blīnd 'lan·diŋ }

BL Lacertae objects   A class of extragalactic sources of extremely intense, highly variable electromagnetic radiation which are related to quasars but have a featureless optical spectrum, and display strong optical polarization and a radio spectrum that increases in intensity at shorter wavelengths. { ¦be¦el lə'ser·tē ₁äb·jiks }

blowdown tunnel   A wind tunnel in which stored compressed gas is allowed to expand through a test section to provide a stream of gas or air for model testing. { 'blō₁daȯn ₁tən·əl }

blowdown turbine   A turbine attached to a reciprocating engine which receives exhaust gases separately from each cylinder, utilizing the kinetic energy of the gases. { 'blō͵daún ͵tər·bən }

blowing boundary-layer control   A technique that is used in addition to purely geometric means to control boundary-layer flow; it consists of reenergizing the retarded flow in the boundary layer by supplying high-velocity flow through slots or jets on the surface of the body. { 'blō·iŋ 'baún·drē ͵lā·ər kən'trōl }

blowoff   The action of applying an explosive force and separating a package section away from the remaining part of a rocket vehicle or reentry body, usually to retrieve an instrument or to obtain a record made during early flight. { 'blō͵óf }

blue band   A dark band which appears around the polar caps of Mars as they shrink during the spring and early summer. { ˈblü 'band }

blue edge   The curve on the Hertzsprung-Russell diagram given by the maximum temperature, as a function of luminosity, at which a star of specified composition is unstable against small-amplitude pulsations. { 'blü 'ej }

blue flash   See green flash. { 'blü ͵flash }

blue-green flame   See green flash. { ˈblüˈgrēn 'flām }

blue haze   A condition of the Martian atmosphere that sometimes causes it to be opaque to radiation near the blue end of the visible spectrum. { 'blü 'hāz }

blue shift   A displacement of lines in the spectrum of a celestial object toward shorter wavelengths, indicating motion of the object toward thè observer. { 'blü ͵shift }

blue star   A star of spectral type O, B, A, or F according to the Draper catalog. { 'blü ͵stär }

blue straggler star   A member of a star cluster that lies above the turnoff point of the cluster's Hertzsprung-Russell diagram, and lies near the main sequence. { ˈblü 'strag·lər ͵stär }

bluff body   A body having a broad, flattened front, as in some reentry vehicles. { ˈbləf ˈbäd·ē }

BN object   See Becklin-Neugebauer object. { ˈbē'en ͵äb·jəkt }

boattail   Of an elongated body such as a rocket, the rear portion having decreasing cross-sectional area. { 'bōt͵tāl }

Bode's law   An empirical law giving mean distances of planets to the sun by the formula $a = 0.4 + 0.3 \times 2^n$, where a is in astronomical units and n equals $-\infty$ for Mercury, 0 for Venus, 1 for Earth, and so on; the asteroids are included as planets. Also known as Titius-Bode law. { 'bōdz ͵ló }

body   **1.** The main part or main central portion of an airplane, airship, rocket, or the like; a fuselage or hull. **2.** Any fabrication, structure, or other material form, especially one aerodynamically or ballistically designed; for example, an airfoil is a body designed to produce an aerodynamic reaction. { 'bäd·ē }

body angle   The angle which the longitudinal axis of the airframe makes with some selected line. { 'bäd·ē ͵aŋ·gəl }

body axis   Any one of a system of mutually perpendicular reference axes fixed in an aircraft or a similar body and moving with it. { 'bäd·ē ͵ak·səs }

bogey *See* bogie. { 'bō·gē }

bogie A type of landing-gear unit consisting of two sets of wheels in tandem with a central strut. Also spelled bogey; bogy. { 'bō·gē }

bogy *See* bogie. { 'bō͵gē }

boiler-plate model A metal copy of a flight vehicle, the structure or components of which are heavier than the flight model. { 'bȯil·ər ͝plāt ͵mäd·əl }

boiling The telescopic appearance of the limbs of the sun and planets when the earth's atmosphere is turbulent, characterized by a constant rippling motion and lack of a clearly defined edge. { 'bȯil·iŋ }

bolide A brilliant meteor, especially one which explodes; a detonating fireball meteor. { 'bō͵līd }

bolometric correction The difference between the bolometric and visual magnitude. { ͝bō·lə͝me·trik kə'rek·shən }

bolometric magnitude The magnitude of a celestial object, as calculated from the total amount of radiation received from the object at all wavelengths. { ͝bō·lə͝me·trik 'mag·nə͵tüd }

bomb bay The compartment or bay in the fuselage of a bomber where the bombs are carried for release. { ͝bäm ͝bā }

bomber An airplane specifically designed to carry and drop bombs. Also known as bombardment aircraft. { 'bäm·ər }

Boo *See* Boötes.

boost **1.** An auxiliary means of propulsion such as by a booster. **2.** To supercharge. **3.** To launch or push along during a portion of a flight. **4.** *See* boost pressure. { büst }

booster *See* booster engine; booster rocket; launch vehicle. { 'büs·tər }

booster engine An engine, especially a booster rocket, that adds its thrust to the thrust of the sustainer engine. Also known as booster. { 'büs·tər ͵en·jən }

booster rocket Also known as booster. **1.** A rocket motor, either solid- or liquid-fueled, that assists the normal propulsive system or sustainer engine of a rocket or aeronautical vehicle in some phase of its flight. **2.** A rocket used to set a vehicle in motion before another engine takes over. { 'büs·tər ͵räk·ət }

boost-glide vehicle An air vehicle capable of aerodynamic lift which is projected to an extreme altitude by reaction propulsion and then coasts down with little or no propulsion, gliding to increase its range when it reenters the sensible atmosphere. { ͝büst ͝glīd 'vē·ə·kəl }

boost pressure Manifold pressure greater than the ambient at atmospheric pressure, obtained by supercharging. Also known as boost. { 'büst ͵presh·ər }

Boot *See* Boötes. { büt }

Boötes A constellation which lies south and east of Ursa Major; the star Arcturus is a member of the group. Abbreviated Boo; Boot. Also known as Bear Driver. { bō'ō͵tēz }

bootstrap process   A self-generating or self-sustaining process; specifically, the operation of liquid-propellant rocket engines in which, during main-stage operation, the gas generator is fed by the main propellants pumped by the turbopump, and the turbopump in turn is driven by hot gases from the gas generator system. { 'büt‚strap ‚präs·əs }

bow   The forward section of an aircraft. { bau̇ }

bowl crater   A type of lunar crater whose interior cross section is a smooth curve, with no flat floor. { 'bōl ‚krād·ər }

bowshock   The shock wave set up by the interaction of the supersonic solar wind with a planet's magnetic field. { 'bau̇‚shäk }

Bradley aberration   Stellar aberration with a maximum of 20.5 seconds of arc; can be used to compute an approximate velocity for light. { 'brad·lē ab·ə'rā·shən }

braking ellipses   A series of ellipses, decreasing in size due to aerodynamic drag, followed by a spacecraft in entering a planetary atmosphere. { 'bra·kiŋ i'lip‚sēz }

braking rocket   See retrorocket. { 'bra·kiŋ ‚räk·ət }

breakaway phenomenon   See breakoff phenomenon. { 'brāk·ə‚wā fə'näm·ə‚nän }

breakoff phenomenon   The feeling which sometimes occurs during high-altitude flight of being totally separated and detached from the earth and human society. Also known as breakaway phenomenon. { 'brā‚kȯf fə‚näm·ə‚nän }

Breguet range equation   An equation for the range of an aircraft stating that the range is equal to K(PE/SFC)(L/D) ln (TOW/LW), where PE is propeller efficiency, SFC is specific fuel consumption, L/D is lift-to-drag ratio, TOW is takeoff weight, LW is landing weight, and K is a constant (equal to 375 if the range is expressed in miles and the specific fuel consumption is expressed in pounds per horsepower-hour). { ˈbre·gā ˈrānj i‚kwā·zhən }

brennschluss   1. The cessation of burning in a rocket, resulting from consumption of the propellants, from deliberate shutoff, or from other cause. 2. The time at which this cessation occurs. { 'bren‚shlu̇s }

bright diffuse nebula   A nebula which is illuminated by the action of embedded or nearby stars. { ˈbrīt dəˈfyüs 'neb·yə·lə }

bright points   Relatively small regions on the sun, distributed uniformly over the solar disk, from which there is increased x-ray and ultraviolet emission, having lifetimes on the order of 8 hours. { 'brīt ‚pȯins }

bright rim structures   Bright edges exhibited by many diffuse-emission nebulae, usually on the side facing the exciting star. { 'brīt ‚rim ‚strək·chərz }

bright stars catalog   A catalog of stars brighter than 6.5 magnitude, giving positions, motions, parallaxes, and spectral classes. { ˈbrīt ˈstärz 'kad·ə‚läg }

brown dwarf   A black dwarf that radiates its internal heat. { ˈbrau̇n ˈdwȯrf }

B star   See B-type star. { 'bē ‚stär }

B Tauri   A daytime meteor shower that occurs at the end of June and has its radiant near the star. { ˈbē 'tȯr·ē }

B-type star   A type in a classification based on stellar spectral characteristics; has strong HeI absorption. Also known as B star. { 'bē ˌtīp ˌstär }

buffeting   1. The beating of an aerodynamic structure or surfaces by unsteady flow, gusts, and so forth. 2. The irregular shaking or oscillation of a vehicle component owing to turbulent air or separated flow. { 'bəf·əd·iŋ }

buffeting Mach number   The free-stream Mach number of an aircraft when the local Mach number over the tops of the wings approaches unity. { ¦bəf·əd·iŋ 'mäk ˌnəm·bər }

bulkhead   A wall, partition, or such in a rocket, spacecraft, airplane fuselage, or similar structure, at right angles to the longitudinal axis of the structure and serving to strengthen, divide, or help give shape to the structure. { 'bəlkˌhed }

Bull   See Taurus. { bəl }

bump Cepheid   A Cepheid variable star with a period of 5-15 days that displays a prominent secondary maximum (bump) in its light and velocity curves. { 'bəmp 'sef·ē·əd }

bumpiness   An atmospheric condition causing aircraft to experience sudden vertical jolts. { 'bəm·pē·nəs }

bumping   See chugging. { 'bəm·piŋ }

burning-rate constant   A constant, related to initial grain temperature, used in calculating the burning rate of a rocket propellant grain. { 'bər·niŋ ˌrāt ˌkän·stənt }

burnout   1. An act or instance of fuel or oxidant depletion or of depletion of both at once. 2. The time at which this depletion occurs. 3. The point on a rocket trajectory at which this depletion occurs. { 'bərnˌaůt }

burnout velocity   The velocity of a rocket at the time when depletion of the fuel or oxidant occurs. Also known as all-burnt velocity; burnt velocity. { 'bərnˌaůt və'läs·əd·ē }

burnt velocity   See burnout velocity. { ¦bərnt və'läs·əd·ē }

burst disk   A diaphragm designed to burst at a predetermined pressure differential; sometimes used as a valve, for example, in a liquid-propellant line in a rocket. Also known as rupture disk. { 'bərst ˌdisk }

burster   A celestial source of radiation, such as x-rays or gamma rays, that is very intense for brief periods of time and whose nature has not yet been established. { 'bər·stər }

bus   A spacecraft or missile that is designed to carry one or more separable devices, such as probes or warheads. { bəs }

buzz   Sustained oscillation of an aerodynamic control surface caused by intermittent flow separation on the surface, or by a motion of shock waves across the surface, or by a combination of flow separation and shock-wave motion on the surface. { bəz }

C

cabane The arrangement of struts used on early types of airplanes to brace the wings. { kə′ban }

Cae *See* Caelum.

Caelum A southern constellation, right ascension 5 hours, declination 40°S. Abbreviated Cae. Also known as Chisel. { ′sē·ləm }

calcium star A term sometimes used to denote a star of spectral class F, which has prominent absorption bands of calcium. { ′kal·se·əm ′stär }

calendar A system for everyday use in which time is divided into days and longer periods, such as weeks, months, and years, and a definite order for these periods and a correspondence between them are established. { ′kal·ən·dər }

calendar day The period from midnight to midnight; it is 24 hours of mean solar time in length and coincides with the civil day. { ′kal·ən·dər ′dā }

calendar month The month of the calendar, varying from 28 to 31 days in length. { ′kal·ən·dər ′mənth }

calendar year The year in the Gregorian calendar, common years having 365 days and leap years 366. Also known as civil year. { ′kal·ən·dər ′yir }

calibrated airspeed The airspeed as read from a differential-pressure airspeed indicator which has been corrected for instrument and installation errors; equal to true airspeed for standard sea-level conditions. { ′kal·ə′brād·əd ′er′spēd }

Callipic cycle Four Metonic cycles, or 76 years. { kə′lip·ik ′sī·kəl }

Callisto A satellite of Jupiter orbiting at a mean distance of 1,884,000 kilometers. Also known as Jupiter IV. { kə′lis′tō }

Caloris Basin A large depression on Mercury, about 1300 kilometers in diameter. { kə′lȯr·əs ′bā·sən }

Calypso A small, irregularly shaped satellite of Saturn that librates about the leading Lagrangian point of Tethys's orbit. { kə′lip·sō }

Cam *See* Camelopardalis.

camber The rise of the curve of an airfoil section, usually expressed as the ratio of the departure of the curve from a straight line joining the extremities of the curve to the length of this straight line. { ′kam·bər }

Camelopardalis

Camelopardalis Latin name for the Giraffe constellation of the northern hemisphere. Abbreviated Cam; Caml. Also known as Camelopardus; Giraffe. { ka‚mel·ə'pärd·əl· əs }

Camelopardus *See* Camelopardalis. { ka‚mel·ə'pär·dəs }

Camilla An asteroid with a diameter of about 210 kilometers, mean distance from the sun of 3.49 astronomical units, and C-type surface composition. { kə'mil·ə }

Caml *See* Camelopardalis. { 'kam·əl }

canard **1.** An aerodynamic vehicle in which horizontal surfaces used for trim and control are forward of the wing or main lifting surface. **2.** The horizontal trim and control surfaces in such an arrangement. { kə'närd }

Cancer A constellation with right ascension 9 hours, declination 20°N. Abbreviated Canc. Also known as Crab. { 'kan·sər }

Canes Venatici A northern constellation with right ascension 13 hours, declination 40°N, between Ursa Major and Boötes. Abbreviated CVn. Also known as Hunting Dogs. { 'kä‚nēz və'nad·ə‚sē }

Canes Venatici I cloud A relatively nearby, loosely clustered group of galaxies consisting chiefly of late-type spirals and irregular galaxies, with recession velocities near 220 miles (350 kilometers) per second. { 'kä‚nēz və'nad·ə‚sē 'wən ‚klaůd }

Canis Major A constellation with right ascension 7 hours, declination 20°S. Abbreviated CMa. Also known as Greater Dog. { ‚kā·nəs 'mā·jər }

Canis Minor A constellation with right ascension 8 hours, declination 5°N. Abbreviated CMi. Also known as Lesser Dog. { ‚kā·nəs 'mī·nər }

cannular combustion chambers The separate combustion chambers in an aircraft gas turbine. Also known as can-type combustors. { 'kan·yə·lər kəm'bəs·chən ‚chām· bərz }

canonical change A periodic change in one of the components of the orbit of a celestial object. { kə'nän·ə·kəl 'chānj }

canonical time unit For geocentric orbits, the time required by a hypothetical satellite to move one radian in a circular orbit of the earth's equatorial radius, that is, 13.447052 minutes. { kə'nän·ə·kəl 'tīm ‚yü·nət }

Canopus A star that is 180 light-years from the sun; spectral classification F0Ia. Also known as α Carinae. { kə'nō·pəs }

canopy **1.** The umbrellalike part of a parachute which acts as its main supporting surface. **2.** The overhead, transparent enclosure of an aircraft cockpit. { 'kan·ə·pē }

can-type combustors *See* cannular combustion chambers. { ¦kan ‚tīp kəm'bəs·tərz }

Canc *See* Cancer.

Cap *See* Capricornus.

Capella A star that is 45 light-years from the sun; spectral classification G0IIIp. Also known as α Aurigae. { kə'pel·ə }

Capricornus A constellation with right ascension 21 hours, declination 20°S. Abbreviated Cap. Also known as Sea Goat. { ¦kap·rə¦kȯr·nəs }

capsule A small, sealed, pressurized cabin with an internal environment that will support human or animal life during extremely high-altitude flight, space flight, or escape. { 'kap·səl }

captive balloon A moored balloon, usually held by steel cables. { 'kap·tiv bə'lün }

capture **1.** The process in which a missile is taken under control by the guidance system. **2.** Of a central force field, as of a planet, to overcome by gravitational force the velocity of a passing body and bring the body under the control of the central force field, in some cases absorbing its mass. { 'kap·chər }

carbon-detonation supernova model A model for a supernova in a star of 4 to 9 solar masses through the explosive ignition of carbon in a high-density, electron-degenerate core by the formation and propagation of a detonation wave. { 'kär·bən ₁det·ən'ā·shən ¦sü·pər'nō·və ₁mäd·əl }

carbon sequence Wolf-Rayet stars in which carbon emission bands dominate the spectrum. { 'kär·bən ₁sē·kwəns }

carbon star Any of a class of stars with an apparently high abundance ratio of carbon to hydrogen; a majority of these are low-temperature red giants of the C class. { 'kär·bən ₁stär }

Carina A constellation, right ascension 9 hours, declination 60°S. Abbreviated Car. Also known as Keel. { kə'rī·nə }

Carina Nebula A gaseous nebula near the star η Carinae in the Milky Way. { kə'ri·nə 'neb·yə·lə }

Carme A small satellite of Jupiter with a diameter of about 19 miles (31 kilometers), orbiting with retrograde motion at a mean distance of 1.4×10^7 miles (2.3×10^7 kilometers). Also known as Jupiter XI. { 'kär·mā }

carrier rocket A rocket vehicle used to carry something, as the carrier rocket of the first artificial earth satellite. { 'kar·ē·ər ₁räk·ət }

Carrington rotation number A method of numbering rotations of the sun based on a mean rotation period of sunspots of 27.2753 days, and starting with rotation number 1 on November 9, 1853. { 'kar·iŋ·tən rō'tā·shən ₁nəm·bər }

cartographic satellite An applications satellite that is used to prepare maps of the earth's surface and of the culture on it. { ¦kärd·ə¦graf·ik 'sad·əl₁īt }

cartridge-actuated initiator An item designed to provide gas pressure for activating various aircraft components such as canopy removers, thrusters, and catapults. { 'kär·trij 'ak·chə₁wād·əd in'ish·ē₁ād·ər }

Cartwheel A ring galaxy found in the southern hemisphere. { 'kärt₁wēl }

Cas *See* Cassiopeia.

Cassini's division The gap, 2500 miles (4000 kilometers) wide, that separates ring A from ring B of the planet Saturn. { kə'sē·nēz di'vizh·ən }

Cassiopeia A constellation with right ascension 1 hour, declination 60°N. Abbreviated Cas. { ₁kas·ē·ə'pē·ə }

Cassiopeia A   One of the strongest discrete radio sources, located in the constellation Cassiopeia, associated with patches of filamentary nebulosity which are probably remnants of a supernova. { ˌkas·ē·ə′pē·ə ′ā }

Castor   A multiple star of spectral classification A0 in the constellation Gemini; the star α Geminorum. { ′kas·tər }

cataclysmic variable   A star showing a sudden increase in the magnitude of light, followed by a slow fading of light; examples are novae and supernovae. Also known as explosive variable. { ¦kad·ə¦kliz·mik ′ver·ē·ə·bəl }

catalog number   The designation of a star composed of the name of a particular star catalog and the number of the star as listed there. { ′kad·əlˌäg ˌnəm·bər }

catapult   **1.** A power-actuated machine or device for hurling an object at high speed, for example, a device which launches aircraft from a ship deck. **2.** A device, usually explosive, for ejecting a person from an aircraft. { ′kad·əˌpəlt }

CAVU   An operational term commonly used in aviation, which designates a condition wherein the ceiling is more than 10,000 feet (3048 meters) and the visibility is more than 10 miles (16 kilometers). Derived from ceiling and visibility unlimited.

CD galaxy   A supergiant elliptical galaxy with an extended envelope, the largest known type of galaxy. { ¦sē¦dē ′gal·ik·sē }

ceiling and visibility unlimited   See CAVU. { ′sē·liŋ ən ˌviz·ə′bil·əd·ē ən′lim·əd·əd }

ceiling balloon   A small balloon used to determine the height of the cloud base; the height is computed from the ascent velocity of the balloon and the time required for its disappearance into the cloud. { ′sē·liŋ bə′lün }

celestial body   Any aggregation of matter in space constituting a unit for astronomical study, as the sun, moon, a planet, comet, star, or nebula. Also known as heavenly body. { sə′les·chəl ′bäd·ē }

celestial coordinates   Any set of coordinates, such as zenithal distance, altitude, celestial latitude, celestial longitude, local hour angle, azimuth and declination, used to define a point on the celestial sphere. { sə′les·chəl kō′órd·nəts }

celestial equator   The primary great circle of the celestial sphere in the equatorial system, everywhere 90° from the celestial poles; the intersection of the extended plane of the equator and the celestial sphere. Also known as equinoctial. { sə′les·chəl i′kwäd·ər }

celestial equator system of coordinates   See equatorial system. { sə′les·chəl i′kwäd·ər ¦sis·təm əv kō′órd·nəts }

celestial globe   A small globe representing the celestial sphere, on which the apparent positions of the stars are located. Also known as star globe. { sə′les·chəl ′glōb }

celestial horizon   That great circle of the celestial sphere which is formed by the intersection of the celestial sphere and a plane through the center of the earth and is perpendicular to the zenith-nadir line. Also known as rational horizon. { sə′les·chəl hə′rīz·ən }

celestial latitude   Angular distance north or south of the ecliptic; the arc of a circle of latitude between the ecliptic and a point on the celestial sphere, measured northward or southward from the ecliptic through 90°, and labeled N or S to indicate the direction of measurement. Also known as ecliptic latitude. { sə′les·chəl ′lad·əˌtüd }

celestial longitude Angular distance east of the vernal equinox, along the ecliptic; the arc of the ecliptic or the angle at the ecliptic pole between the circle of latitude of the vernal equinox and the circle of latitude of a point on the celestial sphere, measured eastward from the circle of latitude of the vernal equinox, through 360°. Also known as ecliptic longitude. { sə'les·chəl 'län·jə₁tüd }

celestial mechanics The calculation of motions of celestial bodies under the action of their mutual gravitational attractions. Also known as gravitational astronomy. { sə'les·chəl mə'kan·iks }

celestial meridian A great circle on the celestial sphere, passing through the two celestial poles and the observer's zenith. { sə'les·chəl mə'rid·ē·ən }

celestial parallel See parallel of declination. { sə'les·chəl 'par·ə₁lel }

celestial pole Either of the two points of intersection of the celestial sphere and the extended axis of the earth, labeled N or S to indicate the north celestial pole or the south celestial pole. { sə'les·chəl 'pōl }

celestial sphere An imaginary sphere of indefinitely large radius, which is described about an assumed center, and upon which positions of celestial bodies are projected along radii passing through the bodies. { sə'les·chəl 'sfir }

Cen See Centaurus.

Centaurus A constellation with right ascension 13 hours, declination 50°S. Abbreviated Cen. { sen'tȯr·əs }

Centaurus A A strong, discrete radio source in the constellation Centaurus, associated with the peculiar galaxy NGC 5128. { sen'tȯr·əs 'ā }

Centaurus cluster A large cluster of galaxies that shows a composite structure, with a concentration of galaxies having recession velocities of about 3000 kilometers (1900 miles) per second, and a weaker concentration having recession velocities of about 4500 kilometers (2800 miles) per second. { sen'tȯr·əs ₁kləs·tər }

Centaurus X-3 A source of x-rays that pulses with a period of 4.8 seconds and is eclipsed every 2.1 days; believed to be a binary star, one of whose members is a rotating neutron star. Abbreviated Cen X-3. { sen'tȯr·əs ₁eks 'thrē }

center of lift The mean of all the centers of pressure on an airfoil. { 'sen·tər əv 'lift }

center of pressure The point in the chord of an airfoil section which is at the intersection of the chord (prolonged if necessary) and the line of action of the combined air forces (resultant air force). { 'sen·tər əv 'presh·ər }

center-of-pressure coefficient The ratio of the distance of a center of pressure from the leading edge of an airfoil to its chord length. { 'sen·tər əv 'presh·ər ₁kō·ə'fish·ənt }

center of thrust See thrust axis. { 'sen·tər əv 'thrəst }

central condensation The bright, central portion of the coma of a comet, containing one or more nuclei. { 'sen·trəl ₁kän·dən'sā·shən }

central control The place, facility, or activity at which the whole action incident to a test launch and flight is coordinated and controlled, from the make-ready at the launch site and on the range, to the end of the rocket flight down-range. { 'sen·trəl kən'trōl }

central eclipse   An eclipse in which the eclipsing body passes centrally (midpoints in line) over the body eclipsed. { 'sen·trəl i'klips }

central meridian   The meridian of a planet that crosses the center of the visible face of the planet at a given instant. { 'sen·trəl mə'rid·ē·ən }

central-meridian transit   The passage of an object on the surface of a planet across the central meridian. { 'sen·trəl mə'rid·ē·ən 'tranz·ət }

central peak   A mountain located at the center of the floor of a lunar crater. { 'sen·trəl 'pēk }

Cen X-3   See Centaurus X-3.

Cep   See Cepheus.

Cepheid   One of a subgroup of periodic variable stars whose brightness does not remain constant with time and whose period of variation is a function of intrinsic mean brightness. { 'sē·fē·əd }

Cepheus   A constellation with right ascension 22 hours, declination 70°N. Abbreviated Cep. { 'sē·fē·əs }

Ceres   The largest asteroid, with a diameter of about 960 kilometers, mean distance from the sun of 2.766 astronomical units, and C-type surface composition. { 'sir,ēz }

cesium-ion engine   An ion engine that uses a stream of cesium ions to produce a thrust for space travel. { 'sē·zē·əm ¦ī·ən 'en·jən }

Cet   See Cetus.

Cetus   A constellation with right ascension 2 hours, declination 10°S. Abbreviated Cet. Also known as Whale. { 'sēd·əs }

Cha   See Chamaeleon.

Chamaeleon   A constellation, right ascension 11 hours, declination 80°S. Abbreviated Cha. Also spelled Chameleon. { kə'mēl·yən }

chamber capacity   See chamber volume. { 'chām·bər kə'pas·əd·ē }

chamber pressure   The pressure of gases within the combustion chamber of a rocket engine. { 'chām·bər ,presh·ər }

chamber volume   The volume of the rocket combustion chamber, including the convergent portion of the nozzle up to the throat. Also known as chamber capacity. { 'chām·bər ,väl·yəm }

Chameleon   See Chamaeleon. { kə'mēl·yən }

Chandrasekhar limit   A limiting mass of about 1.44 solar masses above which a white dwarf cannot exist in a stable configuration. { ,chən·drə'shā,kär ,lim·ət }

Chandrasekhar-Schönberg limit   A mass limit for the isothermal, helium core of a main-sequence star above which the star must rapidly increase in radius and evolve away from the main sequence. Also known as Schönberg-Chandrasekhar limit. { ,chən·drə'shā,kär 'shərn,bərg ,lim·ət }

channel wing   A wing that is trough-shaped so as to surround partially a propeller to get increased lift at low speeds from the slipstream. { 'chan·əl ,wiŋ }

characteristic chamber length   The length of a straight, cylindrical tube having the same volume as that of the chamber of a rocket engine if the chamber had no converging section. { ˌkar·ik·təˈris·tik ˈchām·bər ˌleŋkth }

characteristic exhaust velocity   Of a rocket engine, a descriptive parameter, related to effective exhaust velocity and thrust coefficient. Also known as characteristic velocity. { ˌkar·ik·təˈris·tik igˈzȯst vəˈläs·əd·ē }

characteristic velocity   See characteristic exhaust velocity. { ˌkar·ik·təˈris·tik vəˈläs·əd·ē }

Charles' Wain   See Big Dipper. { ˈchärlz ˈwān }

Charon   The only known satellite of Pluto, with an orbital period of 6.387 days, distance from Pluto of approximately 18,000 kilometers, and diameter of approximately 1500 kilometers. { ˈka·rən }

chase pilot   A pilot who flies an escort airplane and advises another pilot who is making a check, training, or research flight in another craft. { ˈchās ˌpī·lət }

chaser   The vehicle that maneuvers in order to effect a rendezvous with an orbiting object. { ˈchās·ər }

check flight   1. A flight made to check or test the performance of an aircraft, rocket, or spacecraft, or a piece of its equipment, or to obtain measurements or other data on performance. 2. A familiarization flight in an aircraft, or a flight in which the pilot or the aircrew are tested for proficiency. { ˈchek ˌflīt }

chemical pressurization   The pressurization of propellant tanks in a rocket by means of high-pressure gases developed by the combustion of a fuel and oxidizer or by the decomposition of a substance. { ˈkem·i·kəl ˌpresh·ə·rəˈzā·shən }

cherry picker   A crane used to remove the aerospace capsule containing astronauts from the top of the rocket in the event of a malfunction. { ˈcher·ē ˌpik·ər }

Chiron   An object circling the sun in an eccentric orbit which takes it from inside the orbit of Saturn out to near the orbit of Uranus, and which has a period of 50.7 years. { ˈkīˌrän }

Chisel   See Caelum. { ˈchiz·əl }

chord   1. A straight line intersecting or touching an airfoil profile at two points. 2. Specifically, that part of such a line between two points of intersection. { kȯrd }

chord length   The length of the chord of an airfoil section between the extremities of the section. { ˈkȯrd ˌleŋkth }

chromosphere   A transparent, tenuous layer of gas that rests on the photosphere in the atmosphere of the sun. { ˈkrȯ·məˌsfir }

chromospheric network   A large-scale cellular pattern into which the motion of gas in the chromosphere is ordered by magnetic folds, and which is visible in spectroheliograms taken at the Hα (hydrogen alpha) line at a wavelength of about 656 nanometers and in other spectral regions. { ˈkrō·məˌsfir·ik ˈnetˌwərk }

CH star   A type of metal-poor carbon star that shows especially strong CH, CN, and C_2 bands in its spectra as well as enhanced bands due to the s-process elements; found in the halo of the Milky Way Galaxy. { ˈsēˈäch ˌstär }

chuffing

chuffing See chugging. { 'chəf·iŋ }

chugging Also known as bumping; chuffing. **1.** A form of combustion instability in a rocket engine, characterized by a pulsing operation at a fairly low frequency, sometimes defined as occurring between particular frequency limits. **2.** The noise that is made in this kind of combustion. { 'chəg·iŋ }

Cir See Circinus.

Circinus A constellation, right ascension 15 hours, declination 60°S. Abbreviated Cir. Also known as Compasses. { 'sərs·ən·əs }

circle of declination See hour circle. { 'sər·kəl əv ˌdek·lə'nā·shən }

circle of equal declination See parallel of declination. { 'sər·kəl əv 'ē·kwəl ˌdek·lə'nā·shən }

circle of equal probability A measure of the accuracy with which a rocket or missile can be guided; the radius of the circle at a specific distance in which 50% of the reliable shots land. Also known as circle of probable error; circular error probable. { 'sər·kəl əv 'ē·kwəl präb·ə'bil·əd·ē }

circle of latitude A great circle of the celestial sphere passing through the ecliptic poles, and hence perpendicular to the plane of the ecliptic. Also known as parallel of latitude. { 'sər·kəl əv 'lad·əˌtüd }

circle of longitude A circle of the celestial sphere, parallel to the ecliptic. { 'sər·kəl əv 'län·jəˌtüd }

circle of perpetual apparition That circle of the celestial sphere, centered on the polar axis and having a polar distance from the elevated pole approximately equal to the latitude of the observer, within which celestial bodies do not set. { 'sər·kəl əv pər'pech·ə·wəl ap·ə'rish·ən }

circle of perpetual occultation That circle of the celestial sphere, centered on the polar axis and having a polar distance from the depressed pole approximately equal to the latitude of the observer, within which celestial bodies do not rise. { 'sər·kəl əv pər'pech·ə·wəl ˌäk·əl'tā·shən }

circle of probable error See circle of equal probability. { 'sər·kəl əv 'präb·ə·bəl 'er·ər }

circle of right ascension See hour circle. { 'sər·kəl əv 'rīt ə'sen·shən }

circular error probable See circle of equal probability. { 'sər·kyə·lər ˌer·ər 'präb·ə·bəl }

circular orbit An orbit comprising a complete constant-altitude revolution around the earth. { 'sər·kyə·lər 'òr·bət }

circulating current A current that circulated in an abnormal direction in the atmosphere of the southern hemisphere of Jupiter between 1919 and 1934; its presence was indicated by the behavior of dark spots in the region. { 'sər·kyəˌlād·iŋ 'kər·ənt }

circumlunar Around the moon; generally applied to trajectories. { ˌsər·kəm'lü·nər }

circummeridian altitude See exmeridian altitude. { ˌsər·kəm·mə'rid·ē·ən 'al·təˌtüd }

circumpolar   Revolving about the elevated pole without setting. { ˈsər·kəm'pō·lər }

circumpolar star   A star with its polar distance approximately equal to or less than the latitude of the observer. { ˈsər·kəm'pō·lər 'stär }

circumstellar disk   A flattened cloud of gas or small particles that undergoes approximately circular motion about a star, and in which the material velocity is determined primarily by the balance of gravity and centrifugal force. { ˌsər·kəmˈstel·ər 'disk }

cislunar   Of or pertaining to phenomena, projects, or activity in the space between the earth and moon, or between the earth and the moon's orbit. { ˈsis'lü·nər }

civil day   A mean solar day beginning at midnight instead of at noon; may be based on either apparent solar time or mean solar time. { 'siv·əl 'dā }

civil time   Solar time in a day (civil day) that begins at midnight; may be either apparent solar time or mean solar time. { ˈsi·vəl ˈtīm }

civil twilight   The interval of incomplete darkness between sunrise (or sunset) and the time when the center of the sun's disk is 6° below the horizon. { ˈsi·vəl ˈtwīˌlīt }

civil year   See calendar year. { ˈsi·vəl ˈyir }

classical T Tauri star   A T Tauri star that exhibits strong emission lines in its optical spectrum, emits a strong stellar wind, and accretes material from a circumstellar disk. { ˈklas·ə·kəl ˈtē ˈtȯr·ē 'stär }

cleanup   Improving the external shape and smoothness of an aircraft to reduce its drag. { 'klēˌnəp }

climb   The gain in altitude of an aircraft. { klīm }

Clock   See Horologium. { kläk }

clock star   Any star that is used to measure time; always a bright star, whose right ascension is well known. { 'kläk ˌstär }

closed ecological system   A system used in spacecraft that provides for the maintenance of life in an isolated living chamber through complete reutilization of the material available, in particular, by means of a cycle wherein exhaled carbon dioxide, urine, and other waste matter are converted chemically or by photosynthesis into oxygen, water, and food. { ˈklōzd ek·ə'läj·ə·kəl ˌsis·təm }

closed universe   A cosmological model in which the volume of the universe is finite and in which the expansion of the universe will slow to a halt billions of years in the future, and the universe will then contract, becoming progressively denser, until it ends in a fireball similar to the big bang. { ˈklōzd 'yü·nəˌvərs }

closest approach   1. The event that occurs when two planets or other celestial bodies are nearest each other as they orbit about the sun or other primary. 2. The place or time of such an event. { 'klō·səst ə'prōch }

closing rate   The speed at which two aircraft or missiles come closer together. { 'klōz·iŋ ˌrāt }

closure parameter   The ratio of the actual mean mass density of the observable universe to the critical density for a Friedmann universe. { 'klō·zhər pəˌram·əd·ər }

cluster   See star cluster. { 'kləs·tər }

cluster cepheids

cluster cepheids   See RR Lyrae stars. { 'kləs·tər 'sef·ē·ədz }

cluster variables   See RR Lyrae stars. { ¦kləs·tər ¦ver·ē·ə·bəlz }

CMa   See Canis Major.

cmHg   See centimeter of mercury.

CMi   See Canis Minor.

CM Tauri   A supernova observed by the Chinese and Japanese in 1054; remnants are still seen as the Crab Nebula. { ¦sē¦em 'taúr·ē }

Coalsack   An area in one of the brighter regions of the Southern Milky Way which to the naked eye appears entirely devoid of stars and hence dark with respect to the surrounding Milky Way region. { 'kōl‚sak }

coasting flight   The flight of a rocket between burnout or thrust cutoff of one stage and ignition of another, or between burnout and summit altitude or maximum horizontal range. { 'kō·stiŋ ‚flīt }

cockpit   A space in an aircraft or spacecraft where the pilot sits. { 'käk‚pit }

coffin corner   The range of Mach numbers between the buffeting Mach number and the stalling Mach number within which an aircraft must be operated. { 'kò·fən ‚kòr·nər }

cold dark matter   A hypothetical type of dark matter consisting of particles that would have been in thermal equilibrium while traveling at nonrelativistic velocities in the early universe; possibilities include axions, photinos, gravitinos, heavy magnetic monopoles, and weakly interacting massive particles. { ¦kōld 'därk ‚mad·ər }

cold-flow test   A test of a liquid rocket without firing it to check or verify the integrity of a propulsion subsystem, and to provide for the conditioning and flow of propellants (including tank pressurization, propellant loading, and propellant feeding). { ¦kōld ¦flō ‚test }

coleopter   An aircraft having an annular (barrel-shaped) wing, the engine and body being mounted within the circle of the wing. { 'kō·lē‚äp·tər }

collimation error   The amount by which the angle between the optical axis of a transit telescope and its east-west mechanical axis deviates from 90°. { ‚käl·ə'mā·shən ‚er·ər }

collision parameter   In orbit computation, the distance between a center of attraction of a central force field and the extension of the velocity vector of a moving object at a great distance from the center. { kə'lizh·ən pə'ram·əd·ər }

color-color diagram   A graph whose coordinates are both color indices, showing the distribution of stars or other objects. { 'kəl·ər 'kəl·ər ‚dī·ə‚gram }

color equation   A measure of the color sensitivity and response of a method of observation; photographic, visual, or photoelectric techniques may be employed. { 'kəl·ər i'kwā·zhən }

color excess   The difference between the observed color index of a star and the color index corresponding to its spectral type. { 'kəl·ər 'ek‚ses }

color index   Abbreviated CI. **1.** Of a star, the numerical difference between the apparent photographic magnitude and the apparent photovisual magnitude. **2.** More generally, the difference in apparent magnitudes between two specified spectral regions. { 'kəl·ər ˌin·deks }

color-magnitude diagram   A graph of the apparent or absolute magnitudes of a group of stars versus their color indices. { 'kəl·ər ˈmag·nə·tüd ˌdī·ə·gram }

Columba   A constellation, right ascension 6 hours, declination 35°S. Abbreviated Col. Also known as Dove. { kə'ləm·bə }

colure   A great circle of the celestial sphere through the celestial poles and either the equinoxes or solstices, called respectively the equinoctial colure or the solstitial colure. { kə'lür }

Com   *See* Coma Berenices.

coma   The gaseous envelope that surrounds the nucleus of a comet. Also known as head. { 'kō·mə }

Coma Berenices   A constellation, right ascension 13 hours, declination 20°N. Abbreviated Com. Also known as Berenice's Hair. { 'kō·mə ˌber·ə'nī·sēz }

Coma cluster   **1.** A group of over 1000 bright galaxies having a recession velocity of about 4300 miles (6900 kilometers) per second. **2.** An open cluster of about 100 stars at a distance of about 80 parsecs (1.6×10^{15} miles or 2.6×10^{15} kilometers). { 'kō·mə ˌkləs·tər }

Coma supercluster   A supercluster that is centered on the Coma cluster of galaxies and has several extensions, including the Great Wall. { ˈkō·mə 'sü·pərˌkləs·tər }

combination spectrum   The composite spectrum characteristic of a symbiotic star. { ˌkäm·bə'nā·shən 'spek·trəm }

combustion chamber   That part of the rocket engine in which the combustion of propellants takes place at high pressure. Also known as firing chamber. { kəm'bəs·chən ˌchām·bər }

combustion instability   Unsteadiness or abnormality in the combustion of fuel, as may occur in a rocket engine. { kəm'bəs·chən ˌin·stə'bil·əd·ē }

comes   The smaller star in a binary system. Also known as companion. { 'kō·mēz }

comet   A nebulous celestial body having a fuzzy head surrounding a bright nucleus, one of two major types of bodies moving in closed orbits about the sun; in comparison with the planets, the comets are characterized by their more eccentric orbits and greater range of inclination to the ecliptic. { 'käm·ət }

cometary kilometric radiation   Radio waves detected by space probes encountering Comet Halley, consisting of several different emission patterns ranging from intense, sporadic bursts of broad-band noise to continuously rising and falling tones. { 'käm·əˌter·ē ˈkil·əˌme·trik ˌrād·ē'ā·shən }

cometary nebula   A fan-shaped reflection nebula that resembles a comet in appearance. { 'käm·əˌter·ē 'neb·yə·lə }

comet family   Those short-period comets whose aphelia correspond closely to Jupiter's orbit. { 'käm·ət ˌfam·lē }

comet group   A division of comets on the basis of their period; the short-period group (periods of less than 200 years) contains orbits that show a strong preference for the plan of the solar system; the planes of long-period comets are randomly distributed. { 'käm·ət ˌgrüp }

command guidance   The guidance of a missile, rocket, or spacecraft by means of electronic signals sent to receiving devices in the vehicle. { kə'mand ˌgīd·əns }

command module   The spacecraft module that carries the crew, the main communication and telemetry equipment, and the reentry capsule during cruising flight. { kə'mand ˌmäj·ül }

commensurable motions   Mean motions of the planets, or of the satellites of a planet, which satisfy simple arithmetic relationships. { kə'mens·rə·bəl 'mō·shənz }

commensurate orbits   Orbits of two celestial objects about a common center of gravity so that the period of one is a rational fraction of that of the other. { kə'mench·ə·rət 'or·bəts }

common year   A calendar year of 365 days. { ¦käm·ən ¦yir }

communications satellite   An orbiting, artificial earth satellite that relays radio, television, and other signals between ground terminal stations thousands of miles apart. Also known as radio relay satellite; relay satellite. { kəˌmyü·nə'kā·shənz 'sad·əˌlīt }

compact H II region   A region of dense ionized hydrogen in interstellar space, not greater than 1 parsec (1.9 × 10¹³ miles or 3.1 × 10¹³ kilometers) in diameter. { 'kämˌpakt 'āch 'tü ˌrē·jən }

compact radio source   A source of radio-frequency radiation outside the solar system whose flux at an intermediate radio frequency is dominated by the contribution from a single bright component less than 1 kiloparsec (1.9 × 10¹⁶ miles or 3.1 × 10¹⁶ kilometers) in diameter. { 'käm·pakt 'rād·ē·ō ˌsórs }

companion   See comes. { kəm'pan·yən }

companion body   A nose cone, last-stage rocket, or other body that orbits along with an earth satellite or follows a space probe. { kəm'pan·yən ˌbäd·ē }

comparison star   A star of known brightness used as a standard for comparison in determining the magnitude of a nearby celestial object. { kəm'par·ə·sən ˌstär }

Compasses   See Circinus. { 'käm·pə·səz }

Compton-Getting effect   The sidereal diurnal variation of the intensity of cosmic rays which would be expected from the rotation of the galaxy if cosmic radiation originated in extragalactic regions and was isotropic in intergalactic space, and if this radiation was unaffected at entry to and passage through the galaxy. { ¦käm·tən 'ged·iŋ i'fekt }

comptonization   The redistribution in the energies of photons in interstellar space that results from their scattering from electrons. { ˌkäm·tə·nə'zā·shən }

Comstock refraction formula   A formula for the apparent angular displacement of an object outside the earth's atmosphere due to refraction, in terms of the barometric pressure, the temperature of the atmosphere, and the observed zenith distance. { 'kämˌstäk ri'frak·shən ˌfòr·myə·lə }

concentric ring structures   A formation on the moon's surface consisting of two craters, one inside the other, with approximately the same center. { kən'sen·trik 'riŋ ˌstrək·chərz }

cone of visibility   Generally, the right conical space which has its apex at some ground target and within which an aircraft must be located if the pilot is to be able to discern the target while flying at a specified altitude. { 'kōn əv ˌviz·ə'bil·əd·ē }

configuration   A particular type of specific aircraft, rocket, or such, which differs from others of the same model by the arrangement of its components or by the addition or omission of auxiliary equipment; for example, long-range configuration or cargo configuration. { kənˌfig·yə'rā·shən }

conical point   See inner Lagrangian point. { 'kän·ə·kəl 'pȯint }

conjunction   **1.** The situation in which two celestial bodies have either the same celestial longitude or the same sidereal hour angle. **2.** The time at which this conjunction takes place. { kən'jəŋk·shən }

consanguineous ring structures   A formation on the moon's surface consisting of two or more craters that are similar in form and very close to each other. { ˈkän·saŋˈgwin·ē·əs 'riŋ ˌstrək·chərz }

constant-level balloon   A balloon designed to float at a constant pressure level. Also known as constant-pressure balloon. { ˈkän·stənt ˈlev·əl bə'lün }

constant of aberration   The maximum aberration of a star observed from the surface of the earth, equal to 20.49 seconds of arc. { 'kän·stənt əv ab·ə'rā·shən }

constant-pressure balloon   See constant-level balloon. { ˈkän·stənt ˈpresh·ər bə'lün }

constant-speed propeller   A variable-pitch propeller having a governor which automatically changes the pitch to maintain constant engine speed. { ˈkän·stənt ˈspēd prə'pel·ər }

constellation   **1.** Any one of the star groups interpreted as forming configurations in the sky; examples are Orion and Leo. **2.** Any one of the definite areas of the sky. { ˌkän·stə'lā·shən }

constituent day   The duration of one rotation of the earth on its axis with respect to an astre fictif, that is, a fictitious star representing one of the periodic elements in the tidal forces; approximates the length of a lunar or solar day. { kən'stich·ə·wənt 'dā }

constrictor   The exit portion of the combustion chamber in some designs of ramjets, where there is a narrowing of the tube at the exhaust. { kən'strik·tər }

construction weight   The weight of a rocket exclusive of propellant, load, and crew if any. Also known as structural weight. { kən'strək·shən ˌwāt }

contact binary   A binary system at least one of whose components fills its Roche lobe and in which mass exchange is taking place. { 'känˌtakt 'bī·ner·ē }

contiguous arc   A crater arc in which successive craters are in contact. { kən'tig·yə·wəs 'ärk }

contiguous chain   A crater chain in which successive craters are in contact. { kən'tig·yə·wəs 'chān }

contiguous craters   A formation on the moon's surface consisting of two craters in contact; the walls at the point of contact are low, broken, or entirely absent. { kən'tig·yə·wəs 'krād·ərz }

contraorbit missile A missile that is sent backward along the calculated orbit of an aerospace weapon, satellite, or spacecraft for the purpose of destroying it in a head-on collision with an explosive warhead or through use of a secondary missile. { ˈkän·trəˈȯr·bət 'mis·əl }

control column A cockpit control lever pivoted or sliding in front of the pilot; controls operation of the elevator and aileron. { kən'trōl ˌkäl·əm }

control feel The impression of the stability and control of an aircraft that a pilot receives through the cockpit controls, either from the aerodynamic forces acting on the control surfaces or from forces simulating these aerodynamic forces. { kən'trōl ˌfēl }

controllability The quality of an aircraft or guided weapon which determines the ease of producing changes in flight direction or in altitude by operation of its controls. { kənˌtrōl·ə'bil·əd·ē }

controlled-leakage system A system that provides for the maintenance of life in an aircraft or spacecraft cabin by a controlled escape of carbon dioxide and other waste from the cabin, with replenishment provided by stored oxygen and food. { kənˈtrōld ˈlēk·ij ˌsis·təm }

control-moment gyro An internal momentum storage device that applies torques to the attitude-control system through large rotating gyros. { kən'trōl ˌmō·mənt ˌjī·rō }

control plane An aircraft from which the movements of another craft are controlled remotely. { kən'trōl ˌplān }

control rocket A vernier engine, retrorocket, or other such rocket used to change the attitude of, guide, or make small changes in the speed of a rocket, spacecraft, or the like. { kən'trōl ˌräk·ət }

control surface **1.** Any movable airfoil used to guide or control an aircraft, guided missile, or the like in the air, including the rudder, elevators, ailerons, spoiler flaps, and trim tabs. **2.** In restricted usage, one of the main control surfaces, such as the rudder, an elevator, or an aileron. { kən'trōl ˌsər·fəs }

control vane A movable vane used for control, especially a movable air vane or jet vane on a rocket used to control flight altitude. { kən'trōl ˌvān }

convective zone A region of instability just below the photosphere of the sun in which part of the heat is carried outward by convective currents. { kən'vek·div ˌzōn }

convertiplane A hybrid form of heavier-than-air craft capable, because of one or more horizontal rotors or units acting as rotors, of taking off, hovering, and landing in a fashion similar to a helicopter; and once aloft and moving forward, capable, by means of a mechanical conversion, of flying purely as a fixed-wing aircraft, especially in higher speed ranges. { kən'vərd·əˌplān }

cool star A low-temperature star, generally visible in the infrared range of the electromagnetic spectrum. { ˈkül ˈstär }

Copernican principle The idea that the earth occupies a typical or unexceptional position in the universe. { kə'pər·nə·kən ˈprin·sə·pəl }

Copernican system The system of planetary motions according to Copernicus, who maintained that the earth revolves about an axis once every day and revolves around the sun once every year while the other planets also move in orbits centered near the sun. { kə'pər·nə·kən ˌsis·təm }

Cordelia A satellite of Uranus orbiting at a mean distance of 30,910 miles (49,750 kilometers) with a period of 8 hours 4 minutes, and with a diameter of about 16 miles (26 kilometers); the inner shepherding satellite for the outermost ring of Uranus. { kȯr'dēl·yə }

core-halo galaxy A radio galaxy characterized by a relatively large region of diffuse radio emission surrounding a central region of more intense emission. { 'kȯr ¦hā· lō ˌgal·ik·sē }

corona See solar corona. { kə'rō·nə }

Corona Australis A constellation, right ascension 19 hours, declination 40°S. Abbreviated CrA. Also known as Southern Crown. { kə'rō·nə ȯs'tral·əs }

Corona Borealis A constellation, right ascension 16 hours, declination 30°N. Abbreviated CrB. Also known as Northern Crown. { kə'rō·nə bȯr·ē'al·əs }

coronagraph An instrument for photographing the corona and prominences of the sun at times other than at solar eclipse. { kə'rō·nəˌgraf }

coronal green line The strongest emission line in the visible spectrum of the solar corona, located at a wavelength of 530.3 nanometers and resulting from the emission of iron atoms that have lost 13 of their electrons. { 'kȯr·ən·əl grēn ˌlīn }

coronal hole A large-scale, apparently open structure in the solar corona, devoid of any soft x-ray emission and surrounded by diverging boundary structures. { kə'rō· nəl ˌhōl }

corotating interaction regions Regions of enhanced magnetic field bounded by jumps in the solar wind speed that form at distances from the sun greater than 2.5 astronomical units. { ¦kō'rōˌtād·iŋ ˌin·tər'ak·shən ˌrē·jənz }

Corvus A constellation, right ascension 12 hours, declination 20°S. Abbreviated Crv. Also known as Crow. { 'kȯr·vəs }

cosmic Pertaining to the cosmos, the vast extraterrestrial regions of the universe. { 'käz·mik }

cosmic abundance The amount of a substance believed to be present in the entire universe, relative to other substances. { 'käz·mik ə'bən·dəns }

cosmic background radiation See cosmic microwave radiation. { 'käz·mik ¦bakˌgraȯnd ˌrād·ēˌā·shən }

cosmic censorship hypothesis The hypothesis that a system which evolves according to the equations of general relativity from an initial state that does not have singularities or any unusual properties will not develop any space-time singularities that would be visible from large distances. { 'käz·mik 'sen·sərˌship hī∕päth·ə·səs }

cosmic dust Fine particles of solid matter forming clouds in interstellar space. { 'käz·mik 'dəst }

cosmic electrodynamics The science concerned with electromagnetic phenomena in ionized media encountered in interstellar space, in stars, and above the atmosphere. { 'käz·mik iˌlek·trō·də'nam·iks }

47

cosmic expansion   The recession of all distant galaxies from each other, as manifested in the red shift of their spectral lines. { 'käz·mik ik'span·shən }

cosmic light   The contribution to the brightness of the night sky from all unresolved extragalactic sources. { 'käz·mik 'līt }

cosmic microwave background   *See* cosmic microwave radiation. { 'käz·mik 'mī·krō‚wāv 'bak‚graȯnd }

cosmic microwave radiation   A nearly uniform flux of microwave radiation that is believed to permeate all of space and to have originated in the big bang. Also known as cosmic background radiation; cosmic microwave background; microwave background. { 'käz·mik 'mī·krō‚wāv ‚rād·ē'ā·shən }

cosmic radio waves   Radio waves reaching the earth from interstellar or intergalactic sources. { 'käz·mik 'rād·ē·ō ‚wāvz }

cosmic string   A hypothetical relic of the early universe, postulated to have a diameter of the order of 10^{-35} meter and a linear density of the order of 4×10^{22} kilograms per meter, and to be either infinitely long or in the form of a closed curve. { 'käz·mik 'striŋ }

cosmic year   The period of rotation of the Milky Way Galaxy, about 220 million years. { 'käz·mik 'yir }

cosmochemistry   The branch of science which treats of the chemical composition of the universe and its origin. { ¦käz·mō¦kem·ə·strē }

cosmogony   Study of the origin and evolution of specific astronomical systems and of the universe as a whole. { käz'mäg·ə·nē }

cosmological   Relating to the overall structure of the universe. { ¦käz·mə¦läj·ə·kəl }

cosmological principle   The assumption made in most theories of cosmology that the universe is homogeneous on a large scale. { ¦käz·mə¦läj·ə·kəl 'prin·sə·pəl }

cosmological redshift   The red shift that can be ascribed entirely to the general expansion of space-time initiated by the big bang. { ¦käz·mə¦läj·ə·kəl 'red‚shift }

cosmology   The study of the overall structure of the physical universe. { käz'mäl·ə·jē }

cosmonaut   A Russian astronaut. { 'käz·mə‚nȯt }

cotidal hour   The average interval expressed in solar or lunar hours between the moon's passage over the meridian of Greenwich and the following high water at a specified place. { ‚kō'tīd·əl 'aȯ·ər }

count   **1.** To proceed from one point to another in a countdown or plus count, normally by calling a number to signify the point reached. **2.** To proceed in a countdown, for example, T minus 90 and counting. { kaȯnt }

countdown   **1.** The process in the engineering definition, used in leading up to the launch of a large or complicated rocket vehicle, or in leading up to a captive test, a readiness firing, a mock firing, or other firing test. **2.** The act of counting inversely during this process. { 'kaȯnt‚daȯn }

counter sun   *See* anthelion. { 'kaȯnt·ər‚sən }

48

counterglow See gegenschein. { 'kaùnt·ər,glō }

Cowell method A method of orbit computation using direct step-by-step integration in rectangular coordinates of the total acceleration of the orbiting body. { 'kaù· əl ,meth·əd }

cowling The streamlined metal cover of an aircraft engine. { 'kaù·liŋ }

CrA See Corona Australis.

Crab Nebula A gaseous nebula in the constellation Taurus; an amorphous mass which radiates a continuous spectrum involved in a mesh of filaments that radiate a bright-line spectrum. { 'krab 'neb·yə·lə }

Crab pulsar A pulsar found in the center of the Crab Nebula with a period of about 0.033 second and that emits radiation at all wavelengths from the radio to the x-ray region. { 'krab 'pəl,sär }

Crane See Grus. { krān }

Crater A constellation, right ascension 11 hours, declination 15°S. Abbreviated Crt. Also known as Cup. { 'krād·ər }

crater arc A series of lunar craters located along a curved line. { 'krād·ər ,ärk }

crater chain A series of lunar craters located along a straight line. { 'krād·ər ,chān }

craterlet A very small lunar crater, with diameter less than about 5 miles (8 kilometers), that still has raised walls. { 'krād·ər·lət }

crater pit A small lunar crater with no raised walls surrounding it. { 'krād·ər ,pit }

CrB See Corona Borealis.

crepuscular rays Streaks of light radiating from the sun shortly before and after sunset which shine through breaks in the clouds or through irregular spaces along the horizon. { krə'pəs·kyə·lər 'rāz }

crescent phase A phase of the moon or an inferior planet in which less than half of the visible hemisphere is illuminated. { 'kres·ənt ,fāz }

Cressida A satellite of Uranus orbiting at a mean distance of 38,380 miles (61,770 kilometers) with a period of 11 hours 9 minutes, and with a diameter of about 41 miles (66 kilometers). { 'kres·əd·ə }

critical altitude The maximum altitude at which a supercharger can maintain a pressure in the intake manifold of an engine equal to that existing during normal operation at rated power and speed at sea level without the supercharger. { 'krid·ə·kəl 'al·tə,tüd }

critical angle of attack The angle of attack of an airfoil at which the flow of air about the airfoil changes abruptly so that lift is sharply reduced and drag is sharply increased. Also known as stalling angle of attack. { 'krid·ə·kəl !aŋ·gəl əv ə'tak }

critical density The mass density above which, it is believed, the expansion of the universe will slow down and reverse. { 'krid·ə·kəl 'den·səd·ē }

critical equatorial velocity In rotating early-type stars, the velocity at which the cen-

critical Mach number

trifugal force at the equator equals the force of gravity there. { 'krid·ə·kəl ˌek·wə'tōr·ē·əl və'läs·əd·ē }

critical Mach number   The free-stream Mach number at which a local Mach number of 1.0 is attained at any point on the body under consideration. { 'krid·ə·kəl 'mäk ˌnəm·bər }

critical velocity   In rocketry, the speed of sound at the conditions prevailing at the nozzle throat. Also known as throat velocity. { 'krid·ə·kəl və'läs·əd·ē }

Cross   See Crux. { kròs }

crossed-field accelerator   A plasma engine for space travel in which plasma serves as a conductor to carry current across a magnetic field, so that a resultant force is exerted on the plasma. { 'kròst ˌfēld ik'sel·ə‚rād·ər }

cross-flow   A flow going across another flow, as a spanwise flow over a wing. { 'kròs ˌflō }

cross-flow plane   A plane at right angles to the free-stream velocity. { 'kròs ˌflō ˌplān }

Crow   See Corvus. { krō }

Crt   See Crater.

Cru   See Crux.

cruciform wing   An aircraft wing in the shape of a cross. { 'krü·sə‚fórm ˌwiŋ }

cruise missile   A pilotless airplane that can be launched from a submarine, surface ship, ground vehicle, or another airplane; range can be up to 1500 miles (2400 kilometers), flying at a constant altitude that can be as low as 200 feet (60 meters). { 'krüz ˌmis·əl }

Crux   A constellation having four principal bright stars which form the figure of a cross; right ascension 12 hours, declination 60°S. Abbreviated Cru. Also known as Cross; Southern Cross. { krùks }

Crv   See Corvus.

C-type asteroid   A type of asteroid whose surface is very dark and neutral-colored, and probably is of carbonaceous composition similar to primitive carbonaceous chondritic meteorites. { 'sē ˌtīp 'as·tə‚ròid }

culmination   1. The position of a heavenly body when at highest apparent altitude. 2. For a heavenly body which is continually above the horizon, the position of lowest apparent altitude. { kəl·mə'nā·shən }

Cup   See Crater. { kəp }

curtate distance   The distance between the earth or the sun and the foot of a perpendicular from a planet or comet to the plane of the earth's orbit. { 'kər‚tāt ˌdis·təns }

curvature correction   A correction applied to the mean of a series of observations on a star or planet to take account of the divergence of the apparent path of the star or planet from a straight line. { 'kər·və·chər kə'rek·shən }

curve of growth A graph of the equivalent width of an absorption line versus the number of atoms that produce it. { 'kərv əv 'grōth }

cusp cap One of the 10 bright areas observed near one of the extremities of the illuminated portion of Venus during the crescent phase. { 'kəsp ˌkap }

cutoff The shutting off of the propellant flow in a rocket, or the stopping of the combustion of the propellant. { 'kətˌȯf }

CVn *See* Canes Venatīci.

cyanogen absorption Bands in the absorption spectra of stars at wavelengths near 418 nanometers, caused by atmospheric cyanogen; used as a measure of absolute stellar magnitude. { sī'an·ə·jən əb'sȯrp·shən }

Cybele An asteroid with a diameter of about 177 miles (295 kilometers), mean distance from the sun of 3.423 astronomical units, and C-type surface composition. { 'sib·ə·lē }

cycle checkout The periodic action of carrying out a complete series of operational and calibrational tests on missiles held in alert status. { 'sī·kəl 'chekˌaut }

Cyg *See* Cygnus.

Cygnus A conspicuous northern summer constellation; the five major stars are arranged in the form of a cross, but the constellation is represented by a swan with spread wings flying southward; right ascension 21 hours, declination 40°N. Abbreviated Cyg. Also known as Northern Cross; Swan. { 'sig·nəs }

Cygnus A A strong, discrete radio source in the constellation Cygnus, associated with two spiral galaxies in collision. { 'sig·nəs 'ā }

Cygnus loop A supernova remnant about 17,000 years old, and 30-40 parsecs across and probably about 770 parsecs distant that emits radio waves and x-rays as well as visible light. Also known as Veil Nebula. { 'sig·nəs ˌlüp }

Cygnus X-1 A source of x-rays whose intensity varies in an irregular manner, associated with a weak variable radio source and a ninth-magnitude spectroscopic binary star, designated HDE226868, that consists of a blue supergiant and an invisible companion, which may be a black hole. Abbreviated Cyg X-1. { 'sig·nəs ˌeks 'wən }

Cygnus X-3 A variable source of x-rays, with a period of 4.8 hours, associated with a variable radio source that flared up to enormous levels in September 1972 with no observed increase in x-ray emission. Abbreviated Cyg X-3. { 'sig·nəs ˌeks 'thrē }

Cyg X-1 *See* Cygnus X-1.

Cyg X-3 *See* Cygnus X-3.

D

daily aberration See diurnal aberration. { ˈdā·lē ab·əˈrā·shən }

dark cloud A relatively dense, cool cloud of interstellar gas, chiefly molecular, whose dust particles obscure the light of stars behind it. { ˈdärk ˈklaůd }

dark-eclipsing variables A binary star system, comprising a bright star and an almost dark companion that revolve about each other. { ˈdärk əˌklip·siŋ ˈver·ē·ə·bəlz }

dark matter Matter that is postulated to exist to explain the rotational motion of the Milky Way Galaxy and other galaxies, to explain the motions of galaxies in clusters, and, in certain cosmological theories, to achieve the critical density of matter in the universe that is just sufficient to close the universe. Also known as missing mass. { ˈdärk ˌmad·ər }

dark nebula A cloud of solid particles which absorbs or scatters away radiation directed toward an observer and becomes apparent when silhouetted against a bright nebula or rich star field. Also known as absorption nebula. { ˈdärk ˌneb·yə·lə }

dark of the moon 1. The time period of approximately a week at the time of a new moon, when the light of the moon is absent at night. 2. Any period in which the light of the moon is obscured. { ˈdärk əv thə ˈmün }

dark satellite Satellite that gives no information to a friendly ground environment, either because it is controlled or because the radiating equipment is inoperative. { ˈdärk ˈsad·əlˌīt }

dark star A star that is not visible but is a part of a binary star system; in particular, a star which causes, in an eclipsing variable, a primary eclipse. { ˈdärk ˈstär }

dart configuration An aerodynamic configuration in which the control surfaces are at the tail of the vehicle. { ˈdärt kənˌfig·yəˈrā·shən }

Darwin ellipsoids Ellipsoidal figures of equilibrium of homogeneous bodies moving about each other in circular orbits, calculated by making certain approximations about their mutual tidal influences. { ˈdär·wən əˈlipˌsòidz }

Davida An asteroid with a diameter of about 280 kilometers, mean distance from the sun of 3.191 astronomical units, and C-type surface composition. { ˈdä·və·də }

Davis wing A narrow-chord wing that has comparatively low drag and a stable center of pressure and develops lift at relatively small angles of attack. { ˈda·vəs ˌwiŋ }

dawn The first appearance of light in the eastern sky before sunrise, or the time of that appearance. Also known as daybreak. { dòn }

dawn side That side of a celestial object, such as a planet, which points in the direction of its orbital movement. { dȯn ˌsīd }

day One of various units of time equal to the period of rotation of the earth with respect to one or another direction in space; specific examples are the mean solar day and the sidereal day. { dā }

daybreak See dawn. { 'dāˌbrāk }

dayglow Airglow of the day sky. { 'dāˌglō }

daylight Light of the day, from sun and sky. { 'dāˌlīt }

daylight saving meridian The meridian used for reckoning daylight saving time; generally 15° east of the zone of standard meridian. { ¦dāˌlīt 'sāv·iŋ məˈrid·ē·ən }

daylight saving noon Twelve o'clock daylight saving time, or the instant the mean sun is over the upper branch of the daylight saving meridian; during a war, when daylight saving time may be used throughout the year and called war time, the expression war noon applies. Also known as summer noon. { ¦dāˌlīt 'sāv·iŋ 'nün }

daylight saving time A variation of zone time, usually 1 hour more advanced than standard time, frequently kept during the summer to make better use of daylight. Also known as summer time. { ¦dāˌlīt ˌsāv·iŋ ˌtīm }

db galaxy A dumbbell-shaped radio galaxy, believed to consist of two elliptical nuclei surrounded by a common extended envelope. { ¦dē¦bē 'gal·ik·sē }

dead stick The propeller of an airplane that is not rotating because the engine has stopped. { 'ded ˌstik }

debriefing The relating of factual information by a flight crew at the termination of a flight, consisting of flight weather encountered, the condition of the aircraft, or facilities along the airways or at the airports. { dē'brēf·iŋ }

deceleration parachute See drogue. { dēˌsel·əˈrā·shən 'par·əˌshüt }

deceleron A lateral control surface of an airplane that is divided so as to combine the functions of an airbrake and an aileron. { dē'sel·əˌrän }

December solstice Winter solstice in the Northern Hemisphere. { di'sem·bər 'säl·stəs }

declination The angular distance of a celestial object north or south of the celestial equator. { ˌdek·ləˈnā·shən }

decoupling era The time about 300,000 years after the big bang when matter and radiation, which had previously been strongly coupled, practically ceased to interact, electrons were able to attach to nuclei and form atoms, and photons could propagate freely. { dē'kəp·liŋ ˌir·ə }

decremental arc A crater arc in which the diameters of the craters decrease from one end of the arc to the other. { 'dek·rəˈment·əl 'ärk }

decremental chain A crater chain in which the diameters of the craters decrease from one end of the chain to the other. { 'dek·rəˈment·əl ˌchān }

deep space Space beyond the gravitational influence of the earth. { ¦dēp 'spās }

Deep Space Network   A spacecraft network operated by NASA which tracks, commands, and receives telemetry for all types of spacecraft sent to explore deep space, the moon, and solar system planets. Abbreviated DSN. { ¦dēp ¦spās 'net‚wərk }

deep-space probe   A spacecraft designed for exploring space beyond the gravitational and magnetic fields of the earth. { ¦dēp ¦spās 'prōb }

deferent   An imaginary circle around the earth, postulated by Ptolemy, in whose circumference a celestial body or its epicycle is supposed to move. { 'def·ə·rənt }

deicer   Any device to keep the wings and propeller of an airplane free of ice. { dē'īs·ər }

Deimos   A satellite of Mars orbiting at a mean distance of 14,600 miles (23,500 kilometers). { 'dā‚mós }

de Laval nozzle   A converging-diverging nozzle used in certain rockets. Also known as Laval nozzle. { də·lä'väl ‚näz·əl }

delayed repeater satellite   Satellite which stores information obtained from a ground terminal at one location, and upon interrogation by a terminal at a different location, transmits the stored message. { di'lād ri¦pēd·ər 'sad·əl‚īt }

Delphinus   A northern constellation, right ascension 21 hours, declination 10° north. Also known as Dolphin. { del'fē·nəs }

δ Aquarids   A meteor shower consisting of relatively long, slow-moving meteors that has its maximum around July 30 and radiant near the star δ Aquarii. { ¦del·tə 'ak·wə‚ridz }

δ Cephei   A cepheid variable, from which the name of this type of star is derived; it has a period of 5.3 days. { 'del·tə 'sef·ē‚ī }

δ Scuti stars   A class of pulsating variable stars of spectral type A and with periods of less than 8 hours, relatively small amplitude variations, and masses between 1 and 3 solar masses. { ¦del·tə 'sküd·ē ‚stärz }

delta wing   A triangularly shaped wing of an aircraft. { 'del·tə ‚wiŋ }

Dembowska   The only moderately large asteroid whose surface composition resembles that of ordinary chondritic meteorites; has a diameter of about 65 miles (140 kilometers) and a mean distance from the sun of 2.924 astronomical units. { dem'bóf·skə }

Demon Star   See Algol. { 'dē·mən ‚stär }

Deneb   A white star of spectral classification A2-Ia in the constellation Cygnus; the star α Cygni. { 'den‚eb }

Denebola   A white star of stellar magnitude 2.2, spectral classification A2, in the constellation Leo; the star β Leonis. { də'neb·ə·lə }

density airspeed   Calibrated airspeed corrected for pressure altitude and true air temperature. { 'den·səd·ē 'er‚spēd }

density correction   A correction made necessary because the airspeed indicator is calibrated only for standard air pressure; it is applied to equivalent airspeed to obtain true airspeed, or to calibrated airspeed to obtain density airspeed. { 'den·səd·ē kə'rek·shən }

density error The error in the indications of a differential-pressure-type airspeed indicator due to nonstandard atmospheric density. { 'den·səd·ē ,er·ər }

density specific impulse The product of the specific impulse of a propellant combination and the average specific gravity of the propellants. { 'den·səd·ē spə,sif·ik 'im,pəls }

density-wave theory A theory explaining the spiral structure of galaxies by a periodic variation in space in the density of matter which rotates with a fixed angular velocity while the angular velocity of the matter itself varies with distance from the galaxy's center. { 'den·səd·ē ,wāv ,thē·ə·rē }

deorbit To recover a spacecraft from earth orbit by providing a new orbit which intersects the earth's atmosphere. { dē'òr·bət }

descending node **1.** That point at which an earth satellite crosses to the south side of the equatorial plane of its primary. Also known as southbound node. **2.** The point at which a planet, planetoid, or comet crosses the ecliptic from north to south. { di'sen·diŋ 'nōd }

descent Motion of a craft in which the path is inclined with respect to the horizontal. { di'sent }

descriptive astronomy Astronomy as presented by graphic and verbal description. { di'skrip·tiv ə'strän·ə·mē }

Desdemona A satellite of Uranus orbiting at a mean distance of 38,935 miles (62,660 kilometers) with a period of 11 hours 24 minutes, and with a diameter of about 36 miles (58 kilometers). { ,dez·də'mōn·ə }

design gross weight The gross weight at takeoff that an aircraft, rocket, or such is expected to have, used in design calculations. { di'zīn ˌgrōs 'wāt }

despin To stop or reduce the rotation of a spacecraft or one of its components. { ,dē'spin }

Despoina A satellite of Neptune orbiting at a mean distance of 32,500 miles (52,500 kilometers) with a period of 8.0 hours, and with a diameter of about 110 miles (180 kilometers). { des'pòin·ə }

destruct The deliberate action of destroying a rocket vehicle after it has been launched, but before it has completed its course. { di'strəkt }

destruct line On a rocket test range, a boundary line on each side of the down-range course beyond which a rocket cannot fly without being destroyed under destruct procedures; or a line beyond which the impact point cannot pass. { di'strəkt ,līn }

detached binary A binary system in which the components do not fill their Roche lobes and have little tidal distortion, and in which significant mass exchange is not taking place. { di'tacht 'bī,ner·ē }

developed planform The plan of an airfoil as drawn with the chord lines at each section rotated about the airfoil axis into a plane parallel to the plane of projection and with the airfoil axis rotated or developed and projected into the plane of projection. { də'vel·əpt 'plan,fòrm }

D galaxy A giant galaxy consisting of an elliptically shaped nucleus surrounded by an unusually large envelope. { 'dē ,gal·ik·sē }

diagram on the plane of the celestial equator   See time diagram. { 'dī·ə‚gram ȯn thə 'plān əv thə sə'les·chəl ē'kwäd·ər }

diagram on the plane of the equinoctial   See time diagram. { 'dī·ə‚gram ȯn thə 'plān əv thə ē·kwə'näk·chəl }

diamond-ring effect   A phenomenon observed just before and after the central phase of a total solar eclipse, in which the last Baily's bead glows brightly compared with other visible features, and the solar corona forms a band that is visible on the rest of the lunar edge. { ¦dī·mənd 'riŋ i‚fekt }

dichotomy   The phase of the moon or an inferior planet at which exactly half of its disk is illuminated and the terminator is a straight line. { dī'käd·ə·mē }

differential correction   A method for finding from the observed residuals minus the computed residuals (O − C) small corrections which, when applied to the orbital elements or constants, will reduce the deviations from the observed motion to a minimum. { ‚dif·ə'ren·chəl kə'rek·shən }

diffuse galactic light   Starlight that has been scattered or reflected by interstellar dust near the galactic plane. { də'fyüs gə'lak·tik 'līt }

diffuse nebula   A type of nebula ranging from huge masses presenting relatively high surface brightness down to faint, milky structures that are detectable only with long exposures and special filters; may contain both dust and gas or may be purely gaseous. { də'fyüs 'neb·yə·lə }

diffuse skylight   See diffuse sky radiation. { də'fyüs 'skī‚līt }

diffuse sky radiation   Solar radiation reaching the earth's surface after having been scattered from the direct solar beam by molecules or suspensoids in the atmosphere. Also known as diffuse skylight; skylight; sky radiation. { də¦fyüs ¦skī ‚rād·ē'ā·shən }

digital flight-control computer   A device that contains a digital model of the aerodynamic performance of an aircraft under various conditions of flight and uses this information to interpret pilot commands into optimum motions of the aircraft's control surfaces. { 'dij·əd·əl 'flīt kən‚trōl kəm‚pyüd·ər }

dihedral   The upward or downward inclination of an airplane's wing or other supporting surface in respect to the horizontal; in some contexts, the upward inclination only. { dī'hē·drəl }

Dione   A satellite of Saturn that orbits at a mean distance of 2.35 × 10⁵ miles (3.78 × 10⁵ kilometers) and has a diameter of about 700 miles (1120 kilometers). { 'dī·ə‚nē }

dipole anisotropy   A deviation of the equivalent blackbody temperature of the cosmic microwave radiation from its average value which is proportional to the cosine of the angle with some given direction, thus resembling the form of radiation from a dipole antenna. { 'dī‚pōl ‚an·ə'sä·trə·pē }

direct air cycle   A thermodynamic propulsion cycle involving a nuclear reactor and gas turbine or ramjet engine, in which air is the working fluid. Also known as direct cycle. { də¦rekt ¦er ‚sī·kəl }

direct cycle   See direct air cycle. { də¦rekt 'sī·kəl }

directional gyro   A flight instrument incorporating a gyro that holds its position in

directional stability

azimuth and thus can be used as a directional reference. Also known as direction indicator. { də'rek·shən·əl 'jī·rō }

directional stability   The property of an aircraft, rocket, or such, enabling it to restore itself from a yawing or side-slipping condition. Also known as weathercock stability. { də'rek·shən·əl stə'bil·əd·ē }

direction indicator   See directional gyro. { də'rek·shən ‚in·də‚kād·ər }

direct motion   Eastward, or counterclockwise, motion of a planet or other object as seen from the North Pole (motion in the direction of increasing right ascension). { dəǀrekt 'mō·shən }

direct solar radiation   That portion of the radiant energy received at the actinometer direct from the sun, as distinguished from diffuse sky radiation, effective terrestrial radiation, or radiation from any other source. { dəǀrekt ǀsō·lər rād·ē'ā·shən }

dirigible   A lighter-than-air craft equipped with means of propelling and steering for controlled flight. { də'rij·ə·bəl }

dirty ice   Interstellar ice particles with particles of graphite or other impurities adsorbed on their surfaces. { 'dər·dē 'īs }

dirty snowball model   A model of comet structure in which the nucleus of the comet resembles a large dirty snowball. { ǀdər·dē 'snō‚ból ‚mäd·əl }

disc   See disk. { disk }

DISCOS   See disturbance compensation system. { 'dis‚kōs }

discrete radio source   A source of radio waves coming from a small area of the sky. { di'skrēt 'rād·ē·ō ‚sórs }

disk   A relatively thin layer of material distributed in the central plane of a spiral galaxy, in contrast to the nucleus or halo. Also spelled disc. { disk }

disk loading   A measure which expresses the design gross weight of a helicopter as a function of the swept areas of the lifting rotor. { 'disk ‚lōd·iŋ }

disk population   The older Population I stars such as the sun. { 'disk ‚päp·yə'lā·shən }

dispersion   1. Deviation from a prescribed flight path; specifically, circular dispersion especially as applied to missiles. 2. The frequency dependence of the retardation of radio waves (such as those emitted by a pulsar) when they pass through an ionized gas. { də'spər·zhən }

dispersion measure   A quantity that describes the dispersion of a radio signal, proportional to the product of the density of interstellar electrons and the distance to the source. { də'spər·zhən ‚mezh·ər }

distance-luminosity relation   The relation in which the light intensity from a star is inversely proportional to the square of its distance. { ǀdis·təns lü·mə'näs·əd·ē ri'lā·shən }

distance modulus   See modulus of distance. { 'dis·təns ‚mäj·ə·ləs }

disturbance compensation system   A system applied to navigational satellites to remove the along-the-track component of drag and radiation forces. Abbreviated DISCOS. { də'stər·bəns käm·pən'sā·shən ˌsis·təm }

disturbed-sun noise   Noise at times of sunspot or solar flare activity. { dəˈstərbd 'sən ˌnȯiz }

ditching   A forced landing on water, or the process of making such a landing. { 'dich·iŋ }

diurnal aberration   Aberration caused by the rotation of the earth; its value varies with the latitude of the observer and ranges from zero at the poles to 0.31˙ second of arc. Also known as daily aberration. { dī'ərn·əl ˌab·ə'rā·shən }

diurnal arc   That part of a celestial body's diurnal circle which lies above the horizon of the observer. { dī'ərn·əl 'ärk }

diurnal circle   The apparent daily path of a celestial body, approximating a parallel of declination. { dī'ərn·əl 'sər·kəl }

diurnal motion   The apparent daily motion of a celestial body as observed from a rotating body. { dī'ərn·əl 'mō·shən }

diurnal parallax   *See* geocentric parallax. { dī'ərn·əl 'par·əˌlaks }

dive   A rapid descent by an aircraft or missile, nose downward, with or without power or thrust. { 'dīv }

dive bomber   An aircraft designed to release bombs during a steep dive. { 'dīv ˌbäm·ər }

dive brake   An air brake designed for operation in a dive; flaps at the following edge of one wing that can be extended into the airstream to increase drag and hold the aircraft to its "never exceed" dive speed in a vertical dive; used on dive bombers and sailplanes. { 'dīv ˌbrāk }

divergence speed   The speed of an aircraft above which no statically stable equilibrium condition exists and the deformation will increase to a point of structural failure. { də'vər·jəns ˌspēd }

diverging yaw   In the flight of a projectile, an angle of yaw increasing from the initial yaw, so that the projectile is unstable. { də'vərj·iŋ 'yȯ }

division circle   A large circular structure attached to the horizontal axis of a transit circle with accurately calibrated markings; used to determine the inclination of the instrument. { də'vizh·ən ˌsər·kəl }

docking   The mechanical coupling of two or more human-made orbiting objects. { däk·iŋ }

Dog Star   *See* Sirius. { 'dȯg ˌstär }

Dolphin   *See* Delphinus. { 'däl·fən }

dome   A shallow raised structure on the moon's surface with a smooth convex cross section and a diameter anywhere from a few kilometers up to about 80 kilometers (50 miles). { dōm }

domestic satellite   A satellite in stationary orbit 22,300 miles (35,680 kilometers) above the equator for handling up to 12 separate color television programs, up to 14,000 private-line telephone calls, or an equivalent number of channels for other communication services within the United States. Abbreviated DOMSAT. { də'mes·tik 'sad·əlˌīt }

DOMSAT See domestic satellite. { 'dämˌsat }

Dorado A constellation of the southern hemisphere, right ascension 5 hours, declination 65° south. Also known as Swordfish. { də'rä·dō }

double cluster A pair of globular clusters that are physically close to each other, near the northern boundary of the constellation Perseus. { ¦dəb·əl 'kləs·tər }

double star A star which appears as a single point of light to the eye but which can be resolved into two points by a telescope. { ¦dəb·əl 'stär }

Dove See Columba. { dəv }

down lock An airplane mechanism that locks the landing gear in a down position after the gear is lowered. { 'daún ˌläk }

downrange Any area along the flight course of a rocket or missile test range. { 'daúnˌrānj }

DQ Herculis star See intermediate polar. { ¦dē¦kyü 'hər·kyə·ləs ˌstär }

Dra See Draco.

Drac See Draco.

Draco A long, serpentine constellation that surrounds half of the Little Dipper in the north. Abbreviated Dra; Drac. Also known as Dragon. { 'drāˌkō }

Draconids Several meteor showers whose radiants lie in the constellation Draco. { drə'kän·ədz }

draconitic month See nodical month. { ˌdra·kə'nid·ik 'mənth }

Draco system A dwarf elliptical galaxy in the Local Group about 330,000 light-years (1.9 × 10¹⁸ miles or 3.1 × 10¹⁸ kilometers) distant having a diameter of about 4500 light-years (2.6 × 10¹⁶ miles or 4.3 × 10¹⁶ kilometers) and consisting chiefly of older stars. { 'drā·kō ˌsis·təm }

drag chute See drag parachute. { 'drag ˌshüt }

drag direction In stress analysis of a given airfoil, the direction of the relative wind. { 'drag də'rek·shən }

Dragon See Draco. { 'drag·ən }

drag parachute Any of various types of parachutes that can be deployed from the rear of an aircraft, especially during landings, to decrease speed and also, under certain flight conditions, to control and stabilize the aircraft. Also known as drag chute. { ¦drag 'par·əˌshüt }

drag rope A long, heavy rope carried in the basket of a balloon and permitted to hang over the side and drag on the ground in order to lighten the basket. { 'drag ˌrōp }

drag truss A truss that is positioned horizontally between the wing spars; used to stiffen the wing structure and as a resistance for drag forces acting on the airplane wing. { 'drag ˌtrəs }

drag-weight ratio   The ratio of the drag of a missile to its total weight. { ˈdrag ˈwāt 'rā·shō }

drag wire   A part of the truss in an airplane wing and also in the wing support; used to sustain the backward reaction due to the wing's drag. { 'drag ˌwīr }

Drake equation   An equation which gives the number of advanced technological civilizations curently active in the Galaxy as the product of the rate at which new stars are born in the Galaxy, the probability (actually a product of probabilities) that any one of these stars will possess the necessary conditions for life to originate and to slowly evolve to a technological civilization, and the average longevity of such civilizations. { 'drāk iˌkwā·zhən }

Draper catalog   A nine-volume catalog of stars completed in 1924; it gives positions, magnitudes, and spectral classes of 225,300 stars. { 'drā·pər 'kad·əlˌäg }

Drift I   A group of stars that tend to move in a stream, traveling in the direction of the constellation Orion; it comprises 60% of the stars whose proper motions are known. { ˈdrift ˈwən }

Drift II   A group of stars that tend to move in a stream, traveling in the direction of the constellation Scutum; it comprises 40% of the brighter stars. { ˈdrift ˈtü }

drogue   1. A small parachute attached to a body for stabilization and deceleration. Also known as deceleration parachute. 2. A funnel-shaped device at the end of the hose of a tanker aircraft in flight, to receive the probe of another aircraft that will take on fuel. { drōg }

drone   A pilotless aircraft usually subordinated to the controlling influences of a remotely located command station, but occasionally preprogrammed. { drōn }

drooped ailerons   Ailerons that are of the hinged trailing-edge type and are so arranged that both the right and left one have a 10 to 15° positive downward deflection with the control column in a neutral position. { ˈdrüpt 'ā·ləˌräns }

drop tank   A fuel tank on an airplane that may be jettisoned. { 'dräp ˌtaŋk }

dry-fuel rocket   A rocket that uses a mixture of rapidly burning powders; used especially as a booster rocket. { 'drī ˈfyül 'räk·ət }

dry start   The starting up of a liquid-fuel rocket engine without having previously filled the regenerative cooling tubes. { 'drī 'stärt }

D2 radio source   A radio source consisting of a small, variable nuclear component sometimes coincident with an optical object, and a second, larger component with a much steeper radio spectrum. { ˈdēˈtü 'rād·ē·ō ˌsòrs }

DSN   *See* Deep Space Network.

dual thrust   A rocket thrust derived from two propellant grains and using the same propulsion section of a missile. { 'dü·əl 'thrəst }

dual-thrust motor   A solid-propellant rocket engine built to obtain dual thrust. { 'dü·əl ˈthrəst 'mōd·ər } .

ducted-fan engine   An aircraft engine incorporating a fan or propeller enclosed in a duct; especially, a jet engine in which an enclosed fan or propeller is used to ingest ambient air to augment the gases of combustion in the jetstream. { ˈdək· təd ˌfan ˈen·jən }

ducted rocket   See rocket ramjet. { ˈdək·təd ˈräk·ət }

duct propulsion   A means of propelling a vehicle by ducting a surrounding fluid through an engine, adding momentum by mechanical or thermal means, and ejecting the fluid to obtain a reactive force. { ˈdəkt prə·pəl·shən }

Dumbbell Nebula   A planetary nebula of large apparent diameter and low surface brightness in the constellation Vulpecula, about 220 parsecs (4.2×10^{15} miles or 6.8×10^{15} miles or 6.8×10^{15} kilometers) away. { ˈdəm·bel ˈneb·yə·lə }

dusk   That part of either morning or evening twilight between complete darkness and civil twilight. { dəsk }

dusk side   The side of a planet or other celestial body pointing away from its orbital movement direction. { ˈdəsk ˌsīd }

dust tail   A comet tail that consists of particles, typically 1 micrometer in diameter and primarily silicate in composition, and is usually curved with a length in the range from 10^6 to 10^7 kilometers. { ˈdəst ˌtāl }

dwarf Cepheids   A class of pulsating variable stars with periods of less than 6 hours and spectral type A or F; similar to δ Scuti stars but sometimes distinguished from them by the slightly larger amplitudes of their light curves. Also known as AI Velorum stars. { ˈdwȯrf ˈsef·ē·ədz }

dwarf galaxy   An elliptical galaxy with low mass and low luminosity, having at most a few tens of millions of stars. { ˈdwȯrf ˈgal·ik·sē }

dwarf novae   A class of irregular variable stars which undergo rapid increases in brightness of several magnitudes at semiperiodic intervals, and then decrease more slowly to the normal minimum; they may be divided into U Geminorum stars and Z Camelopardalis stars. { ˈdwȯrf ˈnō·vī }

dwarf spheroidal galaxy   One of the smallest and faintest of the dwarf galaxies, with an effective radius of 200-1000 parsecs and an absolute visual magnitude between -8 and -13. { ˈdwȯrf sfir·ȯid·əl ˈgal·ik·sē }

dwarf star   A star that typically has surface temperature of 5730 K, radius of 428,000 miles (690,000 kilometers), mass of 2×10^{33} grams, and luminosity of 4×10^{33} ergs per second. Also known as main sequence star. { ˈdwȯrf ˈstär }

dynamical halo model   A model for the behavior of cosmic rays in the Galaxy in which the cosmic rays are produced in a thin disk near the central plane and then diffuse through the disk and into an outwardly convecting halo to an outer boundary at a distance of perhaps several kiloparsecs from the central plane. { dī′nam·ə·kəl ′hā· lō ˌmäd·əl }

dynamical parallax   A parallax of binary stars that is computed from the sum of the masses of the binary system. { dī′nam·ə·kəl ′par·ə·laks }

dynamic factor   A ratio formed from the load carried by any airplane part when the airplane is accelerating or subjected to abnormal conditions to the load carried in the conditions of normal flight. { dī′nam·ik ′fak·tər }

dynamic load   With respect to aircraft, rockets, or spacecraft, a load due to an acceleration of craft, as imposed by gusts, by maneuvering, by landing, by firing rockets, and so on. { dī¦nam·ik ′lōd }

dynamic parallax   A value for the parallax of a binary star computed from the observations of the period and angular dimensions of the orbit by assuming a value for the mass of the binary system. Also known as hypothetical parallax. { dī¦nam· ik ′par·ə،laks }

E

Eagle Nebula A large emission nebula in the constellation Serpens, about 2500 parsecs away. { 'ē·gəl 'neb·yə·lə }

early-type spiral A spiral galaxy with a large nuclear bulge and tightly wound arms. { 'ər·lē ¦tīp 'spī·rəl }

early-type star A star with relatively high surface temperature, in spectral class O or B. { 'ər·lē ¦tīp 'stär }

earth The third planet in the solar system, lying between Venus and Mars; sometimes capitalized. { ərth }

earthlight The illumination of the dark part of the moon's disk, produced by sunlight reflected onto the moon from the earth's surface and atmosphere. Also known as earthshine. { 'ərth‚līt }

earth orbit The elliptical motion of the earth about the sun (eccentricity 0.01675, average radius 9.290×10^7 miles or 1.496×10^8 kilometers) in a little over a year. { ¦ərth 'ór·bət }

earth rate The angular velocity or rate of the earth's rotation. { 'ərth ‚rāt }

earth resources technology satellite One of a series of satellites designed primarily to measure the natural resources of the earth; functions include mapping, cataloging water resources, surveying crops and forests, tracing sources of water and air pollution, identifying soil and rock formations, and acquiring oceanographic data. Abbreviated ERTS. { ¦ərth ri¦sór·səz tek¦näl·ə·je 'sad·əl‚īt }

earthrise The rising of the earth above the horizon of the moon, as viewed from the moon. { 'ərth‚rīz }

earth rotation Motion about the earth's axis that occurs 365.2422 times over a year's period. { ¦ərth rō¦tā·shən }

earth satellite **1.** An artificial satellite placed into orbit about the earth. **2.** A natural body that revolves about the earth, such as the moon. { 'ərth ‚sad·əl‚īt }

earthshine *See* earthlight. { 'ərth‚shīn }

earth's way The angle between the direction of the earth's motion and the apparent direction of a star. { 'ərths ‚wā }

east-west effect The phenomenon due to the fact that a greater number of cosmic-ray particles approach the earth from a westerly direction than from an easterly. { ¦ēst ¦west i‚fekt }

eccentric anomaly   For a planet in an elliptical orbit, the eccentric angle corresponding to the planet's location. { ek¦sen·trik ə′näm·ə·lē }

eccentric orbit   An orbit of a celestial body that deviates markedly from a circle. { ek¦sen·trik ′ȯr·bət }

eccentric ring structure   A formation on the moon's surface consisting of two craters, one inside the other, with the inner crater touching the wall of the outer one at one point. { ek¦sen·trik ′riŋ ˌstrək·chər }

eclipse   1. The reduction in visibility or disappearance of a body by passing into the shadow cast by another body. 2. The apparent cutting off, wholly or partially, of the light from a luminous body by a dark body coming between it and the observer. Also known as astronomical eclipse. { i′klips }

eclipse seasons   The two times when the sun is near enough to one of the nodes of the moon's orbit for eclipses to occur; this positioning occurs at nearly opposite times of the year, and the eclipse seasons vary yearly because of westward regression of the nodes. { i′klips ˌsēz·ənz }

eclipse year   The interval between two successive conjunctions of the sun with the same node of the moon's orbit, equal to 346.62 sidereal days. { i′klips ˌyir }

eclipsing binary   See eclipsing variable star. { i′klips·iŋ′bī·nər·ē }

eclipsing variable star   A binary star whose orbit is such that every time one star passes between the observer and its companion an eclipse results. Also known as eclipsing binary; photometric binary. { i′klips·iŋ ¦ver·ē·ə·bəl ′stär }

ecliptic   1. The apparent annual path of the sun among the stars; the intersection of the plane of the earth's orbit with the celestial sphere. 2. The plane of the earth's orbit around the sun. { i′klip·tik }

ecliptic coordinate system   A celestial coordinate system in which the ecliptic is taken as the primary and the great circles perpendicular to it are then taken as secondaries. { i′klip·tik kō′ȯrd·ən·ət ˌsis·təm }

ecliptic diagram   A diagram of the zodiac indicating positions of certain celestial bodies in the ecliptic region. { i¦klip·tik ′dī·əˌgram }

ecliptic latitude   See celestial latitude. { i¦klip·tik ′lad·əˌtüd }

ecliptic limits   The distance of the sun from a node of the moon's orbit such that a solar eclipse cannot occur, or the greatest distance of the moon from a node such that an eclipse of the moon cannot occur. { i¦klip·tik ′lim·əts }

ecliptic longitude   See celestial longitude. { i¦klip·tik ′län·jəˌtüd }

ecliptic pole   On the celestial sphere, either of two points 90° from the ecliptic. { i¦klip·tik ′pōl }

E corona   The component of the light seen from the solar corona which consists of radiation emitted from the corona itself, as opposed to scattered light. Also known as emission-line corona. { ′ē kəˌrō·nə }

Eddington limit   A limit on the radiation emitted by a star above which the star becomes unstable. { ′ed·iŋ·tən ˌlim·ət }

Eddington's model   A model of a star in which energy is transported by radiation throughout the star and the ratio of radiation pressure to gas pressure is assumed to be constant. { 'ed·iŋ·tənz ˌmäd·əl }

eddy-current damper A device used to damp nutation and other unwanted vibration in spacecraft, based on the principle that eddy currents induced in conducting material by motion relative to magnets tend to counteract that motion. { 'ed·ē ˌkə·rənt ˌdam·pər }

effective angle of attack That part of a given angle of attack that lies between the chord of an airfoil and a line representing the resultant velocity of the disturbed airflow. { əˈfek·tiv ˌaŋ·gəl əv əˈtak }

effective exhaust velocity A fictitious exhaust velocity that yields the observed value of jet thrust in calculations. { əˈfek·tiv igˈsȯst vəˌläs·əd·ē }

effective pitch The distance traveled by an airplane along its flight path for one complete turn of the propeller. { əˈfek·tiv 'pich }

effective radius The distance from the center of an external galaxy within which half its luminosity is included. { əˈfek·tiv 'rād·ē·əs }

effective temperature A measure of the temperature of a star, deduced by means of the Stefan-Boltzmann law, from the total energy that is emitted per unit area. { əˈfek·tiv 'tem·prə·chər }

effective thrust In a rocket motor or engine, the theoretical thrust less the effects of incomplete combustion and friction flow in the nozzle. { əˈfek·tiv 'thrəst }

E galaxy See elliptical galaxy. { 'ē ˌgal·ik·sē }

Egeria An asteroid with a diameter of about 140 miles (230 kilometers), mean distance from the sun of 2.576 astronomical units, and C-type surface composition. { eˈgir·ē·ə }

Egg Nebula A reflection nebula consisting of two optical components separated by about 8 arc-seconds, with an infrared source between them. { 'eg ˌneb·yə·lə }

egress The departure of the moon from the shadow of the earth in an eclipse, or of a planet from the disk of the sun, or of a satellite (or its shadow) from the disk of the parent planet. { 'ē·gres }

ejection capsule In an aircraft or spacecraft, a detachable compartment (serving as a cockpit or cabin) or a payload capsule which may be ejected as a unit and parachuted to the ground. { ēˈjek·shən ˌkap·səl }

ejection seat Emergency device which expels the pilot safely from a high-speed airplane. { ēˈjek·shən 'sēt }

Elara A small satellite of Jupiter with a diameter of about 20 miles (32 kilometers), orbiting at a mean distance of 7.29 × 10⁶ miles (11.73 × 10⁶ kilometers). Also known as Jupiter VII. { eˈlar·ə }

Electra A small, irregularly shaped satellite of Saturn that librates about the leading Lagrangian point of Dione's orbit. { iˈlek·trə }

electric engine A rocket engine in which the propellant is accelerated by some electric device. Also known as electric propulsion system; electric rocket. { iˈlek·trik 'en·jən }

67

electric propulsion   A general term encompassing all the various types of propulsion in which the propellant consists of electrically charged particles which are accelerated by electric or magnetic fields, or both. { i⁀lek·trik prə′pəl·shən }

electric propulsion system   See electric engine. { i⁀lek·trik prə′pəl·shən ˌsis·təm }

electric rocket   See electric engine. { i⁀lek·trik ′räk·ət }

electromagnetic propulsion   Motive power for flight vehicles produced by electromagnetic acceleration of a plasma fluid. { i⁀lek·trō·mag′ned·ik prə′pəl·shən }

electropulse engine   An engine, for propelling a flight vehicle, that is based on the use of spark discharges through which intense electric and magnetic fields are established for periods ranging from microseconds to a few milliseconds; a resulting electromagnetic force drives the plasma along the leads and away from the spark gap. { i′lek·trō‚pəls ˌen·jən }

electrothermal propulsion   Propulsion of spacecraft by using an electric arc or other electric heater to bring hydrogen gas or other propellant to the high temperature required for maximum thrust; an arc-jet engine is an example. { i⁀lek·trō′thər·məl prə′pəl·shən }

Elektra   An asteroid with a diameter of about 140 miles (235 kilometers), mean distance from the sun of 3.117 astronomical units, and C-type surface composition. { i′lek·trə }

elementary ring structure   A formation on the moon's surface consisting of a simple wall of uniform cross section enclosing a circular area which has the same elevation as the surrounding surface. Also known as simple ring. { ˌel·ə′men·trē ′riŋ ˌstrək·chər }

elements   A set of quantities specifying the orbit of a member of the solar system or of a binary star system, used to calculate the body's position at any time. { ′el·ə·mənts }

elephant ear   Thick metal plating that reinforces a missile's skin. { ′el·ə·fənt ˌir }

elephant trunks   Long, dark regions that encroach into the bright matter in diffuse nebulae, usually bordered by bright rims. { ′el·ə·fənt ˌtrəŋks }

elevated pole   . The celestial pole that appears above the horizon. { ′el·əˌvād·əd ′pōl }

elevator   The hinged rear portion of the longitudinal stabilizing surface or tail plane of an aircraft, used to obtain longitudinal or pitch-control moments. { ′el·əˌvād·ər }

elevator angle   The angular displacement of the elevator from its neutral position; it is positive when the trailing edge of the elevator is below the neutral position, and negative when it is above. { ′el·əˌvād·ər ˌaŋ·gəl }

elevon   The hinged rear portion of an aircraft wing, moved in the same direction on each side of the aircraft to obtain longitudinal control and differentially to obtain lateral control; elevon is a combination of the words elevator and aileron to denote that an elevon combines the functions of aircraft elevators and ailerons. { ′el·əˌvän }

elliptical galaxy   A galaxy whose overall shape ranges from a spheroid to an ellipsoid, without any noticeable structural features. Also known as E galaxy; spheroidal galaxy. { ə′lip·tə·kəl ′gal·ik·sē }

elliptical ring structure   A lunar crater enclosed by a wall that is elliptical in shape. { ə'lip·tə·kəl 'riŋ ˌstrək·chər }

ellipticity   The difference between the equatorial and polar radii of a planet divided by the mean radius. { ēˌlip'tis·əd·ē }

elongation   The difference between the celestial longitude of the moon or a planet, as measured from the earth, and that of the sun. { ēˌloŋ'gā·shən }

Emden equation   An equation for stellar structure which arises in a model based on the assumption that the star is a gaseous sphere in adiabatic equilibrium, in which the pressure is proportional to $\rho\gamma$, where ρ is the density and γ is a constant; the equation is $d^2y/dx^2 + (2/x)dy/dx + y^n = 0$, where $n = 1/(\gamma - 1)$, x is proportional to the distance from the center of the sphere, and y is proportional to $\rho^{1/n}$. Also known as Lane-Emden equation. { 'em·dən iˌkwā·zhən }

Emden function   A solution of the Emden equation with the boundary conditions $y = 1$ and $dy/dx = 0$ at $x = 0$. Also known as Lane-Emden function. { 'em·dən ˌfəŋk·shən }

emersion   The reappearance of a celestial body after an eclipse or occultation. { ē'mer·zhən }

emission-line corona   See E corona. { i'mish·ən ¦līn kə'rō·nə }

emission-line galaxy   A galaxy whose spectrum displays narrow, high-excitation emission lines. { i'mish·ən ¦līn 'gal·ik·sē }

emission nebula   A type of bright diffuse nebula whose luminosity results from the excitation and ionization of its gas atoms by ultraviolet radiation from a nearby O- or B-type star. { i'mish·ən 'neb·yə·lə }

empennage   The assembly at the rear of an aircraft; it comprises the horizontal and vertical stabilizers. Also known as tail assembly. { ¦am·pə¦näzh }

Enceladus   A satellite of Saturn orbiting at a mean distance of 153,600 miles (238,000 kilometers). { ˌen·se'lä·dŭs }

Encke division   A faint line that splits the outer ring of Saturn into two. { 'eŋ·kə dəˌvizh·ən }

Encke's Comet   A very faint comet with the shortest period of any known comet, 3.3 years. { 'eŋ·kəz 'käm·ət }

energetic solar particles   Electrons and atomic nuclei produced in association with solar flares, with energies mostly in the range 1-100 million electronvolts, but occasionally as high as 15 billion electronvolts. Also known as solar cosmic rays. { ˌen·ər'jed·ik ¦sō·lər 'pärd·i·kəlz }

energy management   In rocketry, the monitoring of the expenditure of fuel for flight control and navigation. { 'en·ər·jē ˌman·ij·mənt }

engine spray   That part of a pad deluge that is directed at cooling a rocket's engine during launch. { 'en·jən ˌsprā }

entry corridor   Depth of the region between two trajectories which define the design limits of a vehicle about to enter a planetary atmosphere, or define the desired landing area (footprint). { 'en·trē ˌkär·əˌdȯr }

ephemeris

ephemeris A periodical publication tabulating the predicted positions of celestial bodies at regular intervals, such as daily, and containing other data of interest to astronomers. Also known as astronomical ephemeris. { ə'fem·ə·rəs }

ephemeris day A unit of time equal to 86,400 ephemeris seconds (International System of Units). { ə'fem·ə·rəs 'dā }

ephemeris second The fundamental unit of time of the International System of Units of 1960, equal to 1/31556925.9747 of the tropical year defined by the mean motion of the sun in longitude at the epoch 1900 January 0 day 12 hours. { ə'fem·ə·rəs 'sek·ənd }

ephemeris time The uniform measure of time defined by the laws of dynamics and determined in principle from the orbital motions of the planets, specifically the orbital motion of the earth as represented by Newcomb's Tables of the Sun. Abbreviated E.T. { ə'fem·ə·rəs 'tīm }

Epimetheus A satellite of Saturn which orbits at a mean distance of 151,000 kilometers (94,000 miles), near Saturn's rings, in nearly the same orbit as Janus, and has an irregular shape with an average diameter of 120 kilometers (75 miles). { ˌep·ə'mē·thē·əs }

epoch A particular instant for which certain data are valid; for example, star positions in an astronomical catalog, epoch 1950.0. { 'ep·ək }

ε Argus A star of visual magnitude 1.74, spectral type K0. { 'ep·sə/län 'är·gəs }

ε Canis Majoris See Adhara. { ¦ed·ə ˌkā·nəs 'mā·jər·is }

equal-areas law The second of Kepler's laws, which states that the line joining a planet and the sun sweeps over equal areas in equal periods of time. { 'ē·kwəl ¦er·ē·əz ˌlȯ }

equation of the center The angle between the actual longitude of the moon and the longitude of an imaginary body that moves with constant angular velocity with the same period as the moon. { i'kwā·zhən əv thə 'sen·tər }

equation of time The addition of a quantity to mean solar time to obtain apparent solar time; formerly, when apparent solar time was in common use, the opposite convention was used; apparent solar time has annual variation as a result of the sun's inclination in the ecliptic and the eccentricity of the earth's elliptical orbit. { i'kwā·zhən əv 'tīm }

equatorial acceleration A state in which the equatorial atmosphere of a celestial body has a larger absolute angular velocity than the more poleward portions of the atmosphere; exhibited by the sun, Jupiter, and Saturn. { ˌe·kwə'tȯr·ē·əl ak/sel·ə'rā·shən }

equatorial horizontal parallax The parallax of a member of the solar system measured from positional observations made at the same time at two stations on earth, whose distance apart is the earth's equatorial radius. { ˌe·kwə'tȯr·ē·əl ˌhär·əˌzänt·əl 'par·əˌlaks }

equatorial orbit An orbit in the plane of the earth's equator. { ˌe·kwə'tȯr·ē·əl 'ȯr·bət }

equatorial plane The plane passing through the equator of the earth, or of another celestial body, perpendicular to its axis of rotation and equidistant from its poles. { ˌe·kwə'tȯr·ē·əl 'plān }

equatorial system A set of celestial coordinates based on the celestial equator as the primary great circle; usually declination and hour angle or sidereal hour angle. Also known as celestial equator system of coordinates; equinoctial system of coordinates. { ˌe·kwə'tȯr·ē·əl 'sis·təm }

equinoctial See celestial equator. { ˌē·kwə'näk·shəl }

equinoctial colure The great circle of the celestial sphere through the celestial poles and the equinoxes; the hour circle of the vernal equinox. { ˌē·kwə'näk·shəl kə'lür }

equinoctial point See equinox. { ˌē·kwə'näk·shəl 'pȯint }

equinoctial system of coordinates See equatorial system. { ˌē·kwə'näk·shəl ¦sis·təm əv kō'ȯrd·ən·əts }

equinox 1. Either of the two points of intersection of the ecliptic and the celestial equator, occupied by the sun when its declination is 0°. Also known as equinoctial point. 2. That instant when the sun occupies one of the equinoctial points. { 'ē·kwəˌnäks }

equivalent airspeed The product of the true airspeed and the square root of the density ratio; used in structural design work to designate various design conditions. { i'kwiv·ə·lənt 'erˌspēd }

Equl See Equuleus.

Equuleus A northern constellation near Aquarius, right ascension 21 hours, declination 10° north. Abbreviated Equl. Also known as Little Horse. { e'kwül·ē·əs }

Eri See Eridanus.

Erid See Eridanus.

Eridanus A southern constellation made up of a long, crooked line of stars beginning near Rigel in the foot of Orion, and winding west and south to the first-magnitude star Achernar. Abbreviated Eri; Erid. Also known as River Po. { ˌer·ə'dan·əs }

Eros An asteroid that is about 20 miles (32 kilometers) in diameter; its closest approach to the earth is every 44 years. { 'eˌräs }

ERTS See earth resources technology satellite.

eruptive prominence A prominence on the sun that is formed from active material above the chromosphere and reaches high altitudes on the sun at great speed. { i'rəp·tiv 'präm·ə·nəns }

eruptive star A star that has a rapid change in its intensity because of the physical change it undergoes; examples are flare stars, recurrent novae, novae, supernovae, and nebular variables. { ə'rəp·tiv 'stär }

escape orbit One of various paths that a body or particle escaping from a central force field must follow in order to escape. { ə'skāp ˌȯr·bət }

escape rocket A small rocket engine attached to the leading end of an escape tower, to provide additional thrust to the capsule in an emergency; it helps separate the capsule from the booster vehicle and carries it to an altitude where parachutes can be deployed. { ə'skāp ˌräk·ət }

71

escape tower   A trestle tower placed on top of a space capsule, connecting the capsule to the escape rocket on top of the tower; used for emergencies. { ə'skāp ˌtau̇·ər }

escape velocity   The minimum speed away from a parent body that a particle must acquire to escape permanently from the gravitational attraction of the parent. { ə'skāp vəˌläs·əd·ē }

escort fighter   A fighter designed or equipped for long-range missions, usually to accompany heavy bombers on raids. { 'esˌkȯrt ˌfīd·ər }

estival   Of or pertaining to the summer. Also spelled aestival. { 'es·tə·vəl }

E.T.   See ephemeris time.

η Aquarids   A meteor shower associated with Halley's Comet that occurs in the first week of May with radiant near the star η Aquarii. { ¦ā·də 'ak·wəˌridz }

Eugenia   An asteroid with a diameter of about 225 kilometers, mean distance from the sun of 2.721 astronomical units, and C-type surface composition. { yü'jēn·yə }

Eunomia   An asteroid with a diameter of about 153 miles (255 kilometers), mean distance from the sun of 2.642 astronomical units, and S-type surface composition. { yü'nō·mē·ə }

Euphrosyne   An asteroid with a diameter of about 150 miles (250 kilometers), mean distance from the sun of 3.156 astronomical units, and C-type surface composition. { yü'fräz·ən·ē }

Europa   1. A satellite of Jupiter with a mean distance from Jupiter of 4.17 × 10⁵ miles (6.71 × 10⁵ kilometers), orbital period of 3.6 days, and diameter of about 1950 miles (3100 kilometers). Also known as Jupiter II. 2. An asteroid with a diameter of about 168 miles (280 kilometers), mean distance from the sun of 3.096 astronomical units, and C-type surface composition. { yu̇'rō·pə }

evection   A perturbation of the moon in its orbit due to the attraction of the sun. { ē'vek·shən }

evening star   A misnomer for a planet that can be seen without a telescope when it sets after the sun. { ¦ev·niŋ 'stär }

evening twilight   The period of time between sunset and darkness. { ¦ev·niŋ 'twīˌlīt }

Evershed effect   A displacement of spectral lines of sunspots near the sun's limb, caused by outward motion of gases from the center of the sunspot. { 'ev·ərˌshed iˌfekt }

exhaust nozzle   The terminal portion of a jet engine tail pipe. { ig'zȯst ˌnäz·əl }

exhaust stream   The stream of matter or radiation emitted from the nozzle of a rocket or other reaction engine. { ig'zȯst ˌstrēm }

exmeridian altitude   An altitude of a celestial body near the celestial meridian of the observer to which a correction is to be applied to determine the meridian altitude. Also known as circummeridian altitude. { eks·mə'rid·ē·ən 'al·təˌtüd }

exmeridian observation   1. Measurement of the altitude of a celestial body near the celestial meridian of the observer, for conversion to a meridian altitude. 2. The altitude so measured. { eks·mə'rid·ē·ən ˌäb·zər'vā·shən }

expandable space structure A structure which can be packaged in a small volume for launch and then erected to its full size and shape outside the earth's atmosphere. { ik¦span·də·bəl 'spās ˌstrək·chər }

expanding arm A spiral arm of the Galaxy consisting of neutral hydrogen that lies between 2.5 and 4 kiloparsecs beyond the galactic center and is moving out from it at about 85 miles (135 kilometers) per second. { ik'spand·iŋ 'ärm }

expanding universe Explanation of the red shift observed in spectral lines from distant galaxies as due to a mutual recession of galaxies away from each other. { ik¦spand· iŋ 'yü·nə·vərs }

expendable rocket See expendable vehicle. { ik'spen·də·bəl 'räk·ət }

expendable vehicle A rocket that is used only once to place a payload in orbit. Also known as expendable rocket. { ik'spen·də·bəl 've̅·ə·kəl }

explosive bolt A bolt designed to contain a remote-initiated explosive charge which, upon detonation, will shear the bolt or cause it to fail otherwise; applicable to such uses as stage separation of rockets, jettison of expended fuel tanks, and ejection of parachutes. { ik'splō·siv 'bōlt }

explosive decompression A sudden loss of pressure in a pressurized cabin, cockpit, or the like, so rapid as to be explosive, as when punctured by gunfire. { ik'splō· siv ˌdē·kəm'presh·ən }

explosive nucleosynthesis Nucleosynthetic processes that are believed to occur in supernovae, such as the r process. { ik'splō·siv ˌnü·klē·ō'sin·thə·səs }

explosive variable See cataclysmic variable. { ik'splō·siv 'ver·ē·ə·bəl }

extended source A radio source that has a large angular extent and is strongest at longer wavelengths, as distinguished from a compact source. { ik'stend·əd 'sȯrs }

extensive air shower See Auger shower. { ik¦sten·siv 'er ˌshau̇·ər }

external aileron An aileron offset from the wing; that is, not forming a part of the wing. { ek'stərn·əl 'ā·lə,rän }

external galaxy Any galaxy known to exist, besides the Milky Way. { ek¦stərn·əl 'gal· ik·sē }

extinction The reduction in the apparent brightness of a celestial object due to absorption and scattering of its light by the atmosphere and by interstellar dust; it is greater at low altitudes. { ek'stiŋk·shən }

extraction parachute An auxiliary parachute designed to release and extract cargo from aircraft in flight and to deploy cargo parachutes. { ik'strak·shən 'par·ə,shüt }

extragalactic Beyond the Milky Way. { ¦ek·strə·gə'lak·tik }

extragalactic background light The contribution to the brightness of the sky from light coming from outside the Galaxy, chiefly distant galaxies, excluding resolved galaxies. { ¦ek·strə·gə¦lak·tik 'bak,graund ˌlīt }

extragalactic radio source A source of radio emission outside the Milky Way. { ¦ek· strə·gə'lak·tik 'rad·ē·ō ˌsȯrs }

extraterrestrial intelligence The potential existence beyond the earth of other ad-

vanced civilizations with a technology at least as developed as that on earth. { ˈek·
strə·tə′res·trē·əl in′tel·ə·jəns }

extraterrestrial radiation   Electromagnetic radiation which originates outside the earth
or its atmosphere, as in the sun or stars. { ˈek·strə·tə′res·trē·əl ˌrād·ē′ā·shən }

extravehicular activity   Activity conducted outside a spacecraft during space flight.
{ ˈek·strə·və′hik·yə·lər ak′tiv·əd·ē }

extrinsic variable star   A variable star, such as an eclipsing variable, whose variation
in apparent brightness is due to some external cause, rather than to actual variaiton
in the amount of radiation emitted. { ekˈstrinz·ik ˌver·ē·ə·bəl ′stär }

F

Faber-Jackson relation A relation between the spectral dispersion caused by the random motions of stars in an elliptical galaxy and the galaxy's intrinsic luminosity. { ˈfāb·ər ˈjak·sən riˌlā·shən }

facula Any of the large patches of bright material forming a veined network in the vicinity of sunspots; faculae appear to be more permanent than sunspots and are probably due to elevated clouds of luminous gas. { ˈfak·yə·lə }

fairing A structure or surface on an aircraft or rocket that functions to reduce drag, such as the streamlined nose of a satellite-launching rocket. { ˈfer·iŋ }

fairlead A guide through which an airplane antenna or control cable passes. { ˈferˌlēd }

falcate Crescent-shaped; applied usually to the appearance of the moon, Venus, and Mercury during their crescent phases. { ˈfalˌkat }

fall 1. Of a spacecraft or spatial body, to drop toward a spatial body under the influence of its gravity. 2. *See* autumn. { fȯl }

fallaway section A section of a rocket vehicle that is cast off from the vehicle during flight, especially such a section that falls back to the earth. { ˈfȯl·əˌwā ˌsek·shən }

fanjet A turbojet engine whose performance has been improved by the addition of a fan which operates in an annular duct surrounding the engine. { ˈfanˌjet }

fast nova A nova whose brightness rises quickly to a maximum, remains near maximum for a short time, and then decreases to the original value in a few years or less. { ˈfast ˈnō·və }

fast pulsar A pulsar with a very short period, of the order of a millisecond. Also known as millisecond pulsar. { ˈfast ˈpəlˌsär }

F corona The outer portion of the solar corona, consisting of sunlight that has been scattered from interplanetary dust between the sun and the earth. Also known as Fraunhofer corona. { ˈef kəˌrō·nə }

fence A stationary plate or vane projecting from the upper surface of an airfoil, substantially parallel to the airflow, used to prevent spanwise flow. { fens }

fictitious year The period between successive returns of the fictitious mean sun to a sidereal hour angle of 80° (right ascension 18 hours 40 minutes; about January 1); the length of the fictitious year is the same as that of the tropical year, since both are based upon the position of the sun with respect to the vernal equinox. Also known as Besselian year. { fikˈtish·əs ˈyir }

field galaxy

field galaxy   An isolated galaxy that does not belong to a cluster. { 'fēld ,gal·ik·sē }

field-line annihilation   See field line reconnection. { 'fēld ,līn ə,nī·ə'lā·shən }

field-line reconnection   A topological rearrangement of the magnetic field lines surrounding an astronomical body, for example, the transfer of lines between open and closed configurations in the terrestrial magnetotail; a possible source of the energy released explosively in solar flares and magnetospheric substorms. Also known as field line annihilation; magnetic merging. { 'fēld ,līn ,rē·kə'nek·shən }

field stars   Background stars when a specific object is being observed. { 'fēld ,stärz }

fighter aircraft   A military aircraft designed primarily to destroy other aircraft in the air; may also be used to bomb military targets; it is maneuverable and has a high rate of climb. { ¦fīd·ər 'er,kraft }

fighter bomber   A fighter aircraft that is designed to have bombs, or rockets, added to it so that it may be used as a bomber. { 'fīd·ər ,bäm·ər }

fighter interceptor   A fighter aircraft designed to intercept and shoot down enemy aircraft. { 'fīd·ər ,in·tər'sep·tər }

filament   A prominence, seen as a dark marking on the solar disk. { 'fil·ə·mənt }

fin   A fixed or adjustable vane or airfoil affixed longitudinally to an aerodynamically or ballistically designed body for stabilizing purposes. { fin }

final mass   The mass of a rocket after its propellants are consumed. { ¦fīn·əl 'mas }

fineness ratio   The ratio of the length of a streamlined body, as that of a fuselage or airship hull, to its maximum diameter. { 'fīn·nəs ,rā·shō }

fireball   A bright meteor with luminosity equal to or exceeding that of the brightest planets. { 'fīr,bȯl }

firing chamber   See combustion chamber. { 'fīr·iŋ ,chām·bər }

first lunar meridian   The great circle on the moon which passes through the poles and through the center of the side of the moon that faces the earth. { ¦fərst ¦lün·ər mə'rid·ē·ən }

first motion   The first indication of motion of a rocket, missile, or test vehicle from its launcher. { 'fərst 'mō·shən }

first point of Aries   See vernal equinox. { ¦fərst ¦pȯint əv 'er·ēz }

first point of Cancer   See summer solstice. { ¦fərst ¦pȯint əv 'kan·sər }

first point of Libra   See autumnal equinox. { ¦fərst ¦pȯint əv 'lē·brə }

first quarter   The phase of the moon when it is near east quadrature, when the western half of it is visible to an observer on the earth. { 'fərst 'kwȯrd·ər }

fixed fin   A nonadjustable vane or airfoil affixed longitudinally to an aerodynamically or ballistically designed body for stabilizing purposes. { ¦fikst 'fin }

fixed star   A misnomer to indicate those stars which kept apparently the same position with respect to other stars, in contrast to the planets which were termed wandering stars. { ˈfikst ˈstär }

flame bucket A deep, cavelike construction built beneath a rocket launchpad, open at the top to receive the hot gases of the rocket, and open on one or three sides below, with a thick metal fourth side bent toward the open side or sides so as to deflect the exhaust gases. { ˈflām ˌbək·ət }

flame deflector 1. In a vertical launch, any of variously designed obstructions that intercept the hot gases of the rocket engine so as to deflect them away from the ground or from a structure. 2. In a captive test, an elbow in the exhaust conduit or flame bucket that deflects the flame into the open. { ˈflām diˌflek·tər }

flameholder A device that sustains combustion in a flowing mixture within the combustion chamber of some types of jet engines. { ˈflāmˌhōl·dər }

flameout The extinguishing of the flame in a reaction engine, especially in a jet engine. { ˈflāmˌaút }

Flamsteed's number A number sometimes used with the possessive form of the Latin name of the constellation to identify a star, for example, 72 Ophiuchi. { ˈflamˌstēdz ˌnəm·bər }

flap 1. Any control surface, such as a speed brake, dive brake, or dive-recovery brake, used primarily to increase the lift or drag on an airplane, or to aid in recovery from a dive. 2. Any rudder attached to a rocket and acting either in the air or within the jet stream. { flap }

flaperon A control surface used both as a flap and as an aileron. { ˈflap·əˌrän }

flare 1. To descend in a smooth curve, making a transition from a relatively steep descent to a direction substantially parallel to the surface, when landing an aircraft. 2. A bright eruption from the sun's chromosphere; flares may appear within minutes and fade within an hour, cover a wide range of intensity and size, and tend to occur between sunspots or over their penumbrae. { fler }

flareout That portion of the approach path of an aircraft in which the vertical component is modified to lessen the impact of landing. { ˈflerˌaút }

flare stars *See* UV Ceti stars. { ˈfler ˌstärz }

flash A thermal instability that occurs in late stages of stellar evolution, according to numerical calculations. { flash }

flash spectrum The emission spectrum of the sun's chromosphere, observed for a few seconds just before and just after a total solar eclipse. { ˈflash ˌspek·trəm }

flatness problem The problem of explaining why, after 10^{10} years of expansion, the density parameter is of the order of 1, whereas the standard big-bang theory suggests that once this parameter deviates even slightly from 1 it very quickly approaches an asymptotic value far away from 1 for open or closed universes. { ˈflat·nəs ˌpräb·ləm }

flicker control Control of an aircraft, rocket, or such in which the control surfaces are deflected to their maximum degree with only a slight motion of the controller. { ˈflik·ər kənˌtrōl }

flight The movement of an object through the atmosphere or through space, sustained by aerodynamic reaction or other forces. { flīt }

flight characteristic

flight characteristic A characteristic exhibited by an aircraft, rocket, or the like in flight, such as a tendency to stall or to yaw, or an ability to remain stable at certain speeds. { 'flīt ˌkar·ik·tə͵ris·tik }

flight deck In certain airplanes, an elevated compartment occupied by the crew for operating the airplane in flight. { 'flīt ˌdek }

flight dynamics The study of the motion of an aircraft or missile; concerned with transient or short-term effects relating to the stability and control of the vehicle, rather than to calculating such performance as altitude or velocity. { 'flīt dī͵nam· iks }

flight envelope The boundary depicting, for a specific aircraft, the limits of speed, altitude, and acceleration which that aircraft cannot safely exceed. { 'flīt ͵en· və͵lōp }

flight instrument An aircraft instrument used in the control of the direction of flight, attitude, altitude, or speed of an aircraft, for example, the artificial horizon, airspeed indicator, altimeter, compass, rate-of-climb indicator, accelerometer, turn-and-bank indicator, and so on. { 'flīt ͵in·strə·mənt }

flight level A surface of constant atmospheric pressure which is related to the standard pressure datum. { 'flīt ͵lev·əl }

flight path The path made or followed in the air or in space by an aircraft, rocket, or such. { 'flīt ͵path }

flight-path angle The angle between the horizontal (or some other reference angle) and a tangent to the flight path at a point. Also known as flight-path slope. { 'flīt ͵path ͵aŋ·gəl }

flight-path slope See flight-path angle. { 'flīt ͵path ͵slōp }

flight profile A graphic portrayal or plot of the flight path of an aeronautical vehicle in the vertical plane. { 'flīt ͵prō͵fīl }

flight science The sum total of all knowledge that enables humans to accomplish flight; it is compounded of both science and engineering, and is concerned with airplanes, missiles, and crewed and crewless space vehicles. { 'flīt ͵sī·əns }

flight simulator A training device or apparatus that simulates certain conditions of actual flight or of flight operations. { 'flīt ͵sim·yə͵lād·ər }

flight stability The property of an aircraft or missile to maintain its attitude and to resist displacement, and, if displaced, to tend to restore itself to the original attitude. { 'flīt stə͵bil·əd·ē }

flight test 1. A test by means of actual or attempted flight to see how an aircraft, spacecraft, space-air vehicle, or missile flies. 2. A test of a component part of a flying vehicle, or of an object carried in such a vehicle, to determine its suitability or reliability in terms of its intended function by making it endure actual flight. { 'flīt ͵test }

flocculus A patch in the sun's surface seen in the light of calcium or hydrogen; the patch may be bright or dark and is usually in the vicinity of sunspots. { 'fläk·yə· ləs }

flux unit A unit of energy flux density of radio-astronomical sources, equal to 10^{-26} watt per square meter per hertz. Abbreviated fu. { 'fləks ͵yü·nət }

Fly See Musca. { flī }

flyby A close approach of a space vehicle to a target planet in which the vehicle does not impact the planet or go into orbit around it. Also known as swing-by. { 'flī‚bī }

fly-by-wire system A flight control system that uses electric wiring instead of mechanical or hydraulic linkages to control the actuators for the ailerons, flaps, and other control surfaces of an aircraft. { ¦flī bī ¦wīr ‚sis·təm }

flying angle The acute angle between the longitudinal axis of an aircraft and the horizontal axis in normal level flight, or the angle of attack of a wing in normal level flight. { 'flī·iŋ ‚aŋ·gəl }

flying boat A seaplane with a fuselage that acts as a hull and is the means of the plane's support on water. { ¦flī·iŋ ¦bōt }

flying-crane helicopter A heavy-lift helicopter used in rapid loading and unloading of, for example, cargo ships. { 'flī·iŋ ‚krān 'hel·ə‚käp·tər }

Flying Fish See Volan. { ¦flī·iŋ ¦fish }

flying hour rate See utilization rate. { ¦flī·iŋ ¦aúr 'rāt }

folding fin A fin hinged at its base to lie flat, especially a fin on a rocket that lies flat until the rocket is in flight. { 'fōld·iŋ 'fin }

following limb The half of the limb of a celestial body with an observable disk that appears to follow the body in its apparent motion across the field of view of a fixed telescope. { 'fäl·ə·wiŋ ‚lim }

footpad A somewhat flat base on the leg of a spacecraft to distribute weight and thereby minimize sinking into a surface. { 'fút‚pad }

footpoint The intersection of tubes of magnetic field lines with the surface of the photosphere. { 'fút‚póint }

Forbush decrease A sudden decrease in cosmic-ray intensity which occurs a day or two after a solar flare, and at the same time as the commencement of magnetic storms and auroral activity. { 'fòr‚búsh di'krēs }

Fornax A A peculiar giant elliptical galaxy on the periphery of the Fornax cluster which is a strong double radio source. { 'fòr‚naks 'ā }

Fornax cluster A cluster of galaxies with a few tens of members, about 30 megaparsecs (6 × 10^{19} miles or 9 × 10^{19} kilometers) distant. { 'fòr‚naks ‚kləs·tər }

Fornax system A dwarf elliptical galaxy in the Local Group, about 800,000 light-years (4.7 × 10^{18} miles or 7.6 × 10^{18} kilometers) distant, having a diameter of about 15,000 light-years (9 × 10^{16} miles or 1.4 × 10^{17} kilometers) and a mass and luminosity about 2 × 10^7 that of the sun. { 'fòr‚naks ‚sis·təm }

fortnightly nutation Nutation caused by the change in declination of the moon, having a displacement of up to 0.1 second of arc and a period of 15 days. { ‚fòrt¦nīt·lē nü'tā·shən }

Fortuna An asteroid with a diameter of about 130 miles (220 kilometers), mean distance from the sun of 2.442 astronomical units, and C-type surface composition. { fòr'tü·nə }

Fraunhofer corona

Fraunhofer corona See F corona. { 'fraún₁hōf·ər kə₁rō·nə }

free balloon A balloon that ascends without a tether, propulsion or guidance; it is made to descend by the release of gas. { ¦frē bə'lün }

free-stream Mach number The Mach number of the total airframe (entire aircraft) as contrasted with the local Mach number of a section of the airframe. { 'frē ₁strēm 'mäk ₁nəm·bər }

French division See Lyot division. { 'french də'vizh·ən }

Friedmann universe A nonstatic, homogeneous, isotropic model of the universe that displays expansion or contraction and has nonzero matter density. { 'frēd·mən 'yü· nə₁vərs }

Frise aileron A type of aileron having its leading edge projecting well ahead of the hinge axis. { 'frēz 'ā·lə₁rän }

frontal passage The transit of an aircraft through a frontal zone. { ¦frənt·əl 'pas·ij }

f spot One of a pair of sunspots that appears to follow the other across the face of the sun, or whose magnetic polarity is that normally found in such a sunspot during that sunspot cycle and in that hemisphere of the sun. { 'ef ₁spät }

F star A star whose spectral type is F; surface temperature is 7000 K, and color is yellowish. { 'ef ₁stär }

fu See flux unit.

fuel shutoff 1. The action of shutting off the flow of liquid fuel into a combustion chamber or of stopping the combustion of a solid fuel. 2. The event or time marking this action. { 'fyül ₁shəd₁óf }

fuel structure ratio See fuel-weight ratio. { 'fyül ₁strək·chər ₁rā·shō }

fuel-weight ratio The ratio of the weight of a rocket's fuel to the weight of the unfueled rocket. Also known as fuel structure ratio. { ¦fyül ¦wāt ₁rā·shō }

full moon The moon at opposition, with a phase angle of 0°, when it appears as a round disk to an observer on the earth because the illuminated side is toward the observer. { ¦fúl 'mün }

full pressure suit A pressure suit which completely encloses the body and in which a gas pressure sufficiently above ambient pressure for maintenance of function may be sustained. { 'fúl 'presh·ər ₁süt }

fundamental star places The apparent right ascensions and declinations of 1535 standard comparison stars obtained by leading observatories and published annually under the sponsorship of the International Astronomical Union. { ¦fən·də¦ment· əl 'stär ₁plās·əz }

funneling The convergence of the evolutionary paths of stars from different parts of the main sequence into the red giant region on a Hertzsprung-Russell diagram. { 'fən· əl·iŋ }

fuselage In an airplane, the central structure to which wings and tail are attached; it accommodates flight crew, passengers, and cargo. { 'fyü·sə₁läzh }

G

galactic bulge A spheroidal distribution of stars that is centered on the nucleus of the Milky Way Galaxy and extends to a distance of about 3 kiloparsecs from the center. { gə¦lak·tik 'bəlj }

galactic center The gravitational center of the Milky Way Galaxy; the sun and other stars of the Galaxy revolve about this center. { gə'lak·tik 'sen·tər }

galactic circle See galactic equator. { gə'lak·tik 'sər·kəl }

galactic cluster See open cluster. { gə'lak·tik 'kləs·tər }

galactic concentration A measure of the increasing density of stars toward the galactic plane, equal to the ratio of the density of stars of a given magnitude at the galactic plane to that at the galactic poles. { gə'lak·tik ˌkäns·ən'trā·shən }

galactic coordinates See galactic system. { gə'lak·tik kō'órd·ən·əts }

galactic corona A low-density gaseous region extending away from the dense gas of the disk of the Milky Way Galaxy into the halo for distances estimated to be at least 3000 parsecs. { gə¦lak·tik kə'rōn·ə }

galactic disk The flat distribution of stars and interstellar matter in the spiral arms and plane of the Milky Way Galaxy. { gə'lak·tik 'disk }

galactic equator A great circle of the celestial sphere, inclined 62° to the celestial equator, coinciding approximately with the center line of the Milky Way, and constituting the primary great circle for the galactic system of coordinates; it is everywhere 90° from the galactic poles. Also known as galactic circle. { gə'lak·tik i'kwād·ər }

galactic halo The spherical distribution of oldest stars that are centered about the galactic center of the Milky Way Galaxy. { gə'lak·tik 'hā·lō }

galactic latitude Angular distance north or south of the galactic equator; the arc of a great circle through the galactic poles, between the galactic equator and a point on the celestial sphere, measured northward or southward from the galactic equator through 90° and labeled N or S to indicate the direction of measurement. { gə'lak·tik 'lad·əˌtüd }

galactic light The part of the illumination of the night sky that is due to light emitted from stars but diffused through interstellar space. { gə'lak·tik 'līt }

galactic longitude Angular distance east of sidereal hour angle 94.4° along the galactic equator; the arc of the galactic equator or the angle at the galactic pole between the great circle through the intersection of the galactic equator and the celestial equator in Sagittarius (SHA 94.4°) and a great circle through the galactic poles, measured eastward from the great circle through SHA 94.4° through 360°. { gə'lak·tik 'län·jəˌtüd }

galactic nebula   A nebula that is in or near the galactic system known as the Milky Way. { gə'lak·tik 'neb·yə·lə }

galactic noise   Radio-frequency noise that originates outside the solar system; it is similar to thermal noise and is strongest in the direction of the Milky Way. { gə'lak·tik 'nȯiz }

galactic nova   One of the novae that are concentrated largely in a band 10° on each side of the plane of the galaxy and are most frequent toward the center of the galaxy. { gə'lak·tik 'nō·və }

galactic nucleus   The center area in the galaxy about which there is a large spherical distribution of stars and from which the spiral arms emanate. { gə'lak·tik 'nü·klē·əs }

galactic plane   The plane that may be drawn through the galactic equator; the plane of the Milky Way Galaxy. { gə'lak·tik 'plān }

galactic pole   On the celestial sphere, either of the two points 90° from the galactic equator. { gə'lak·tik 'pōl }

galactic radiation   Radiation emanating from the Milky Way Galaxy. { gə'lak·tik rād·ē'ā·shən }

galactic rotation   The rotation of the Milky Way about an axis through the center and perpendicular to the plane of the Galaxy; the rotation is apparent from the highly flattened shape and from relative stellar motion. { gə'lak·tik rō'tā·shən }

galactic system   An astronomical coordinate system using latitude measured north and south from the galactic equator, and longitude measured in the sense of increasing right ascension from 0 to 360°. Also known as galactic coordinates. { gə'lak·tik 'sis·təm }

galactic windows   The regions near the equator of the Milky Way where there is low absorption of light by interstellar clouds so that some distant external galaxies may be seen through them. { gə'lak·tik 'winˌdōz }

Galatea   A satellite of Neptune orbiting at a mean distance of 38,500 miles (62,000 kilometers) with a period of 10.3 hours, and a diameter of about 90 miles (150 kilometers). { ˌgal·ə'tē·ə }

galaxy   A large-scale aggregate of stars, gas, and dust; the aggregate is a separate system of stars covering a mass range from 10^7 to 10^{12} solar masses and ranging in diameter from 1500 to 300,000 light-years. { 'gal·ik·sē }

Galaxy   *See* Milky Way Galaxy. { 'gal·ik·sē }

galaxy cluster   A collection of from two to several hundred galaxies which are much more densely distributed than the average density of galaxies in space. { 'gal·ik·sē ˌkləs·tər }

Galilean satellites   The four largest and brightest satellites of Jupiter (Io, Europa, Ganymede, and Callisto). { ˌgal·ə¦lē·ən 'sad·əlˌīts }

82

gamma-ray astronomy   The study of gamma rays from extraterrestrial sources, especially gamma-ray bursts. { 'gam · ə ˌrā ə'strän · ə · mē }

gamma-ray bursts   Intense blasts of soft gamma rays of unknown origin, which range in duration from a tenth of a second to tens of seconds and occur several times a year from sources widely distributed over the sky. { 'gam · ə ˌrā ˌbərsts }

gamma-ray telescope   Any device for detecting and determining the directions of extraterrestrial gamma rays, using coincidence or anticoincidence circuits with scintillation or semiconductor detectors to obtain directional discrimination. { 'gam · ə ˌrā 'tel · ə ˌskōp }

Ganymede   A satellite of Jupiter orbiting at a mean distance of 664,000 miles (1,071,000 kilometers). Also known as Jupiter III. { 'gan · ə ˌmēd }

gardening   A phenomenon in which the lunar regolith is constantly churning at a very slow rate because of successive impacts; the result is that bottom material is brought up to the top and surface material is buried. { 'gärd · ən · iŋ }

gas-bounded nebula   An emission nebula whose central star is hot enough, or in which the density of the cloud is small enough, to ionize the entire cloud. { 'gas ˈbaund · əd 'neb · yə · lə }

gaseous nebulae   Clouds of gas, such as the Network Nebula in Cygnus, that are members of the Milky Way galactic system and are small compared with its overall dimensions. { ˈgash · əs 'neb · yə · lē }

GAT   *See* Greenwich apparent time.

Gaussian constant   The acceleration caused by the attraction of the sun at the mean distance of the earth from the sun. { ˈgaủ · sē · ən 'kän · stənt }

Gaussian year   The period, according to Kepler's laws, of a body of negligible mass traveling in an orbit about the sun whose semimajor axis is 1 astronomical unit; equal to about 365.2569 days. { 'gaủs · ē · ən 'yir }

gegenschein   A round or elongated, faint, ill-defined spot of light in the sky at a point 180° from the sun. Also known as counterglow; zodiacal counterglow. { 'gāg · ən ˌshīn }

Gemini   A northern constellation; right ascension 7 hours, declination 20°N. Also known as Twins. { 'jem · ə ˌnē }

Geminids   A meteor shower that reaches maximum about December 13. { 'jem · ə · nidz }

general aviation   All aviation activity not associated with either certificated air carriers or the military, including business uses, commuter airlines, air taxi operators, various commercial applications, and personal flying. { 'jen · rəl ˌā · vē'ā · shən }

general precession   The resultant motion of the components causing precession of the equinoxes westward along the ecliptic at the rate of about 50.3″ per year. { ˈjen · rəl prē'sesh · ən }

geocentric   Relative to the earth as a center; that is measured from the center of the earth. { ˈjē · ōˈsen · trik }

geocentric coordinates   Coordinates that define the position of a point with respect

geocentric coordinate system

to the center of the earth; can be either cartesian (x, y, and z) or spherical (latitude, longitude, and radial distance). Also known as geocentric coordinate system; geocentric position. { ¦jē·ō¦sen·trik kō'órd·ən·əts }

geocentric coordinate system   See geocentric coordinates. { ¦jē·ō¦sen·trik kō'órd·ən·ət ˌsis·təm }

geocentric latitude   The latitude of a celestial body from the center of the earth. { ¦jē·ō¦sen·trik 'lad·əˌtüd }

geocentric longitude   The celestial longitude of the position of a body projected on the celestial sphere when the body is viewed from the center of the earth. { ¦jē·ō¦sen·trik 'län·jəˌtüd }

geocentric parallax   The difference in the apparent direction or position of a celestial body, measured in seconds of arc, as determined from the center of the earth and from a point on its surface; this varies with the body's altitude and distance from the earth. Also known as diurnal parallax. { ¦jē·ō¦sen·trik 'par·əˌlaks }

geocentric position   See geocentric coordinates. { ¦jē·ō¦sen·trik pə'zish·ən }

geocentric zenith   The point where a line from the center of the earth through a point on its surface meets the celestial sphere. { ¦jē·ō¦sen·trik 'zē·nith }

geodetic satellite   An artificial earth satellite used to obtain data for geodetic triangulation calculations. { ¦jē·ə¦ded·ik 'sad·əlˌīt }

geographical position   That point on the earth at which a given celestial body is in the zenith at a specified time. { ¦jē·ə¦graf·ə·kəl pə'zish·ən }

Geographos   An asteroid whose orbit has a semimajor axis of 1.25 astronomical units and an eccentricity of 0.335, giving it a perihelion inside the earth's orbit. { jē'äg·rəˌfōs }

geoidal horizon   That circle of the celestial sphere formed by the intersection of the celestial sphere and a plane tangent to the sea-level surface of the earth at the zenith-nadir line. { jē'óid·əl hə'rīz·ən }

geometrical pitch   The distance a component of an airplane propeller would move forward in one complete turn of the propeller if the path it was moving along was a helix that had an angle equal to an angle between a plane perpendicular to the axis of the propeller and the chord of the component. { ¦jē·ə¦me·trə·kəl 'pich }

geostationary satellite   A satellite that orbits the earth from west to east at such a speed as to remain fixed over a given place on the earth's equator at approximately 22,300 miles (35,900 kilometers) altitude; makes one revolution in 24 hours, synchronous with the earth's rotation. Also known as geosynchronous satellite; synchronous satellite. { ¦jē·ō¦stā·shəˌner·ē 'sad·əlˌīt }

geosynchronous satellite   See geostationary satellite. { ˌjē·ō¦siŋ·krə·nəs 'sad·əlˌīt }

GHA   See Greenwich hour angle.

Giacobinids   A meteor shower that reaches maximum about October 10, associated with Comet P/Giacobini-Zinner. { jə'kä·bəˌnidz }

giant planets   The planets Jupiter, Saturn, Uranus, and Neptune. { ¦jī·ənt 'plan·əts }

84

giant star   One of a class of stars that is 20 or 30 or more times larger than the sun and over 100 times more luminous. { ¦jī·ənt 'stär }

gibbous moon   The shape of the moon's visible surface when the sun is illuminating more than half of the side facing the earth. { 'jib·əs 'mün }

gimbaled motor   A rocket engine mounted on a gimbal. { 'gim·bəld 'mōd·ər }

Giraffe   See Camelopardalis. { jə'raf }

Gledhill disk   The outer magnetosphere of Jupiter, which forms a disk-shaped region of hot plasma near the plane of Jupiter's magnetic equator. { 'gled͵hil ͵disk }

glide   Descent of an aircraft at a normal angle of attack, with little or no thrust. { glīd }

glide angle   See gliding angle. { 'glīd ͵aŋ·gəl }

glide path   **1.** The flight path of an aeronautical vehicle in a glide, seen from the side. Also known as glide trajectory. **2.** The path used by an aircraft or spacecraft in a landing approach procedure. { 'glīd ͵path }

glider   A fixed-wing aircraft designed to glide, and sometimes to soar; usually does not have a power plant. { 'glīd·ər }

glide rocket   A rocket that is kept within or near the sensible atmosphere so that it assumes a flat, gliding attitude when power is shut off. { 'glīd ͵räk·ət }

glide slope   See gliding angle. { 'glīd ͵slōp }

glide trajectory   See glide path. { 'glīd trə͵jek·trē }

gliding angle   The angle between the horizontal and the glide path of an aircraft. Also known as glide angle; glide slope. { 'glīd·iŋ ͵aŋ·gəl }

glitch   A sudden change in the period of a pulsar, believed to result from a phenomenon analogous to an earthquake that changes the pulsar's moment of inertia. { glich }

globular star cluster   A group of many thousands of stars that are much closer to each other than the stars around the group and that are traveling through space together; a globular cluster has a slightly flattened spheroidal shape. { 'gläb·yə·lər 'stär ͵kləs·tər }

globule   A black volume of cosmic dust viewed against the brighter background of bright nebulae. { 'gläb·yəl }

GMT   See Greenwich mean time.

gnomic   Pertaining to the gnomon of a sundial. { 'nō·mik }

Gould's belt   A belt of bright stars inclined about 20° to the Milky Way and including most of the bright stars in Orion, Scorpio, Carina, and Centaurus, apparently resulting from a slight tilt of the spiral arm of the Milky Way Galaxy containing the sun, with respect to the galactic plane. { 'gülz ͵belt }

gradual phase   The second phase of a solar flare, characterized by emission of relatively low-energy (soft) x-radiation which appears soon after the beginning of the impulsive phase, grows in intensity as the impulsive bursts wane, and lasts up to several hours. Also known as thermal phase. { 'graj·ə·wəl ͵fāz }

granulation The small "rice grain" markings on the sun's photosphere. Also known as photospheric granulation. { ˌgran·yə'lā·shən }

granule A convective cell in the solar photosphere, about 600 miles (1000 kilometers) in diameter. { 'gran·yül }

gravitational astronomy See celestial mechanics. { ˌgrav·ə'tā·shən·əl ə'strän·ə·mē }

gravitational clustering A theory that attributes the hierarchy structure of the universe to growth of density fluctuations in a statistically uniform and isotropic universe. { ˌgrav·ə'tā·shən·əl 'kləs·təˌriŋ }

gravitational collapse The implosion of a star or other astronomical body from an initial size to a size hundreds or thousands of times smaller. { ˌgrav·ə'tā·shən·əl kə'laps }

gravitational encounter An approach of two massive bodies in which the directions of motion of both bodies are altered by their mutual gravitational attraction. { ˌgrav·ə'tā·shən·əl in'kaúnt·ər }

gravitational equilibrium The condition of a star in which the weight of overlying layers at each point is balanced by the total pressure at that point. { ˌgrav·ə'tā·shən·əl ˌē·kwə'lib·rē·əm }

gravitational lens A massive galaxy or other massive object whose gravitational field focuses light from a distant quasar near or along its line of sight, giving a double or multiple image of the quasar. { ˌgrav·ə'tā·shən·əl 'lenz }

gravity-gradient attitude control A device that regulates automatically attitude or orientation of an aircraft or spacecraft by responding to changes in gravity acting on the craft. { ˈgrav·əd·ē ˈgrād·ē·ənt 'ad·əˌtüd kənˌtrōl }

gravity simulation The spinning of part or all of a space vehicle so that the centripetal force on bodies within the vehicle near the outer periphery mimics the force of gravity on objects at the earth's surface. { 'grav·əd·ē ˌsim·yəˌlā·shən }

grazing-incidence telescope An instrument for forming images of celestial x-ray or gamma-ray sources in which the total external reflection of the x-rays or gamma rays from a surface at sufficiently shallow angles of incidence is used to focus them. { 'grāz·iŋ ˈin·səd·əns 'tel·əˌskōp }

Great Attractor A great supercluster of galaxies and dark matter, approximately 150 × 10⁶ light-years distant, whose existence has been hypothesized to account for the peculiar motions of galaxies, including the Milky Way Galaxy. { ˈgrāt ə'trak·tər }

great cluster A galaxy cluster containing thousands of member galaxies and having a radius of 5 × 10⁶ to 20 × 10⁶ light-years. { ˈgrāt ˈkləs·tər }

Greater Dog See Canis Major. { 'grād·ər ˈdȯg }

greatest elongation The maximum angular distance of a body of the solar system from the sun, as observed from the earth. { 'grād·əst ˌēˌloŋ'gä·shən }

Great Nebula of Orion See Orion Nebula. { ˈgrāt 'neb·yə·lə əv ə'rī·ən }

Great Rift An apparent break in the Milky Way between Cygnus and Sagittarius caused by a series of large, dark overlapping clouds about 100 parsecs (2 × 10¹⁵ miles or 3 × 10¹⁵ kilometers) distant in the equatorial plane of the Galaxy. { 'grāt 'rift }

Great Wall A layer of several thousand galaxies, estimated to extend for about 500 × 10⁶ by 200 × 10⁶ light-years but to be less than 15 × 10⁶ light-years thick, constituting the largest known structure in the universe. { ¦grāt ′wȯl }

great year The period of one complete cycle of the equinoxes around the ecliptic, about 25,800 years. Also known as platonic year. { ¦grāt ′yir }

Greek group The group of Trojan planets which lies near the Lagrangian point 60° ahead of Jupiter. Also known as Achilles group. { ′grēk ¦grüp }

green flash A brilliant green coloration of the upper limb of the sun occasionally observed just as the sun's apparent disk is about to sink below a distant clear horizon. Also known as blue flash; blue-green flame; green segment; green sun. { ′grēn ¦flash }

green segment See green flash. { ′grēn ¦seg·mənt }

green sun See green flash. { ′grēn ¦sən }

Greenwich apparent noon Local apparent noon at the Greenwich meridian; twelve o'clock Greenwich apparent time, or the instant the apparent sun is over the upper branch of the Greenwich meridian. { ′gren·ich ə′par·ənt ¦nün }

Greenwich apparent time Local apparent time at the Greenwich meridian. Abbreviated GAT. { ′gren·ich ə′par·ənt ¦tīm }

Greenwich civil time See Greenwich mean time. { ′gren·ich ′siv·əl ¦tīm }

Greenwich hour angle Angular distance west of the Greenwich celestial meridian; the arc of the celestial equator, or the angle at the celestial pole, between the upper branch of the Greenwich celestial meridian and the hour circle of a point on the celestial sphere, measured westward from the Greenwich celestial meridian through 360°. Abbreviated GHA. { ′gren·ich ′au̇r ¦aŋ·gəl }

Greenwich interval An interval based on the moon's transit of the Greenwich celestial meridian, as distinguished from a local interval based on the moon's transit of the local celestial meridian. { ′gren·ich ′in·tər·vəl }

Greenwich lunar time Local lunar time at the Greenwich meridian; the arc of the celestial equator, or the angle at the celestial pole, between the lower branch of the Greenwich celestial meridian and the hour circle of the moon, measured westward from the lower branch of the Greenwich celestial meridian through 24 hours. { ′gren·ich ′lün·ər ¦tīm }

Greenwich mean noon Local mean noon at the Greenwich meridian, twelve o'clock Greenwich mean time, or the instant the mean sun is over the upper branch of the Greenwich meridian. { ′gren·ich ′mēn ¦nün }

Greenwich mean time Mean solar time at the meridian of Greenwich. Abbreviated GMT. Also known as Greenwich civil time; universal time; Z time; zulu time. { ′gren·ich ′mēn ¦tīm }

Greenwich sidereal time Local sidereal time at the Greenwich meridian. Abbreviated GST. { ′gren·ich sī′dir·ē·əl ¦tīm }

Gregorian calendar The calendar used for civil purposes throughout the world, replacing the Julian calendar and closely adjusted to the tropical year. { grə′gȯr·ē·ən ′kal·ən·dər }

ground   To forbid (an aircraft or individual) to fly, usually for a relatively short time. { graúnd }

ground effect   Increase in the lift of an aircraft operating close to the ground caused by reaction between high-velocity downwash from its wing or rotor and the ground. { 'graúnd i⸝fekt }

ground handling equipment   *See* ground support equipment. { 'graúnd ¦hand· liŋ i⸝kwip·mənt }

ground loop   A sharp, uncontrollable turn made by an aircraft on the ground during landing, taking off, or taxiing. { 'graúnd ⸝lüp }

ground start   A propulsion starting sequence of a rocket or missile that is initiated and carried through to ignition of the main-stage engines on the ground. { 'graúnd ⸝stärt }

ground support equipment   That equipment on the ground, including all implements, tools, and devices (mobile or fixed), required to inspect, test, adjust, calibrate, appraise, gage, measure, repair, overhaul, assemble, disassemble, transport, safeguard, record, store, or otherwise function in support of a rocket, space vehicle, or the like, either in the research and development phase or in an operational phase, or in support of the guidance system used with the missile, vehicle, or the like. Abbreviated GSE. Also known as ground handling equipment. { 'graúnd sə⸝pórt i⸝kwip·məmt }

group   A number of stars moving in the same direction with the same speed. { grüp }

growth factor   The additional weight of fuel and structural material required by the addition of 1 pound (0.45 kilogram) of payload to the original payload. { 'gröth ⸝fak·tər }

Grus   A constellation, right ascension 22 hours, declination 45°S. Also known as Crane. { grüs }

GSE   *See* ground support equipment.

G star   A star of spectral type G; many metallic lines are seen in the spectra, with hydrogen and potassium being strong; G stars are yellow stars, with surface temperatures of 4200-5500 K for giants, 5000-6000 K for dwarfs. { 'jē ⸝stär }

GST   *See* Greenwich sidereal time.

guidance system   The control devices used in guidance of an aircraft or spacecraft. { 'gīd·əns ⸝sis·təm }

guillotine factor   A quantity that expresses the sharp reduction in the opacity of a gas which occurs when its temperature becomes sufficiently high to ionize the atoms down to their K shells. { 'gē·ə⸝tēn ⸝fak·tər }

gull wing   An airplane wing that slants upward from the fuselage for a short distance and then levels out. { 'gəl ⸝wiŋ }

Gum Nebula   A giant nebula about 250 parsecs (5×10^{15} miles or 8×10^{15} kilometers) in diameter, with its near edge about 300 parsecs (6×10^{15} miles or 9×10^{15} kilometers) distant, which is both an old supernova remnant and an H II region. { 'gəm 'neb·yə·lə }

gust-gradient distance   The horizontal distance along an aircraft flight path from the "edge" of a gust to the point at which the gust reaches its maximum speed. { 'gəst¦grād·ē·ənt ‚dis·təns }

gust tunnel   A type of wind tunnel that has an enclosed space and is used to test the effect of gusts on an airplane model in free flight to determine how atmospheric gusts affect the flight of an airplane. { 'gəst ‚tən·əl }

gyroplane   A rotorcraft whose rotors are not power-driven. { 'jī·rō‚plān }

H

Hadar *See* Centauri. { ha′där }

hadron era The period in the early universe when the physical forces (gravity, weak, strong, and electromagnetic) diverged from a condition of rough equivalence to increasing disparity, roughly the time between about 10^{-43} and 10^{-4} second after the big bang. { ′had‚rän ‚ir·ə }

Hale cycle The variation of the sun′s magnetic field over a period of approximately 22 years, during which the field reverses and is restored to its original polarity; one such cycle comprises two successive sunspot cycles. { ′hāl ‚sī·kəl }

half-moon The moon as seen in the first quarter and the last quarter. { ′haf ‚mün }

Halley′s Comet A member of the solar system, with an orbit and a period of about 76 years; its nucleus is about 9 miles (15 kilometers) in diameter; next due to appear in 2061. { ′hal·ēz ¦käm·ət }

halo A type of ray system in which many short, filamentary streaks form a complex network of bright matter surrounding the lunar crater. Also known as nimbus. { ′hā·lō }

halo population *See* Population II. { ′hā·lō ‚päp·yə‚lā·shən }

Hamal A second-magnitude star in the constellation Aries; the star α Ari. { hə′mäl }

hang glider A flexible, deployable, steerable, kitelike glider from which a harnessed rider hangs during flight. { ′haŋ ‚glīd·ər }

hard landing A landing made without deceleration, as by impact on the moon. { ′härd ¦land·iŋ }

harmonic law The third of Kepler′s laws, which states that the squares of the periods of revolution of any two planets are proportional to the cubes of their mean distances from the sun. { här′män·ik ′lȯ }

harness 1. Straps arranged to hold an occupant of a spacecraft or aircraft in the seat. 2. Straps worn by a parachutist or used to suspend a load from a parachute. { ′här·nəs }

Harvard-Draper sequence A system of classification of stellar spectra based on features that are found to vary in a smooth way from one star to another, and on the star′s color. { ¦här·vərd ′drā·pər ‚sē·kwəns }

harvest moon A full moon that is seen nearest the autumnal equinox. { ′här·vəst ¦mün }

Hayashi track   A vertical track on the Hertzsprung-Russell diagram along which a star of small mass descends during its early stages of formation, when convective heat transport prevails over most of the star. { ha'ya·shē ˌtrak }

HdC star   A type of hydrogen-deficient supergiant carbon star that resembles the R Coronae Borealis stars but does not display significant variability. { ˌāch ˌdē'sē ˌstär }

head   *See* coma. { hed }

heat barrier   *See* thermal barrier. { 'hēt ˌbar·ē·ər }

heatsink   **1.** A type of protective device capable of absorbing heat and used as a heat shield. **2.** In nuclear propulsion, any thermodynamic device, such as a radiator or condenser, that is designed to absorb the excess heat energy of the working fluid. Also known as heat dump. { 'hētˌsiŋk }

heavenly body   *See* celestial body. { 'hev·ən·lē 'bäd·ē }

heavier-than-air craft   Any aircraft weighing more than the air it displaces. { 'hev·ē·ər thən 'er ¦kraft }

heavy bomber   Any large bomber considered to be relatively heavy, such as a bomber having a gross weight, including bomb load, of 250,000 pounds (113,000 kilograms) or more, as the B-36 and the B-52. { 'hev·ē 'bäm·ər }

heavy-metal star   A member of a class of peculiar giants that includes the barium stars and S stars, characterized by unusually strong lines of heavy metals, including barium and zirconium. { 'hev·ē ¦med·əl 'stär }

Hebe   An asteroid with a diameter of about 200 kilometers, mean distance from the sun of 2.426 astronomical units, and S-type surface composition. { 'hē·bē }

Hektor   An asteroid, believed to be the largest of the Trojan planets, which circles the sun in the orbit of and approximately 60° ahead of Jupiter; diameter is about 130 miles (210 kilometers) and surface composition is unusual. { 'hek·tər }

heliacal rising   The rising of a celestial body at the same time or just before that of the sun. { hi'lī·ə·kəl 'rīz·iŋ }

heliacal setting   The setting of a celestial body at the same time or just after that of the sun. { hi'lī·ə·kəl 'sed·iŋ }

helicopter   An aircraft fitted to sustain itself by motor-driven horizontal rotating blades (rotors) that accelerate the air downward, providing a reactive lift force, or accelerate the air at an angle to the vertical, providing lift and thrust. { 'hel·əˌkäp·tər }

heliocentric   Relative to the sun as a center. { ¦hē·lē·ō¦sen·trik }

heliocentric coordinates   A coordinate system relative to the sun as a center. { ¦hē·lē·ō¦sen·trik kō'ȯrd·ən·əts }

heliocentric Julian date   The Julian date corrected to the time at which light from the celestial object in question reaches the sun (rather than the earth). Abbreviated HJD. { ˌhē·lē·ō'sen·trik 'jül·yən 'dāt }

heliocentric latitude   Sun-centered coordinate of angular distance perpendicular to the ecliptic plane. { ¦hē·lē·ō¦sen·trik 'lad·əˌtüd }

heliocentric longitude The angular distance east or west from a given point on the sun's equator. { ˈhē·lē·ōˌsen·trik 'län·jəˌtüd }

heliocentric orbit An orbit relative to the sun as a center. { ˈhē·lē·ōˌsen·trik 'ȯr·bət }

heliocentric parallax See annual parallax. { ˈhē·lē·ōˌsen·trik 'par·əˌlaks }

heliographic latitude On the sun, angular distance north or south of its equator. { ˌhē·lē·ə'graf·ik 'lad·əˌtüd }

heliographic longitude On the sun, angular distance east or west from given point on the equator of the sun. { ˌhē·lē·ə'graf·ik 'lan·jəˌtüd }

helioseismology The analysis of wave motions of the solar surface to determine the structure of the sun's interior. { ˌhē·lē·ō·sīz'mäl·ə·jē }

heliosphere The region surrounding the sun where the solar wind dominates the interstellar medium. Also known as solar cavity. { 'hē·lē·əˌsfir }

helium flash The onset of runaway helium burning in the degenerate core of a red giant star and the resulting expansion of the core. { 'hē·lē·əm ˌflash }

helium stars The class B stars. { 'hē·lē·əm ˈstärz }

Helix Nebula A planetary nebula in Aquarius about 140 parsecs (2.7 × 10^15 miles or 4.3 × 10^15 kilometers) distant that has a high helium abundance and the largest known diameter of any planetary nebula. { 'hēˌliks 'neb·yə·lə }

Hellas The largest impact basin on Mars, approximately 1240 miles (2000 kilometers) across and 2.5 miles (4 kilometers) deep, appearing as a bright circular region in earth-based telescopes. { 'hel·əs }

Hellespontus A surface region of the planet Mars between the regions Hellas and Noachis. { ˈhel·əsˌpän·təs }

Henyey track An almost horizontal track on the Hertzsprung-Russell diagram that a star of small mass follows in an early stage of evolution after leaving the Hayashi track and before reaching the main sequence, during which the star is almost wholly in radiative equilibrium. { 'hen·yē ˌtrak }

Herbig emission star A relatively massive star in early stages of formation, still surrounded by a nebula which makes it variable in luminosity and renders its spectrum very peculiar. { 'hər·bik iˈmish·ən ˌstär }

Herbig-Haro object A bright patch on the surface of a dark cloud of gas and dust, consisting of light that has been scattered and reflected from a newborn star embedded in the cloud. { ˈhər·big 'hä·rō ˌäb·jəkt }

Hercules A constellation with no stars brighter than third magnitude; right ascension 17 hours, declination 30° north. { 'hər·kyəˌlēz }

Hercules cluster A cluster of about 75 bright galaxies with a recession velocity of 6200 miles (10,000 kilometers) per second. { 'hər·kyəˌlēz ˌkləs·tər }

Hercules superclusters A pair of superclusters with recession velocities around 10,000 kilometers (6200 miles) per second, one of which contains the Hercules cluster. { ˈhərk·yəˌlēz ˈsü·pərˌkləs·tərz }

Hercules X-1

Hercules X-1 A source of x-rays that pulses with a period of 1.237 seconds, and is eclipsed for 6 of every 42 hours, associated with a variable star, designated HZ Herculis, that also has a period of 42 hours and faint 1.237-second pulsations; believed to be a binary star whose invisible member is a rotating neutron star. Abbreviated Her X-1. { 'hər·kyəˌlēz ˈeks 'wən }

Hermes A very small asteroid which passed within 485,000 miles (780,000 kilometers) of the earth in 1937, the closest known approach of a celestial body other than the moon. { 'hərˌmēz }

Hertzsprung gap A gap on the Hertzsprung-Russell diagram between giant stars of spectral types A0 and G0, caused by the fact that the movement of stars across this region occupies a relatively brief time. { 'hert·sprúŋ ˌgap }

Hertzsprung-Russell diagram A plot showing the relation between the luminosity and surface temperature of stars; other related quantities frequently used in plotting this diagram are the absolute magnitude for luminosity, and spectral type or color index for the surface temperatures. Abbreviated H-R diagram. Also known as Russell diagram. { 'hert·sprúŋ 'rəs·əl 'dī·əˌgram }

Her X-1 *See* Hercules X-1.

Hesperus Greek name for the planet Venus as an evening star. { 'hes·prəs }

Hess diagram A diagram showing the frequencies of occurrence of stars at various positions on the Hertzsprung-Russell diagram. { 'hes ˌdī·əˌgram }

Hidalgo The asteroid with the second largest known mean distance from the sun, about 5.8 astronomical units. { hi'däl·gō }

high-energy astrophysics A science concerned with studies of acceleration of charged particles to high energies in space, cosmic rays, radio galaxies, pulsars, and quasistellar sources. { 'hī ˌen·ər·jē as·trə'fiz·iks }

high-mass x-ray binary A binary system consisting of a massive (greater than 5 solar masses), early-type star and a neutron star or black hole that accretes material through a stellar wind or Roche-lobe overflow, resulting in the emission of hard x-rays. Abbreviated HMXRB. { ˈhīˌmas ˈeksˌrā'bīˌner·ē }

high-velocity cloud A rapidly moving interstellar cloud with a radial velocity greater than about 12 miles (20 kilometers) per second, consisting primarily of neutral atomic hydrogen, observed in the ultraviolet. { 'hī vəˈläs·əd·ē 'klaúd }

high-velocity star A star that moves across the galactic track along which the majority of the stars execute their galactic rotation, thus exhibiting high velocity with respect to the sun and low velocity with respect to the galactic center. { 'hī vəˈläs·əd·ē 'stär }

Hilda group A group of asteroids whose periods of revolution about the sun are approximately two-thirds that of Jupiter, and whose motions are in resonance with Jupiter. { 'hil·də ˌgrüp }

Hiltner-Hall effect The polarization of the light received from distant stars; this effect is thought to take place in interstellar space. { ˈhilt·nər 'hól iˌfekt }

Himalia A small satellite of Jupiter with a diameter of about 35 miles (56 kilometers), orbiting at a mean distance of 7.12 × 10⁶ miles (11.46 × 10⁶ kilometers). Also known as Jupiter VI. { hi'mäl·ē·ə }

Hind's Nebula   A reflection nebula illuminated by the star T Tauri that undergoes marked changes in brightness. { 'hīnz 'neb·yə·lə }

hinge moment   The tendency of an aerodynamic force to produce motion about the hinge line of a control surface. { 'hinjd ¦mō·mənt }

Hirayama family   A clustering of asteroids whose orbits have similar values of semimajor axis, eccentricity, and inclination; over 100 such families have been tabulated. { ‚hi·rä'yä·mä ‚fam·lē }

HJD   See heliocentric Julian date.

Hohmann orbit   A minimum-energy-transfer orbit. { 'hō·mən ‚ȯr·bət }

Hohmann trajectory   The minimum-energy trajectory between two planetary orbits, utilizing only two propulsive impulses. { 'hō·mən trə‚jek·tə·rē }

hold   A scheduled or unscheduled pause in a testing or launching sequence or countdown of a missile or space vehicle. { hōld }

Holmberg radius   The radius of an external galaxy at which the surface brightness is such that the light emitted from one square arc-second equals that from a star of magnitude 26.6. { 'hōm‚bərg ‚rād·ē·əs }

homologous transformation   A mathematical transformation in the study of stellar models. { hə'mäl·ə·gəs ‚tranz·fər'mā·shən }

H I region   A region of interstellar space where neutral hydrogen is present. { ¦āch 'wən ‚rē·jən }

horizon   **1.** The apparent boundary line between the sky and the earth or sea. Also known as apparent horizon. **2.** The distance a light-ray could have traveled since the big-bang explosion at any given epoch in the evolution of the universe. { hə'rīz·ən }

horizon problem   The problem of explaining the observed uniformity of the universe, and in particular of the cosmic background radiation, when, according to the standard big-bang theory, sources of radiation coming from opposite directions in the sky were separated by manyfold the horizon distance at the time of emission, and thus could not possibly have been in physical contact. { hə'rīz·ən ‚präb·ləm }

horizon system of coordinates   A set of celestial coordinates based on the celestial horizon as the primary great circle. { hə'rīz·ən ¦sis·təm əv kō'ȯrd·ən·əts }

horizontal branch   A region in the Hertzsprung-Russell diagram of a typical globular cluster that extends in the blue direction from the giant branch at an absolute bolometric magnitude of 0.3 and consists of stars that are burning helium in their cores and hydrogen in their surrounding envelopes. { ‚här·ə'zänt·əl 'branch }

horizontal parallax   The geocentric parallax of a celestial object when it is rising or setting. { ‚här·ə'zänt·əl 'par·ə‚laks }

Horologium   A constellation with right ascension 3 hours, declination 60° south. Also known as Clock. { ‚hȯr·ə'lō·jē·əm }

Horologium superclusters   Two superclusters in approximately the same direction, with recession velocities around 12,000 kilometers (7500 miles) and 18,000 kilometers (11,200 miles) per second. { ‚hȯr·ə‚lō·gē·əm 'sü·pər‚kləs·tərz }

Horsehead Nebula

Horsehead Nebula   A cloud of obscuring particles between the earth and a gaseous emission nebula in the constellation Orion. { 'hȯrs‚hed 'neb·yə·lə }

hot dark matter   A hypothetical type of dark matter consisting of entities that were not in thermal equilibrium in the early universe; possibilities include massive neutrinos and cosmic strings. { ¦hät ¦därk 'mad·ər }

hotshot wind tunnel   A wind tunnel in which electrical energy is discharged into a pressurized arc chamber, increasing the temperature and pressure in the arc chamber so that a diaphragm separating the arc chamber from an evacuated chamber is ruptured, and the heated gas from the arc chamber is then accelerated in a conical nozzle to provide flows with Mach numbers of 10 to 27 for durations of 10 to 100 milliseconds. { 'hät¦shät 'win ‚tən·əl }

hour angle   Angular distance west of a celestial meridian or hour circle; the arc of the celestial equator, or the angle at the celestial pole, between the upper branch of a celestial meridian or hour circle and the hour circle of a celestial body or the vernal equinox, measured westward through 360°. { 'aür ‚aŋ·gəl }

hour-angle difference   *See* meridian angle difference. { 'aür ‚aŋ·gəl 'dif·rəns }

hour circle   An imaginary great circle passing through the celestial poles on the celestial sphere above which declination is measured. Also known as circle of declination; circle of right ascension. { 'aür ‚sər·kəl }

H-R diagram   *See* Hertzsprung-Russell diagram. { ¦āch 'är ‚dī·ə‚gram }

H II region   A region of interstellar space occupied by gas that is largely atomic hydrogen and mostly ionized. { ¦āch 'tü ‚rē·jən }

hubble   A unit of astronomical distance equal to 10^9 light-years or 9.4605×10^{24} meters. { 'həb·əl }

Hubble constant   The rate at which the velocity of recession of the galaxies increases with distance; the value is about 30 kilometers per second per million light-years (or 3.2×10^{-18} s^{-1}) with an uncertainty of about ±15 kilometers per second. { 'həb·əl ‚kän·stənt }

Hubble effect   *See* redshift. { 'həb·əl i‚fekt }

Hubble flow   The mutual recession of celestial objects from each other by virtue of the cosmological expansion of the universe. { 'həb·əl ‚flō }

Hubble law   The principle that the distance of external galaxies from the earth is proportional to their redshift. { 'həb·əl ‚lȯ }

Hubble's Variable Nebula   A variable-brightness nebula associated with variable stars and fan-shaped in appearance. { 'həb·əlz ¦ver·ē·ə·bəl 'neb·yə·lə }

Hubble time   The reciprocal of the Hubble constant. { 'həb·əl ‚tīm }

hunt   **1.** Of an aircraft or rocket, to weave about its flight path, as if seeking a new direction or another angle of attack; specifically, to yaw back and forth. **2.** Of a control surface, to rotate up and down or back and forth without being detected by the pilot. { hənt }

hunter's moon   The full moon next following the harvest moon. { 'hən·tərz ¦mün }

Hunting Dogs   *See* Canes Venatici. { 'hənt·iŋ ‚dȯgz }

Hyades A V-shaped open star cluster about 150 light-years from the sun, which appears in the constellation Taurus near the star Aldebaran. { 'hī·ə‚dēz }

hybrid propulsion Propulsion utilizing energy released by a liquid propellant with a solid propellant in the same rocket engine. { 'hī·brəd prə'pəl·shən }

hybrid rocket A rocket with an engine utilizing a liquid propellant with a solid propellant in the same rocket engine. { 'hī·brəd 'räk·ət }

Hydra A large constellation of the southern hemisphere, right ascension 10 hours, declination 20° south. Also known as Water Monster. { 'hī·drə }

Hydra-Centaurus-Pavo supercluster The nearest supercluster outside the local supercluster; includes the Centaurus cluster, the Hydra I cluster, and a number of smaller clusters in the constellation Pavo. { ¦hī·drə sen¦tȯr·əs ¦pä·vō 'sü·pər‚kləs·tər }

Hydra I cluster A large cluster of galaxies with recession velocities around 3500 kilometers (2200 miles) per second, part of the Hydra-Centaurus-Pavo supercluster. { ¦hī·drə ‚wən 'kləs·tər }

hydrogen burning Thermonuclear reactions occurring in the cores of main-sequence stars, in which nuclei of hydrogen fuse to form helium nuclei. { 'hī·drə·jən ‚bərn·iŋ }

hydrogen star A star of spectral class A, a white star with a surface temperature of 8000 to 11,000 K. { 'hī·drə·jən ‚stär }

Hydrus A southern constellation, right ascension 2 hours, declination 75°S. Also known as Water Snake. { 'hī·drəs }

Hygiea The fourth largest asteroid, with a diameter of about 254 miles (410 kilometers), mean distance from the sun of 3.151 astronomical units, and C-type surface composition. { hī'jē·ə }

hyperbolic flareout A flareout obtained by changing the glide slope from a straight line to a hyperbolic curve at an appropriate distance from touchdown at an airport. { ¦hī·pər¦bäl·ik 'fler‚aut }

hyperbolic trajectory A trajectory entered by a spacecraft when its velocity exceeds the escape velocity of a planet, satellite, or star. { ¦hī·pər¦bäl·ik trə'jek·trē }

Hyperion A satellite of Saturn approximately 300 miles (480 kilometers) in diameter. { hī'pir·ē·ən }

hypersonic flight Flight at speeds well above the local velocity of sound; by convention, hypersonic regime starts at about five times the speed of sound and extends upward indefinitely. { ¦hī·pər'sän·ik 'flīt }

hypersonic glider An unpowered vehicle, specifically a reentry vehicle, designed to fly at hypersonic speeds. { ¦hī·pər'sän·ik 'glīd·ər }

hypothetical parallax *See* dynamic parallax. { ¦hī·pə¦thed·ə·kəl 'par·ə‚laks }

Iapetus   A satellite of Saturn that orbits at a mean distance of 2.207 × 10⁶ miles (3.560 × 10⁶ kilometers) and has a diameter of about 900 miles (1500 kilometers). { ˌyap·əd·əs }

Icarus   An asteroid with an orbit of highest known eccentricity and smallest perihelion and distance of all the asteroids. { ˌik·ə·rəs }

ideal rocket   A rocket motor or rocket engine that would have a velocity equal to the velocity of its jet gases. { ī′dēl ′räk·ət }

igneous theory   *See* volcanic theory. { ′ig·nē·əs ˌthē·ə·rē }

immersion   The disappearance of a celestial body either by passing behind another or passing into another's shadow. { ə′mər·zhən }

impact predictor   A device which takes information from a trajectory measuring system and continuously computes the point (in real time) at which the rocket will strike the earth. { ′imˌpakt prəˌdik·tər }

impact theory   A theory which holds that most features of the moon's surface were formed by the impact of meteorites. Also known as meteoric theory; meteoritic theory. { ′imˌpakt ˌthē·ə·rē }

impulsive phase   The first phase of a solar flare, in which x-radiation rises to a maximum in a few seconds or minutes, and can then vary rapidly for several minutes in bursts of decreasing amplitude with rise times as short as 10 milliseconds. { im′pəl·siv ˌfāz }

inclination of axis   The angle between a planet's axis of rotation and the perpendicular to the plane of its orbit. { ˌiŋ·klə′nā·shən əv ′ak·səs }

inclination of planetary orbits   The angle between the plane of the orbit and the plane of the ecliptic, which is the plane of the earth's orbit. { ˌiŋ·klə′nā·shən əv ˈplan·əˌter·ē ′òr·bəts }

inclined orbit   A satellite orbit which is inclined with respect to the earth's equator. { in′klīnd ′òr·bət }

index catalog   A supplement to the New General Catalog of nebulae. { ′inˌdeks ˌkad·əlˌäg }

Indian   *See* Indus. { ′in·dē·ən }

indicated airspeed   The airspeed as shown by a differential-pressure airspeed indicator, uncorrected for instrument and installation errors; a simple computation for altitude and temperature converts indicated airspeed to true airspeed. Abbreviated IAS. { 'in·dəˌkād·əd 'erˌspēd }

indicated altitude   The uncorrected reading of a barometric altimeter. { 'in·dəˌkād·əd 'al·təˌtüd }

induced angle of attack   The downward vertical angle between the horizontal and the velocity (relative to the wing of an aircraft) of the airstream passing over the wing. { in'düst ¦aŋ·gəl əv ə'tak }

Indus   A constellation, right ascension 21 hours, declination 55° south. Also known as Indian. { 'in·dəs }

inertial orbit   The path described by an object that is subject only to gravitational forces, such as a celestial body or a spacecraft that is not under any type of propulsive power. { in'ər·shəl 'òr·bət }

infall process   A process in which gas falls upon a very compact object such as a neutron star or black hole, reaching a high velocity and forming a hot plasma; postulated as a model for x-ray sources such as Centaurus X-1 and Hercules X-1. { 'inˌfòl ˌprä·səs }

infall zone   The region that forms between the tidal radius of a planet in formation and the actual surface of the planet when the planet contracts from the tidal radius, so that any matter that enters this region falls to the planet's surface. { 'inˌfòl ˌzōn }

inferior conjunction   A type of configuration in which two celestial bodies have their least apparent separation; the smaller body is nearer the observer than the larger body, about which it orbits; for example, Venus is closest to the earth at its inferior conjunction. { in'fir·ē·ər kən'jəŋk·shən }

inferior planet   A planet that circles the sun in an orbit that is smaller than the earth's. { in'fir·ē·ər 'plan·ət }

inflationary universe cosmology   A theory of the evolution of the early universe which asserts that at some early time the observable universe underwent a period of exponential expansion, during which the scale of the universe increased by at least 28 orders of magnitude. { in'flā·shəˌner·ē 'yü·nəˌvərs käz'mäl·ə·jē }

inflight start   An engine ignition sequence that takes place after takeoff and during flight. { 'in¦flīt 'stärt }

infrared astronomy   The study of electromagnetic radiation in the spectrum between 0.75 and 1000 micrometers emanating from astronomical sources. { ¦in·frə¦red ə'strän·ə·mē }

infrared galaxy   A galaxy or quasar whose nucleus emits enormous amounts of infrared radiation, in some cases more than 1000 times the output of the entire Milky Way Galaxy at all wavelengths. { ¦in·frə¦red 'gal·ik·sē }

infrared star   A star that emits a large amount of radiant energy in the infrared portion of the electromagnetic spectrum. { ¦in·frə¦red ¦stär }

ingress   The entrance of the moon into the shadow of the earth in an eclipse, of a planet into the disk of the sun; or of a satellite (or its shadow) onto the disk of the parent planet. { 'inˌgres }

inhibitor A substance bonded, taped, or dip-dried onto a solid propellant to restrict the burning surface and to give direction to the burning process. { in'hib·əd·ər }

initial mass The mass of a rocket missile at the beginning of its flight. { i'nish·əl 'mas }

initial mass function The distribution of the masses of stars at the time of their formation. { i'nish·əl 'mas ˌfəŋk·shən }

injection The process of placing a spacecraft into a specific trajectory, such as an earth orbit or an encounter trajectory to Mars. Also known as insertion. { in'jek·shən }

inner Lagrangian point A Lagrangian point that lies between two primary bodies on the line passing through their centers of mass, and through which mass transfer may occur between them. Also known as conical point. { ¦in·ər lə'gran·jē·ən ˌpȯint }

inner planet Any of the four planets (Mercury, Venus, Earth, and Mars) in the solar system whose orbits are closest to the sun. { ¦in·ər 'plan·ət }

insertion See injection. { in'sər·shən }

insolation 1. Exposure of an object to the sun. 2. Solar energy received, often expressed as a rate of energy per unit horizontal surface. { ˌin·sō'lā·shən }

instability strip A portion of the Hertzsprung-Russell diagram occupied by pulsating stars; stars traverse this region at least once after they leave the main sequence. { ˌin·stə'bil·əd·ē ˌstrip }

integrated profile See mean profile. { 'in·tə·ˌgrād·əd 'prō·ˌfīl }

Interamnia An asteroid with a diameter of about 190 miles (320 kilometers), mean distance from the sun of 3.057 astronomical units, and C-type surface composition. { ˌin·tər'am·nē·ə }

intercalary day A day inserted or introduced among others in a calendar, as February 29 during leap years. { in'tər·kə·ˌler·ē 'dā }

interceptor A manned aircraft utilized for the identification or engagement of airborne objects. { ˌin·tər'sep·tər }

intercombination line A spectral line emitted in a transition between energy levels that have different multiplicities, that is, different values of the total spin quantum number. { ¦in·tər·ˌkäm·bə'nā·shən ˌlīn }

intergalactic Pertaining to the space between the galaxies. { ¦in·tər·gə'lak·tik }

intergalactic matter The material between the galaxies. { ˌin·tər·gə¦lak·tik 'mad·ər }

interlocking ring structures Two lunar craters that overlap, but both have their walls intact, indicating that they were formed at the same time. { ¦in·tər¦läk·iŋ 'riŋ ˌstrək·chərz }

intermediate polar A member of a class of cataclysmic variable stars whose x-ray and optical light curves display large pulses on time scales of minutes. Also known as DQ Herculis star. { ˌin·tər'mēd·ē·ət 'pōl·ər }

international date line A jagged arbitrary line, roughly equal to the 180° meridian, where a date change occurs: if the line is crossed from east to west a day is skipped, if from west to east the same day is repeated. { ¦in·tər¦nash·ən·əl 'dāt ˌlīn }

interplanetary dust   Dust particles between the planets. { ¦in·tər′plan·ə⋅ter·ē ′dəst }

interplanetary flight   Flight through the region of space between the planets, under the primary gravitational influence of the sun. { ¦in·tər′plan·ə⋅ter·ē ′flīt }

interplanetary magnetic field   The magnetic field between the planets. { ¦in·tər′plan· ə⋅ter·ē mag¦ned·ik ′fēld }

interplanetary medium   That part of space containing electromagnetic radiation, dust, gas, and plasma between the planets. { ¦in·tər′plan·ə⋅ter·ē ′mēd·ē·əm }

interplanetary probe   An instrumented spacecraft that flies through the region of space between the planets. { ¦in·tər′plan·ə⋅ter·ē ′prōb }

interplanetary space   The region that extends beyond near-space away from earth to the other planets in the solar system. { ¦in·tər′plan·ə⋅ter·ē ′spās }

interplanetary spacecraft   A spacecraft designed for interplanetary flight. { ¦in·tər ′plan·ə⋅ter·ē ′spās⋅kraft }

interplanetary transfer orbit   An elliptical trajectory tangent to the orbits of both the departure planet and the target planet. { ¦in·tər′plan·ə⋅ter·ē ′tranz·fər ⋅ór·bət }

interstellar   Between the stars. { ¦in·tər¦stel·ər }

interstellar extinction   The dimming of light from stars due to its absorption and scattering by dust grains in the interstellar medium. { ¦in·tər¦stel·ər ik′stiŋk·shən }

interstellar lines   Dark, narrow lines in the spectra of stars, caused by absorption of radiation by a gaseous medium in space. { ¦in·tər¦stel·ər ′līnz }

interstellar matter   The gaseous and dust material between the stars. { ¦in·tər¦stel· ər ′mad·ər }

interstellar probe   An instrumentated spacecraft propelled beyond the solar system to obtain specific information about interstellar environment. { ¦in·tər¦stel·ər ′prōb }

interstellar space   The space between the stars. { ¦in·tər¦stel·ər ′spās }

interstellar travel   Space flight between stars. { ¦in·tər¦stel·ər ′trav·əl }

intracluster medium   A hot, tenuous gas that fills the space between the members of a cluster of galaxies and emits x-rays. { ⋅in·trə′kləs·tər ⋅mēd·ē·əm }

intrinsic luminosity   The total amount of radiation emitted by a star over a specified range of wavelengths. { in′trin·sik ⋅lü·mə′näs·əd·ē }

intrinsic variable star   A star that is variable not because of an eclipse. { in′trin· sik ¦ver·ē·ə·bəl ′stär }

invariant plane   The plane that is perpendicular to the total angular momentum of the solar system and passes through its center of mass. { in′ver·ē·ənt ′plān }

Io   A satellite of Jupiter; its diameter is 2300 miles (3700 kilometers). Also known as Jupiter I. { ′ī⋅ō }

ion engine   An engine which provides thrust by expelling accelerated or high-velocity ions; ion engines using energy provided by nuclear reactors are proposed for space vehicles. { 'ī‚än ‚en·jən }

ionization front   A transition region that separates interstellar gas in which a given atomic species (usually hydrogen) is mostly ionized from interstellar gas in which it is mostly neutral. { ‚ī·ə·nə'zā·shən ‚frənt }

ion propulsion   Vehicular motion caused by reaction from the high-speed discharge of a beam of electrically charged minute particles ejected behind the vehicle. { 'ī‚än prə'pəl·shən }

Io torus   A doughnut-shaped region of dense plasma that orbits Jupiter at the radial distance of the satellite Io and results from ionization by solar ultraviolet radiation of gases emitted from Io in volcanic eruptions. { ¦ī‚ō 'tȯr·əs }

iron meteorite   A type of meteorite that consists mainly of iron and nickel and is several times heavier than any ordinary rock. { 'ī·ərn 'mēd·ē·ə‚rīt }

irregular cluster   A type of galaxy cluster that has an overall amorphous appearance, usually showing little overall symmetry or central concentration and often composed of several distinct clumps of galaxies. { i'reg·yə·lər 'kləs·tər }

irregular galaxy   A galaxy which shows no definite order or shape, except that of a general flattened appearance. { i'reg·yə·lər 'gal·ik·sē }

irregular variable star   A star with no fixed period. { i'reg·yə·lər ¦ver·ē·ə·bəl 'stär }

isotropic universe   A universe postulated to have the same properties when viewed from all directions. { ¦ī·sə¦trä·pik 'yü·nə‚vərs }

J

Jacobi ellipsoid A triaxial ellipsoid that can be formed by the surface of a homogeneous, self-gravitating body rotating uniformly with sufficient high angular velocity. { jä′kō·bē i′lip,sȯid }

jansky A unit of measurement of flux density, in units of watt·meter^{-2}·hertz^{-1}; 1 jansky is 10^{-26} W·m^{-2}·Hz^{-1}. Abbreviated Jy. { ′jans·kē }

Janus A satellite of Saturn which orbits at a mean distance of 151,000 kilometers (94,000 miles) and has an irregular shape with an average diameter of 190 kilometers (120 miles). { ′jā·nəs }

JATO engine Derived from jet-assisted-takeoff engine. **1.** An auxiliary jet-producing unit or units, usually rockets, for additional thrust. **2.** A JATO bottle or unit; the complete auxiliary power system used for assisted takeoff. { ′jā·dō ,en·jən }

Jeans flux For a particular constituent of a planetary atmosphere, the number of atoms or molecules that escape from the atmosphere, per unit area per unit time, by virtue of their thermal motions. { ′jēnz ,fləks }

Jeans length A critical length such that oscillations in homogeneous, infinite media with wavelengths greater than this length are gravitationally unstable. { ′jēnz ,leŋkth }

jet A narrow, elongated feature in the radio or optical map of an active galaxy, quasar, or object in the Milky Way Galaxy, believed to represent an energetic outflow of gas from a compact astronomical object. { jet }

jet aircraft An aircraft with a jet engine or engines. { ′jet ′er,kraft }

jet engine An aircraft engine that derives all or most of its thrust by reaction to its ejection of combustion products (or heated air) in a jet and that obtains oxygen from the atmosphere for the combustion of its fuel. { ¦jet ¦en·jən }

jet flap A sheet of fluid discharged at high speed close to the trailing edge of a wing so as to induce lift over the whole wing. { ′jet ′flap }

jet propulsion The propulsion of a rocket or other craft by means of a jet engine. { ¦jet prə¦pəl·shən }

jet stream The stream of gas or fluid expelled by any reaction device, in particular the stream of combustion products expelled from a jet engine, rocket engine, or rocket motor. { ′jet ,strēm }

Jovian planet Any of the four major planets (Jupiter, Saturn, Uranus, and Neptune)

Jovian Van Allen belts

that are at a greater distance from the sun than the terrestrial planets (Mercury, Venus, Earth, and Mars). { 'jō·vē·ən ¦plan·ət }

Jovian Van Allen belts The extended belts of high-energy charged particles that are trapped in Jupiter's magnetic field and cause the microwave nonthermal emission of radio waves observed in the band from about 3 to 70 centimeters. { 'jō·vē·ən ‚van 'al·ən ‚belts }

joystick A lever used to control the motion of an aircraft; fore-and-aft motion operates the elevators while lateral motion operates the ailerons. { 'jȯi‚stik }

Julian calendar A calendar (replaced by the Gregorian calendar) in which the year was 365.25 days, with the fraction allowing for an extra day every fourth year (leap year); there were 12 months, each 30 or 31 days except for February which had 28 days or in leap year 29. { 'jül·yən 'kal·ən·dər }

Julian date The sum of the Julian day number and the fraction of a day elapsed since the previous noon. { 'jül·yən ¦dāt }

Julian day The number of each day, as reckoned consecutively since the beginning of the present Julian period on January 1, 4713 B.C.; it is used primarily by astronomers to avoid confusion due to the use of different calendars at different times and places; the Julian day begins at noon, 12 hours later than the corresponding civil day. { 'jül·yən ¦dā }

Julian ephemeris century The unit of ephemeris time (ET) in Simon Newcomb's formulas which relate the orbital position of the earth to ephemeris time; the Julian ephemeris century is subdivided into 36,525 days, and 1 ephemeris day = 86,400 ephemeris seconds. { 'jül·yən ə'fem·ə·rəs 'sen·chə·rē }

Juliet A satellite of Uranus orbiting at a mean distance of 39,990 miles (64,360 kilometers) with a period of 11 hours 52 minutes, and with a diameter of about 52 miles (84 kilometers). { 'jül·ē·ət }

June solstice Summer solstice in the Northern Hemisphere. { 'jün 'säl·stəs }

Juno An asteroid with a diameter of about 140 miles (235 kilometers), mean distance from the sun of 2.668 astronomical units, and S-type surface composition; it is grouped with Ceres, Pallas, and Vesta as the Big Four. { 'jü·nō }

Jupiter The largest planet in the solar system, and the fifth in order of distance from the sun; semimajor axis = 485×10^6 miles (780×10^6 kilometers); sidereal revolution period = 11.86 years; mean orbital velocity = 8.2 miles per second (13.2 kilometers per second); inclination of orbital plane to ecliptic = 1.03; equatorial diameter = 88,700 miles (142,700 kilometers); polar diameter = 82,800 miles (133,300 kilometers); mass = about 318.4 (earth = 1). { 'jü·pəd·ər }

Jupiter I See Io. { 'jü·pəd·ər 'wən }

Jupiter II See Europa. { 'jü·pəd·ər 'tü }

Jupiter III See Ganymede. { 'jü·pəd·ər 'thrē }

Jupiter IV See Callisto. { 'jü·pəd·ər 'fȯr }

Jupiter V See Amalthea. { 'jü·pəd·ər 'fīv }

Jupiter VI See Himalia. { 'jü·pəd·ər 'siks }

Jupiter VII See Elara. { 'jü·pəd·ər 'sev·ən }

Jupiter VIII   *See* Pasiphae. { 'jü·pəd·ər 'āt }

Jupiter IX   *See* Sinope. { 'jü·pəd·ər 'nīn }

Jupiter X   *See* Lysithea. { 'jü·pəd·ər 'ten }

Jupiter XI   *See* Carme. { 'jü·pəd·ər ə'lev·ən }

Jupiter XII   *See* Ananke. { 'jü·pəd·ər 'twelv }

Jupiter XIII   *See* Leda. { 'jü·pəd·ər 'thər'tēn }

Jupiter XIV   *See* Thebe. { 'jü·pəd·ər 'fȯr,tēn }

Jupiter XV   *See* Adrastea. { 'jü·pəd·ər 'fif,tēn }

Jupiter XVI   *See* Metis. { 'jü·pəd·ər 'siks,tēn }

K

Kapetyn selected areas Certain areas in the Milky Way Galaxy that the astronomer J.C. Kapetyn suggested be studied intensively in order to determine the structure of the galaxy. Also known as selected areas. { 'kap·əd·ən si¦lek·təd 'er·ē·əz }

Kapetyn's star A star 13.0 light-years from the solar system, absolute magnitude 11.2, spectrum type M0; has a large proper motion. { 'kap·əd·ənz ¡stär }

K corona The inner portion of the sun's corona, having a continuous spectrum caused by electron scattering. { 'kä kə¡rō·nə }

Keel *See* Carina. { kēl }

Kelvin-Helmholtz contraction A contraction of a star once it is formed and before it is hot enough to ignite its hydrogen; the contraction converts gravitational potential energy into heat, some of which is radiated, with the remainder used to raise the internal temperature of the star. { 'kel·vən 'helm¡hōlts kən¡trak·shən }

Kelvin time scale The time that would be required for a star to contract gravitationally from infinity to its present radius solely through radiation of thermal energy. Also known as thermal time scale. { 'kel·vən 'tīm ¡skāl }

Keplerian ellipse *See* Keplerian orbit. { ke'plir·ē·ən i'lips }

Keplerian motion Orbital movement of a body about another that is not disturbed by the presence of a third celestial body. { ke'plir·ē·ən 'mō·shən }

Keplerian orbit An elliptical orbit of a celestial body about another, the latter at a focus of the ellipse. Also known as Keplerian ellipse. { ke'plir·ē·ən 'òr·bət }

Kepler's equations The mathematical relationship between two different systems of angular measurements of the position of a body in an ellipse. { 'kep·lərz i'kwā·zhənz }

Kepler's laws Three laws, determined by Johannes Kepler, that describe the motions of planets in their orbits: the orbits of the planets are ellipses with the sun at a common focus; the line joining a planet and the sun sweeps over equal areas during equal intervals of time; the squares of the periods of revolution of any two planets are proportional to the cubes of their mean distances from the sun. { 'kep·lərz 'lòz }

Kepler's supernova A supernova that appeared in the constellation Ophiuchus in October 1604 and was visible until March 1606. { 'kep·lərz ¦sü·pər'nō·və }

kiloparsec A distance of 1000 parsecs (3260 light-years). { ¦kil·ə'pär¡sek }

Kirkwood gaps

Kirkwood gaps Regions in the main zone of asteroids where almost no asteroids are found. { 'kərkˌwùd ˌgaps }

Kleinmann-Low Nebula A cool, extended source of infrared radiation in the Orion Nebula, probably a collapsing cloud of gas containing embedded protostars. Abbreviated KL Nebula. { 'klīnˌmän 'lō 'neb·yə·lə }

Klein's hypothesis A theory of the overall structure of the universe that regards the visible universe as part of a large but finite astronomical system called a metagalaxy, which may itself belong to a much larger bounded system. { 'klīnz hī·ˌpäth·ə·səs }

KL Nebula *See* Kleinmann-Low Nebula. { 'kā 'el 'neb·yə·lə }

Kochab The brighter of the two stars called the Guardian of the Pole in the constellation Ursa Minor. { 'kä·ˌkäb }

Kohoutek's comet A comet that was discovered on March 7, 1973, at a distance of 4 astronomical units from the sun, and reached a perihelion of less than 0.1 astronomical unit at the end of 1973. { kə'hō·teks ˌkäm·ət }

Kollsman window A small window on the dial face of an aircraft pressure altimeter in which the altimeter setting in inches of mercury is indicated. { 'kōls·mən ˌwin·dō }

K ratio The ratio of propellant surface to nozzle throat area. { 'ka ˌrā·shō }

K star A star of spectral type K, a cool orange to red star with a surface temperature of about 3600-5000 K (6000-8500°F), and a spectrum resembling that of sunspots in which hydrogen lines have been greatly weakened. { 'kā ˌstär }

kytoon A captive balloon used to maintain meteorological equipment aloft at approximately a constant height; it is streamlined, and combines the aerodynamic properties of a balloon and a kite. { 'kīˌtün }

L

Lacaille's constellations The 14 southern constellations identified by N. L. de Lacaille in 1763: Antlia, Callum, Circinus, Crux, Fornax, Horologium, Mensa, Microscopium, Norma, Octans, Pictor, Reticulum, Sculptor, and Telescopium. { lə'kāz ˌkän·stə'lā·shənz }

Lacerta A small northern constellation lying between Cygnus and Andromeda, and adjoining the northern boundary of Pegasus. Also known as Lizard. { lə'sərd·ə }

Lagoon Nebula A patchy, luminous gaseous nebula that appears to be surrounded by a much larger region of cold, neutral hydrogen. { lə'gün 'neb·yə·lə }

Lagrangian points Five points in the orbital plane of two massive objects orbiting about a common center of gravity at which a third object of negligible mass can remain in equilibrium; three points of instable equilibrium are located on the line passing through the centers of mass of the two bodies, and two points of stable equilibrium are located in the orbit of the less massive body, 60° ahead of or behind it. { lə'grän·jē·ən ˌpoins }

laminar flow control The removal of a small amount of boundary-layer air from the surface of an aircraft wing with the result that the airflow is laminar rather than turbulent; frictional drag is greatly reduced. { 'lam·ə·nər 'flō kən'trōl }

laminar wing A low-drag wing in which the distribution of thickness along the chord is so selected as to maintain laminar flow over as much of the wing surface as possible. { 'lam·ə·nər 'wiŋ }

land Of an aircraft, to alight on land or a ship deck. { land }

lander A spacecraft that is designed to land on a celestial body. { 'lan·dər }

landing area An area intended primarily for landing and takeoff of aircraft. { 'land·iŋ ˌer·ē·ə }

landing circle The approximately circular path flown by an airplane to get into the landing pattern; used particularly with naval aircraft landing on an aircraft carrier. { 'land·iŋ ˌsər·kəl }

landing flap A movable airfoil-shaped structure located aft of the rear beam or spar of the wing; extends about two-thirds of the span of the wing and functions to substantially increase the lift, permitting lower takeoff and landing speeds. { 'land·iŋ ˌflap }

landing gear Those components of an aircraft or spacecraft that support and provide mobility for the craft on land, water, or other surface. { 'land·iŋ ˌgir }

landing light One of the floodlights mounted on the leading edge of the wing and below the nose of the fuselage to enable an airplane to land at night. { 'land· iŋ ˌlīt }

landing load The load on an aircraft's wings produced during landing; depends on descent velocity and landing attitude. { 'land· iŋ ˌlōd }

landing strip A portion of the landing area prepared for the landing and takeoff of aircraft in a particular direction; it may include one or more runways. Also known as air strip. { 'land· iŋ ˌstrip }

land mobile satellite A geosynchronous satellite employed in the land mobile satellite service. { 'land ˌmō· bəl 'sad· əlˌīt }

Lane-Emden equation See Emden equation. { 'lān 'em· dən iˌkwā· zhən }

Lane-Emden function See Emden function. { 'lān 'em· dən ˌfəŋk· shən }

Lane's law For the contraction of a star that is assumed to be a sphere of perfect gas, the law that the temperature of the perfect-gas sphere is inversely proportional to its radius. { 'lānz ˌló }

Large Magellanic Cloud An irregular cloud of stars in the constellation Doradus; it is 150,000 light-years away and nearly 30,000 light-years in diameter. Abbreviated LMC. Also known as Nubecula Major. { 'lärj ˌmaj· əˌlan· ik 'klaüd }

Larissa A satellite of Neptune orbiting at a mean distance of 45,700 miles (73,600 kilometers) with a period of 13.3 hours, and with a diameter of about 120 miles (190 kilometers). { lə'ris· ə }

last quarter The phase of the moon at western quadrature, half of the illuminated hemisphere being visible from the earth; has the characteristic half-moon shape. { 'last 'kwȯrd· ər }

lateral acceleration The component of the linear acceleration of an aircraft or missile along its lateral, or Y, axis. { 'lad· ə· rəl akˌsel· ə'rā· shən }

lateral controller A primary flight control mechanism, generally a part of the longitudinal controller, which controls the ailerons; often resembles an automobile steering wheel but may be a control column. { 'lad· ə· rəl kən'trōl· ər }

late-type star A star with relatively low surface temperature, in spectral class K or M. { 'lāt ˌtīp ˌstär }

launch 1. To send off a rocket vehicle under its own rocket power, as in the case of guided aircraft rockets, artillery rockets, and space vehicles. 2. To send off a missile or aircraft by means of a catapult or by means of inertial force, as in the release of a bomb from a flying aircraft. 3. To give a space probe an added boost for flight into space just before separation from its launch vehicle. { lȯnch }

launch complex The composite of facilities and support equipment needed to assemble, check out, and launch a rocket vehicle. { 'lȯnch ˌkämˌpleks }

launching angle The angle between the horizontal plane and the longitudinal axis of a rocket or missile at the time of launching. { 'lȯn· chiŋ ˌaŋ· gəl }

launching ramp A ramp used for launching an aircraft or missile into the air. { 'lȯn· chiŋ ˌramp }

launching site 1. A site from which launching is done. 2. The platform, ramp, rack, or other installation at such a site. { 'lȯn·chiŋ ˌsīt }

launch pad The load-bearing base or platform from which a rocket vehicle is launched. Also known as launching pad; pad. { 'lȯnch ˌpad }

launch vehicle A rocket or other vehicle used to launch a probe, satellite, or the like. Also known as booster. { 'lȯnch ˌve·ə·kəl }

launch window The time period during which a spacecraft or missile must be launched in order to achieve a desired encounter, rendezvous, or impact. { 'lȯnch ˌwin·dō }

Laval nozzle See de Laval nozzle. { lə'väl ˌnäz·əl }

law of equal areas The second of Kepler's laws. { 'lȯ əv ¦ē·kwəl 'er·ē·əz }

leading edge The front edge of an airfoil or wing. { 'lēd·iŋ 'ej }

leading edge slat A small airfoil attached to the leading edge of a wing of an aircraft that automatically improves airflow at large angles of attack. { 'lēd·iŋ ¦ej ˌslat }

leap year A year with 366, and not 365, days. { 'lēp ˌyir }

Leda A small satellite of Jupiter with a diameter probably less than 5 miles (8 kilometers), orbiting at a mean distance of 6.88 × 10⁶ miles (1.11 × 10⁷ kilometers). Also known as Jupiter XIII. { 'lēd·ə }

LEM See lunar excursion module. { lem }

lenticular galaxy A galaxy of type S0, consisting of a nucleus surrounded by a disklike structure without arms, and containing little gas and few if any young stars. { len'tik·yə·lər 'gal·ik·sē }

Leo A northern constellation, right ascension 11 hours, declination 15° north. Also known as Lion. { 'lē·ō }

Leo Minor A northern constellation, right ascension 10 hours, declination 35° north. Also known as Lesser Lion. { 'lē·ō 'mīn·ər }

Leonids A meteor shower, the radiant of which lies in the constellation Leo; it is visible between November 10 and 15. { 'lē·ə·nədz }

Leo I system A dwarf elliptical galaxy about 900,000 light-years distant, having a diameter of about 5000 light-years, and a luminosity about 10⁶ that of the sun. { 'lē·ō 'wən ˌsis·təm }

Leo II system A dwarf elliptical galaxy about 750 light-years distant, having a diameter of about 5000 light-years and a luminosity about 800,000 times that of the sun. { 'lē·ō 'tü ˌsis·təm }

lepton era The period in the early universe, following the hadron era, during which electrons, positrons, neutrinos, and photons were present in nearly equal numbers; roughly between 10⁻⁴ and 20 seconds after the big bang. { 'lep·tän·ir·ə }

Lepus A southern constellation, right ascension 5.5 hours, declination 20°S. Also known as Hare. { 'lē·pəs }

Lesser Dog See Canis Minor. { 'les·ər ¦dȯg }

letdown   Gradual and orderly reduction in altitude, particularly in preparation for landing. { 'let₁daún }

level error   **1.** The difference between the apparent altitude of a celestial object above the apparent horizon and its true altitude above the celestial horizon. **2.** The angle between the east-west mechanical axis of a transit telescope and the horizontal plane. { 'lev·əl ₁er·ər }

level off   To bring an aircraft to level flight after an ascent or descent. { 'lev·əl 'óf }

level-off position   That position over which a craft ends an ascent or descent and begins relatively horizontal motion. { 'lev·əl ¦óf pə₁zish·ən }

Lexell's Comet   A small comet that approached to within 2,000,000 miles (3,200,000 kilometers) of earth in 1770; it has not been seen since. { 'lek·selz ₁käm·ət }

Libra   A southern constellation, right ascension 15 hours, declination 15° south. Also known as Balance. { 'lē·brə }

libration in latitude   See lunar libration. { lī'brā·shən in 'lad·ə₁tüd }

lift coefficient   The quantity $C_L = 2L/\rho V^2 S$, where L is the lift of a whole airplane wing, ρ is the mass density of the air, V is the free-stream velocity, and S is the wing area; this is also applicable to other airfoils. { 'lift ₁kō·i₁fish·ənt }

lift-drag ratio   The lift of an aerodynamic form, such as an airplane wing, divided by the drag. { 'lift 'drag ₁rā·shō }

lift fan   A special turbofan engine used primarily for lift in VTOL/STOL aircraft and often mounted in a wing with vertical thrust axis. { 'lift ₁fan }

lifting body   A maneuverable, rocket-propelled, wingless craft that can travel both in the earth's atmosphere, where its lift results from its shape, and in outer space, and that can land on the ground. { 'lift·iŋ ₁bäd·ē }

lifting reentry   A reentry into the atmosphere by a space vehicle where aerodynamic lift is used, allowing a more gradual descent, greater accuracy in landing at a predetermined spot; it can accommodate greater errors in the guidance system and greater temperature control. { 'lift·iŋ rē'en·trē }

lifting reentry vehicle   A space vehicle designed to utilize aerodynamic lift upon entering the atmosphere. { 'lift·iŋ rē'en·trē ₁vē·ə·kəl }

lift-off   The action of a rocket vehicle as it leaves its launch pad in a vertical ascent. { 'lif₁tóf }

light bomber   Any bomber with a gross weight of less than 100,000 pounds (45,000 kilograms), including bombs; for example, the A-20 and A-26 bombers in World War II. { 'līt 'bäm·ər }

light curve   A graph showing the variations in brightness of a celestial object; the stellar magnitude is usually shown on the vertical axis, and time is the horizontal coordinate. { 'līt ₁kərv }

light cylinder   See velocity-of-light cylinder. { 'līt ₁sil·ən·dər }

light-day   The distance traveled by light in 1 day in a vacuum. { 'līt₁dā }

lighter-than-air craft An aircraft, such as a dirigible, that weighs less than the air it displaces. { 'līd·ər thən !er ‚kraft }

light-hour The distance traveled by light in 1 hour in a vacuum. { 'līt‚aú·ər }

light radius See velocity-of-light radius. { 'līt ‚rād·ē·əs }

light ratio A number (2.512) that expresses the ratio of a star's light to that of another star that is one magnitude fainter or brighter. { 'līt ‚rā·shō }

light time The time required for light to travel from a distant object to the earth. { 'līt ‚tīm }

light-year A unit of measurement of astronomical distance; it is the distance light travels in one sidereal year and is equivalent to 9.461 × 10^{12} kilometers or 5.879 × 10^{12} miles. { 'līt ‚yir }

limb The circular outer edge of a celestial body; the half with the greater altitude is called the upper limb, and the half with the lesser altitude, the lower limb. { limb }

limb brightening An observed increase in the intensity of radio, extreme ultraviolet, or x-radiation from the sun or another star from its center to its limb. { 'lim ‚brīt·ən·iŋ }

limb darkening An observed darkening near the surface of the sun's limb as compared to its brighter center. { 'lim ‚där·kə·niŋ }

lineament A prominent linear feature on the lunar surface. { 'lin·ē·ə·mənt }

line displacement Widening or shifting of spectral lines of celestial objects arising from several causes, such as gas under high pressure. { 'līn di‚splās·mənt }

line of apsides 1. The line connecting the two points of an orbit that are nearest and farthest from the center of attraction, as the perigee and apogee of the moon or the perihelion and aphelion of a planet. 2. The length of this line. { 'līn əv 'ap·sə‚dēz }

line profile A curve that indicates the internal variation in intensity of a spectral line of a celestial body. { 'līn ‚prō‚fīl }

Lion See Leo. { 'lī·ən }

lithium star A peculiar giant star of spectral type G or M whose spectrum displays a high abundance of lithium. { 'lith·ē·əm ‚stär }

Little Bear See Ursa Minor. { 'lid·əl 'ber }

Little Dipper See Ursa Minor. { 'lid·əl 'dip·ər }

Little Fox See Vulpecula. { 'lid·əl 'fäks }

Little Horse See Equuleus. { 'lid·əl 'hòrs }

Little Ruler See Regulus. { 'lid·əl 'rül·ər }

Lizard See Lacerta. { 'liz·ərd }

LM See lunar excursion module.

LMC

LMC *See* Large Magellanic Cloud.

LMXRB *See* low-mass x-ray binary.

local apparent noon Twelve o'clock local apparent time, or the instant the apparent sun is over the upper branch of the local meridian. { 'lō·kəl ə¦par·ənt ¦nün }

local apparent time The arc of the celestial equator, or the angle at the celestial pole, between the lower branch of the local celestial meridian and the hour circle of the apparent or true sun, measured westward from the lower branch of the local celestial meridian through 24 hours. { 'lō·kəl ə¦par·ənt ¦tīm }

local arm *See* Orion arm. { 'lō·kəl 'ärm }

local civil time United States terminology during 1925-1952 for local mean time. { 'lō·kəl ¦siv·əl ¦tīm }

local cluster of stars *See* local star system. { 'lō·kəl ¦kləs·tər əv ¦stärz }

Local Group A group of at least 20 known galaxies in the vicinity of the sun; the Andromeda Spiral is the largest of the group, and the Milky Way Galaxy is the second largest. { 'lō·kəl 'grüp }

local hour angle Angular distance west of the local celestial meridian. { 'lō·kəl 'aür ¸aŋ·gəl }

local lunar time The arc of the celestial equator, or the angle at the celestial pole, between the lower branch of the local celestial meridian and the hour circle of the moon, measured westward from the lower branch of the local celestial meridian through 24 hours; local hour angle of the moon, expressed in time units, plus 12 hours; local lunar time at the Greenwich meridian is called Greenwich lunar time. { 'lō·kəl ¦lü·nər ¦tīm }

local Mach number The Mach number of an isolated section of an airplane or its airframe. { 'lō·kəl 'mäk ¸nəm·bər }

local mean noon Twelve o'clock local mean time, or the instant the mean sun is over the upper branch of the local meridian; local mean noon at the Greenwich meridian is called Greenwich mean noon. { 'lō·kəl ¦mēn ¦nün }

local mean time The arc of the celestial equator, or the angle at the celestial pole, between the lower branch of the local celestial meridian and the hour circle of the mean sun, measured westward from the lower branch of the local celestial meridian through 24 hours. { 'lō·kəl ¦mēn ¦tīm }

local meridian The meridian through any particular position which serves as the reference for local time. { 'lō·kəl mə'rid·ē·ən }

local noon Noon at the local meridian. { 'lō·kəl 'nün }

local sidereal noon Zero hour local sidereal time, or the instant the vernal equinox is over the upper branch of the local meridian; local sidereal noon at the Greenwich meridian is called Greenwich sidereal noon. { 'lō·kəl sə¦dir·ē·əl ¦nün }

local sidereal time The arc of the celestial equator, or the angle at the celestial pole which is between the upper branch of the local celestial meridian and the hour circle of the vernal equinox. { 'lō·kəl sə¦dir·ē·əl ¦tīm }

local standard of rest   A frame of reference in which the velocities of neighboring stars average out to zero. { 'lō·kəl 'stan·dərd əv 'rest }

local star system   The group of stars of which the sun is a member. Also known as local cluster of stars; local star cloud. { 'lō·kəl 'stär ˌsis·təm }

Local Supercluster   A great flattened system of groups and clusters of galaxies, about 1.5 to 2 × 10^8 light-years (1.4 to 1.9 × 10^{24} meters) across, which includes the local group of galaxies and the Virgo Cluster. Also known as Virgo Supercluster. { 'lō·kəl 'sü·pərˌkləs·tər }

local time   1. Time based upon the local meridian as reference, as contrasted with that based upon a zone meridian, or the meridian of Greenwich. 2. Any time kept locally. { 'lō·kəl 'tīm }

longeron   A principal longitudinal member of the structural framework of a fuselage, nacelle, or empennage boom. { 'lan·jəˌrän }

longitudinal controller   A primary flight control mechanism which controls pitch attitude; located in the cockpit, this may be a control column or a side stick. { ˌlän·jə'tüd·ən·əl kən'trōl·ər }

long-period variable   A variable star with a period from about 100 to more than 600 days. { 'lȯŋ ˌpir·ē·əd 'ver·ē·ə·bəl }

look angle   The elevation and azimuth at which a particular satellite is predicted to be found at a specified time. { 'lùk ˌaŋ·gəl }

look-back time   The time in the past at which the light now being received from a distant object was emitted. { 'lùk ˌbak ˌtīm }

loop   A flight maneuver in which an airplane flies a circular path in an approximately vertical plane, with the lateral axis of the airplane remaining horizontal, that is, an inside loop. { lüp }

Loop Nebula   A large, bright gaseous nebula in the Large Magellanic Cloud; its diameter is about 260 light-years. Also known as 30 Doradus; Tarantula. { 'lüp 'neb·yə·lə }

loop of retrogression   A loop in the apparent path of a planet, relative to the stars, that is described when the planet undergoes retrograde motion. { 'lüp əv ˌre·trə'gresh·ən }

lower branch   That half of a meridian or celestial meridian from pole to pole which passes through the antipode or nadir of a place. { 'lō·ər ˈbranch }

lower limb   That half of the outer edge of a celestial body having the least altitude. { 'lō·ər 'lim }

lower transit   Transit across the lower branch of the celestial meridian. Also known as lower culmination. { 'lō·ər 'trans·ət }

low-mass x-ray binary   A binary system consisting of a low-mass (typically less than 1 solar mass), late-type star and a neutron star or black hole that accretes material through Roche-lobe overflow, resulting in the emission of relatively soft x-rays. Abbreviated LMXRB. { ˈlō ˈmas ˈeksˌrā 'bīˌner·ē }

low-velocity star   One of the Population I stars in the spiral arms of a galaxy which participate in the galactic rotation, thus exhibiting low velocity with respect to the sun and high velocity with respect to the galactic center. { 'lō və!läs·əd·ē 'stär }

luminosity classes   A classification of stars in an orderly sequence according to their absolute brightness. { ,lü·mə'näs·əd·ē ,klas·əz }

luminosity function   The functional relationship between stellar magnitude and the number and distribution of stars of each magnitude interval. Also known as relative luminosity factor. { ,lü·mə'näs·əd·ē ,fəŋk·shən }

luminous blue variable   Any of a small group of high-luminosity, unstable, hot supergiant stars that have irregular eruptions or ejections with greatly enhanced mass outflow (10⁻⁵ to 10⁻⁴ solar mass per year). { 'lüm·ən·əs !blü 'ver·ē·ə·bəl }

luminous mass   The mass of a celestial object inferred from its luminosity or the luminosities of its components. { 'lü·mə·nəs 'mas }

luminous nebula   A nebula made bright by radiation from stars in the vicinity. { 'lü·mə·nəs 'neb·yə·lə }

Luna   A name for the moon. { 'lü·nə }

lunabase   The basic rocks that make up the dark portions of the lunar surface. Also known as marebase; marial rocks. { 'lü·nə,bās }

Luna program   A series of Soviet space probes launched for flight missions to the moon. { 'lü·nə ,prō·grəm }

lunar appulse   An eclipse of the moon in which the penumbral shadow of the earth falls on the moon. Also known as penumbral eclipse. { 'lü·nər 'a,pəls }

lunar atmosphere   The volatile elements postulated to have been present on the moon's surface at one time. { 'lü·nər 'at·mə,sfir }

lunar crater   A crater on the moon's surface. { 'lü·nər 'krād·ər }

lunar crust   The outer layer of the moon. { 'lü·nər 'krəst }

lunar day   The time interval between two successive crossings of the meridian by the moon. { 'lü·nər 'dā }

lunar dust   Small particles adhering to the moon's surface. { 'lü·nər 'dəst }

lunar eclipse   Obscuration of the full moon when it passes through the shadow of the earth. { 'lü·nər i'klips }

lunar ephemeris   A computed list of positions the moon will occupy in the sky on certain dates. { 'lü·nər i'fem·ə·rəs }

lunar excursion module   A manned spacecraft designed to be carried on top of the Apollo service module and having its own power plant for making a manned landing on the moon and a return from the moon to the orbiting Apollo spacecraft. Abbreviated LEM. Also known as lunar module (LM). { 'lü·nər ik!skər·zhən !maj·ül }

lunar flight   Flight by a spacecraft to the moon. { 'lü·nər 'flīt }

lunar geology   See selenology. { 'lü·nər jē'äl·ə·jē }

lunar inequality   Variation in the moon's motion in its orbit, due to attraction by other bodies of the solar system. { 'lü·nər ,in·i'kwäl·əd·ē }

lunar interval   The difference in time between the transit of the moon over the Greenwich meridian and a local meridian; the lunar interval equals the difference between the Greenwich and local intervals of a tide or current phase. { 'lü·nər 'in·tər·vəl }

lunarite   The rocks that make up the bright portions of the lunar surface. { 'lü·nəˌrīt }

lunar libration   **1.** The effect wherein the face of the moon appears to swing east and west about 8° from its central position each month. Also known as apparent libration in longitude. **2.** The state wherein the inclination of the moon's polar axis allows an observer on earth to see about 59% of the moon's surface. Also known as libration in latitude. **3.** The small oscillation with which the moon rocks back and forth about its mean rotation rate. Also known as physical libration of the moon. { 'lü·nər lī'brā·shən }

lunar magnetic field   The magnetic field of the moon. { 'lü·nər magˌned·ik 'fēld }

lunar mass   The mass of the moon. { 'lü·nər 'mas }

lunar meteoroid   A meteoric particle before it strikes the moon. { 'lü·nər 'mēd·ē·əˌroid }

lunar module   *See* lunar excursion module. { 'lü·nər 'mäj·ül }

lunar month   The period of revolution of the moon about the earth, especially a synodical month. { 'lü·nər 'mənth }

lunar mountain   A mountain on the moon. { 'lü·nər 'maunt·ən }

lunar node   A node of the moon's orbit. { 'lü·nər 'nōd }

lunar nodule   A rock nodule found on the moon. { 'lü·nər 'näj·ül }

lunar noon   The instant at which the sun is over the upper branch of any meridian of the moon. { 'lü·nər 'nün }

lunar nutation   A nodding motion of the earth's axis caused by the inclination of the moon's orbit to the ecliptic; it can displace the celestial pole by 9 seconds of arc from its mean position and has a period of 18.6 years. { 'lü·nər nü'tā·shən }

lunar orbit   Orbit of a spacecraft around the moon. { 'lü·nər 'or·bət }

lunar polarization   Polarization of light by the moon's surface. { 'lü·nər ˌpō·lə·rə'zā·shən }

lunar pole   A pole of the moon. { 'lü·nər 'pōl }

lunar probe   Any space probe launched for flight missions to the moon. { 'lü·nər 'prōb }

lunar rock   Rock found on the moon. { 'lü·nər 'räk }

lunar satellite   A satellite making one or more revolutions about the moon. { 'lü·nər 'sad·əlˌīt }

lunar spacecraft   A spacecraft designed for flight to the moon. { 'lü·nər 'spāsˌkraft }

lunar time   **1.** Time based upon the rotation of the earth relative to the moon; it may be designated as local or Greenwich, as the local or Greenwich meridian is used as the reference. **2.** Time on the moon. { 'lü·nər 'tīm }

lunar topology   Topology of the moon. { 'lü·nər tə'päl·ə·jē }

lunar year   A time interval comprising 12 lunar (synodic) months. { 'lü·nər 'yir }

lunation   The time period between two successive new moons. { lü'nā·shən }

lunisolar precession   Precession of the earth's equinox caused by the gravitational attraction of the sun and moon. { ¦lü·nə'sō·lər prē'sesh·ən }

Lupus   A southern constellation lying between Centaurus and Scorpius. Also known as Wolf. { 'lü·pəs }

Lupus Loop   A very old supernova remnant, about 400-600 parsecs distant, that forms an extended source of radio waves and soft x-rays. { 'lü·pəs ˌlüp }

Lyot division   The gap between rings B and C of Saturn. Also known as French division. { 'lyō diˌvizh·ən }

Lyra   A northern constellation; right ascension 19 hours, declination 40° north; its first-magnitude star, Vega, is a navigational star and the most brilliant star in this part of the sky. { 'lī·rə }

Lyrids   An important meteor shower occurring about April 22; it is regular and predictable, but not heavy, the hourly rate usually being about 7-10. { 'lī·rədz }

Lysithea   A small satellite of Jupiter with a diameter of about 15 miles (24 kilometers), orbiting at a mean distance of about 7.30×10^6 miles (11.75×10^6 kilometers). Also known as Jupiter X. { lī'sith·ē·ə }

M

Maclaurin spheroid A spheroid formed by the surface of a homogeneous, self-gravitating mass in uniform rotation. { mə'klȯr·ən 'sfir‚ȯid }

Maffei system A cluster of external galaxies that lie very close to the galactic plane in the constellation Perseus and are heavily obscured by galactic dust. { mä'fā·ē ‚sis·təm }

Magellanic Clouds Two irregular clouds of stars that are the nearest galaxies to the galactic system; both the Large and Small Magellanic Clouds are identified as Irregular in the classification of E.P. Hubble. Also known as Nubeculae. { ˈmaj·əˈlan·ik 'klaůdz }

Magellanic Stream A long, thin inhomogeneous filament of gas which extends 120° from the region between the Magellanic Clouds to a point near the south galactic pole. { ˈmaj·əˈlan·ik 'strēm }

Magellanic System An envelope of neutral hydrogen that includes both the Magellanic Clouds. { ˈmaj·əˈlan·ik 'sis·təm }

magnetic merging See field line reconnection. { mag'ned·ik 'mər·jiŋ }

magnetic star A star with an unusually strong magnetic field. { mag'ned·ik 'stär }

magnetohydrodynamic arcjet An electromagnetic propulsion system utilizing a plasma that is heated in an electric arc and then adiabatically expanded through a nozzle and further accelerated by a crossed electric and magnetic field. { magˈnēd·ȯ‚hī·drə·dī'nām·ik 'ärk‚jet }

magnitude The relative luminance of a celestial body; the smaller (algebraically) the number indicating magnitude, the more luminous the body. Also known as stellar magnitude. { 'mag·nə‚tüd }

magnitude ratio The ratio (2.512) of relative brightness of two celestial bodies differing in magnitude by 1.0. { 'mag·nə‚tüd ˈrā·shō }

magnitude system A system for designating the relative brightness of stars when photography is used; emulsions of different color sensitivities, used with color filters, permit measurements of starlight of different wavelengths with corresponding determination of magnitude at these wavelengths. { 'mag·nə‚tüd ‚sis·təm }

main sequence The band in the spectrum luminosity diagram which has the great majority of stars; their energy derives from core burning of hydrogen into helium. { 'mān 'sē·kwəns }

main sequence star   1. Any of those stars in the smooth curve termed the main sequence in a Hertzsprung-Russell diagram. **2.** *See* dwarf star. { 'mān ¦sē·kwəns 'stär }

main stage   1. In a multistage rocket, the stage that develops the greatest amount of the thrust, with or without booster engines. **2.** In a single-stage rocket vehicle powered by one or more engines, the period when full thrust (at or above 90%) is attained. **3.** A sustainer engine, considered as a stage after booster engines have fallen away. { 'mān 'stāj }

major planet   Any of the four planets that are larger than earth: Jupiter, Saturn, Neptune, and Uranus. { 'mā·jər 'plan·ət }

Malus   *See* Pyxis. { 'mä·ləs }

manganese star   A star that has an anomalously high ratio of manganese to iron. { 'maŋ·gə‚nēs ‚stär }

Manger   *See* Praesepe. { 'mān·jər }

manned orbiting laboratory   An earth-orbiting satellite which contains instrumentation and personnel for continuous measurement and surveillance of the earth, its atmosphere, and space. Abbreviated MOL. { 'mand 'ȯr·bəd·iŋ 'lab·rə‚tȯr·ē }

manned spacecraft   A vehicle capable of sustaining a person above the terrestrial atmosphere. { 'mand 'spās‚kraft }

March equinox   *See* vernal equinox. { 'märch 'ē·kwə‚näks }

mare   1. One of the large, dark, flat areas on the lunar surface. **2.** One of the less well-defined areas on Mars. { 'mär·ā, mer }

marebase   *See* lunabase. { 'mär·ā‚bās }

marial rocks   *See* lunabase. { 'mär·ē·əl ‚räks }

Mars   The planet fourth in distance from the sun; it is visible to the naked eye as a bright red star, except for short periods when it is near its conjunction with the sun; its diameter is about 4150 miles (6700 kilometers). { märz }

Mars probe   A United States uncrewed spacecraft intended to be sent to the vicinity of the planet Mars, such as in the Mariner or Viking programs. { 'märz ‚prōb }

mass-luminosity relation   A relation between stellar magnitudes and mass of the stars; when the absolute magnitudes of stars are plotted versus the logarithms of their masses, the points fall closely along a smooth curve. { 'mas ‚lü·mə'näs·əd·ē ri‚lā·shən }

mass ratio   The ratio of the mass of the propellant charge of the rocket to the total mass of the rocket when charged with the propellant. { 'mas 'rā·shō }

matter era   The period in the evolution of the universe, beginning roughly 10^5 years after the big bang, when the universe had cooled to the point at which electrons and protons were able to form neutral hydrogen atoms, and continuing to the present time, during which matter, in the form of atoms, is dominant over radiation. { 'mad·ər ‚ir·ə }

maunder minimum   A period of time from about 1650 to 1710 when the sun did not appear to have sunspots. { 'mȯn·dər 'min·ə·məm }

Mayall's object A peculiar object that consists of a ring, a cigar-shaped galaxy, and a bridge that appears to connect them. { 'mā·ȯlz ˌäb·jikt }

mean camber line A line on a cross section of a wing of an aircraft which is equidistant from the upper and lower surfaces of the wing. { 'mēn 'kam·bər ˌlīn }

mean chord That chord of an airfoil that is equal to the sum of all the airfoil's chord lengths divided by the number of chord lengths; equivalently, that chord whose length is equal to the area of the airfoil section divided by the span. { 'mēn 'kȯrd }

mean motion The speed which a planet or its satellite would have if it were moving in a circular orbit with radius equal to its distance from the sun or a central planet with a period equal to its actual period. { 'mēn 'mō·shən }

mean noon Twelve o'clock mean time, or the instant the mean sun is over the upper branch of the meridian; it may be either local or Greenwich, depending upon the reference meridian. { 'mēn 'nün }

mean place The position of a star on the celestial sphere as it would be observed from the center of the sun, referred to the mean celestial equator and celestial equinox for the beginning of the year of observation. { 'mēn 'plās }

mean profile The waveform of a pulsar's periodic emission, averaged synchronously over several hundred pulses or more. Also known as integrated profile; pulse window. { 'mēn 'prō·fīl }

mean sidereal time Sidereal time adjusted for nutation, to eliminate slight irregularities in the rate. { 'mēn si'dir·ē·əl 'tīm }

mean solar day The duration of one rotation of the earth on its axis, with respect to the mean sun; the length of the mean solar day is 24 hours of mean solar time or $24^h\ 03^m\ 56.555^s$ of mean sidereal time. { 'mēn 'sō·lər 'dā }

mean solar second A unit equal to 1/86,400 of a mean solar day. { 'mēn 'sō·lər 'sek·ənd }

mean solar time Time that has the mean solar second as its unit, and is based on the mean sun's motion. { 'mēn 'sō·lər 'tīm }

mean sun A fictitious sun conceived to move eastward along the celestial equator at a rate that provides a uniform measure of time equal to the average apparent time; used as a reference for reckoning time, such as mean time or zone time. { 'mēn 'sən }

mean time Time based on the rotation of the earth relative to the mean sun. { 'mēn 'tīm }

megaparsec A unit equal to 1,000,000 parsecs. { ˌmeg·ə'pär·sek }

Mercury The planet nearest to the sun; it is visible to the naked eye shortly after sunset or before sunrise when it is nearest to its greatest angular distance from the sun. { 'mər·kyə·rē }

mercury-manganese star A star of spectral type B8 or B9 that has a variable spectrum displaying excesses of phosphorus, manganese, gallium, strontium, yttrium, zirconium, platinum, and mercury, and lacks a strong global magnetic field. { 'mər·kyə·rē 'maŋ·gə·nēs 'stär }

meridian   1. A great circle passing through the poles of the axis of rotation of a planet or satellite. 2. *See* celestial meridian. { mə′rid·ē·ən }

meridian altitude   The altitude of a celestial body when it is on the celestial meridian of the observer, bearing 000° or 180° true. { mə′rid·ē·ən ‚al·tə‚tüd }

meridian angle   Angular distance east or west of the local celestial meridian; the arc of the celestial equator, or the angle at the celestial pole, between the upper branch of the local celestial meridian and the hour circle of a celestial body, measured eastward or westward from the local celestial meridian through 180°, and labeled E or W to indicate the direction of measurement. { mə′rid·ē·ən ‚aŋ·gəl }

meridian angle difference   The difference between two meridian angles, particularly between the meridian angle of a celestial body and the value used as an argument for entering into a table. Also called hour angle difference. { mə′rid·ē·ən ‚aŋ· gəl ′dif·rəns }

meridian observation   Measurement of the altitude of a celestial body on the celestial meridian of the observer, or the altitude so measured. { mə′rid·ē·ən ‚äb·sər′vā· shən }

meridian passage   The passage of a celestial body across an observer's meridian. { mə′rid·ē·ən ‚pas·ij }

meridian photometer   An instrument in which mirrors are used to bring the light from two stars which are at or near the celestial meridian simultaneously, but at different altitudes, to a common focus, to compare their brightness. { mə′rid·ē·ən fə′täm· əd·ər }

Messier number   A number by which star clusters and nebulae are listed in Messier's catalog; for example, the Andromeda Galaxy is M 31. { me′syä ‚nəm·bər }

Messier's catalog   A listing of 103 star clusters and nebulae compiled in 1784. { me′syäz ′kad·əl‚äg }

metagalaxy   The total assemblage of recognized galaxies; essentially this represents the entire material universe. { ¦med·ə′gal·ik·sē }

metal   In stellar spectroscopy, any element heavier than helium. { ′med·əl }

metal-enhanced star formation   The hypothesis that stars form preferentially from regions with higher-than-average atomic number in a chemically inhomogeneous interstellar medium. { ′med·əl in¦hanst ′stär fȯr‚mā·shən }

metal-rich star   A star in which the ratio of metals (elements heavier than helium) to hydrogen is greater than that of the Hyades. { ′med·əl ¦rich ′stär }

meteor   The phenomena which accompany a body from space (a meteoroid) in its passage through the atmosphere, including the flash and streak of light and the ionized trail. { ′mēd·ē·ər }

meteor bumper   A thin shield around a space vehicle designed to dissipate the energy of impacting meteoric particles. { ′mēd·ē·ər ‚bəm·pər }

meteoric ionization   Ionization resulting from collisional interactions of a meteoroid and its vaporization products with the air. { ‚mēd·ē′ȯr·ik ‚ī·ə·nə′zā·shən }

meteoric theory   *See* impact theory. { ‚mēd·ē′ȯr·ik ′thē·ə·rē }

meteoroid   Any solid object moving in interplanetary space that is smaller than a planet or asteroid but larger than a molecule. { 'med·ē·ə,roid }

meteorological satellite   Earth-orbiting spacecraft carrying a variety of instruments for measuring visible and invisible radiations from the earth and its atmosphere. { ,med·ē·ə·rə'läj·ə·kəl 'sad·əl,īt }

meteor shower   A number of meteors with approximately parallel trajectories. { 'mēd·ē·ər ,shaú·ər }

meteor stream   A group of meteoric bodies with nearly identical orbits. { 'mēd·ē·ər ,strēm }

Metis   The innermost known satellite of Jupiter, having an orbital radius of 79,510 miles (127,960 kilometers) and a radius of 12 miles (20 kilometers). Also known as Jupiter XVI. { 'mēd·əs }

metonic cycle   A time period of 235 lunar months, or 19 years; after this period the phases of the moon occur on the same days of the same months. { me'tän·ik 'sī·kəl }

M82 galaxy   An active, variable spiral galaxy that exhibits strong emission from its center in the radio band, 10^4 to 10^6 times greater than that of normal spirals, and ejection of gases at speeds up to 620 miles (1000 kilometers) per second. { ¦em ¦ād·ē¦tü 'gal·ik·sē }

micrometeorite   A very small meteorite or meteoritic particle with a diameter generally less than a millimeter. { ¦mī·krō'mē·dē·ə,rīt }

micrometeorite penetration   Penetration of the thin outer shell (skin) of space vehicles by small particles traveling in space at high velocities. { ¦mī·krō'mē·dē·ə,rīt ,pen·ə'trā·shən }

micrometeoroid   A very small meteoroid with diameter generally less than a millimeter. { ¦mī·krō'mē·dē·ə,roid }

microwave background   *See* cosmic microwave radiation. { 'mī·krə,wāv 'bak,graúnd }

Midas   A two-object trajectory-measuring system whereby two complete cotar antenna systems and two sets of receivers at each station, with the multiplexing done after phase comparison, are utilized in tracking more than one object at a time. { 'mīd·əs }

midcourse correction   A change in the course of a spacecraft some time between the end of the launching phase and some arbitrary point when terminal guidance begins. { 'mid,kórs kə'rek·shən }

midnight sun   The sun when it is visible at midnight; occurs during the summer in high latitudes, poleward of the circle at which the latitude is approximately equal to the polar distance of the sun. { 'mid,nīt 'sən }

military aircraft   Aircraft that are designed or modified for highly specialized use by the armed services of a nation. { 'mil·i,ter·ē 'er,kraft }

military satellite   An artificial earth satellite used for military purposes; the six mission categories are communication, navigation, geodesy, nuclear test detection, surveillance, and research and technology. { 'mil·i,ter·ē 'sad·əl,īt }

Milky Way

Milky Way   The faint band of light which encircles the sky and results from the combined light of the many stars near the plane of our galaxy. { 'mil·kē 'wā }

Milky Way Galaxy   The large aggregation of stars and interstellar gas and dust of which the sun is a member. Also known as Galaxy. { 'mil·kē 'wā 'gal·ik·sē }

millisecond pulsar   See fast pulsar. { 'mil·ə‚sek·ənd 'pəl·sär }

Mimas   A satellite of Saturn orbiting at a mean distance of 115,300 miles (186,000 kilometers). { 'mē·mäs }

Mimosa   See Crucis. { mə'mō·sə }

minimum flight altitude   The lowest altitude at which aircraft may safely operate. { 'min·ə·məm 'flīt ‚al·tə‚tüd }

minitrack   A satellite tracking system consisting of a field of separate antennas and associated receiving equipment interconnected so as to form interferometers which track a transmitting beacon in the payload itself. { 'min·ē‚trak }

minor planet   1. Those planets smaller than the earth, specifically Mercury, Venus, Mars, and Pluto. 2. See asteroid. { 'mīn·ər 'plan·ət }

Mira   The first star recognized to be a periodic variable; has a period of 332 ± 9 days and its spectrum changes from M5e at maximum to M9e at minimum;it is the prototype of long-period variable stars. { 'mir·ə }

Miranda   A satellite of Uranus orbiting at a mean distance of 76,880 miles (124,000 kilometers). { mə'ran·də }

Mira variables   A group of over 1300 stars having the same type of variability as the star Mira. { 'mir·ə ‚ver·ē·ə·bəls }

missing mass   See dark matter. { ‚mis·iŋ 'mas }

mixture ratio   The ratio of the weight of oxidizer used per unit of time to the weight of fuel used per unit of time. { 'miks·chər ‚rā·shō }

MJD   See modified Julian date.

MKK system   See MK system. { ¦em¦kā'kā ‚sis·təm }

MK system   A system of classifying stars in which suffixes are added to the designations of the Harvard-Draper sequence to indicate luminosity, ranging from I for supergiants to VI for subdwarfs and white dwarfs. Also known as MKK system; spectral/luminosity classification; Yerkes system. { ¦em‚kā ‚sis·təm }

mock moon   See paraselene. { 'mäk 'mün }

mock sun   See paranthelion; parhelion. { 'mäk 'sən }

mock sun ring   See parhelic circle. { 'mäk 'sən ‚riŋ }

modified Julian date   The Julian date minus 2,400,000.5. Abbreviated MJD. { 'mäd·ə‚fīd 'jül·yən 'dāt }

module   A self-contained unit which serves as a building block for the overall structure in space technology; usually designated by its primary function, such as command module or lunar landing module. { 'mäj·ül }

modulus of distance   The quantity m-M, where M is the absolute magnitude of a given star and m is its apparent magnitude. Also known as distance modulus. { 'mäj·ə·ləs əv 'dis·təns }

MOL   See manned orbiting laboratory.

molecular cloud   A dense cloud of interstellar gas in which molecules have formed in appreciable abundance. { mə'lek·yə·lər 'klaůd }

moment coefficient   The coefficients used for moment are similar to coefficients of lift, drag, and thrust, and are likewise dimensionless; however, these must include a characteristic length, in addition to the area; the span is used for rolling or yawing moment, and the chord is used for pitching moment. { 'mō·mənt ˌkō·i'fish·ənt }

Monoceros   A constellation, right ascension 7 hours, declination 5° south; it has mostly faint stars. { mə'näs·ə·rəs }

Monoceros Loop   A filamentary loop nebula about 1000 parsecs (2×10^{16} miles or 3×10^{16} kilometers) distant, which is the remnant of a supernova that took place 50,000-100,000 years ago. { mə'näs·ə·rəs 'lüp }

Monoceros R2 molecular cloud   A massive rotating gas cloud with an abundance of various molecules that contains a compact H II region and is a region of active star formation. { mə'näs·ə·rəs ˈärˌtü mə'lek·yə·lər klaůd }

monocoque   A type of construction, as of a rocket body, in which all or most of the stresses are carried by the skin. { 'män·əˌkäk }

monofuel propulsion   Propulsion system which obtains its power from a single fuel; in rocket units, the fuel furnishes both oxygen supply and the hydrocarbon for combustion. { 'män·ōˌfyül prə'pəl·shən }

month   1. The period of the revolution of the moon around the earth (sidereal month). 2. The period of the phases of the moon (synodic month). 3. The month of the calendar (calendar month). { mənth }

moon   1. The natural satellite of the earth. 2. A natural satellite of any planet. { mün }

moonrise   The crossing of the visible horizon by the upper limb of the ascending moon. { 'münˌrīz }

moonset   The crossing of the visible horizon by the upper limb of the descending moon. { 'münˌset }

moon shot   The launching of a rocket intended to travel to the vicinity of the moon. { 'mün ˌshät }

mooring mast   A mast or pole with fittings at the top to secure any lighter-than-air craft, such as a dirigible or blimp. { 'můr·iŋ ˌmast }

morning star   A misnomer given to a planet visible to the naked eye, when it rises before the sun. { 'mȯrn·iŋ ˌstär }

morning twilight   The period of time between darkness and sunrise. { 'mȯrn·iŋ ˈtwī·līt }

127

morphological astronomy   A branch of astronomy in which the forms of celestial objects, such as galaxies, are observed, and an attempt is made to draw conclusions from these observations. { ˈmȯr·fəˈläj·ə·kəl ə'strän·ə·mē }

moving cluster   **1.** A star cluster with common motions. **2.** An open star cluster near the sun such that measurements may be made of the individual proper motions of the stars. { 'müv·iŋ 'kləs·tər }

M region   Any of the areas on the surface of the sun that are theoretically responsible for magnetic disturbances on the earth. { 'em ˌrē·jən }

M star   A spectral classification for a star whose spectrum is characterized by the presence of titanium oxide bands; M stars have surface temperatures of 3000 K for giants and 3400 K for dwarfs. { 'em ˌstär }

multiple-stage rocket   See multistage rocket. { 'məl·tə·pəl ˈstāj 'räk·ət }

multiple star   A system of three or more stars which appear to the naked eye as a single star. { 'məl·tə·pəl 'stär }

multipropellant   A rocket propellant consisting of two or more substances that are fed separately to the combustion chamber. { ˈməl·tə·prə'pel·ənt }

multiring structure   A formation on the moon's surface consisting of two or more craters within a larger crater. { 'məl·təˌriŋ ˌstrək·chər }

multistage rocket   A vehicle having two or more rocket units, each unit firing after the one in back of it has exhausted its propellant; normally, each unit, or stage, is jettisoned after completing its firing. Also known as multiple-stage rocket; step rocket. { 'məl·tēˌstāj 'räk·ət }

Musca   A southern constellation, right ascension 12 hours, declination 70°S. Also known as Fly. { 'məs·kə }

Myklestad method   A method of determining the mode shapes and frequencies of the lateral bending modes of space vehicles, taking into account secondary effects of shear and rotary inertia, in which one imagines masses to be concentrated at a finite number of points along the beam, with elastic properties remaining constant between consecutive mass points. { 'mik·əlˌstad ˌmeth·əd }

N

nacelle A separate streamlined enclosure on an airplane for sheltering or housing something, as the crew or an engine. { nə'sel }

nadir That point on the celestial sphere vertically below the observer, or 180° from the zenith. { 'nā·dər }

Naiad A satellite of Neptune orbiting at a mean distance of 30,000 miles (48,000 kilometers) with a period of 7.1 hours, and a diameter of about 34 miles (54 kilometers). { 'nī,ad }

naked T Tauri star *See* weak-line T Tauri star. { ¦nāk·əd ¦tē ¦tȯr·ē 'stär }

natural laminar flow Airflow over a portion of the wing such that local pressure decreases in the direction of flow and flow in the boundary layer is laminar rather than turbulent; frictional drag on the aircraft is greatly reduced. { ¦nach·rəl 'lam·ə·nər 'flō }

nautical twilight The interval of incomplete darkness between sunrise or sunset and the time at which the center of the sun's disk is 12° below the celestial horizon. { 'nȯd·ə·kəl 'twī,līt }

navigational satellite An artificial earth-orbiting satellite designed for use in at least four widely different navigational systems. { ,nav·ə'gā·shən·əl 'sad·əl,īt }

navigation dome *See* astrodome. { ,nav·ə'gā·shən ,dōm }

near stars Those stars in the celestial neighborhood of the sun, sometimes taken as those 22 stars within 13 light-years of the sun. { 'nir 'stärz }

nebula Interstellar clouds of gas or small particles; an example is the Horsehead Nebula in Orion. { 'neb·yə·lə }

nebular hypothesis A theory, proposed in 1796 by Laplace, supposing that the planets originated from the solar nebula surrounding the proto-sun; as the sun cooled, it contracted, rotated faster, and thus caused a ringlike bulging at the equator; this bulge eventually broke off and formed the planets; Laplace further theorized that the sun and other stars formed from clouds of nebulous matter; the theory in this form is not accepted. { 'neb·yə·lər hī'päth·ə·səs }

nebular lines The spectral lines formed in the glow of bright nebulae; they arise from forbidden atomic transition which can take place because of the very low pressure in the nebula itself. { 'neb·yə·lər 'līnz }

nebular redshift A systematic shift observed in the spectra of all distant galaxies; the

nebular transitions

wavelength shift toward the red increases with the distance of the galaxies from the earth. { 'neb·yə·lər 'red₁shift }

nebular transitions   Those electronic transitions for doubly ionized argon and chlorine that yield the nebular lines seen in the spectra of gaseous nebulae. { 'neb·yə·lər tran'zish·ənz }

nebular variable   *See* T Tauri star. { 'neb·yə·lər 'ver·ē·ə·bəl }

Nemesis   A hypothetical, undetected, brown-dwarf companion of the sun, in a highly elongated orbit that would cause cometary material in Oort's Cloud to fall toward the inner region of the solar system approximately once every 2.8×10^7 years. { 'nem·ə·səs }

Neptune   The outermost of the four giant planets, and the next to last planet, from the sun; it is 30 astronomical units from the sun, and the sidereal revolution period is 164.8 years. { 'nep·tün }

Nereid   The outermost known satellite of Neptune, orbiting at a mean distance of 3,425,900 miles (5,513,400 kilometers) with a period of 360 days, 3.1 hours, and with a diameter of about 210 miles (340 kilometers). { 'nir·ē·əd }

Nestor   One of a group of asteroids whose period of revolution is approximately equal to that of Jupiter, or about 12 years (it is one of the Trojan planets). { 'nes·tər }

Net   *See* Reticulum. { net }

net thrust   The gross thrust of a jet engine minus the drag due to the momentum of the incoming air. { 'net 'thrəst }

neutral region   A region on the sun's surface where the longitudinal magnetic field nearly vanishes; generally found between regions of opposite polarity. { 'nü·trəl ₁rē·jən }

neutrino telescope   Any device for detecting and determining the directions of extraterrestrial neutrinos, such as the deep underwater muon and neutrino detector. { nü'trē·nō 'tel·ə₁skōp }

neutron drip   The rapid increase in the abundance of free neutrons that occurs when matter becomes sufficiently dense that electrons are absorbed into nuclei. { 'nü₁trän ₁drip }

neutron matter   Degenerate matter such as occurs in neutron stars in which there are 8 to 12 times as many neutrons as protons. { 'nü₁trän ₁mad·ər }

neutron star   A star that is supposed to occur in the final stage of stellar evolution; it consists of a superdense mass mainly of neutrons, and has a strong gravitational attraction from which only neutrinos and high-energy photons could escape so that the star is invisible. { 'nü₁trän ₁stär }

new inflationary cosmology   A modification of the original inflationary universe cosmology in which the breaking of grand unified symmetry does not involve a tunneling process and is, instead, analogous to a process in which a ball rolls down from a hill with an extremely flat top. { 'nü in'flā·shə₁ner·ē käz'mäl·ə·jē }

new moon   The moon at conjunction, when little or none of it is visible to an observer on the earth because the illuminated side is turned away. { 'nü 'mün }

Ney-Allen nebula   An extended source of infrared radiation in the Trapezium region of

Orion which displays intense emission at a wavelength of 10 millimeters. { 'nī 'al·ən 'neb·yə·lə }

N galaxy   A galaxy that has the optical appearance of a strongly concentrated object with a semistellar nucleus that is surrounded by a faint halo or extension. { 'en ˌgal·ik·sē }

night   The period of darkness between sunset and sunrise. { nīt }

nimbus   See halo. { 'nim·bəs }

nitrogen sequence   Wolf-Rayet stars in which nitrogen emission bands dominate the spectrum. { 'nī·trə·jən ˌsē·kwəns }

Nix Olympica   See Olympus Mons. { 'niks ə'lim·pə·kə }

no-atmospheric control   Any device or system designed or set up to control a guided rocket missile, rocket craft, or the like outside the atmosphere or in regions where the atmosphere is of such tenuity that it will not affect aerodynamic controls. { 'nō ˌat·mə'sfir·ik kən'trōl }

nodal line   The line passing through the ascending and descending nodes of the orbit of a celestial body. { 'nōd·əl ˌlīn }

node   **1.** One of two points at which the orbit of a planet, planetoid, or comet crosses the plane of the ecliptic. **2.** One of two points at which a satellite crosses the equatorial plane of its primary. { nōd }

node cycle   The period of time needed for the regression of the moon's nodes to conclude a circuit of 360° of longitude; approximately equal to 18.61 Julian years. { 'nōd ˌsī·kəl }

nodical month   The average period of revolution of the moon about the earth with respect to the moon's ascending node, a period of 27 days 5 hours 5 minutes 35.8 seconds, or approximately $27\frac{1}{4}$ days. Also known as draconitic month. { 'näd·ə·kəl 'mənth }

nonimpinging injector   An injector used in rocket engines which employs parallel streams of propellant usually emerging normal to the face of the injector. { 'nän·imˌpin·jiŋ in'jek·tər }

noon   The instant at which a time reference is over the upper branch of the reference meridian. { nün }

noon interval   The predicted time interval between a given instant, usually the time of a morning observation, and local apparent noon; it is used to predict the time for observing the sun on the celestial meridian. { 'nün 'in·tər·vəl }

Norma   A southern constellation; right ascension 16 hours, declination 50°S. Also known as Rule. { 'nor·mə }

normal spiral galaxy   A galaxy that has a lens-shaped central portion with two arms that begin to coil in the same plane and in the same fashion immediately upon emerging from opposite sides of it. { 'nor·məl 'spī·rəl 'gal·ik·sē }

North American Nebula   A cloud of dust and gas in the constellation Cygnus; the density of this gas and dust is possibly a thousand times greater than the average density of interstellar gas; a much denser cloud of dust between the nebula and earth

northbound node

obscures portions of the emission nebula to create the appearance of the "Gulf of Mexico" and the "Atlantic Ocean." { 'nȯrth ə'mer·i·kən 'neb·yə·lə }

northbound node See ascending node. { 'nȯrth‚baůnd 'nōd }

northerly turning error An acceleration error in the magnetic compass of an aircraft in a banked attitude during a turn, so called because it was first noted and is most pronounced during turns made from initial north-south courses; during a turn the magnetic needle is tilted from the horizontal, due to acceleration and the banking of the aircraft; in this position the compass needle will be acted upon by the vertical as well as the horizontal component of the earth's magnetic field; in addition, the compass needle is mechanically restricted in movement, due to tilt. Also known as turning error. { 'nȯr·thər·lē ¦tərn·iŋ ‚er·ər }

Northern Cross See Cygnus. { 'nȯr·thərn 'krȯs }

Northern Crown See Corona Borealis. { 'nȯr·thərn 'kraůn }

north point The point on the celestial sphere, due north of the observer, at which the celestial meridian intersects the celestial horizon. { 'nȯrth ‚pȯint }

north polar distance The angular distance between a celestial object and the north celestial pole. { 'nȯrth ¦pō·lər 'dis·təns }

north polar sequence A list of stars in the vicinity of the north celestial pole whose photographic magnitudes have been measured as accurately as possible, and which are used as a basis for determining the magnitudes of other stars. { 'nȯrth ¦pō·lər 'sē·kwəns }

North Polar Spur A region of radio and soft x-ray emission, having a continuous spectral distribution, that extends from the galactic plane to the north galactic pole; believed to be the remnant of an old supernova. { 'nȯrth 'pō·lər 'spər }

north pole The north celestial pole that indicates the zenith of the heavens when viewed from the north geographic pole. { 'nȯrth 'pōl }

North Star See Polaris. { 'nȯrth 'stär }

nose cone A protective cone-shaped case for the nose section of a missile or rocket; may include the warhead, fusing system, stabilization system, heat shield, and supporting structure and equipment. { 'nōz ‚kōn }

nose-heavy Pertaining to an airframe in which the nose tends to sink when the longitudinal control is released in any attitude of normal flight. { 'nōz ‚hev·ē }

nova A star that suddenly becomes explosively bright, the term is a misnomer because it does not denote a new star but the brightening of an existing faint star. { 'nō·və }

novalike symbiotic A symbiotic star consisting of a red giant combined with a white dwarf, in which thermonuclear reactions of hydrogen and helium from the red giant accreted in the surface layers of the white dwarf are believed to produce outbursts of energy similar to those observed in a nova. Also known as symbiotic nova. { 'nō·və‚līk ‚sim·bē'äd·ik }

nozzle blade Any one of the blades or vanes in a nozzle diaphragm. Also known as nozzle vane. { 'näz·əl ‚blād }

nozzle thrust coefficient A measure of the amplification of thrust due to gas expansion in a particular nozzle as compared with the thrust that would be exerted if the chamber pressure acted only over the throat area. Also known as thrust coefficient. { 'näz·əl ┆thrəst ‚kō·i‚fish·ənt }

N star   An obsolete classification for a star in the carbon sequence; has about the same temperature as an M star in the Draper catalog. { 'en ‚stär }

Nubeculae   See Magellanic Clouds. { nü'bek·yə‚lē }

Nubecula Major   See Large Magellanic Cloud. { nü'bek·yə·lə 'mā·jər }

Nubecula Minor   See Small Magellanic Cloud. { nü'bek·yə·lə 'mīn·ər }

nuclear-electric propulsion   A system of propulsion utilizing a nuclear reactor to generate electricity which is then used in an electric propulsion system or as a heat source for the working fluid. { 'nü·klē·ər i┆lek·trik prə‚pəl·shən }

nuclear-electric rocket engine   A rocket engine in which a nuclear reactor is used to generate electricity that is used in an electric propulsion system or as a heat source for the working fluid. { 'nü·klē·ər i┆lek·trik 'räk·ət ‚en·jən }

nuclear rocket   See atomic rocket. { 'nü·klē·ər 'räk·ət }

nuclear time scale   The time it takes for a star to evolve a significant distance from the main sequence when a certain fraction of the hydrogen in its core has been converted to helium by thermonuclear reactions. { 'nü·klē·ər 'tīm ‚skāl }

nucleogenesis   The origin of chemical elements in the universe. { ‚nü·klē·ə'jen·ə·səs }

nucleosynthesis   The formation of the various nuclides present in the universe by various nuclear reactions, occurring chiefly in the early universe following the big bang, in the interiors of stars, and in supernovae. { ┆nü·klē·ō'sin·thə·səs }

nucleus   The small permanent body of a comet, believed to have a diameter between one and a few tens of kilometers, and to be composed of water and volatile hydrocarbons. { 'nü·klē·əs }

nutation   A slight, slow, nodding motion of the earth's axis of rotation which is superimposed on the precession of the equinoxes; it is the combination of a number of perturbations (lunar, solar, and fortnightly nutation). { nü'tā·shən }

Nysa   An asteroid whose surface composition resembles that of the aubrites; it has a diameter of approximately 40 miles (70 kilometers) and a mean distance from the sun of 2.422 astronomical units. { 'nī·sə }

O

OB association A grouping of very young, very hot massive stars of spectral types O and B that has not had time to disperse. { ¦ō′bē ə‚sō·sē′ā·shən }

Oberon One of the five satellites of Uranus; diameter about 870 miles (1400 kilometers). { ′ō·bə‚rän }

oblateness The distortion from a spherical shape in which the diameter at the equator exceeds that at the poles. { ä′blāt·nəs }

oblique ascension The arc of the celestial equator, or the angle at the celestial pole, between the hour circle of the vernal equinox and the hour circle through the intersection of the celestial equator and the eastern horizon at the instant a point on the oblique sphere rises, measured eastward from the hour circle of the vernal equinox through 24 hours. { ə′blēk ə′sen·chən }

oblique rotator A star model in which the axis of the magnetic field does not coincide with the axis of rotation. { ə′blēk ′rō‚tād·ər }

oblique sphere The celestial sphere as it appears to an observer between the equator and the pole, where celestial bodies appear to rise obliquely to the horizon. { ə′blēk ′sfir }

obliquity of the ecliptic The acute angle between the plane of the ecliptic and the plane of the celestial equator, about 23°27′. { ə′blik·wəd·ē əv thə i′klip·tik }

occultation The disappearance of the light of a celestial body by intervention of another body of larger apparent size; especially, a lunar eclipse of a star or planet. { ‚ä·kəl′tā·shən }

occulting bar A bar placed in the focal plane of a telescope eyepiece to cover part of the field of view, usually to cover a bright object in order to permit observation of a nearby faint object. { ə′kəlt·iŋ ‚bär }

occulting disk A small metal disk placed in the focal plane of the eyepiece of a telescope, usually to cover a bright object in order to permit observation of a faint one. { ə′kəlt·iŋ ‚disk }

off-airways Pertaining to any aircraft course or track that does not lie within the bounds of prescribed airways. { ′ȯf ′er‚wāz }

Olbers' paradox If the universe were static, of infinite age, and the galaxies distributed isotropically, the distance attenuation of their light would be exactly balanced by the increase in number in successive spherical shells centered at the earth; hence the night sky would be of daylight brightness instead of dark. { ′ōl·bərz ′par·ə‚däks }

old inflationary cosmology   The original version of the inflationary universe cosmology in which a quantum-mechanical tunneling process is responsible for the phase transition of the universe to a state in which grand unified symmetry is broken. { 'ōld in'flā·shə‚ner·ē käz'mäl·ə·jē }

Olympus Mons   The largest volcano on Mars; it is approximately 360 miles (600 kilometers) across at its base and stands approximately 16 miles (26 kilometers) above the surrounding terrain. Also known as Nix Olympica. { ə'lim·pəs 'mänz }

Omega Nebula   A bright H II region in the constellation Sagittarius that is both a bright far-infrared source and a double radio source. Also known as Swan Nebula. { ō'meg·ə 'neb·yə·lə }

on-top flight   Flight above an overcast. { 'ón 'täp 'flīt }

Oort dark matter   Matter of unknown nature that is postulated to exist in the disk of the Milky Way Galaxy in order to account for the spatial and velocity distributions of stars in the direction perpendicular to the galactic plane. { ¦órt 'därk ‚mad·ər }

Oort's Cloud   A cloud of comets at distances from 75,000 to 150,000 astronomical units from the sun, which has been proposed as a source of comets that pass near the sun. { 'órts ‚klaúd }

open arc   A crater arc in which the craters do not touch each other. { 'ō·pən 'ärk }

open chain   A crater chain in which the craters do not touch each other. { 'ō·pən 'chān }

open cluster   One of the groupings of stars that are concentrated along the central plane of the Milky Way; most have an asymmetrical appearance and are loosely assembled, and the stars are concentrated in their central region; they may contain from a dozen to many hundreds of stars. Also known as galactic cluster. { 'ō·pən 'kləs·tər }

open universe   A cosmological model in which the volume of the universe is infinite and its expansion will continue forever. { 'ō·pən 'yü·nə‚vərs }

Ophelia   A satellite of Uranus orbiting at a mean distance of 33,400 miles (53,760 kilometers) with a period of 9 hours 3 minutes, and a diameter of about 20 miles (32 kilometers); the outer shepherding satellite for the outermost ring of Uranus. { ō'fēl·yə }

Oppenheimer-Volkoff limit   The upper limit on the mass of a neutron star, above which there is no stable equilibrium configuration and it is predicted that matter will collapse into a black hole. { 'äp·ən‚hī·mər 'fól‚kóf ‚lim·ət }

opposition   The situation of two celestial bodies having either celestial longitudes or sidereal hour angles differing by 180°; the term is usually used only in relation to the position of a superior planet or the moon with reference to the sun. { ‚äp·ə'zish·ən }

optical double star   Two stars not formally a physical system but that appear to be a typical double star; a false binary star whose components happen to lie nearby in the same line of sight. { 'äp·tə·kəl 'dəb·əl 'stär }

optical galaxy   One of the galaxies that appear as nearly starlike, generally having compact nuclei. { 'äp·tə·kəl 'gal·ik·sē }

optimum flight   An aircraft flight so planned and navigated that it is completed under the optimum conditions of minimum time and minimum exposure to dangerous flying weather. { 'äp·tə·məm 'flīt }

orbital curve One of the tracks on a primary body's surface traced by a satellite that orbits about it several times in a direction other than normal to the primary body's axis of rotation; each track is displaced in a direction opposite and by an amount equal to the degrees of rotation between each satellite orbit. { 'or·bəd·əl 'kərv }

orbital decay The lessening of the eccentricity of the elliptical orbit of an artificial satellite. { 'or·bəd·əl di'kā }

orbital direction The direction that the path of an orbiting body takes; in the case of an earth satellite, this path may be defined by the angle of inclination of the path to the equator. { 'or·bəd·əl di'rek·shən }

orbital node One of the two points at which the orbit of a planet or satellite crosses the plane of the ecliptic or equator. { 'or·bəd·əl 'nōd }

orbital period The interval between successive passages of a satellite through the same specified point in its orbit. { 'or·bəd·əl 'pir·ē·əd }

orbital rendezvous **1.** The meeting of two or more orbiting objects with zero relative velocity at a preconceived time and place. **2.** The point in space at which such an event occurs. { 'or·bəd·əl 'rän·də₁vü }

orbital velocity The instantaneous velocity at which an earth satellite or other orbiting body travels around the origin of its central force field. { 'or·bəd·əl və'läs·əd·ē }

orbit point A geographically defined reference point over land or water, used in stationing airborne aircraft. { 'or·bət ₁point }

Origem Loop A loop of gas on the boundary between Orion and Gemini about 60 parsecs (1.2×10^{15} miles or 1.8×10^{15} kilometers) in radius and 1000 parsecs (2×10^{16} miles or 3×10^{16} kilometers) distant, with at least five nebulae embedded in it. { 'or·ə₁jem ₁lüp }

Orion A northern constellation near the celestial equator, right ascension 5 hours, declination 5° north. Also known as Warrior. { ə'rī·ən }

Orion arm The spiral arm of the Milky Way Galaxy that has a spur in which the sun is located. Also known as local arm. { ə'rī·ən ₁ärm }

Orionids A meteor shower seen in October in the northern hemisphere; its radiant lies in the constellation Orion. { ə'rī·ə₁nidz }

Orion molecular clouds Two molecular clouds in the Orion Nebula; one has about 300,000 hydrogen molecules per cubic centimeter and contains the Becklin-Nengebauer object and the Kleinmann-Low Nebula, while the other is centered on a cluster of infrared sources. { ə'rī·ən mə'lek·yə·lər 'klaudz }

Orion Nebula A luminous cloud surrounding Ori, the northern star in Orion's dagger; visible to the naked eye as a hazy object. Also known as Great Nebula of Orion. { ə'rī·ən 'neb·yə·lə }

Orion spur That portion of the Orion arm within which the sun is located. { ə'rī·ən 'spər }

orrery A model of the solar system equipped with mechanical devices to make the planets move at their correct relative velocities around the sun. { 'or·ər·ē }

oscillating universe   An extension of the closed universe model in which the universe, after contracting toward a singularity, undergoes another big bang to begin a new cycle, and thenceforth oscillates between successive expansions and contractions, each contraction followed by a new big bang. { 'äs·ə‚lād·iŋ 'yü·nə‚vərs }

osculating orbit   The orbit which would be followed by a body such as an asteroid or comet if, at a given time, all the planets suddenly disappeared, and it then moved under the gravitational force of the sun alone. { 'äs·kyə‚lād·iŋ 'ȯr·bət }

O star   A star of spectral type O, a massive, very hot blue star with a surface temperature of at least 35,000 K (63,000°F), and a spectrum in which lines of singly ionized helium are prominent. { 'ō ‚stär }

Ostriker-Peebles halo   A spherical distribution of matter of unknown nature that is postulated to exist to account for the stability of the highly flattened visible disk of the Milky Way Galaxy. { ¦äs·trīk·ər 'pēb·əlz ‚hā‚lō }

O-type star   A spectral-type classification in the Draper catalog of stars; a star having spectral type O; a very hot, blue star in which the spectral lines of ionized helium are prominent. { 'ō ¦tīp 'stär }

outer planets   The planets with orbits larger than that of Mars: Jupiter, Saturn, Uranus, Neptune, and Pluto. { 'au̇d·ər 'plan·əts }

outer space   A general term for any region that is beyond the earth's atmosphere. { 'au̇d·ər 'spās }

outgassing   The ejection of gases trapped within a planet so that they are added to the planet's atmosphere. { 'au̇t‚gas·iŋ }

overall efficiency   The efficiency of a jet engine, rocket engine, or rocket motor in converting the total heat energy of its fuel first into available energy for the engine, then into effective driving energy. { ¦ō·vər¦ȯl i'fish·ən·sē }

Owl Nebula   A large planetary nebula in Ursa Major which has two large, circular darker areas in an otherwise opaque spherical shell. { 'au̇l 'neb·yə·lə }

oxidizer   A substance, not necessarily containing oxygen, that supports the combustion of a fuel or propellant. { 'äk·sə‚dīz·ər }

oxygen-hydrocarbon engine   A rocket engine that uses a propellant consisting of liquid oxygen as the oxidizer, and a hydrocarbon, such as a petroleum derivative, as the fuel. { 'äk·sə·jən ¦hī·drə'kär·bən ‚en·jən }

P

Pacific Standard Time   *See* Pacific time. { pə'sif·ik 'stan·dərd 'tīm }

Pacific time   The time for a given time zone that is based on the 120th meridian and is the eighth zone west of Greenwich. Also known as Pacific Standard Time. { pə'sif·ik 'tīm }

pad   *See* launch pad. { pad }

pad deluge   Water sprayed on certain launch pads during rocket launching in order to reduce the temperatures of critical parts of the pad or the rocket. { 'pad 'del‚yüj }

paddle   A large, flat, paddle-shaped support for solar cells, used on some satellites. { 'pad·əl }

Pallas   The second-largest asteroid, with a diameter of about 324 miles (540 kilometers), mean distance from the sun of 2.769 astronomical units, and C-type surface composition. { 'pal·əs }

pancake landing   Landing of an aircraft at a low forward speed and at a very high rate of descent. { 'pan‚kāk ¦land·iŋ }

Pandora   A satellite of Saturn which orbits at a mean distance of 88,000 miles (142,000 kilometers), just outside the F ring; together with Prometheus, it holds this ring in place. { Pan'dȯr·ə }

parabolic flight   A space flight occurring in a parabolic orbit. { ¦par·ə¦bäl·ik 'flīt }

parabolic orbit   An orbit whose overall shape is like a parabola; the orbit represents the least eccentricity for escape from an attracting body. { ¦par·ə¦bäl·ik 'ȯr·bət }

parabolic velocity   The velocity attained by a celestial body in a parabolic orbit. { ¦par·ə¦bäl·ik və'läs·əd·ē }

parachute   1. A contrivance that opens out somewhat like an umbrella and catches the air so as to retard the movement of a body attached to it. 2. The canopy of this contrivance. { 'par·ə‚shüt }

parachute-opening shock   The shock or jolt exerted on a suspended parachute load when the parachute fully catches the air. { 'par·ə‚shüt ‚ōp·ə·niŋ ‚shäk }

paraglider   A triangular device on a rocket or spacecraft that consists of two flexible sections and resembles a kite; deployed to assist in guiding or landing a spacecraft or in recovering a launching rocket. { 'par·ə‚glīd·ər }

parallactic displacement

parallactic displacement The apparent changes in the position of a star due to changes in the position of the earth as it moves around the sun. Also known as parallactic shift. { ¦par·əǀlak·tik di′splās·mənt }

parallactic ellipse An annual apparent elliptical course of a celestial body on the celestial sphere about its mean position; caused by the elliptical orbital motion of the earth. { ¦par·əǀlak·tik i′lips }

parallactic equation An inequality in the moon's motion caused by the sun's perturbing effect on the moon being greater in that half of the moon's apparent orbit around the earth when at new moon rather than at full moon. Also known as parallactic inequality. { ¦par·əǀlak·tik i′kwä·zhən }

parallactic inequality See parallactic equation. { ¦par·əǀlak·tik ‚in·i′kwäl·əd·ē }

parallactic motion An apparent motion of stars away from the point in the celestial sphere toward which the sun is moving. { ¦par·əǀlak·tik ′mō·shən }

parallactic orbit The apparent orbit of a star as it appears to move once around in the sky each year; the motion is caused by the earth's orbital motion around the sun. { ¦par·əǀlak·tik ′òr·bət }

parallactic shift See parallactic displacement. { ¦par·əǀlak·tik ′shift }

parallax-second See parsec. { ′par·ə‚laks ǀsek·ənd }

parallel of altitude A circle on the celestial sphere parallel to the horizon connecting all points of equal altitude. Also known as almucantar; altitude circle. { ′par·ə‚lel əv ′al·tə‚tüd }

parallel of declination A small circle of the celestial sphere parallel to the celestial equator. Also known as celestial parallel; circle of equal declination. { ′par·ə‚lel əv ‚dek·lə′nā·shən }

parallel of latitude See circle of longitude; parallel. { ′par·ə‚lel əv ′lad·ə‚tüd }

parallel sphere The celestial sphere as it appears to an observer at the pole, where celestial bodies appear to move parallel to the horizon. { ′par·ə‚lel ′sfir }

paranthelion A refraction phenomenon similar to a parhelion, but occurring generally at a distance of 120° (occasionally 90° and 140°) from the sun, on the parhelic circle. Also known as mock sun. { ‚par·ən′thē·lē‚än }

paraselene A weakly colored lunar halo identical in form and optical origin to the solar parhelion; paraselenae are observed less frequently than are parhelia, because of the moon's comparatively weak luminosity. Also known as mock moon. { ¦par·ə·sə′lēn }

paraselenic circle A halo phenomenon consisting of a horizontal circle passing through the moon, corresponding to the parhelic circle through the sun, and produced by reflection of moonlight from ice crystals. { ¦par·ə·sə′len·ik ′sər·kəl }

parasheet A simple form of parachute in which the canopy is a single piece of material or two or more pieces sewed together; it may have any geometrical form, such as square or hexagonal, and the hem may be gathered to assist in the development of a crown when the parasheet is opened. { ′par·ə‚shēt }

parhelic circle A halo consisting of a faint white circle passing through the sun and running parallel to the horizon for as much as 360° of azimuth. Also known as mock sun ring. { pär'hē·lik }

parhelion Either of two colored luminous spots that appear at points 22° (or somewhat more) on both sides of the sun and at the same elevation as the sun; the solar counterpart of the lunar paraselene. Also known as mock sun; sun dog. { pär'hēl·yən }

Parker bound An upper bound on the density of magnetic monopoles that is obtained from arguments based on the existence of a galactic magnetic field. { ¦pär·kər ¦baund }

Parker model A model of the solar wind that assumes the solar wind is driven by the thermal pressure of the hot coronal gas. { 'pär·kər ˌmäd·əl }

parking orbit A temporary earth orbit during which the space vehicle is checked out and its trajectory carefully measured to determine the amount and time of increase in velocity required to send it into a final orbit or into space in the desired direction. { 'pärk·iŋ ˌȯr·bət }

parsec The distance at which a star would have a parallax equal to 1 second of arc; 1 parsec equals 3.258 light-years or 3.08572 × 10^13 kilometers. Derived from parallax-second. { 'pär·sek }

partial eclipse An eclipse in which only part of the source of light is obscured. { 'pär·shəl i'klips }

partial pressure suit A skintight suit which does not completely enclose the body but which is capable of exerting pressure on the major portion of the body in order to counteract an increased oxygen pressure in the lungs. { 'pär·shəl 'presh·ər ˌsüt }

Pasiphae A small satellite of Jupiter with a diameter of about 35 miles (56 kilometers), orbiting with retrograde motion at a mean distance of about 1.46 × 10^7 miles (2.35 × 10^7 kilometers). Also known as Jupiter VIII. { pə'sif·əˌē }

pass 1. A single circuit of the earth made by a satellite; it starts at the time the satellite crosses the equator from the Southern Hemisphere into the Northern Hemisphere. 2. The period of time in which a satellite is within telemetry range of a data acquisition station. { pas }

passive communications satellite A satellite that reflects communications signals between stations, without providing amplification; an example is the Echo satellite. Also known as passive satellite. { 'pas·iv kəˌmyü·nə'kā·shənz ˌsad·əlˌīt }

passive satellite See passive communications satellite. { 'pas·iv 'sad·əlˌīt }

Patientia An asteroid with a diameter of about 146 miles (235 kilometers), mean distance from the sun of 3.061 astronomical units, and C-type surface composition. { ˌpä·shē'en·chə }

Patroclus group See pure Trojan group. { pə'trō·kləs ˌgrüp }

pattern The flight path flown by an aircraft, or prescribed to be flown, as in making an approach to a landing. { 'pad·ərn }

Pavo A southern constellation; right ascension 20 hours, declination 65°S. Also known as Peacock. { 'pä·vō }

payload

payload That which an aircraft, rocket, or the like carries over and above what is necessary for the operation of the vehicle in its flight. { 'pā,lōd }

payload-mass ratio Of a rocket, the ratio of the effective propellant mass to the initial vehicle mass. { 'pā,lōd ¦mas ,rā·shō }

P Cygni star An explosive variable star of spectral type B, with broad emission lines and strong absorption of violet light. { ¦pē 'sig·nē ,stär }

peculiar star A star that does not fit into a standard spectral classification. { pə'kyül·yər 'stär }

peculiar velocity Superposed on the systematic rotation of the galaxy are individual motions of the stars; each star moves in a somewhat elliptical orbit and therefore shows a velocity of its own (peculiar velocity) to the local standard of rest, the standard moving in a circular orbit around the galactic center. { pə'kyül·yər və'läs·əd·ē }

Pegasus A northern constellation; right ascension 22 hours, declination 20°N. Also known as Winged Horse. { 'peg·ə·səs }

penetration That phase of the letdown from high altitude to a specified approach altitude. { ,pen·ə'trā·shən }

penumbra The outer, relatively light part of a sunspot. { pə'nəm·brə }

penumbral eclipse See lunar appulse. { pə'nəm·brəl i'klips }

penumbral waves Waves that are often observed to propagate outward across the penumbrae of large sunspots when the penumbrae are viewed in the light of the Hα spectral line of hydrogen. { pə'nəm·brəl 'wāvz }

perfect cosmological principle The assumption that the universe is homogeneous and isotropic, and does not change with time. { 'pər·fikt ,käz·mə'läj·ə·kəl 'prin·sə·pəl }

periapsis The orbital point nearest the center of attraction of an orbiting body. { ,per·ē'ap·səs }

periastron The coordinates and time when the two stars of a binary star system are nearest to each other in their orbits. { ¦per·ē¦as·trən }

pericronus The nearest point of a satellite in its orbit about Saturn. Also known as perisaturnium. { ¦per·ə'krō·nəs }

pericynthion The point in the orbit of a satellite around the moon that is nearest to the moon. { ,per·ə'sin·thē,än }

perigalacticon The point in the orbit of a star that is closest to the center of the Galaxy. { ,per·i·gə'lak·tē,kän }

perigee The point in the orbit of the moon or other satellite when it is nearest the earth. { 'per·ə,jē }

perigee-to-perigee period See anomalistic period. { 'per·ə,jē tü 'per·ə,jē ,pir·ē·əd }

perihelion That orbital point nearest the sun when the sun is the center of attraction. { ¦per·ə¦hēl·yən }

perijove   The nearest point of a satellite in its orbit about Jupiter. { 'per·ə₁jōv }

period   The average time interval for a variable star to complete a cycle of its variations. { 'pir·ē·əd }

periodic perturbation   Small deviations from the computed orbit of a planet or satellite; the deviations extend through cycles that generally do not exceed a century. { ¦pir·ē¦äd·ik pər·tər'bā·shən }

period-luminosity relation   Relation between the periods of Cepheid variable stars and their absolute magnitude; the absolutely brighter the star, the longer the period. { 'pir·ē·əd ₁lü·mə'näs·əd·ē ri₁lā·shən }

perisaturnium   See pericronus. { 'per·ə₁sə'tər·nē·əm }

perpetual calendar   A table or mechanical device used to determine the day of the week corresponding to any given date over a period of many years. { pər'pech·ə·wəl 'kal·ən·dər }

Perseids   A meteor shower whose radiant lies in the constellation Perseus; it reaches a maximum about August 12. { 'pər·sē·ədz }

Perseus   A northern constellation; right ascension 3 hours; declination 45°N. { 'pər·sē·əs }

Perseus A   A strong radio source, having a redshift $z = 0.018$ and centered on the Seyfert galaxy NGC 1275, that undergoes extremely violent outbursts. { 'pər·sē·əs 'ā }

Perseus arm   A spiral arm of the Milky Way galaxy visible in the constellation Perseus, located (as viewed from the earth) in the direction opposite that of the galactic center. { 'pər·sē·əs ₁ärm }

Perseus cluster   An irregular, diffuse cluster of galaxies centered on the Seyfert galaxy NGC 1275, with redshift $z = 0.018$. { 'pər·sē·əs ₁kləs·tər }

Perseus-Pisces supercluster   A dominant supercluster that occurs in the south galactic hemisphere and includes the Perseus cluster toward one end of a long, filamentary central condensation. { ¦pər·sē·əs ¦pī₁sēz 'sü·pər₁kləs·tər }

Perseus X-1   The strongest known x-ray source outside the Milky Way galaxy, centered on the Seyfert galaxy NGC 1275. { 'pər·sē·əs 'eks 'wən }

perturbation   A deviation of an astronomical body from its computed orbit because of the attraction of another body or bodies. { ₁pər·tər'bā·shən }

phase   One of the cyclically repeating appearances of the moon or other orbiting body as seen from earth. { fāz }

Phobos   A satellite of Mars; it is the larger of the two satellites, with a diameter of about 15 miles (24 kilometers). { 'fō₁bòs }

Phoebe   A satellite of the planet Saturn; its diameter is judged to be about 190 miles (320 kilometers); it has an eccentric orbit and retrograde revolution. { 'fē·bē }

Phoenix   A southern constellation; right ascension 1 hour, declination 50°S. { 'fē·niks }

photoelectric magnitude   The magnitude of a celestial object, as measured by a photoelectric photometer attached to a telescope. { ¦fōd·ō·i'lek·trik 'mag·nə‚tüd }

photographic magnitude   The magnitude of a star, as obtained by measuring the apparent size of a star's image on a photographic emulsion sensitive to blue light at wavelengths between 400 and 500 nanometers. { ¦fōd·ə¦graf·ik 'mag·nə‚tüd }

photographic meteor   A meteor which has been photographed for the purpose of determining its origin, velocity, and other characteristics. { ¦fōd·ə¦graf·ik 'mēd·ē·ər }

photometric binary   See eclipsing variable star. { ¦fōd·ō¦me·trik 'bī‚ner·ē }

photometric parallax   The annual parallax of a star too far away for its parallax to be measured directly, as calculated from its apparent magnitude and its absolute magnitude inferred from its spectral type. { ¦fōd·ə¦me·trik 'par·ə‚laks }

photon sail   See solar sail. { 'fō‚tän ‚sāl }

photosphere   The intensely bright portion of the sun visible to the unaided eye; it is a shell a few hundred miles in thickness marking the boundary between the dense interior gases of the sun and the more diffuse cooler gases in the outer portions of the sun. { 'fōd·ə‚sfir }

photospheric granulation   See granulation. { ¦fōd·ə¦sfir·ik ‚gran·yə'lā·shən }

photovisual magnitude   The magnitude of a star, obtained by measuring the size of the star's image on an isochromatic photographic emulsion, using a filter transmitting only the longer wavelengths between 500 and 600 nanometers; nearly identical with visual magnitude. { ¦fōd·ō'vizh·ə·wəl 'mag·nə‚tüd }

phugoid   Pertaining to variations in the longitudinal motion or course of the center of mass of an aircraft. { 'fü‚góid }

physical libration of the moon   See lunar libration. { 'fiz·ə·kəl lī'brā·shən əv thə 'mün }

pickup   A potentiometer used in an automatic pilot to detect the motion of the airplane around the gyro and initiate corrective adjustments. { 'pik‚əp }

Pictor   A southern constellation; right ascension 6 hours, declination 55°S. Also known as Easel. { 'pik‚tór }

pilot   **1.** A person who handles the controls of an aircraft or spacecraft from within the craft, and guides or controls the craft in flight. **2.** A mechanical system designed to exercise control functions in an aircraft or spacecraft. { 'pī·lət }

pilot chute   A small parachute canopy attached to a larger canopy to actuate and accelerate the opening of the load-bearing canopy. { 'pī·lət ‚shüt }

pilotless aircraft   An aircraft adapted to control by or through a preset self-reacting unit or a radio-controlled unit, without the benefit of a human pilot. { 'pī·lət·ləs 'er‚kraft }

Pisces   A northern constellation; right ascension 1 hour, declination 15°N. Also known as Fishes. { 'pī·sēz }

Pisces Volan   See Volan. { 'pī·sēz 'vō·lən }

144

Piscis Australis   A southern constellation; right ascension 22 hours, declination 30°S. Also known as Southern Fish. { 'pis·kəs 'ȯs·trə·ləs }

pitch indicator   An instrument for indicating the existence and approximate magnitude of the angular velocity about the lateral axis of an airframe. { 'pich ‚in·dəˌkād·ər }

pitchover   The programmed turn from the vertical that a rocket under power takes as it describes an arc and points in a direction other than vertical. { 'pichˌō·vər }

plage   One of the luminous areas that appear in the vicinity of sunspots or disturbed areas on the sun; they may be seen distinctively in spectroheliograms taken in the calcium K line. { pläzh }

Planck era   The epoch in the early universe when the gravitational interaction between particles was as strong as the other interactions. { 'pläŋk ‚ir·ə }

planet   A relatively small, solid celestial body circulating around a star, in particular the star known as the sun (which has nine planets). { 'plan·ət }

planetarium   1. A projection device which accurately portrays the position of the stars and planets at any time in the past, present, or future from any point on the earth or the near region of space; the modern planetarium instrument is a mechanical-electrical analog of space. 2. The name given to the building and gear associated with this device. { ‚plan·ə'ter·ē·əm }

planetary atmosphere   The outer shell of gas around some planets. { 'plan·əˌter·ē 'at·məˌsfir }

planetary nebula   An oval or round nebula of expanding concentric rings of gas associated with a hot central star. { 'plan·əˌter·ē 'neb·yə·lə }

planetary nebula symbiotic   See subdwarf symbiotic. { 'plan·əˌter·ē 'neb·yə·lə ‚sim·bē'äd·ik }

planetary orbit   The path that a planet has as it revolves about the sun. { 'plan·əˌter·ē 'ȯr·bət }

planetary perturbation   A deviation of a planet from its computed orbit because of the attraction of another celestial body or bodies. { 'plan·əˌter·ē ‚pər·tə'bā·shən }

planetary physics   The study of the structure, composition, and physical and chemical properties of the planets of the solar system, including their atmospheres and immediate cosmic environment. { 'plan·əˌter·ē 'fiz·iks }

planetary precession   A comparatively small eastward motion of the equinoxes caused by the action of other planets in altering the plane of the earth's orbit. { 'plan·əˌter·ē pri'sesh·ən }

planetesimal   One of the rocky bodies, of the order of 1 mile (1.6 kilometer) in diameter, that are believed to have formed in the protosolar nebula, and whose accretion formed the rocky cores of the larger planets. { ‚plan·ə'tes·ə·məl }

planetocentric coordinates   Coordinates that indicate the position of a point on the surface of a planet, determined by the direction of a line joining the center of the planet to the point. { pləˌned·ō¦sen·trik kō'ȯrd·ən·əts }

planetographic coordinates   Coordinates that indicate the position of a point on the surface of a planet, determined by the direction of a perpendicular to the mean surface at the point. { pləˌned·ō¦graf·ik kō'ȯrd·ən·əts }

planetography   The descriptive science of the physical features of planets. { ˈplan·əˈtäg·rəˌfē }

planetoid   *See* asteroid. { ˈplan·əˌtȯid }

planetology   Scientific study of the planets, in particular their surface markings. { ˌplan·əˈtäl·ə·jē }

planform   The shape or form of an object, such as an airfoil, as seen from above, as in a plan view. { ˈplanˌfȯrm }

plasma cloud   An aggregate of electrically charged particles that is embedded in the solar wind. { ˈplaz·məˌklau̇d }

plasma engine   An engine for space travel in which neutral plasma is accelerated and directed by external magnetic fields that interact with the magnetic field produced by current flow through the plasma. Also known as plasma jet. { ˈplaz·məˌen·jən }

plasma jet   *See* plasma engine. { ˈplaz·məˌjet }

plasma propulsion   Propulsion of spacecraft and other vehicles by using electric or magnetic fields to accelerate both positively and negatively charged particles (plasma) to a very high velocity. { ˈplaz·məprəˈpəl·shən }

plasma rocket   A rocket that is accelerated by means of a plasma engine. { ˈplaz·məˌräk·ət }

plasma tail   A comet tail that is composed primarily of electrons and molecular ions, the dominant visible ion being positively ionized carbon monoxide, and that is generally straight, with a length in the range from 0.62×10^7 to 0.62×10^8 miles (1×10^7 to 1×10^8 kilometers). { ˈplaz·məˈtāl }

plateau ring structure   A lunar crater whose floor is significantly higher than the surrounding surface. { plaˈtōˈriŋˌstrək·chər }

plate center   The point used as the origin of coordinates for measuring positions of stars on a photographic plate in photographic astrometry, ideally located on the optical axis of the telescope. { ˈplātˌsen·tər }

plate constants   Coefficients that appear in linear equations used to derive the standard coordinates of the position of a star on a photographic plate from the measured coordinates of the star's image on the plate. { ˈplātˌkän·stəns }

plate scale   The ratio of the angular distance between two stars to the linear distance between their images on a photographic plate. { ˈplātˌskāl }

platonic year   *See* great year. { pləˈtän·ikˈyir }

Pleiades   An open cluster of a few hundred stars in the constellation Taurus; six of the stars are easily visible to the naked eye. { ˈplē·əˌdēz }

Pluto   The most distant planet in the solar system; mean distance to the sun is about 3.5×10^9 miles (5.6×10^9 kilometers); it has no known satellite, and its sidereal revolution period is 248.4 years. { ˈplüd·ō }

plutonic theory   *See* volcanic theory. { plüˈtän·ikˈthē·ə·rē }

pod   An enclosure, housing, or detachable container of some kind on an airplane or space vehicle, as an engine pod. { päd }

Pogson scale   An index of brightness used in star catologs; it is the ratio of 2.512 to 1 between the brightness of successive magnitudes. { 'päg·sən ˌskāl }

Pointers   The stars α and β Ursae Majoris, which appear to point toward the north celestial pole and Polaris. { 'pȯint·ərz }

polar   A member of a class of cataclysmic variable stars whose light displays strong circular polarization. Also known as AM Herculis star. { 'pō·lər }

polar cap   Any of the bright areas covering the poles of Mars, believed to be composed of frozen carbon dioxide and water-ice. { 'pō·lər ˌkap }

polar distance   Angular distance from a celestial pole; the arc of an hour circle between a celestial pole, usually the elevated pole, and a point on the celestial sphere, measured from the celestial pole through 180°. { 'pō·lər 'dis·təns }

Polaris   A creamy supergiant star of stellar magnitude 2.0, spectral classification F8, in the constellation Ursa Minor; marks the north celestial pole, being about 1° from this point; the star Ursae Minoris. Also known as North Star; Pole Star. { pə'lar·əs }

polar night   The period of winter darkness in the polar regions, both northern and southern. { 'pō·lər 'nīt }

polar orbit   A satellite orbit running north and south, so the satellite vehicle orbits over both the North Pole and the South Pole. { 'pō·lər 'ȯr·bət }

polar plumes   Columnlike plumes of hot coronal gas that are concentrated at the sun's magnetic poles. { 'pō·lər 'plümz }

polar sequence   A compilation of 96 brightness-standard stars within 2° of the North Pole. { 'pō·lər 'sē·kwəns }

Pole Star   See Polaris. { 'pōl ˌstär }

Pollux   A giant orange-yellow star with visual brightness of 1.16, a little less than 35 light-years from the sun, spectral classification K0-III, in the constellation Gemini; the star β Geminorum. { 'päl·əks }

polygonal ring structure   A lunar crater whose wall approximates a polygon in shape. { pə'lig·ən·əl 'riŋ ˌstrək·chər }

pontoon   A float on an airplane. { pän'tün }

poor cluster   A galaxy cluster that has relatively few member galaxies. { ˈpu̇r ˈkləs·tər }

population I   A class of stars which are relatively young, have relatively low peculiar velocities, and are found chiefly in the spiral arms of galaxies. Also known as arm population. { ˌpäp·yə'lā·shən 'wən }

population II   A class of stars which are relatively old and evolved, have low metallic content and high peculiar velocities from 60 to 300 miles (100 to 500 kilometers) per second, and are found chiefly in the spheroidal halo of a galaxy. Also known as halo population. { ˌpäp·yə'lā·shən 'tü }

population III   A class of stars that condensed from the gas formed in the nucleosynthesis of the big bang, and consist entirely of hydrogen and helium. { ˌpäp·yə'lā·shən 'thrē }

pore   A very small, dark area on the sun formed by the separation of adjacent flocculi. { pȯr }

Portia   A satellite of Uranus orbiting at a mean distance of 41,070 miles (66,100 kilometers) with a period of 12 hours 21 minutes, and with a diameter of about 68 miles (110 kilometers). { 'pȯr·shə }

positional astronomy   The branch of astronomy that deals with the determination of the positions of celestial objects. { pə'zish·ən·əl ə'strän·ə·mē }

position angle   1. The angle formed by the great circle running through two celestial objects and the hour circle running through one of the objects. 2. In measuring double stars, the angle formed between the great circle running through both components and the hour circle going through the primary measured from the north through the east from 0 to 360°. { pə'zish·ən 'aŋ·gəl }

postnova   A nova that has faded to the brightness it had before its outburst. { pōs'nō·ə }

power car   A suspended structure on an airship that houses an engine. { 'paủ·ər ˌkär }

Poynting-Robertson effect   The gradual decrease in orbital velocity of a small particle such as a micrometeorite in orbit about the sun due to the absorption and reemission of radiant energy by the particle. { 'pȯint·iŋ 'räb·ərt·sən iˌfekt }

practical astronomy   That part of astronomy concerned with the use of information acquired by an observer in the solution of problems determining latitude and longitude on sea or land and directions on the earth's surface by the help of celestial objects. { 'prak·ti·kəl ə'strän·ə·mē }

Praesepe   A cluster of faint stars in the center of the constellation Cancer. Also known as Beehive; Manger. { 'prē·səˌpē }

preceding limb   The half of the limb of a celestial body with an observable disk that appears to precede the body in its apparent motion across the field of view of a fixed telescope. { prē'sēd·iŋ 'lim }

precession in declination   The component of general precession of the earth along a celestial meridian, amounting to about 20″ per year. { prē'sesh·ən in ˌdek·lə'nā·shən }

precession in right ascension   The component of general precession of the earth along the celestial equator, amounting to about 46.1″ per year. { prē'sesh·ən in 'rīt ə'sen·shən }

precession of nodes   The gradual change in direction of the orbital plane of a binary system. { prē'sesh·ən əv 'nōdz }

precession of the equinoxes   A slow conical motion of the earth's axis about the vertical to the plane of the ecliptic, having a period of 26,000 years, caused by the attractive force of the sun, moon, and other planets on the equatorial protuberance of the earth; it results in a gradual westward motion of the equinoxes. { prē'sesh·ən əv thə 'ē·kwəˌnäk·səz }

precomputed altitude   The altitude of a celestial body computed before observation with the sextant. Altitude corrections are included in the calculations but are applied with reversed sign. { 'prē·kəmˌpyüd·əd 'al·təˌtüd }

pre-Imbrian   Pertaining to the oldest lunar topographic features and lithologic map units constituting a system of rocks that appear in the mountainous terrae and are well displayed in the southern part of the visible lunar surface and over much of the reverse side. { prē'im·brē·ən }

prenova   A star that is destined to become a nova, but whose outburst has not yet taken place. { prē'nō·və }

pressure ionization   A condition found in white dwarfs and other degenerate matter in which electron orbits overlap to the point that electrons in higher quantum levels are no longer associated with any particular nucleus and must be regarded as free. { 'presh·ər ˌī·ə·nə'zā·shən }

pressure-stabilized   Referring to membrane-type structures that require internal pressure for maintenance of a stable structure. { 'presh·ər 'stā·bə‚līzd }

pressure suit   A garment designed to provide pressure upon the body so that respiratory and circulatory functions may continue normally, or nearly so, under low-pressure conditions such as occur at high altitudes or in space without benefit of a pressurized cabin. { 'presh·ər ‚süt }

pressure thrust   In rocketry, the product of the cross-sectional area of the exhaust jet leaving the nozzle exit and the difference between the exhaust pressure and the ambient pressure. { 'presh·ər ‚thrəst }

pressurized cabin   The occupied portion of an aircraft in which the air pressure has been raised above that of the ambient atmosphere by the compression of the atmosphere into this space. { 'presh·ə‚rīzd 'kab·ən }

prestage   A phase in the process of igniting a large liquid-fuel rocket in which the initial partial flow of propellants into the thrust chamber is ignited, and the combustion is satisfactorily established before the main stage is ignited. { 'prē‚stāj }

primary   **1.** A planet with reference to its satellites, or the sun with reference to its planets. **2.** The brighter star of a double star system. { 'prī ‚mer·ē }

primary body   The celestial body or central force field about which a satellite or other body orbits, or from which it is escaping, or toward which it is falling. { 'prī‚mer·ē'bäd·ē }

primary structure   The main framework, of an aircraft including fittings and attachments; any structural member whose failure would seriously impair the safety of the missile is a part of the primary structure. { 'prī‚mer·ē 'strək·chər }

primordial black holes   Hypothetical black holes which may have formed in the early, highly compressed stages of the universe immediately following the big bang. { prī'mȯrd·ē·əl 'blak 'hōlz }

probe   An instrumented vehicle moving through the upper atmosphere or space or landing upon another celestial body in order to obtain information about the specific environment. { prōb }

Procyon   A star of magnitude 0.3, of spectral type F5, and 11 light-years (1.041 × 10^{17} meters) from earth; one of a binary. Also known as α Canis Minoris. { 'prō·sē‚än }

profile thickness   The maximum distance between the upper and lower contours of an airfoil, measured perpendicular to the mean line of the profile. { ˈprō‚fīl ‚thik·nəs }

prograde motion   1. The apparent motion of a planet around the sun in the direction of the sun's rotation. **2.** *See* prograde orbit. { ¦prō′grād ′mō·shən }

prograde orbit   Orbital motion in the usual direction of celestial bodies within a given system; specifically, of a satellite, motion in the direction of rotation of the primary. Also known as prograde motion. { ¦prō′grād ′ȯr·bət }

program   In missile guidance, the planned flight path events to be followed by a missile in flight, including all the critical functions, preset in a program device, which control the behavior of the missile. { ′prō·grəm *or* ′prō͵gram }

programmed turn   The automatically controlled turn of a ballistic missile into the curved path that will lead to the correct velocity and vector for the final portion of the trajectory. { ′prō͵gramd ′tərn }

program star   A star whose properties are observed or measured during a specified series of observations. { ′prō·grəm ͵stär }

projected planform   The contour of the planform as viewed from above. { prə′jek·təd ′plan͵fórm }

projectile   **1.** Any object, especially a missile, that is fired, thrown, launched, or otherwise projected. **2.** Originally, an object, such as a bullet or artillery shell, projected by an applied external force. { prə′jek·təl }

Prometheus   A satellite of Saturn which orbits at a mean distance of 139,000 kilometers (86,000 miles), just inside the F ring; together with Pandora, it holds this ring in place. { prə′mē·thē·əs }

prominence   A volume of luminous, predominantly hydrogen gas that appears on the sun above the chromosphere; occurs only in the region of horizontal magnetic fields because these fields support the prominences against solar gravity. { ′präm·ə·nəns }

propellant injector   A device for injecting propellants, which include fuel and oxidizer, into the combustion chamber of a rocket engine. { prə′pel·ənt in͵jek·tər }

propellant mass fraction   *See* propellant mass ratio. { prə′pel·ənt ¦mas ͵frak·shən }

propellant mass ratio   Of a rocket, the ratio of the effective propellant mass to the initial vehicle mass. Also known as propellant mass fraction. { prə′pel·ənt ¦mas ͵rā·shō }

propellant weight fraction   The weight of the solid propellant charge divided by weight of the complete solid propellant propulsion unit. { prə′pel·ənt ¦wāt ͵frak·shən }

proper motion   That component of the space motion of a celestial body perpendicular to the line of sight, resulting in the change of a star's apparent position relative to that of other stars; expressed in angular units. { ′präp·ər ′mō·shən }

propfan   An advanced turboprop with very thin, highly swept blades to reduce both compressibility losses and propeller noise during high-speed cruise. { ′präp͵fan }

Prospector   A specific uncrewed spacecraft designed to make a soft landing on the moon to take measurements, photographs, and soil samples, and then return to earth. { ′prä͵spek·tər }

Proteus   A satellite of Neptune orbiting at a mean distance of 73,100 miles (117,600 kilometers) with a period of 26.9 hours, and with a diameter of about 250 miles (400 kilometers). { 'prōd·ē·əs }

protogalaxy   The theoretical precursor of the Galaxy; suggested by James Jeans to be an initial structureless gas cloud, held together by its own gravitation, that broke up into a number of fragments. { ,prōd·ō'gal·ik·sē }

protostar   A flattened mass of gas in space that is hypothesized to form into a star. { 'prōd·ə,stär }

Proxima Centauri   The star that is the sun's nearest neighbor; stellar magnitude is ll, and it is 2° from the bright star α Centauri. { 'präk·sə·mə sen'tór·ē }

prudent limit of endurance   The time during which an aircraft can remain airborne and still retain a given safety margin of fuel. { 'prüd·ənt 'lim·ət əv in'dür·əns }

P spot   One of a pair of sunspots that appears to precede or lead the other across the face of the sun, or whose magnetic polarity is that which is normally found in such a sunspot during that sunspot cycle and in the hemisphere of the sun. { 'pē ,spät }

Psyche   An asteroid with a diameter of about 127 miles (205 kilometers), mean distance from the sun of 2.923 astronomical units, and unusual surface composition. { 'sī·kē }

Ptolemaic system   The movements of the solar system according to Ptolemy; supposedly, the earth was a fixed center, with the sun and moon revolving about it in circular orbits; planets revolved in small circles (epicycles) whose centers revolved about the earth in larger circles (deferents). { ˌtäl·əˌmā·ik 'sis·təm }

Puck   A satellite of Uranus orbiting at a mean distance of 53,440 miles (86,010 kilometers) with a period of 18 hours 20 minutes, and with a diameter of about 96 miles (154 kilometers). { pək }

pulsar   A celestial radio source, emitting intense short bursts of radio emission; the periods of known pulsars range between 33 milliseconds and 3.75 seconds, and pulse durations range from 2 to about 150 milliseconds with longer-period pulsars generally having a longer pulse duration. { 'pəl,sär }

pulsating star   Variable star whose luminosity fluctuates as the star expands and contracts; the variation in brightness is thought to come from the periodic change of radiant energy to gravitational energy and back. { 'pəl,sād·iŋ 'stär }

pulsejet engine   A type of compressorless jet engine in which combustion occurs intermittently so that the engine is characterized by periodic surges of thrust; the inlet end of the engine is provided with a grid to which are attached flap valves; these can be sucked inward by a negative differential pressure to allow a regulated amount of air to flow inward to mix with the fuel. Also known as aeropulse engine. { 'pəls ,jet ,en·jən }

Puppis   A southern constellation; right ascension 8 hours, declination 40° south. Also known as Stern. { 'pəp·əs }

Puppis A   An extended, nonthermal radio source, the remnant of a supernova that exploded about 10,000 years ago, about 1.8 kiloparsecs (3.5 × 10¹⁶ miles or 5.6 × 10¹⁶ kilometers) from the earth. { 'pəp·əs 'ā }

pure Trojan group   The group of Trojan planets which lies near the Lagrangian point 60° behind Jupiter. Also known as Patroclus group. { 'pyùr 'trō·jən ,grüp }

pylon   A suspension device externally installed under the wing or fuselage of an aircraft; it is aerodynamically designed to fit the configuration of specific aircraft, thereby creating an insignificant amount of drag; it includes means of attaching to accommodate fuel tanks, bombs, rockets, torpedoes, rocket motors, or the like. { 'pīˌlän }

Pyxis   A southern constellation; right ascension 9 hours, declination 30° south. Also known as Malus. { 'pik·səs }

Q

Q magnitude   The magnitude of a celestial object based on observations in the infrared at a wavelength of 19.5 micrometers. { 'kyü ˌmag·nəˌtüd }

QSO   See quasar.

QSS   See quasi-stellar radio source.

Quadrantids   A meteor shower whose radiant-right ascension of 15 hours and declination of +48° is in the constellation Boötes; velocity is 27 miles (43 kilometers) per second, and the strength is medium. { kwä′dran·tidz }

quadrature   The right-angle physical alignment of the sun, moon, and earth. { 'kwä·drə·chər }

quark star   A hypothetical star so dense that the nucleons have lost their identity and stability is derived from degenerate quarks. { 'kwärk ˌstär }

quasar   Quasi-stellar astronomical object, often a radio source; all quasars have large red shifts; they have small optical diameter, but may have large radio diameter. Also known as quasi-stellar object (QSO). { 'kwāˌzär }

quasi-stellar object   See quasar. { ˈkwä·zē 'stel·ər 'äb·jekt }

quasi-stellar radio source   A quasar that emits a significant fraction of its energy at radio frequencies ranging from 30 megahertz to 100 gigahertz. Abbreviated QSS. { ˈkwä·zē ˈstel·ər 'rād·ē·ō ˌsȯrs }

quiescent prominence   A vertical sheet of cool gas that is suspended in the solar corona for a period of days to months. { kwē′es·ənt 'präm·ə·nəns }

quiet sun   The sun when it is free from unusual radio wave or thermal radiation such as that associated with sunspots. { 'kwī·ət 'sən }

quiet-sun noise   Electromagnetic noise originating in the sun at a time when there is little or no sunspot activity. { 'kwī·ət 'sən ˌnȯiz }

R

R.A. *See* right ascension.

rack A suspension device permanently fixed to an aircraft; it is designed for attaching, arming, and releasing one or more bombs; it may also be utilized to accommodate other items such as mines, rockets, torpedoes, fuel tanks, rescue equipment, sonobuoys, and flares. { rak }

radar astronomy The study of astronomical bodies and the earth's atmosphere by means of radar pulse techniques, including tracking of meteors and the reflection of radar pulses from the moon and the planets. { 'rā‚där ə'strän‚ə‚mē }

radiant **1.** A point on the celestial sphere through which pass the backward extensions of the trail of a meteor as observed at various locations, or the backward extensions of trails of a number of meteors traveling parallel to each other. **2.** A point on the celestial sphere toward which the stars in a moving cluster appear to travel. { 'rād‚ē‚ənt }

radiation-bounded nebula An emission nebula whose central star is not hot enough to ionize the entire cloud. { ‚rād‚ē'ā‚shən ¦baún‚dəd 'neb‚yə‚lə }

radiation era The period in the early universe, lasting from roughly 20 seconds to 10^5 years after the big bang, when photons dominated the universe. { ‚rād‚ē'ā‚shən ‚ir‚ə }

radiative braking Deceleration of a star's rotation due to emission of electromagnetic radiation. { 'rād‚ē‚ād‚iv 'brāk‚iŋ }

radiative equilibrium The energy transfer through a star by radiation, absorption, and reradiation at a rate such that each section of the star is maintained at the appropriate temperature. { 'rād‚ē‚ād‚iv ‚ē‚kwə'lib‚rē‚əm }

radio astronomy The study of celestial objects by measurement and analysis of their emitted electromagnetic radiation in the wavelength range from roughly 1 millimeter to 30 millimeters. { 'rād‚ē‚ō ə'strän‚ə‚mē }

radio galaxy A galaxy that is emitting much energy in radio frequencies often from regions devoid of visible matter. { 'rād‚ē‚ō 'gal‚ik‚sē }

radio meteor A meteor which has been detected by the reflection of a radio signal from the meteor trail of relatively high ion density (ion column); such an ion column is left behind a meteoroid when it reaches the region of the upper atmosphere between about 50 and 75 miles (80 and 120 kilometers), although occasionally radio meteors are detected at higher altitudes. { 'rād‚ē‚ō 'mēd‚ē‚ər }

radiometric magnitude A celestial body's magnitude as calculated from the total

radio nebula

amount of radiant energy of all the wavelengths that reach the earth's surface. { ˈrād·ē·ōˌme·trik 'mag·nəˌtüd }

radio nebula A nebula that emits nonthermal radio-frequency radiation; derives its luminosity from collisions with the surrounding interstellar medium, or from processes associated with the magnetic fields presumably involved within the nebula; examples are the network nebulae in Cygnus and NGC 443. { 'rād·ē·ō 'neb·yə·lə }

radio relay satellite See communications satellite. { 'rād·ē·ō 'rēˌlā ˌsad·əlˌīt }

radiosonde balloon A balloon used to carry a radiosonde aloft; it is considerably larger than a pilot balloon or a ceiling balloon. { 'rād·ē·ōˌsänd bəˌlün }

radio source A source of extragalactic or interstellar electromagnetic emission in radio wavelengths. { 'rād·ē·ō ˌsȯrs }

radio star A discrete celestial radio source. { 'rād·ē·ō ˌstär }

radio storm A prolonged period of disturbed emission or reception that lasts for periods of hours up to days. { 'rād·ē·ō ˌstȯrm }

radio sun The sun as defined by its electromagnetic radiation in the radio portion of the spectrum. { 'rād·ē·ō ˌsən }

radio tail object An extragalactic object that displays a strong tail or jet at radio frequencies. { 'rād·ē·ō ˌtāl ˌäb·jəkt }

radius vector A line joining the center of an orbiting body with the focus of its orbit located near its primary. { 'rād·ē·əs ˌvek·tər }

ram The forward motion of an air scoop or air inlet through the air. { ram }

Ram See Aries. { ram }

ramjet engine A type of jet engine with no mechanical compressor, consisting of a specially shaped tube or duct open at both ends, the air necessary for combustion being shoved into the duct and compressed by the forward motion of the engine; the air passes through a diffuser and is mixed with fuel and burned, the exhaust gases issuing in a jet from the rear opening. { 'ramˌjet ˌen·jən }

ramjet exhaust nozzle The discharge nozzle in a ramjet engine; hot gas is ejected rearward through this nozzle. { 'ramˌjet igˈzȯst ˌnäz·əl }

ramp weight The static weight of a mission aircraft determined by adding operating weight, payload, flight plan fuel load, and fuel required for ground turbine power unit, taxi, runup, and takeoff. { 'ramp ˌwāt }

ram rocket 1. A rocket motor mounted coaxially in the open front end of a ramjet, used to provide thrust at low speeds and to ignite the ramjet fuel. 2. The entire unit or power plant consisting of the ramjet and such a rocket. { 'ram ˌräk·ət }

range control The operation of an aircraft to obtain the optimum flying time. { 'rānj kənˌtrōl }

range control chart A graph kept in flight on which actual fuel consumption is plotted against distance flown for comparison with planned fuel consumption. { 'rānj kənˌtrōl ˌchärt }

156

Ra-Shalom An Aten asteroid that has a period of 0.759 year and an eccentricity of 0.436. { 'rä shə'lōm }

R association A grouping of stars in a reflection nebula. { 'är ə/sō·sē/ā·shən }

rate climb The climb of an aircraft to higher altitudes at a constant rate. { 'rāt /klīm }

rate descent An aircraft descent from higher altitudes at a constant rate. { 'rāt di/sent }

rate of approach The relative speed of two aircraft when the distance between them is decreasing. { 'rāt əv ə'prōch }

rate of climb Ascent of aircraft per unit time, usually expressed as feet per minute. { 'rāt əv 'klīm }

rate-of-climb indicator A device used to indicate changes in the vertical position of an aircraft by comparing the actual outside air pressure to a reference volume that lags the outside pressure because a calibrated restrictor imposes a lag-time constant to the reference pressure volume. Also known as rate-of-descent indicator; vertical speed indicator. { 'rāt əv 'klīm 'in·də/kād·ər }

rate of departure The relative speed of two aircraft when the distance between them is increasing. { 'rāt əv di'pär·chər }

rate-of-descent indicator See rate-of-climb indicator. { 'rāt əv di'sent 'in·də/kād·ər }

rate of return Aircraft relative to its base, either fixed or moving. { 'rāt əv ri'tərn }

rational horizon See celestial horizon. { 'rash·ən·əl hə'rīz·ən }

rato A rocket system providing additional thrust for takeoff of an aircraft. Derived from rocket-assisted takeoff. { 'rād·ō }

ray One of the broad streaks that radiate from some craters on the moon, especially Copernicus and Tycho; they consist of material of high reflectivity and are seen from earth best at full moon. { rā }

ray crater A large, relatively young lunar crater with visible rays. { 'rā /krād·ər }

ray system The bright streaks radiating outward from a lunar crater. { 'rā /sis·təm }

R Coronae Borealis star A rare type of irregular variable star which has long periods of maximum brightness followed by a sudden, unpredictable reduction in brightness of several magnitudes, and a slower, sometimes erratic return to the original brightness. { 'är kə/rō/nē /bȯr·ē'al·əs /stär }

reactant ratio The ratio of the weight flow of oxidizer to fuel in a rocket engine. { rē'ak·tənt ¦rā·shō }

reaction engine An engine that develops thrust by its reaction to a substance ejected from it; specifically, such an engine that ejects a jet or stream of gases created by the addition of energy to the gases in the engine. Also known as reaction motor. { rē'ak·shən /en·jən }

reaction motor See reaction engine. { rē'ak·shən /mōd·ər }

reaction propulsion Propulsion by means of reaction to a jet of gas or fluid projected

recession of galaxies

rearward, as by a jet engine, rocket engine, or rocket motor. { rē′ak·shən prə‚pəl· shən }

recession of galaxies The increase in the velocity of recession (red shift) of galaxies with distance from an observer on earth. { ri′sesh·ən əv ′gal·ik·sēz }

reconnaissance drone An uncrewed aircraft guided by remote control, with photographic or electronic equipment for providing information about an enemy or potential enemy. { ri′kän·ə·səns ‚drōn }

reconnaissance spacecraft A satellite put into orbit about the earth and containing electronic equipment designed to pick up and transmit back to earth information pertaining to activities such as military. { ri′kän·ə·səns ′spās‚kraft }

reconnection The rejoining of solar magnetic field lines that have been severed at a neutral region. { ‚rē·kə′nek·shən }

recovery 1. The procedure or action that obtains when the whole of a satellite, or a section, instrumentation package, or other part of a rocket vehicle, is retrieved after a launch. 2. The conversion of kinetic energy to potential energy, such as in the deceleration of air in the duct of a ramjet engine. Also known as ram recovery. 3. In flying, the action of a lifting vehicle returning to an equilibrium attitude after a nonequilibrium maneuver. { ri′kəv·ə·rē }

recovery area An area in which a satellite, satellite package, or spacecraft is recovered after reentry. { ri′kəv·ə·rē ‚er·ē·ə }

recovery capsule A space capsule designed to be recovered after reentry. { ri′kəv·ə· rē ‚kap·səl }

recovery package A package attached to a reentry or other body designed for recovery, containing devices intended to locate the body after impact. { ri′kəv·ə·rē ′pak·ij }

recurrent nova A star that has more than one novalike outburst. { ri′kər·ənt ′nō·və }

recycle 1. To stop the count in a countdown and to return to an earlier point. 2. To give a rocket or other object a completely new checkout. { rē′sī·kəl }

red dwarf star A red star of low luminosity, so designated by E. Hertzsprung; dwarf stars are commonly those main-sequence stars fainter than an absolute magnitude of +1, and red dwarfs are the faintest and coolest of the dwarfs. { ′red ‚dwȯrf ′stär }

red giant star A star whose evolution has progressed to the point where hydrogen core burning has been completed, the helium core has become denser and hotter than originally, and the envelope has expanded to perhaps 100 times its initial size. { ′red ‚jī·ənt ′stär }

red giant tip The upper tip of the red giant branch in the Hertzsprung-Russell diagram that represents stars undergoing a flash process. { ′red ‚jī·ənt ′tip }

redshift A systematic displacement toward longer wavelengths of lines in the spectra of distant galaxies and also of the continuous portion of the spectrum; increases with distance from the observer. Also known as Hubble effect. { ′red‚shift }

Red Spot A semipermanent marking of the planet Jupiter; some fluctuations in visibility exist; it does not rotate uniformly with the planet, indicating that it is a disturbance of Jupiter's atmosphere. { ′red ‚spät }

158

reduced proper motion   The proper motion of a star expressed as a linear velocity. { ri'düst 'präp·ər 'mō·shən }

reduction of star places   The computation of mean places of stars from observations of their apparent places. { ri'dək·shən əv 'stär ˌplās·əz }

reduction to the sun   In the spectroscopic determination of a star's radial motion referred to the sun, the correction that is needed to be applied to the observed radial velocity of the star to compensate for the motion of the earth with respect to the sun. { ri'dək·shən tü thə 'sən }

red white-dwarf star   A star type that is considered an anomaly; these are objects 10,000 times fainter than the sun, with surface temperature below 4000 K so that surface radiation has cooled the star at an unexpectedly rapid rate. { 'red 'wīt ¦dwȯrf ˌstär }

reentry   The event when a spacecraft or other object comes back into the sensible atmosphere after being in space. { rē'en·trē }

reentry angle   That angle of the reentry body trajectory and the sensible atmosphere at which the body reenters the atmosphere. { rē'en·trē ˌaŋ·gəl }

reentry body   That part of a space vehicle that reenters the atmosphere after flight above the sensible atmosphere. { rē'en·trē ˌbäd·ē }

reentry nose cone   A nose cone designed especially for reentry, consists of one or more chambers protected by a heat sink. { rē'en·trē 'nōz ˌkōn }

reentry trajectory   That part of a rocket's trajectory that begins at reentry and ends at the target or at the surface. { rē'en·trē trəˌjek·trē }

reentry vehicle   Any payload-carrying vehicle designed to leave the sensible atmosphere and then return through it to earth. { rē'en·trē ˌvē·ə·kəl }

reentry window   The area, at the limits of the earth's atmosphere, through which a spacecraft in a given trajectory can pass to accomplish a successful reentry for a landing in a desired region. { rē'en·trē ˌwin·dō }

reflection nebula   A type of bright diffuse nebula composed mainly of cosmic dust; it is visible because of starlight from nearby stars or nebula stars that is scattered by the dust particles. { ri'flek·shən ˌneb·yə·lə }

reflector satellite   Satellite so designed that radio or other waves bounce off its surface. { ri'flek·tər ˌsad·əlˌīt }

RE galaxy   A type of ring galaxy that consists of a single, relatively empty, ringlike structure, without any prominent condensation or nucleus. { ¦rē'ē ˌgal·ik·sē }

regenerative engine   1. A jet or rocket engine that utilizes the heat of combustion to preheat air or fuel entering the combustion chamber. 2. Specifically, to a type of rocket engine in which one of the propellants is used to cool the engine by passing through a jacket prior to combustion. { rē'jen·rəd·iv 'en·jən }

regression of nodes   The westward movement of the nodes of the moon's orbit; one cycle is completed in about 18.6 years. { ri'gresh·ən əv 'nōdz }

regular cluster   A galaxy cluster that shows a smooth, centrally concentrated distribution of galaxies and an overall symmetric shape. { 'reg·yə·lər 'kləs·tər }

regular variable star   A variable star whose variation in brightness is repeated with a

Regulus

uniform period and light curve from one cycle to the next. { 'reg·yə·lər 'ver·ē·ə· bal 'stär }

Regulus A star of stellar magnitude 1.34, about 67 light-years from the sun, spectral classification B8, in the constellation Leo; the star α Leonis. Also known as Little Ruler. { 'reg·yə·ləs }

relative luminosity factor *See* luminosity function. { 'rel·əd·iv ˌlü·mə'näs·əd·ē ˌfak· tər }

relative orbit The closed path described by the apparent position of the fainter member of a binary system relative to the brighter member. { 'rel·əd·iv 'ȯr·bət }

relative sunspot number A measure of sunspot activity, computed from the formula R = k(10g + f), where R is the relative sunspot number, f the number of individual spots, g the number of groups of spots, and k a factor that varies with the observer (his or her personal equation), the seeing, and the observatory (location and instrumentation). Also known as sunspot number; sunspot relative number; Wolf number; Wolf-Wolfer number; Zurich number. { 'rel·əd·iv 'sən·ˌspät ˌnəm·bər }

relay satellite *See* communications satellite. { 'rē·ˌlā ˌsad·əl·ˌīt }

release altitude Altitude of an aircraft above the ground at the time of release of bombs, rockets, missiles, tow targets, and so forth. { ri'lēs ˌal·tə·ˌtüd }

remotely piloted vehicle A robot aircraft, controlled over a two-wave radio link from a ground station or mother aircraft that can be hundreds of miles away; electronic guidance is generally supplemented by remote control television cameras feeding monitor receivers at the control station. Abbreviated RPV. { ri'mōt·lē ¦pī·ləd· əd 'vē·ə·kəl }

rendezvous **1.** The event of two or more objects meeting with zero relative velocity at a preconceived time and place. **2.** The point in space at which such an event takes place, or is to take place. { 'rän·də·ˌvü }

research rocket A rocket-propelled vehicle used to collect scientific data. { ri'sərch ˌräk·ət }

réseau A grid that is photographed by a separate exposure on the same plate as images of celestial objects. { rā'zō }

reserve aircraft Those aircraft which have been accumulated in excess of immediate needs for active aircraft and are retained in the inventory against possible future needs. { ri'zərv 'er·ˌkraft }

resonant jet A pulsejet engine, exhibiting intensification of power under the rhythm of explosions and compression waves within the engine. { 'res·ən·ənt 'jet }

restart The act of firing a stage of a rocket after a previous powered flight. { 'rē·ˌstärt }

restricted propellant A solid propellant having only a portion of its surface exposed for burning while the other surfaces are covered by an inhibitor. { ri'strik·təd prə'pel·ənt }

restricted proper motion The rate of change of a star's apparent position relative to surrounding stars, corrected for precession, nutation, and aberration. { ri'strik· təd 'präp·ər 'mō·shən }

Reticulum A southern constellation, right ascension 4 hours, declination 60° south. Also known as Net. { rə′tik·yə·ləm }

Reticulum system A globular cluster or dwarf galaxy near the Large Magellanic Cloud. { ri′tik·yə·ləm ˌsis·təm }

retrofire time The computed starting time and duration of firing of retrorockets to decrease the speed of a recovery capsule and make it reenter the earth's atmosphere at the correct point for a planned landing. { ′re·trōˌfīr ˌtīm }

retrograde motion 1. An apparent backward motion of a planet among the stars resulting from the observation of the planet from the planet earth which is also revolving about the sun at a different velocity. Also known as retrogression. 2. See retrograde orbit. { ′re·trəˌgrād ′mō·shən }

retrograde orbit Motion in an orbit opposite to the usual orbital direction of celestial bodies within a given system; specifically, of a satellite, motion in a direction opposite to the direction of rotation of the primary. Also known as retrograde motion. { ′re·trəˌgrād ′ȯr·bət }

retrogression See retrograde motion. { ˌre·trə′gresh·ən }

retrorocket A rocket fitted on or in a spacecraft, satellite, or the like to produce thrust opposed to forward motion. Also known as braking rocket. { ¦re·trō′räk·ət }

reversal speed The speed of an aircraft above which the aeroelastic loads will exceed the control surface loading of a given flight control system; the resultant load will act in the reverse direction from the control surface loading, causing the control system to act in a direction opposite to that desired. { ri′vər·səl ˌspēd }

reversing layer A layer of relatively cool gas forming the lower part of the sun's chromosphere, just above the photosphere, that gives rise to absorption lines in the sun's spectrum. { ri′vərs·iŋ ˌlā·ər }

R galaxy A galaxy that displays rotational symmetry but lacks a clearly defined rotational or elliptical structure. { ′är ˌgal·ik·sē }

RGU system A system for obtaining a complete assessment of a star's magnitude, based on measurements of the star's brightness when viewed through red, green, and ultraviolet filters. { ¦är¦jē′yü ˌsis·təm }

Rhea A satellite of Saturn, with estimated diameter of 740 miles (1200 kilometers). { ′rē·ə }

rib A transverse structural member that gives cross-sectional shape and strength to a portion of an airfoil. { rib }

ribbon parachute A type of parachute having a canopy consisting of an arrangement of closely spaced tapes; this parachute has high porosity with attendant stability and slight opening shock. { ′rib·ən ′par·əˌshüt }

rice grains Bright patches that stand out against the darker background of the surface of the sun; they are short-lived, and the pattern changes in a matter of minutes. { ′rīs ˌgrānz }

rich cluster A galaxy cluster that has relatively many member galaxies. { ¦rich ¦kləs·tər }

161

Rigel

Rigel   A multiple star of stellar magnitude 0.08, 650 light-years from the sun, spectral classification B8-Ia, in the constellation Orion; the star β Orionis. { rī·jəl }

rigging   The shroud lines attached to a parachute. { 'rig·iŋ }

right ascension   A celestial coordinate; the angular distance taken along the celestial equator from the vernal equinox eastward to the hour circle of a given celestial body. Abbreviated R.A. { 'rīt ə'sen·chən }

right sphere   The appearance of the celestial sphere as seen by an observer at the earth's equator. { 'rīt 'sfir }

rigidity   The ratio of the momentum of a cosmic-ray particle to its electric charge, in units of the electron charge. { ri'jid·əd·ē }

Rigil Kent   See Alpha Centauri. { 'rī·jəl 'kent }

rill   A crooked, narrow crack on the moon's surface; may be a kilometer or more in width and a few to several hundred kilometers in length. Also spelled rille. { ril }

rill crater   A lunar crater that forms part of a rill. { 'ril ˌkrād·ər }

rille   See rill. { ril }

ring A   The bright outer ring of Saturn, having an outside diameter of 169,000 miles (272,000 kilometers) and an inner diameter of 150,000 miles (242,000 kilometers). { 'riŋ 'ā }

ring B   The brightest of Saturn's rings, with an outer diameter of 146,000 miles (235,000 kilometers) and an inner diameter of 114,000 miles (183,000 kilometers). { 'riŋ 'bē }

ring C   A faint ring of Saturn inside ring B having an outer diameter of 114,000 miles (183,000 kilometers) and an inner diameter of 91,000 miles (146,000 kilometers). Also known as crepe ring. { 'riŋ 'sē }

ring D   A very faint ring of Saturn that is fainter than ring C and lies between ring C and the planet's surface. { 'riŋ 'dē }

ring E   A diffuse, faint outer ring of Saturn that extends from inside the orbit of Enceladus at about 112,000 miles (181,000 kilometers) from Saturn to outside the orbit of Dione at about 300,000 miles (480,000 kilometers) from the planet. { 'riŋ 'ē }

ring F   A narrow ring of Saturn just outside ring A that consists of more than five separate strands and is held in place by two small satellites. { 'riŋ 'ef }

ring galaxy   A class of galaxy whose ringlike structure has clumps of ionized hydrogen clouds on its periphery, may have a nucleus of stars, and is usually accompanied by a small galaxy; probably formed when a small galaxy crashes through the disk of a spiral galaxy. { 'riŋ ˌgal·ik·sē }

Ring Nebula   A nebula in the summer constellation Lyra; it is an example of the planetary type of gaseous nebulae. { 'riŋ 'neb·yə·lə }

ring plain   A lunar crater of exceptionally large diameter and with a relatively smooth interior. { 'riŋ ˌplān }

rings of Saturn   Circular rings that encircle the planet Saturn at its equator; there are four main regions to the ring system; theory and observations indicate that the rings are composed of separate particles which move independently in the four series of circular coplanar orbits. { 'riŋz əv 'säd·ərn }

ringwall structure A lunar crater whose center lies on the wall, or on the line of the wall, of a larger crater. { 'riŋ‚wól ‚strək·chər }

rip panel A part of a crewed free balloon; it is the panel to which the ripcord is attached and extends about one-fourth to one-fifth of the circumference of the balloon along one of its meridians; it is torn open when the ripcord is pulled so that all the gas in the balloon escapes. { 'rip ‚pan·əl }

rise Of a celestial body, to cross the visible horizon while ascending. { rīz }

River Po *See* Eridanus. { 'riv·ər 'pō }

RK galaxy A type of ring galaxy which consists of a ringlike structure with a large, bright condensation or knot within the ring itself. { ¦är'kā ‚gal·ik·sē }

R magnitude The wavelength of a celestial object based on observations at a wavelength of 680 nanometers. { 'är ‚mag·nə‚tüd }

R Monocerotis An irregular variable star at the tip of the small fan-shaped emission nebula NGC 2261. { 'är ‚män·ə'ser·əd·əs }

RN galaxy A type of ring galaxy which consists of a ringlike structure with a nucleus somewhere within it, the nucleus being somewhat like those seen in ordinary spiral galaxies but typically lying off the center of the ring. { ¦är'en ‚gal·ik·sē }

Roche's limit The limiting distance below which a satellite orbiting a celestial body would be disrupted by the tidal forces generated by the gravitational attraction of the primary; the distance depends on the relative densities of the bodies and on the orbit of the satellite; it is computed by $R = 2.45(Lr)$, where L is a factor that depends on the relative densities of the satellite and the body, R is the radius of the satellite's orbit measured from the center of the primary body, and r is the radius of the primary body; if the satellite and the body have the same density, the relationship is $R = 2.45r$. { 'rō·shəz ‚lim·ət }

rockair A high-altitude sounding system consisting of a small solid-propellant research rocket carried aloft by an aircraft; the rocket is fired while the aircraft is in vertical ascent. { 'räk‚er }

rocket **1.** Any kind of jet propulsion capable of operating independently of the atmosphere. **2.** A complete vehicle driven by such a propulsive system. { 'räk·ət }

rocket airplane An airplane using a rocket or rockets for its chief or only propulsion. { 'räk·ət 'er‚plān }

rocket assist An assist in thrust given an airplane or missile by use of a rocket motor or rocket engine during flight or during takeoff. { 'räk·ət ə‚sist }

rocket-assisted takeoff *See* rato. { 'räk·ət ə¦sis·təd 'tāk‚óf }

rocket astronomy The discipline comprising measurements of the electromagnetic radiation from the sun, planets, stars, and other bodies, of wavelengths that are almost completely absorbed below the 150-mile (250-kilometer) level, by using a rocket to carry instruments above 150 miles to measure these phenomena. { 'räk·ət ə‚strän·ə·mē }

rocket chamber A chamber for the combustion of fuel in a rocket; in particular, that section of the rocket engine in which combustion of propellants takes place. { 'räk·ət ˌchäm·bər }

rocket engine   A reaction engine that contains within itself, or carries along with itself, all the substances necessary for its operation or for the consumption or combustion of its fuel, not requiring intake of any outside substance and hence capable of operation in outer space. Also known as rocket motor. { 'räk·ət ˌen·jən }

rocket igniter   An igniter for the propellant in a rocket. { 'räk·ət igˌnīd·ər }

rocket launcher   A device for launching a rocket, wheel-mounted, motorized, or fixed for use on the ground, rocket launchers are mounted on aircraft, as under the wings, or are installed below or on the decks of ships. { 'räk·ət ˌlón·chər }

rocket motor   See rocket engine. { 'räk·ət ˌmōd·ər }

rocket nose section   The extreme forward portion of a rocket, designed to contain instrumentation, spotting charges, fusing or arming devices, and the like, but does not contain the payload. { 'räk·ət 'nōz ˌsek·shən }

rocket propulsion   Reaction propulsion by a rocket engine. { 'räk·ət proˌpəl·shən }

rocket ramjet   A ramjet engine having a rocket mounted within the ramjet duct, the rocket being used to bring the ramjet up to the necessary operating speed. Also known as ducted rocket. { 'räk·ət 'ramˌjet }

rocketry   1. The science or study of rockets, embracing theory, research, development, and experimentation. 2. The art and science of using rockets, especially rocket ammunition. { 'räk·ə·trē }

rocket sled   A sled that runs on a rail or rails and is accelerated to high velocities by a rocket engine; the sled is used in determining G tolerances and for developing crash survival techniques. { 'räk·ət ˌsled }

rocket-sled testing   A method of subjecting structures and devices to high accelerations or decelerations and aerodynamic flow phenomena under controlled conditions; the test object is mounted on a sled chassis running on precision steel rails and accelerated by rockets or decelerated by water scoops. { 'räk·ət ˈsled ˌtest·iŋ }

rocket staging   The use of successive rocket sections or stages, each having its own engine or engines; each stage is a complete rocket vehicle in itself. { 'räk·ət ˌstāj·iŋ }

rocket thrust   The thrust of a rocket engine. { 'räk·ət ˌthrəst }

rocket tube   1. A launching tube for rockets. 2. A tube or nozzle through which rocket gases are ejected. { 'räk·ət ˌtüb }

rockoon   A high-altitude sounding system consisting of a small solid-propellant research rocket carried aloft by a large plastic balloon. { rä'kün }

Rogallo wing   A glider folded inside a spacecraft; to be deployed during the spacecraft's reentry like a parachute, gliding the spacecraft to a landing. { rō'gäl·ō ˌwiŋ }

Rood-Sastry classification   A classification scheme for galaxy clusters that differentiates between a number of basic cluster morphologies. { ˈrüd ˈsas·trē ˌklas·ə·fə'kā·shən }

Rosalind   A satellite of Uranus orbiting at a mean distance of 43,450 miles (69,930 kilometers) with a period of 13 hours 26 minutes, and with a diameter of about 36 miles (58 kilometers). { 'räz·lind }

Rosette Nebula   A nebula classified as NGC 2237; this nebula contains numerous small dense clouds that have been photographed with large telescopes. { rō'zet 'neb·yə·lə }

rotor   An assembly of blades designed as airfoils that are attached to a helicopter or similar aircraft and rapidly rotated to provide both lift and thrust. { 'rōd·ər }

rough air   An aviation term for turbulence encountered in flight. { 'rəf 'er }

rough burning   Pressure fluctuations frequently observed at the onset of burning and at the combustion limits of a ramjet or rocket. { 'rəf 'bərn·iŋ }

RPV   *See* remotely piloted vehicle.

RR Lyrae stars   Pulsating variable stars with a period of 0.05-1.2 days in the halo population of the Milky Way Galaxy; color is white, and they are mostly stars of spectral class A. Also known as cluster cepheids; cluster variables. { ¦är¦är 'lī·rē ˌstärz }

RS Canum Venaticorum stars   A group of peculiar binary stars with orbital periods between 1 and 14 days, in which the cores of the H and K lines of singly ionized calcium display strong emission, and the hotter of the two stars is of spectral type F or G. { ¦är¦es ¦kan·ən vəˌnad·a¦kór·əm ˌstärz }

R star   A star of spectral type R, having spectral characteristics similar to those of types G and K, except that molecular bands of molecular carbon (C_2), cyanogen radical (CN), and methyldadyne (CH) are prominent. { 'är ˌstär }

Rule   *See* Norma. { 'rül }

runaway star   A star of spectral type O or early B with an unusually high spatial velocity; believed to result from a supernova explosion in a close binary system. { 'rən·ə'wā 'stär }

rupture disk   *See* burst disk. { 'rəp·chər ˌdisk }

Russell diagram   *See* Hertzsprung-Russell diagram. { 'rəs·əl ˌdī·əˌgram }

Russell mixture   A mixture of elements with the same relative proportions as are found in the sun and other stars. { 'rəs·əl ˌmiks·chər }

Russell-Vogt theorem   *See* Vogt-Russell theorem. { 'rəs·əl 'vót 'thir·əm }

RV Tauri stars   A class of stars; they are long-period pulsating variable types with periods from about 50 to 150 days; otherwise they are like the shorter-period W Virginis stars; they are found in both the Milky Way Galaxy and the globular clusters. { ¦är¦vē 'tór·ē ˌstärz }

RW Aurigae stars   A class of stars that are variable, and whose light variations are rapid and irregular. { ¦är¦dəb·əlˌyü ó'rī·gē ˌstärz }

S

Sagitta A small constellation; right ascension 20 hours, declination 10° north. Also known as Arrow. { sə′jid·ə }

Sagittarius A constellation whose major portion lies in the Milky Way; right ascension 19 hours, declination 25° south. Also known as Archer. { ˌsaj·ə′ter·ē·əs }

Sagittarius A An intense radio source in the constellation Sagittarius, apparently comprising a gaseous envelope surrounding a small dense core that is believed to constitute the center of the Milky Way Galaxy. { ˌsaj·ə′ter·ē·əs ′ā }

Sagittarius arm A spiral arm of the Milky Way Galaxy that lies between the sun and the galactic center in the direction of the constellation Sagittarius. { ˌsaj·ə′ter·ē·əs ′ärm }

Sagittarius B2 The richest molecular radio source in the Galaxy, located near the galactic center and consisting of a massive, dense complex of at least seven HII regions and molecular clouds. { ˌsaj·ə′ter·ē·əs ¦bē′tü }

Sagittarius star cloud A large star cloud within the Milky Way; its extension is about 1500 to 6000 light-years (1.42 × 10^{19} to 5.68 × 10^{19} meters) from the sun. { ˌsaj·ə′ter·ē·əs ′stär ˌklaúd }

Sail See Vela. { sāl }

salpeter process See three-alpha process. { sal′pēd·ər ˌpräs·əs }

saros A cycle of time after which the centers of the sun and moon, and the nodes of the moon's orbit return to the same relative position; this period is 18 years 11⅓ days, or 18 years 10⅓ days if 5 rather than 4 leap years are included. { ′saˌräs }

SAS See stability augmentation system.

Sa spiral A class of spiral galaxy, including those galaxies that have the largest center sections and closely wound galactic arms. { ¦es¦ā ′spī·rəl }

satellite 1. A small, solid body moving in an orbit around a planet; the moon is a satellite of earth. 2. See artificial satellite. { ′sad·əlˌīt }

satellite astronomy The study of astronomical objects by using detectors mounted on earth-orbiting satellites or deep-space probes; allows observations that are not obstructed by the earth's atmosphere. { ′sad·əlˌīt ə′strän·ə·mē }

satellite tracking Determination of the positions and velocities of satellites through radio and optical means. { ′sad·əlˌīt ˌtrak·iŋ }

satelloid A vehicle that revolves about the earth or other celestial body, but at such altitudes as to require sustaining thrust to balance drag. { 'sad·əl‚óid }

Saturn 1. One of the very large launch vehicles built primarily for the Apollo program; begun by Army Ordnance but turned over to the National Aeronautics and Space Administration for the manned space flight program to the moon. 2. The second largest planet in the solar system (mass is 95.3 compared to earth's 1) and the sixth in the order of distance to the sun; it is visible to the naked eye as a yellowish first-magnitude star except during short periods near its conjunction with the sun; it is surrounded by a series of rings. { 'sad·ərn }

saturnicentric coordinates Coordinates that indicate the position of a point on the surface of Saturn, determined by the direction of a line joining the center of Saturn to the point. { sə‚tər·nə‚sen·trik kō'órd·ən‚əts }

saturnigraphic coordinates Coordinates that indicate the position of a point on the surface of Saturn, determined by the direction of a line perpendicular to the mean surface at the point. { sə‚tər·nə‚graf·ik kō'órd·ən‚əts }

Saturn Nebula A double-ring planetary nebula in the constellation Aquarius, about 700 parsecs away. { 'sa‚tərn ‚neb·yə·lə }

saucer crater A very shallow type of bowl crater on the moon. { 'sós·ər ‚krād·ər }

Sb spiral galaxy A class of spiral galaxy characterized by smaller central bodies and more open, larger arms. { ‚es‚bē 'spī·rəl 'gal·ik·sē }

scale effect The necessary corrections applied to measurements of a model in a wind tunnel to ascertain corresponding values for a full-sized object. { 'skāl i‚fekt }

Scheat A red giant, irregular, variable star, in the constellation Pegasus. { shē'at }

Schönberg-Chandrasekhar limit See Chandrasekhar-Schönberg limit. { 'shərn‚bərg ‚chan·drə'sā·kər ‚lim·ət }

Schroter effect The occurrence of the dichotomy of Venus earlier than theoretically predicted when it is waning, and later than theoretically predicted when it is waxing. { 'shrōd·ər i‚fekt }

Schwarzschild criterion A criterion for determining the stability of a stellar medium against convective motion, according to which convection takes place when the temperature gradient is greater than the gradient that would exist if the medium were adiabatic. { 'shvärts‚shilt krī‚tir·ē·ən }

Schwassman-Wachmann comet A variable cometlike asteroid whose period is 16 years; its orbit is very nearly circular and lies between the orbits of Saturn and Jupiter. { 'shväs‚män 'vak‚män ‚käm·ət }

Sco-Cen association An association of very young stars within the Gould belt whose brightest member is Antares. { 'skō 'sen ə‚sō·sē‚ā·shən }

Scorpion See Scorpius. { 'skór·pē·ən }

Scorpio X-1 The most intense celestial source of x-rays known, associated with a highly variable radio source and a variable optical source, ranging from the twelfth to fourteenth magnitude. Abbreviated Sco X-1. { 'skór·pē·ō ‚eks'wən }

Scorpius A southern constellation, right ascension 16 hours, declination 40° south; the bright-red star Antares is located in it. Also known as Scorpion. { 'skór·pē·əs }

Scout A four-stage all-solid-propellant rocket, used as a space probe and orbital test vehicle; first launched July 1, 1960, with a 150-pound (68-kilogram) payload. { skaut }

Sco X-1 *See* Scorpio X-1.

scramble To take off as quickly as possible (usually followed by course and altitude instructions). { 'skram·bəl }

scramjet Essentially a ramjet engine, intended for flight at hypersonic speeds. Derived from supersonic combustion ramjet. { 'skram,jet }

screaming A form of combustion instability, especially in a liquid-propellant rocket engine, of relatively high frequency, characterized by a high-pitched noise. { 'skrēm·iŋ }

screeching A form of combustion instability, especially in an afterburner, of relatively high frequency, characterized by a harsh, shrill noise. { 'skrēch·iŋ }

scrub To cancel a scheduled firing, either before or during countdown. { skrəb }

Sc spiral galaxy A class of spiral galaxy characterized by spirals with the largest and most loosely coiled arms and the smallest central portion. { ¦es¦sē ¦spī·rəl 'gal·ik·sē }

SC star A star of a type intermediate between carbon stars and S stars. { ¦es¦sē ,stär }

Sculptor A southern constellation, right ascension 0 hours, declination 30° south. Also known as Sculptor's Apparatus; Workshop. { 'skəlp·tər }

Sculptor Group One of the nearest groups of galaxies beyond the Local Group, consisting of about five large galaxies near the south galactic pole. { 'skəlp·tər ,grüp }

Sculptor's Apparatus *See* Sculptor. { 'skəlp·tərz ,ap·ə 'rad·əs }

Sculptor system A dwarf, elliptical galaxy in the Local Group, about 270,000 light years away. { 'skəlp·tər ,sis·təm }

Scutum A southern constellation, right ascension 19 hours, declination 10° south. Also known as Shield. { 'sküd·əm }

sealed cabin The occupied space of an aircraft or spacecraft characterized by walls which do not allow gaseous exchange between the inner atmosphere and its surrounding atmosphere, and containing its own mechanisms for maintenance of the inside atmosphere. { 'sēld 'kab·ən }

seaplane An airplane that takes off from and alights on the water; it is supported on the water by pontoons, or floats, or by a hull which is a specially designed fuselage. Also known as airboat. { 'sē,plān }

sea rim The apparent horizon as actually observed at sea. { 'sē ,rim }

second pilot A pilot, not necessarily qualified on type, who is responsible for assisting the first pilot to fly the aircraft and is authorized as second pilot. { 'sek·ənd 'pī·lət }

sector boundary The rapid transition from one polarity to another in the interplanetary magnetic field. { 'sek·tər ,baun·drē }

sector structure   The polarity pattern of the interplanetary magnetic field observed during a solar rotation. { 'sek·tər ˌstrək·chər }

secular acceleration   An apparent gradual acceleration of the moon's motion in its orbit, as measured relative to mean solar time. { 'sek·yə·lər akˌsel·ə'rā·shən }

secular parallax   An apparent angular displacement of a star, resulting from the sun's motion. { 'sek·yə·lər 'par·əˌlaks }

secular perturbations   Changes in the orbit of a planet, or of a satellite, that operates in extremely long cycles. { 'sek·yə·lər ˌpər·dər'bā·shənz }

secular variable   A star whose brightness appears to have slowly lessened or increased over a time period of centuries. { 'sek·yə·lər 'ver·ē·ə·bəl }

secular variation   A perturbation of the moon's motion caused by variations in the effect of the sun's gravitational attraction on the earth and moon as their relative distances from the sun vary during the synodic month. { 'sek·yə·lər ˌver·ē'ā·shən }

seed nuclei   Nuclei from which other nuclei are synthesized in stars. { 'sēd ˌnü·klēˌī }

seeing   The clarity and steadiness of an image of a star in a telescope. { 'sē·iŋ }

selected areas   See Kapetyn selected areas. { si'lek·təd 'er·ē·əz }

selenocentric   Pertaining to the moon's center. { səˌlē·nō'sen·trik }

selenodesy   The branch of applied mathematics that determines, by observation and measurement, the exact positions of points on the moon's surface, as well as the shape and size of the moon. { səˌlē·nəˌdes·ē }

selenodetic   Of, or pertaining to, or determined by selenodesy. { səˌlē·nəˌded·ik }

selenofault   A geological fault in the lunar surface. { sə'lē·nəˌfolt }

selenographic coordinates   A coordinate system for specifying positions on the moon's surface relative to the moon's center, consisting of selenographic latitude and longitude, or of a cartesian coordinate system. { səˌlē·nəˌgraf·ik kō'ord·ən·əts }

selenographic latitude   The angular distance, measured along a meridian, between a point on the moon's surface and the moon's equator. { səˌlē·nəˌgraf·ik 'lad·əˌtüd }

selenographic longitude   The angular distance, measured along the moon's equator, between the meridian passing through a point on the moon's surface and the first lunar meridian. { səˌlē·nəˌgraf·ik 'län·jəˌtüd }

selenography   Studies pertaining to the physical geography of the moon; specifically, referring to positions on the moon measured in latitude from the moon's equator and in longitude from a reference meridian. { ˌsel·ə·näg·rə·fē }

selenology   A branch of astronomy that treats of the moon, including such attributes as magnitude, motion and constitution. Also known as lunar geology. { ˌsel·ə'näl·ə·jē }

selenomorphology   The study of landforms on the moon, including their origin, evolution, and distribution. { sə'lē·nō·mor'fäl·ə·jē }

semidetached binary   A binary system whose secondary member fills its Roche lobe but whose primary member does not. { ˌsem·i·di'tacht 'bīˌner·ē }

semidiameter Measured at the observer, half the angle subtended by the visible disk of a celestial body. { ˈsem·i·dīʹam·əd·ər }

semidiurnal Having a period of, occurring in, or related to approximately half a day. { ˈsem·i·dīʹərn·əl }

semimonocoque A fuselage structure in which longitudinal members (stringers) as well as rings or frames which run circumferentially around the fuselage reinforce the skin and help carry the stress. Also known as stiffened-shell fuselage. { ˈsem·iʹmän·əˌkäk }

semiregular variables Variable red giant stars whose variation in brightness is repeated, but whose period and light curve may vary considerably from one cycle to the next; they have absolute magnitude of about 0 or −1 and quasi-periods of from about 40 to 150 days. { ˈsem·iʹreg·yə·lər ʹver·ē·ə·bəlz }

sensible horizon That circle of the celestial sphere formed by the intersection of the celestial sphere and a plane through any point, such as the eye of an observer, and perpendicular to the zenith-nadir line. { ʹsen·sə·bəl həʹrīz·ən }

separation The action of a fallaway section or companion body as it casts off from the remaining body of a vehicle, or the action of the remaining body as it leaves a fallaway section behind it. { ˌsep·əʹrā·shən }

Serpens A constellation, right ascension 17 hours, declination 0°. Also known as Serpent. { ʹsərˌpenz }

Serpent See Serpens. { ʹsər·pənt }

service ceiling The height at which, under standard atmospheric conditions, an aircraft is unable to climb faster than a specified rate (100 feet or 30 meters per minute in the United States, Great Britain, and Canada). { ʹsər·vəs ˌsēl·iŋ }

set Of a celestial body, to cross the visible western horizon while descending. { set }

Sextans A constellation in the southern hemisphere, right ascension 10 hours, declination 0°. Also known as Sextant. { ʹsekˌstanz }

Sextant See Sextans. { ʹsek·stənt }

sextile aspect The position of two celestial bodies when they are 60° apart. { ʹsek·ˌstīl ʹasˌpekt }

Seyfert galaxy A galaxy that has a small, bright nucleus from which violent explosions may occur. { ʹzī·fərt ˌgal·ik·sē }

Seyfert's Sextet A compact collection of galaxies that surrounds the galaxy NGC 6027 and has both spiral and irregular members, most of which interact with each other. { ʹzī·fərts seksʹtet }

shadow bands Rippling bands of shadow that appear on every white surface of flat terrestrial objects a few minutes before the total eclipse of the sun. { ʹshad·ō ˌbanz }

Shahbazian objects Compact collections of the order of 10 galaxies. { shəʹbä·zē·ən ˌäb·jeks }

Shaula A blue-white subgiant star of stellar magnitude 1.7, spectral classification B2-IV, in the constellation Scorpius; the star λ Scorpii. { ʹshaủ·lə }

171

SHED

SHED See solar heat exchanger drive. { shed }

shell star A type of star which is believed to be surrounded by a tenuous envelope of gas, as indicated by bright emission lines in its spectrum. { 'shel ˌstär }

shepherding satellite A satellite that helps to hold in place a given ring of a planet. { ˈshep·ərd·iŋ 'sad·əlˌīt }

Shield See Scutum. { shēld }

Ship See Argo. { ship }

shock strut The primary working part of any landing gear, which supplies the force as the airplane sinks toward the ground, turning the flight path from one intersecting the ground to one parallel to the ground. { 'shäk ˌstrət }

shooting star A small meteor that has the brief appearance of a darting, starlike object. { 'shüd·iŋ 'stär }

short-baseline system A trajectory measuring system using a baseline the length of which is very small compared with the distance of the object being tracked. { 'shȯrt ˈbāsˌlīn ˌsis·təm }

short-period comet A comet whose period is short enough for observations at two or more apparitions to be interrelated; usually taken to be a comet whose period is shorter than 200 years. { 'shȯrt ˈpir·ē·əd 'käm·ət }

short takeoff and landing The ability of an aircraft to clear a 50-foot (15-meter) obstacle within 1500 feet (450 meters) of commencing takeoff, or in landing, to stop within 1500 feet after passing over a 50-foot obstacle. Abbreviated STOL. { 'shȯrt 'tākˌȯf ən 'land·iŋ }

shot An act or instance of firing a rocket, especially from the earth's surface. { shät }

shower meteor A meteor whose direction of arrival is approximately parallel to others belonging to the same meteor shower. { 'shau̇·ər ˌmēd·ē·ər }

shutoff In rocket propulsion, the intentional termination of burning by command from the ground or from a self-contained guidance system. { 'shətˌȯf }

Sickle A group of six stars in the constellation Leo that outline the head of the lion. { 'sik·əl }

sidereal Referring to a quantity, such as time, to indicate that it is measured in relation to the apparent motion or position of the stars. { sī'dir·ē·əl }

sidereal day The time between two successive upper transits of the vernal equinox; this period measures one sidereal day. { sī'dir·ē·əl 'dā }

sidereal hour angle The angle along the celestial equator formed between the hour circle of a celestial body and the hour circle of the vernal equinox, measuring westward from the vernal equinox through 360°. { sī'dir·ē·əl ˈau̇r ˌaŋ·gəl }

sidereal month The time period of one revolution of the moon about the earth relative to the stars; this period varies because of perturbations, but it is a little less than $27\frac{1}{3}$ days. { sī'dir·ē·əl 'mənth }

sidereal noon The instant in time that the vernal equinox is on the meridian. { sī'dir·ē·əl 'nün }

sidereal period   The length of time required for one revolution of a celestial body about its primary, with respect to the stars. { sī'dir·ē·əl 'pir·ē·əd }

sidereal time   Time based on diurnal motion of stars; it is used by astronomers but is not convenient for ordinary purposes. { sī'dir·ē·əl 'tīm }

sidereal year   The time period relative to the stars of one revolution of the earth around the sun; it is about 365.2564 mean solar days. { sī'dir·ē·əl 'yir }

sign of the zodiac   The zodiac is divided into 12 sections, called signs, in each of which the sun is situated for 1 month of the year; each sign, 30° in length, is named from a constellation with which the sign once coincided. { 'sīn əv thə 'zō·dē₁ak }

silo   A missile shelter that consists of a hardened vertical hole in the ground with facilities either for lifting the missile to a launch position, or for direct launch from the shelter. { 'sī·lō }

simple ring   See elementary ring structure. { 'sim·pəl 'riŋ }

simultaneous altitudes   Altitudes of two or more celestial bodies observed at the same time. { ₁sī·məl'tā·nē·əs 'al·tə₁tüdz }

single-stage rocket   A rocket or rocket missile to which the total thrust is imparted in a single phase, by either a single or multiple thrust unit. { 'siŋ·gəl ¦stāj 'räk·ət }

Sinope   A small satellite of Jupiter with a diameter of about 17 miles (27 kilometers), orbiting with retrograde motion at a mean distance of about 1.47×10^7 miles (2.37×10^7 kilometers). Also known as Jupiter IX. { 'sin·ə·pē }

siriometer   A unit of length, formerly used in astronomical measurement, equal to 10^6 astronomical units, or 1.496×10^{17} meters. { ₁sir·ē'äm·əd·ər }

Sirius   The brightest-appearing star in the sky; 8.7 light-years from the sun, spectral class A1V; it has a white dwarf companion. Also known as Dog Star. { 'sir·ē·əs }

skid   The metal bar or runner used as part of the landing gear of helicopters and planes. { skid }

skin   The covering of a body, such as the covering of a fuselage, a wing, a hull, or an entire aircraft. { skin }

skip vehicle   A reentry body which climbs after striking the sensible atmosphere in order to cool the body and to increase its range. { 'skip ₁vē·ə·kəl }

sky   In the daytime the apparent blue dome resting on the earth along the horizon circle; at night the blue becomes nearly black. { skī }

sky diagram   A diagram of the heavens, indicating the apparent positions of various celestial bodies with reference to the horizon system of coordinates. { 'skī ₁dī·ə₁gram }

skyhook balloon   A large plastic constant-level balloon for duration flying at very high altitudes, used for determining wind fields and measuring upper-atmospheric parameters. { 'skī₁húk bə₁lün }

skylight   See diffuse sky radiation. { 'skī₁līt }

sky map   A planar representation of areas of the sky showing positions of celestial bodies. { 'skī ₁map }

sky radiation

sky radiation See diffuse sky radiation. { 'skī ˌrād·ē͵ā·shən }

slat A movable auxiliary airfoil running along the leading edge of a wing, remaining against the leading edge in normal flight conditions, but lifting away from the wing to form a slot at certain angles of attack. { slat }

slenderness ratio A configuration factor expressing the ratio of a missile's length to its diameter. { 'slen·dər·nəs ˌrā·shō }

slope deviation The difference between planned and actual slopes of aircraft travel, expressed in either angular or linear measurement. { 'slōp ˌdē·vē͵ā·shən }

slot 1. An air gap between a wing and the length of a slat or certain other auxiliary airfoils, the gap providing space for airflow or room for the auxiliary airfoil to be depressed in such a manner as to make for smooth air passage on the surface. 2. Any of certain narrow apertures made through a wing to improve aerodynamic characteristics. { slät }

slow nova A nova whose brightness takes a month or more to reach a maximum, and many years to decrease to the original value. { 'slō 'nō·və }

Small Magellanic Cloud The smaller of the two star clouds near the south celestial pole; it is about 170,000 light-years away and contains a wide assortment of giant and variable stars, star clusters, and nebulae. Also known as Nubecula Minor. { 'smȯl ˈmaj·əˌlan·ik 'klau̇d }

SMC X-1 The most luminous x-ray pulsar known, located in the Small Magellanic Cloud.

SNR See supernova remnant.

SNU See solar neutrino unit.

soar To fly without loss of altitude, using no motive power other than updrafts in the atmosphere. { sȯr }

soft landing The act of landing on the surface of a planet or moon without damage to any portion of the vehicle or payload, except possibly the landing gear. { 'sȯft 'land·iŋ }

Sol See sun. { säl }

solar activity Disturbances on the surface of the sun; examples are sunspots, prominences, and solar flares. { 'sō·lər ak'tiv·ədē }

solar antapex The point on the celestial sphere away from which the solar system is moving; it lies in the constellation Columba. { 'sō·lər ant'ā͵peks }

solar apex A point toward which the solar system is moving; it is about 10° southwest of the star Vega. { 'sō·lər 'ā͵peks }

solar bridge A bright, narrow, streak-shaped region which is sometimes observed across a large sunspot, dividing the umbra into two or more parts. { 'sō·lər 'brij }

solar burst A sudden increase in the radio-frequency energy radiated by the sun, generally associated with visible solar flares. { 'sō·lər 'bərst }

solar calendar A calendar based on the time period known as the tropical year, which has 365.24220 days. { 'sō·lər 'kal·ən·dər }

174

solar cavity See heliosphere. { 'sō·lər 'kav·əd·ē }

solar corona The upper, rarefied solar atmosphere which becomes visible around the darkened sun during a total solar eclipse. Also known as corona. { 'sō·lər kə'rō·nə }

solar cosmic rays See energetic solar particles. { 'sō·lər 'käz·mik 'rāz }

solar cycle The periodic change in the number of sunspots; the cycle is taken as the interval between successive minima and is about 11.1 years. { 'sō·lər 'sī·kəl }

solar day A time measurement, the duration of one rotation of the earth on its axis with respect to the sun; this may be a mean solar day or an apparent solar day as the reference is to the mean sun or apparent sun. { 'sō·lər 'dā }

solar eclipse An eclipse that takes place when the new moon passes between the earth and the sun and the shadow formed reaches the earth; may be classified as total, partial, or annular. { 'sō·lər i'klips }

solar energy The energy transmitted from the sun in the form of electromagnetic radiation. { 'sō·lər 'en·ər·jē }

solar faculae Bright streaks or regions on the surface of the sun, especially near solar sunspots. { 'sō·lər 'fak·yə‚lē }

solar flare An abrupt increase in the intensity of the H-α and other emission near a sunspot region; the brightness may be many times that of the associated plage. { 'sō·lər 'fler }

solar flux unit A unit of solar radio emission per unit frequency interval, equal to 10^{-22} watt per square meter per hertz at the earth. { 'sō·lər ‚fləks ‚yü·nət }

solar heat exchanger drive A proposed method of spacecraft propulsion in which solar radiation is focused on an area occupied by a boiler to heat a working fluid that is expelled to produce thrust directly. Abbreviated SHED. { 'sō·lər 'hēt iks‚chān·jər ‚drīv }

solar magnetic field The magnetic field that pervades the ionized and highly conducting gas composing the sun. { 'sō·lər mag'ned·ik 'fēld }

solar month A time interval equal to one-twelfth of the solar year. { 'sō·lər 'mənth }

solar motion The two main motions of the sun: relative motion with respect to the neighboring stars, or motion due to the rotation of the Milky Way of which the sun is a part. { 'sō·lər 'mō·shən }

solar neutrino A neutrino produced in a nuclear reaction inside the sun. { 'sō·lər nü'trē·nō }

solar neutrino unit A unit for measuring the capture rate of neutrinos emanating from the sun, equal to 10^{-36} per second per atom. Abbreviated SNU. { 'sō·lər nü'trē·nō ‚yü·nət }

solar nutation Nutation caused by the change in declination of the sun. { 'sō·lər nü'tā·shən }

solar orbit An orbit of a planet or other celestial body or satellite about the sun. { 'sō·lər 'ȯr·bət }

solar parallax   The sun's mean equatorial horizontal parallax p, which is the angle subtended by the equatorial radius r of the earth at mean distance a of the sun. { 'sō·lər 'par·ə،laks }

solar phase angle   The angular distance between the earth and the sun at a specified planet. { 'sō·lər 'fāz ،aŋ·gəl }

solar physics   The scientific study of all physical phenomena connected with the sun; it overlaps with geophysics in the consideration of solar-terrestrial relationships, such as the connection between solar activity and auroras. { 'sō·lər 'fiz·iks }

solar-powered aircraft   An aircraft in which the energy required for propulsion is collected by arrays of solar photovoltaic cells mounted on the wings. { 'sō·lər ¦paů·ərd 'er،kraft }

solar probe   A space probe whose trajectory passes near the sun so that instruments on board may detect and transmit back to earth data about the sun. { 'sō·lər 'prōb }

solar prominence   Sheets of luminous gas emanating from the sun's surface; they appear dark against the sun's disk but bright against the dark sky, and occur only in regions of horizontal magnetic fields. { 'sō·lər 'präm·ə·nəns }

solar propulsion   Spacecraft propulsion with a system composed of a type of solar engine. { 'sō·lər prə'pəl·shən }

solar radiation   The electromagnetic radiation and particles (electrons, protons, and rarer heavy atomic nuclei) emitted by the sun. { 'sō·lər ،rād·ē'ā·shən }

solar radio emission   Radio-frequency electromagnetic radiation emitted from the sun, and increasing greatly in intensity during sunspots and flares. { 'sō·lər 'rād·ē·ō i،mish·ən }

solar rocket   A rocket designed to carry instruments to measure and transmit parameters of the sun. { 'sō·lər 'räk·ət }

solar sail   A surface of a highly polished material upon which solar light radiation exerts a pressure. Also known as photon sail. { 'sō·lər 'sāl }

solar satellite   A space vehicle designed to enter into orbit about the sun. Also known as sun satellite. { 'sō·lər 'sad·əl،īt }

solar sector   A region of the solar wind in which one magnetic polarity predominates. { 'sō·lər 'sek·tər }

solar spectrum   The spectrum of the sun's electromagnetic radiation extending over the whole electromagnetic spectrum, from wavelengths of 10^{-9} centimeter to 30 kilometers. { 'sō·lər 'spek·trəm }

solar spicule   *See* spicule. { 'sō·lər 'spik·yül }

solar system   The sun and the celestial bodies moving about it; the bodies are planets, satellites of the planets, asteroids, comets, and meteor swarms. { 'sō·lər ،sis·təm }

solar time   Time based on the rotation of the earth relative to the sun. { 'sō·lər 'tīm }

solar tower   A tower which has a coelostat mounted on top to reflect the sun's light vertically downward so that it may be studied with a spectroheliograph or other astronomical instrument at the bottom of the tower. { 'sō·lər ،taů·ər }

solar turboelectric drive A proposed method of spacecraft propulsion in which solar radiation is focused on an area occupied by a boiler to heat a working fluid that drives a turbine generator system, producing electrical energy. Abbreviated STED. { 'sō·lər ¦tər·bō·i¦lek·trik 'drīv }

solar-type star Any of the stars (yellow stars) of spectral type G, so called because the sun is in this class. { 'sō·lər ¦tīp 'stär }

solar ultraviolet radiation That portion of the sun's electromagnetic radiation that has wavelengths from about 400 to about 4 nanometers; this radiation may sufficiently ionize the earth's atmosphere so that propagation of radio waves is affected. { 'sō·lər ¦əl·trə¦vī·lət ˌrād·ē'ā·shən }

solar units A set of units for measuring properties of stars, in which properties of the sun such as mass, diameter, density, and luminosity are set equal to unity. { 'sō·lər ˌyü·nəts }

solar velocity The Sun's velocity with respect to the local standard of rest. { 'sō·lər və'läs·əd·ē }

solid-propellant rocket engine A rocket engine fueled with a solid propellant; such motors consist essentially of a combustion chamber containing the propellant, and a nozzle for the exhaust jet. { 'säl·əd prə¦pel·ənt 'räk·ət ˌen·jən }

solid rocket A rocket that is propelled by a solid-propellant rocket engine. { 'säl·əd 'räk·ət }

solstice The two days (actually, instants) during the year when the earth is so located in its orbit that the inclination (about 23¹/₂°) of the polar axis is toward the sun; the days are June 21 for the North Pole and December 22 for the South Pole; because of leap years, the dates vary a little. { 'sälz·təs }

solstitial colure That great circle of the celestial sphere through the celestial poles and the solstices. { sälz'tish·əl kə'lúr }

solstitial points Those points of the ecliptic that are 90° from the equinoxes north or south at which the greatest declination of the sun is reached. { sälz'tish·əl 'póins }

Sombrero galaxy A spiral galaxy in the constellation Virgo that is seen nearly edge-on, having a recession velocity of approximately 910 kilometers per second (565 miles per second). { səm'brer·ō 'gal·ik·sē }

sonic barrier A popular term for the large increase in drag that acts upon an aircraft approaching acoustic velocity; the point at which the speed of sound is attained and existing subsonic and supersonic flow theories are rather indefinite. Also known as sound barrier. { 'sän·ik 'bar·ē·ər }

sortie An operational flight by one aircraft. { 'sórd·ē }

Sothic cycle A time period of about 1460 years; this cycle is such that the New Year of the calendar used in ancient Egypt was in error by a whole year because the adopted year of 365 days is about a quarter of a day shorter than the mean solar year. { 'sä·thik ˌsī·kəl }

sound barrier See sonic barrier. { 'saúnd ˌbar·ē·ər }

sounding rocket A rocket that carries aloft equipment for making observations of or from the upper atmosphere. { 'saúnd·iŋ ˌräk·ət }

177

source function The emissivity of a stellar or other radiating material divided by its opacity. { 'sȯrs ˌfəŋk·shən }

southbound node See descending node. { 'saüthˌbaünd 'nōd }

Southern Cross See Crux. { 'səth·ərn 'krȯs }

Southern Crown See Corona Australis. { 'səth·ərn 'kraün }

Southern Triangle See Triangulum Australe. { 'səth·ərn 'trīˌaŋ·gəl }

south point That imaginary point on the celestial sphere at which the meridian intersects the horizon; it is due south of the observer. { 'saüth 'pȯint }

south polar distance The angular distance between a celestial object and the south celestial pole. { 'saüth 'pō·lər 'dis·təns }

south tropical disturbance An elongated dark band seen on the surface of Jupiter at about the latitude of the Great Red Spot; it has at times exceeded 180° of longitude in length and, like the Red Spot, appears and disappears intermittently. { 'saüth 'trap·ə·kəl di'stər·bəns }

space 1. Specifically, the part of the universe lying outside the limits of the earth's atmosphere. 2. More generally, the volume in which all celestial bodies, including the earth, move. { spās }

space capsule A container, manned or unmanned, used for carrying out an experiment or operation in space. { 'spās ˌkap·səl }

spacecraft Devices, crewed and uncrewed, which are designed to be placed into an orbit about the earth or into a trajectory to another celestial body. Also known as space ship; space vehicle. { 'spāsˌkraft }

spacecraft launching The setting into motion of a space vehicle with sufficient force to cause it to leave the earth's atmosphere. { 'spāsˌkraft ˌlȯnch·iŋ }

spacecraft propulsion The use of rocket engines to accelerate space vehicles. { 'spāsˌkraft prə'pəl·shən }

space environment The environment encountered by vehicles and living creatures in space, characterized by absence of atmosphere. { 'spās inˌvī·ərn·mənt }

space flight Travel beyond the earth's sensible atmosphere; space flight may be an orbital flight about the earth or it may be a more extended flight beyond the earth into space. { 'spās ˌflīt }

space-flight trajectory The track or path taken by a spacecraft. { 'spās ˈflīt trə'jek·trē }

space mission A journey by a vehicle, manned or unmanned, beyond the earth's atmosphere, usually for the purpose of collecting scientific data. { 'spās ˌmish·ən }

space motion Motion of a celestial body through space. { 'spās ˌmō·shən }

spaceport An installation used to test and launch spacecraft. { 'spāsˌpȯrt }

space power system An on-board assemblage of equipment to generate and distribute electrical energy on satellites and spacecraft. { 'spās 'paü·ər ˌsis·təm }

space probe   An instrumented vehicle, the payload of a rocket-launching system designed specifically for flight missions to other planets or the moon and into deep space, as distinguished from earth-orbiting satellites. { 'spās ˌprōb }

space reconnaissance   Reconnaissance of the surface of a planet from a space ship or satellite. { 'spās riˌkän · ə · səns }

space reddening   Reddening of light from distant stars caused by selective absorption of blue light by interstellar dust clouds. { 'spās ˌred · ən · iŋ }

space research   Research involving studies of all aspects of environmental conditions beyond the atmosphere of the earth. { 'spās riˌsərch }

space satellite   A vehicle, crewed or uncrewed, for orbiting the earth. { 'spās ˌsad · əlˌīt }

space ship   See spacecraft. { 'spās ˌship }

space shuttle   A reusable orbital spacecraft, designed to travel from the earth to an orbital trajectory and then to return. { 'spās ˌshəd · əl }

space simulator   **1.** Any device which simulates one or more parameters of the space environment and which is used to test space systems or components. **2.** Specifically, a closed chamber capable of reproducing approximately the vacuum and normal environments of space. { 'spās ˌsim · yəˌlād · ər }

space station   An autonomous, permanent facility in space for the conduct of scientific and technological research, earth-oriented applications, and astronomical observations. { 'spās ˌstā · shən }

space technology   The systematic application of engineering and scientific disciplines to the exploration and utilization of outer space. { 'spās tekˌnäl · ə · jē }

space vehicle   See spacecraft. { 'spās ˌvē · ə · kəl }

space velocity   A star's true velocity with reference to the sun. { 'spās vəˌläs · əd · ē }

space walk   The movement of an astronaut outside the protected environment of a spacecraft during a space flight; the astronaut wears a spacesuit. { 'spās ˌwȯk }

span   **1.** The dimension of a craft measured between lateral extremities; the measure of this dimension. **2.** Specifically, the dimension of an airfoil from tip to tip measured in a straight line. { span }

spar   A principal spanwise member of the structural framework of an airplane wing, aileron, stabilizer, and such; it may be of one-piece design or a fabricated section. { spär }

special flight   An air transport flight, other than a scheduled service, set up to move a specific load. { 'spesh · əl 'flīt }

specific impulse   A performance parameter of a rocket propellant, expressed in seconds, equal to the thrust in pounds divided by the weight flow rate in pounds per second. Also known as specific thrust. { spə'sif · ik 'imˌpəls }

specific thrust   See specific impulse. { spə'sif · ik 'thrəst }

spectral classification   A classification of stars by characteristics revealed by study of

spectral luminosity classification

their spectra; the six classes B, A, F, G, K, and M include 99% of all known stars. { 'spek·trəl ˌklas·ə·fə'kā·shən }

spectral/luminosity classification   See MK system. { 'spek·trəl ˌlü·mə'näs·əd·ē ˌklas·ə·fə·kā·shən }

spectral type   A label used to indicate the physical and chemical characteristics of a star as indicated by study of the star's spectra; for example, the stars in the spectral type known as class B are blue-white, and are referred to as helium stars because the dominant lines in their spectra are the lines in helium spectra. { 'spek·trəl ˌtīp }

spectroheliogram   A photograph of the sun obtained by means of a spectroheliograph. { ˌspek·trō'hē·lē·ə·ˌgram }

spectroscopic binary star   A binary star that may be distinguished from a single star only by noting the Doppler shift of the spectral lines of one or both stars as they revolve about their common center of mass. { ˌspek·trəˌskäp·ik 'bī·ner·ē 'stär }

spectroscopic parallax   Parallax as determined from examination of a stellar spectrum; critical spectral lines indicate the star's absolute magnitude, from which the star's distance, or parallax, can be deduced. { ˌspek·trəˌskäp·ik 'par·ə·ˌlaks }

spectrum of turbulence   A relationship between the size of turbulent eddies in the sun's atmosphere and their average speed. { 'spek·trəm əv 'tər·byə·ləns }

spectrum variable   A main-sequence star of spectral class A whose spectrum displays anomalously strong lines of metals and rare earths whose intensity varies by about 0.1 magnitude over periods from 1 to 25 days. { 'spek·trəm 'ver·ē·ə·bəl }

speed density metering   A type of aircraft carburetion in which the fuel feed is regulated by the parameters of engine feed and intake manifold pressure. { 'spēd ˌden·səd·ē ˌmēd·ə·riŋ }

spheres of Eudoxus   A theory of Eudoxus from about 400 B.C.; the planets, sun, and moon were on a series of concentric spheres rotating inside one another on different axes. { 'sfirz əv yü'däk·səs }

spheroidal galaxy   See elliptical galaxy. { sfir'óid·əl 'gal·ik·sē }

Spica   A blue-white dwarf star of stellar magnitude 1.0, 160 light-years from the sun, spectral classification B1-V, in the constellation Virgo; the star α Virginis. { 'spī·kə }

spicule   One of an irregular distribution of jets shooting up from the sun's chromosphere. Also known as solar spicule. { 'spik·yül }

spin rocket   A small rocket that imparts spin to a larger rocket vehicle or spacecraft. { 'spin ˌräk·ət }

spin stabilization   Directional stability of a spacecraft obtained by the action of gyroscopic forces which result from spinning the body about its axis of symmetry. { 'spin ˌstā·bə·lə·ˌzā·shən }

spin-up   A sudden increase in the pulse frequency of a pulsar. { 'spin·əp }

spiral arms   The shape of sections of certain galaxies called spirals; these sections are two so-called arms composed of stars, dust, and gas extending from the center of the galaxy and coiled about it. { 'spī·rəl 'ärmz }

180

spiral galaxy A type of galaxy classified on the basis of appearance of its photographic image; this type includes two main groups: normal spirals with circular symmetry of the nucleus and of the spiral arms, and barred spirals in which the dominant form is a luminous bar crossing the nucleus with spiral arms starting at the ends of the bar or tangent to a luminous rim on which the bar terminates. { 'spī·rəl 'gal·ik·sē }

spiral ring structure A lunar crater in which ridges spiral inward from the main wall across the floor. { 'spī·rəl 'riŋ ˌstrək·chər }

splashdown **1.** The landing of a spacecraft or missile on water. **2.** The moment of impact of a spacecraft on water. { 'splashˌdaün }

split-altitude profile Flight profile at two separate altitudes. { 'split ˌal·tə‚tüd 'prō‚fīl }

split flap A hinged plate forming the rear upper or lower portion of an airfoil; the lower portion may be deflected downward to give increased lift and drag; the upper portion may be raised over a portion of the wing for the purpose of lateral control. { 'split 'flap }

spoiler A plate, series of plates, comb, tube, bar, or other device that projects into the airstream about a body to break up or spoil the smoothness of the flow, especially such a device that projects from the upper surface of an airfoil, giving an increased drag and a decreased lift. { 'spói·lər }

sporadic meteor A meteor which is not associated with one of the regularly recurring meteor showers or streams. { spə'rad·ik 'mēd·ē·ər }

Spörer minimum A period of low sunspot activity that occurred between 1420 and 1570. { 'spər·ər 'min·ə·məm }

Spörer's law A relationship to indicate the frequency of occurrence of sunspots and their progressive movement to lower latitudes on the sun. { 'spər·ərz ˌló }

spot group A complex formation of the sun's surface consisting of a sunspot with several umbrae surrounded by a single penumbra, or of several sunspots which are close together and clearly associated. { 'spät ˌgrüp }

spot hover To remain stationary relative to a point on the ground while airborne. { 'spät ˌhəv·ər }

spray An explosive release of gas in all directions from the sun's chromosphere, with velocities as high as 930 miles (1500 kilometers) per second, which normally occurs in the first minutes of a flare. { 'sprā }

spring The period extending from the vernal equinox to the summer solstice; comprises the transition period from winter to summer. { spriŋ }

spring equinox See vernal equinox. { 'spriŋ 'ē·kwəˌnäks }

SS Cygni stars See U Geminorum stars. { ˌesˌes 'sig·nē ˌstärz }

SS 433 A stellar object that shows evidence of ejection of two narrow streams of cool gas travelling in opposite direction from a cool object at a velocity of almost one-quarter the speed of light; the beams execute a repeating, rotating pattern about the central object once every 164 days. { ˌesˌes ˌfórˌthərd·ē'thrē }

SST See supersonic transport.

S star

S star   A spectral classification of stars, comprising red stars with surface temperature of about 2200 K; prominent in the spectra is zirconium oxide. { 'es ₁stär }

stabilator   A one-piece horizontal tail that is swept back and movable; movement is controlled by motion of the pilot's control stick; usually used in supersonic aircraft. { 'stā·bə₁lād·ər }

stability augmentation system   Automatic control devices which supplement a pilot's manipulation of the aircraft controls and are used to modify inherent aircraft handling qualities. Abbreviated SAS. Also known as stability augmentors. { stə'bil·əd·ē óg·mən'tā·shən ₁sis·təm }

stability augmentors   See stability augmentation system. { stə'bil·əd·ē 'óg₁men·tərz }

stabilized flight   Maintenance of desired orientation in flight. { 'stā·bə₁līzd 'flīt }

stabilized platform   See stable platform. { 'stā·bə₁līzd 'plat₁fórm }

stabilizer   Any airfoil or any combination of airfoils considered as a single unit, the primary function of which is to give stability to an aircraft or missile. { 'stā·bə₁līz·ər }

stable platform   A gimbal-mounted platform, usually containing gyros and accelerometers, the purpose of which is to maintain a desired orientation in inertial space independent of craft motion. Also known as stabilized platform. { 'stā·bəl 'plat₁fórm }

stacking   The holding pattern of aircraft awaiting their turn to approach and land at an airport. { 'stak·iŋ }

stage   A self-propelled separable element of a rocket vehicle or spacecraft. { stāj }

staged crew   An aircrew specifically positioned at an intermediate airfield to take over aircraft operating on an air route, thus relieving a complementary crew of flying fatigue and speeding up the traffic rate of the aircraft concerned. { 'stājd 'krü }

staging   The process or operation during the flight of a rocket vehicle whereby a full stage or half stage is disengaged from the remaining body and made free to decelerate or be propelled along its own flightpath. { 'stāj·iŋ }

stall   1. The action or behavior of an airplane (or one of its airfoils) when by the separation of the airflow, as in the case of insufficient airspeed or of an excessive angle of attack, the airplane or airfoil tends to drop; the condition existing during this behavior. 2. A flight performance in which an airplane is made to lose flying speed and to drop by pointing the nose steeply upward. 3. An act or instance of stalling. { stól }

stall flutter   A type of dynamic instability that takes place when the separation of flow around an airfoil occurs during the whole or part of each cycle of a flutter motion. { 'stól ₁fləd·ər }

stalling angle   See angle of stall. { 'stól·iŋ ₁aŋ·gəl }

stalling angle of attack   See critical angle of attack. { 'stól·iŋ 'aŋ·gəl əv ə'tak }

stalling Mach number   The Mach number of an aircraft when the coefficient of lift of the aerodynamic surfaces is the maximum obtainable for the pressure altitude, true airspeed, and angle of attack under which the craft is operated. { 'stȯl·iŋ 'mäk ˌnəm·bər }

stall warning indicator   A device that determines the critical angle of attack for a given aircraft; usually operates from vane sensors, airflow sensors, tabs on leading edges of wings, and computing devices such as accelerometers or airspeed indicators. { 'stȯl ¦wȯrn·iŋ ˌin·dəˌkād·ər }

standard coordinates   A coordinate system used to locate stars on a photographic plate, in which the coordinates are the differences in right ascension and declination between the position of each star and the assumed position of the plate center. { 'stan·dərd kō'ȯrd·ən·əts }

standard noon   Twelve o'clock standard time, or the instant the mean sun is over the upper branch of the standard meridian. { 'stan·dərd 'nün }

standard rate turn   A turn in an aircraft in which heading changes at the rate of 3° per second. { 'stan·dərd ¦rāt 'tərn }

standard star   A star whose position or other data are precisely known so that it is used as a reference to calculate positions of other celestial bodies, or of objects on earth. { 'stan·dərd 'stär }

standard time   The mean solar time, based on the transit of the sun over a specified meridian, called the time meridian, and adopted for use over an area that is called a time zone. { 'stan·dərd 'tīm }

standing operating procedure   A set of instructions covering those features of operations which lend themselves to a definite or standardized procedure without loss of effectiveness; the procedure is applicable unless prescribed otherwise in a particular case; thus, the flexibility necessary in special situations is retained. { 'stand·iŋ 'äp·əˌrād·iŋ prəˌsē·jər }

standstill   An interval in the cycle of a variable star during which its brightness remains nearly constant. { 'stanˌstil }

star   A celestial body consisting of a large, self-luminous mass of hot gas held together by its own gravity; the sun is a typical star. { stär }

star atlas   A series of star maps for different times, for example, for each month; the maps are generally drawn to a small scale and in book form. { 'stär ˌat·ləs }

starburst galaxy   A galaxy that is presently undergoing a period of intense star formation. { 'stärˌbərst ˌgal·ik·sē }

star catalog   A comprehensive tabulation of data concerning the stars listed; the data may include, for example, apparent positions, brightness, motions, parallaxes, and other properties of stars. { 'stär ¦kad·əlˌäg }

star chart   See star map. { 'stär ˌchärt }

star cloud   An aggregation of thousands or of millions of stars spread over hundreds or thousands of light-years. { 'stär ˌklau̇d }

star cluster   A group of stars held together by gravitational attraction; the two chief types are open clusters (composed of from 12 to hundreds of stars) and globular clusters (composed of thousands to hundreds of thousands of stars). Also known as cluster. { 'stär ˌkləs·tər }

star color   The color of a star as a function of its radiation and related to its temperature; colors range from blue-white to deep red. { 'stär ˌkəl·ər }

star count   A count of stars on a photographic plate. { 'stär ˌkaủnt }

star day   The time period between two successive passages of a star across the meridian. { 'stär 'dā }

star density   The average number of stars in a unit volume of space. { 'stär ˌden·səd·ē }

star drift   A description of two star groups in the Milky Way traveling through each other in opposite directions; individual stars have movements that are relative to each other. Also known as star stream. { 'stär ˌdrift }

star finder   A device such as a star map or celestial globe to facilitate the identification of stars. Also known as star identifier. { 'stär ˌfin·dər }

star globe   See celestial globe. { 'stär ˌglōb }

star group   A number of stars that move in the same general direction at the same time. { 'stär ˌgrüp }

star identifier   See star finder. { 'stär ī·den·tə·fī·ər }

star map   A map indicating the relative apparent positions of the stars. Also known as star chart. { 'stär ˌmap }

star model   See stellar model. { 'stär ˌmäd·əl }

star motions   For the Milky Way, this includes rotation within the galaxy, motion which is described with respect to an external frame of reference; superposed on this systematic rotation are the individual motions of a star; each star moves in a somewhat elliptical orbit, with respect to the local standard of rest, the standard moving in a circular orbit around the galactic center. { 'stär ˌmō·shənz }

star names   Nomenclature for the identification of stars; hundreds of stars have proper names that are traditional, for example, Betelgeuse; this star may be also identified as α Orionis (Alpha Orionis), α for its being the brightest visual star in the constellation Orion. { 'stär ˌnāmz }

star place   The position of a star on the celestial sphere, usually measured by its right ascension and declination. { 'stär ˌplās }

starspot   A region of reduced brightness of the surface of a star comparable to a sunspot on the Sun's surface. { 'stärˌspät }

star stream   See star drift. { 'stär 'strēm }

star streaming   A phenomenon that results from the mean random speeds of stars being different in different directions. { 'stär ˌstrēm·iŋ }

static firing   The firing of a rocket engine in a hold-down position to measure thrust and to accomplish other tests. { 'stad·ik 'fīr·iŋ }

static gearing ratio   The ratio of the control-surface deflection in degrees to angular displacement of the missile which caused the deflection of the control surface. { 'stad·ik 'gir·iŋ ˌrā·shō }

static line A line attached to a parachute pack and to a strop or anchor cable in an aircraft so that when the load is dropped the parachute is deployed automatically. { 'stad·ik ˌlīn }

static test In particular, a test of a rocket or other device in a stationary or hold-down position, either to verify structural design criteria, structural integrity, and the effects of limit loads, or to measure the thrust of a rocket engine. { 'stad·ik 'test }

static universe A postulated universe that has a finite static volume and is closed. { 'stad·ik 'yü·nəˌvərs }

stationary orbit A circular, equatorial orbit in which the satellite revolves about the primary body at the angular rate at which the primary body rotates on its axis; from the primary body, the satellite thus appears to be stationary over a point on the primary body; a stationary orbit must be synchronous, but the reverse need not be true. { 'stā·shəˌner·ē 'ȯr·bət }

stationary point A point at which a planet's apparent motion changes from direct to retrograde motion, or vice versa. { 'stā·shəˌner·ē 'pȯint }

stationary satellite A satellite in a stationary orbit. { 'stā·shəˌner·ē 'sad·əlˌīt }

station time Time at which crews, passengers, and cargo are to be on board air transport and ready for the flight. { 'stā·shən ˌtīm }

statistical parallax The mean parallax of a collection of stars that are all at approximately the same distance, as determined from their radial velocities and proper motions. { stə'tis·tə·kəl 'par·əˌlaks }

stay time In rocket engine usage, the average value of the time spent by each gas molecule or atom within the chamber volume. { 'stā ˌtīm }

steady-state theory A cosmological theory which holds that the average density of matter does not vary with space or time in spite of the expansion of the universe; this requires that matter be continuously created. { 'sted·ē ¦stāt 'thē·ə·rē }

STED *See* solar turboelectric drive. { sted }

stellar Relating to or consisting of stars. { 'stel·ər }

stellar association A loose grouping of stars which may have had a common origin. { 'stel·ər əˌsō·sē'ā·shən }

stellar atmosphere The envelope of gas and plasma surrounding a star; consists of about 90% hydrogen atoms and 9% helium atoms, by number of atoms. { 'stel·ər 'at·məˌsfir }

stellar evolution The changes in spectrum and luminosity that take place in the life of a star. { 'stel·ər ˌev·ə'lü·shən }

stellar flare Ejection of material from a star in an eruption that may last from a few minutes to an hour or more. { 'stel·ər 'fler }

stellar light The part of the background illumination of the night sky that results from direct light from stars too faint to be visible to the unaided eye. { 'stel·ər 'līt }

stellar luminosity A star's brightness; it is measured either in ergs per second or in units of solar luminosity or in absolute magnitude. { 'stel·ər lü·mə'näs·əd·ē }

stellar magnetic field   A magnetic field, generally stronger than the earth's magnetic field, possessed by many stars. { 'stel·ər mag'ned·ik 'fēld }

stellar magnitude   See magnitude. { 'stel·ər 'mag·nə‚tüd }

stellar mass   The mass of a star, usually expressed in terms of the sun's mass. { 'stel· ər 'mas }

stellar model   A mathematical characterization of the internal properties of a star. Also known as star model. { 'stel·ər 'mäd·əl }

stellar parallax   The subtended angle at a star formed by the mean radius of the earth's orbit; it indicates distance to the star. { 'stel·ər 'par·ə‚laks }

stellar photometry   The measurement of the brightness of stars. { 'stel·ər phə'täm·ə· trē }

stellar population   Either of two classes of stars, termed population I and population II; population I are relatively young stars, found in the arms of spiral galaxies, especially the blue stars of high luminosity; population II stars are the much older, more evolved stars of lower metallic content; many high luminosity red giants and many variable stars are members of population II. { 'stel·ər ‚päp·yə'lā·shən }

stellar pulsation   Expansion of a star followed by contraction so that its surface temperature and intrinsic brightness undergo periodic variation. { 'stel·ər pəl'sā·shən }

stellar rotation   Axial rotation of stars; surface rotational equatorial velocities of stars range from a few to 500 kilometers per second. { 'stel·ər rō'tā·shən }

stellar scintillation   See astronomical scintillation. { 'stel·ər ‚sint·əl'ā·shən }

stellar spectroscopy   The techniques of obtaining spectra of stars and their study. { 'stel·ər spek'träs·kə·pē }

stellar spectrum   The spectrum of a star normally obtained with a slit spectrograph by black-and-white photography; the spectrum of a star in a large majority of cases shows absorption lines superposed on a continuous background. { 'stel·ər 'spek· trəm }

stellar structure   The mathematical study of a rotating, chemically homogeneous mass of gas held together by its own gravitation; a representative model of the observable properties of a star; thermonuclear reactions are postulated to be the main source of stellar energy. { 'stel·ər ¦strək·chər }

stellar system   A gravitational system of stars. { 'stel·ər ¦sis·təm }

stellar temperature   Any temperature above several million degrees, such as occurs naturally in the interior of the sun and other stars. { 'stel·ər 'tem·prə·chər }

stellar wind   The flow of ionized gas from the surface of a star into interstellar space. { 'stel·ər 'wind }

step-climb profile   The aircraft climbs a specified number of feet whenever its weight reaches a predetermined amount, thus stepping to an optimum altitude as gross weight decreases. { 'step ¦klīm 'prō‚fīl }

Stephan's Quintet   A group of five galaxies which lie close together, one of which has widely divergent red shifts. { 'stef·ənz kwin'tet }

step rocket See multistage rocket. { 'step ˌräk·ət }

stern attack In air intercept, an attack by an interceptor aircraft which terminates with a heading crossing angle of 45° or less. { 'stərn əˌtak }

stiffened-shell fuselage See semimonocoque. { 'stif·ənd ¦shel 'fyü·səˌläzh }

stockage objective The maximum quantities of material to be maintained on hand to sustain current operations; it will consist of the sum of stocks represented by the operating level and the safety level. { 'stä·kij əbˌjek·tiv }

STOL See short takeoff and landing. { 'stōl or ¦es¦tē¦ō'el }

STOL aircraft Heavier-than-air craft that cannot take off and land vertically, but can operate within areas substantially more confined than those normally required by aircraft of the same size. Derived from short takeoff and landing aircraft. { 'stōl ˌer·kraft }

strake The slender forward extension of the inboard region of the wing of a combat aircraft, used to provide increased lift in the high angle-of-attack maneuvering condition. { strāk }

stranger In air intercept, an unidentified aircraft, bearing, distance, and altitude as indicated relative to an aircraft. { 'strān·jər }

strategic airlift The continuous, sustained air movement of units, personnel, and materiel in support of all U.S. Department of Defense agencies between area commands. { strə'tē·jik 'erˌlift }

strategic transport aircraft Aircraft designed primarily for the carriage of personnel or cargo over long distances. { strə'tē·jik 'tranzˌpȯrt 'erˌkraft }

stream takeoff Aircraft taking off in tail/column formation. { 'strēm 'tākˌȯf }

Strömgren four-color index See uvby system. { 'strəm·grən ¦fȯr ¦kəl·ər 'inˌdeks }

Strömgren radius The radius of a sphere surrounding the central star of an emission nebula within which the hydrogen is nearly completely ionized. { 'strəm·grən ˌrād·ē·əs }

Strömgren sphere An approximately spherical region of ionized hydrogen that surrounds a hot star. { 'strəm·grən ˌsfir }

structural weight See construction weight. { 'strək·chə·rəl 'wāt }

structure The construction or makeup of an airplane, spacecraft, or missile, including that of the fuselage, wings, empennage, nacelles, and landing gear, but not that of the power plant, furnishings, or equipment. { 'strək·chər }

strut A bar supporting the wing or landing gear of an airplane. { strət }

S-type asteroid A type of asteroid whose surface is reddish and of moderate albedo, containing pyroxene and olivine silicates, probably mixed with metallic iron, similar to stony iron meteorites. { 'es ¦tīp 'as·təˌrȯid }

subastral point See substellar point. { ¦səb'as·trəl 'pȯint }

subcluster One of the several distinct clumps of galaxies that often compose an irregular cluster. { 'səbˌkləs·tər }

subdwarf star An intermediate star type; luminosity is between that of main sequence stars and the white dwarf stars on the Hertzsprung-Russell diagram; spectral classes F, G, and K are most numerous. { 'səbˌdwȯrf 'stär }

subdwarf symbiotic A type of symbiotic star consisting of a combination of a cool red giant with a small hot subdwarf star, the latter probably the inner core of a former giant or super giant which has shed its outer envelope and is now contracting to become a white dwarf. Also known as planetary nebula symbiotic. { 'səbˌdwȯrf ˌsim·bē'äd·ik }

subgiant CH star A type of star that resembles the CH stars and barium stars but is less luminous and somewhat hotter, with some members of the class lying on or near the main sequence. { ˈsəbˈjī·ənt ˈsē'äch ˌstär }

subgiant star A member of the family of stars whose luminosity is intermediate between giants and the main sequence in the Hertzsprung-Russell diagram; spectral classes G and K are most frequent. { ˈsəb'jī:ənt 'stär }

subluminous star A star that is fainter than those of the same color on the main sequence. { səb'lüm·ə·nəs 'stär }

sublunar point The moon's geographic zenith position at any particular moment in time. { ˈsəb'lü·nər 'pȯint }

submillimeter astronomy Astronomical observations carried out in the region of the electromagnetic spectrum with wavelengths from approximately 0.3 to 1.0 millimeter. { ˌsəbˈmil·əˌmēd·ər ə'strän·ə·mē }

subpulse The weaker component of a pulsar's periodic emission. { 'səbˌpəls }

subsatellite An object that is carried into orbit by, and subsequently released from, an artificial satellite. { 'səbˌsad·əlˌīt }

subsolar point The sun's zenith geographic position at any particular moment in time. { ˈsəb'sō·lər 'pȯint }

subsonic flight Movement of a vehicle through the atmosphere at a speed appreciably below that of sound waves; extends from zero (hovering) to a speed about 85% of sonic speed corresponding to ambient temperature. { ˈsəb'sän·ik 'flīt }

substellar point The geographical position of a star; that point on the earth at which the star is in the zenith at a specified time. Also known as subastral point. { ˈsəb'stel·ər 'pȯint }

suction boundary layer control A technique that is used in addition to purely geometric means to control boundary layer flow; it consists of sucking away the retarded flow in the lower regions of the boundary through slots or perforations in the surface. { 'sək·shən 'baún·drē ˌlā·ər kənˌtrōl }

summer The period from the summer solstice to the autumnal equinox; popularly and for most meteorological purposes, it is taken to include June through August in the Northern Hemisphere, and December through February in the Southern Hemisphere. { 'səm·ər }

summer noon See daylight saving noon. { 'səm·ər 'nün }

summer solstice 1. The sun's position on the ecliptic when it reaches its greatest northern declination. Also known as first point of Cancer. 2. The date, about June 21, on which the sun has its greatest northern declination. { 'səm·ər 'säl·stəs }

summer time   See daylight saving time. { 'səm·ər 'tīm }

sun   The star about which the earth revolves; it is a globe of gas 8.7×10^5 miles (1.4×10^6 kilometers) in diameter, held together by its own gravity; thermonuclear reactions take place in the deep interior of the sun converting hydrogen into helium releasing energy which streams out. Also known as Sol. { sən }

sun dog   See parhelion. { 'sən ˌdȯg }

sun-grazing comet   A comet whose orbit causes it to either collide with the sun or completely disintegrate in the outer solar atmosphere. { 'sən ˌgrāz·iŋ 'käm·ət }

sunrise   The exact moment the upper limb of the sun appears above the horizon. { 'sənˌrīz }

sun satellite   See solar satellite. { 'sən 'sad·əlˌīt }

sunset   The exact moment the upper limb of the sun disappears below the horizon. { 'sənˌset }

sunshine   Direct radiation from the sun, as opposed to the shading of a location by clouds or by other obstructions. { 'sənˌshīn }

sunspot   A dark area in the photosphere of the sun caused by a lowered surface temperature. { 'sənˌspät }

sunspot cycle   Variation of the size and number of sunspots in an 11-year cycle which is shared by all other forms of solar activity. { 'sənˌspät ˌsī·kəl }

sunspot maximum   The time in the solar cycle when the number of sunspots reaches a maximum value. { 'sənˌspät 'mak·sə·məm }

sunspot number   See relative sunspot number. { 'sənˌspät ˌnəm·bər }

sunspot relative number   See relative sunspot number. { 'sənˌspät 'rel·əd·iv ˌnəm·bər }

sun's way   The path of the solar system through space. { 'sənz 'wā }

sun-synchronous orbit   An earth orbit of a spacecraft so that the craft is always in the same direction relative to that of the sun; as a result, the spacecraft passes over the equator at the same spots at the same times. { 'sən ˌsiŋ·krə·nəs 'ȯr·bət }

supercluster   An association of galaxy clusters and groups, typically composed of a few rich clusters and many poorer groups and isolated galaxies. { 'sü·pərˌkləs·tər }

supercritical wing   A wing developed to permit subsonic aircraft to maintain an efficient cruise speed very close to the speed of sound; the middle portion of the wing is relatively flat with substantial downward curvature near the trailing edge; in addition, the forward region of the lower surface is more curved than that of the upper surface with a substantial cusp of the rearward portion of the lower surface. { ˌsü·pər'krid·ə·kəl 'wiŋ }

superdense state   An extremely compact state of matter in which protons and electrons are pressed together to form neutrons, as in a neutron star. { ˌsü·pərˌdens 'stāt }

superdense theory   See big bang theory. { ˌsü·pər'dens ˌthē·ə·rē }

supergalaxy A hypothetical very large group of galaxies which together fill an ellipsoidal space. { ˈsü·pər′gal·ik·sē }

supergiant star A member of the family containing the intrinsically brightest stars, populating the top of the Hertzsprung-Russell diagram; supergiant stars occur at all temperatures from 30,000 to 3000 K and have luminosities from 10^4 to 10^6 times that of the sun; the star Betelgeuse is an example. { ˈsü·pər′gī·ənt ′stär }

supergranulation cells Convective cells in the solar photosphere with primarily horizontal flow and diameters of about 20,000 miles (30,000 kilometers). { ˈsü·pər′gran·yə′lā·shən ‚selz }

superior conjunction A conjunction when an astronomical body is opposite the earth on the other side of the sun. { sə′pir·ē·ər kən′jəŋk·shən }

superior planet Any of the planets that are farther than the earth from the sun; includes Mars, Jupiter, Saturn, Uranus, Neptune, and Pluto. { sə′pir·ē·ər ′plan·ət }

superior transit *See* upper transit. { sə′pir·ē·ər ′tran·zət }

superluminal radio source A radio source whose velocity appears to exceed that of light. { ˈsü·pərˈlüm·ən·əl ′rād·ē·ō ‚sȯrs }

supermassive star A star with a mass exceeding about 50 times that of the sun. { ˈsü·pər′mas·iv ′stär }

super-metal-rich star **1.** A low-luminosity giant star of spectral class K, strongly enhanced cyanogen radical (CN) bands, and apparently strong metal lines. **2.** A star that is significantly richer in metals than those of the Hyades. { ′sü·pər ˈmed·əl ‚rich ′stär }

supernova A star that suddenly bursts into very great brilliance as a result of its blowing up; it is orders of magnitude brighter than a nova. { ˈsü·pər′nō·və }

supernova remnant A nebula consisting of an expanding shell of gas that has been ejected by a supernova. Abbreviated SNR. { ˈsü·pər′nō·və ′rem·nənt }

supersonic aircraft Aircraft capable of supersonic speeds. { ˈsü·pərˈsän·ik ′er‚kraft }

supersonic airfoil An airfoil designed to produce lift at supersonic speeds. { ˈsü·pərˈsän·ik ′er‚fȯil }

supersonic combustion ramjet *See* scramjet. { ˈsü·pərˈsän·ik kəmˈbəs·chən ′ram‚jet }

supersonic inlet An inlet of a jet engine at which single, double, or multiple shock waves form. { ˈsü·pərˈsän·ik ′in‚let }

supersonic transport A transport plane capable of flying at speeds higher than the speed of sound. Abbreviated SST. { ˈsü·pərˈsän·ik ′tranz‚pȯrt }

superthermal particles Particles in the solar corona that have been accelerated by magnetic energy dissipation to very high energies, from 10^2 to 10^6 times the mean thermal energy of particles in the coronal gas. { ˈsü·pər‚thər·məl ′pärd·ə·kəlz }

surge An unusually violent solar prominence that usually accompanies a smaller flare, consisting of a brilliant jet of gas which shoots out into the solar corona with a speed on the order of 180 miles (300 kilometers) per second and reaches a height on the order of 60,000 miles (100,000 kilometers). { sərj }

surveillance satellite   A satellite whose function is to make systematic observations of the earth, usually by photographic means, for military intelligence or for other purposes. { sər'vā·ləns ˌsad·əlˌīt }

sustainer rocket engine   A rocket engine that maintains the velocity of a rocket vehicle once it has achieved its programmed velocity by use of a booster or other engine. { sə'stān·ər 'räk·ət ˌen·jən }

Swan   See Cygnus. { swän }

Swann bands   Particular bands seen in the visible spectra of comets; they arise from the presence of dimeric carbon (C_2) in the comet's tail. { swän ˌbanz }

Swan Nebula   See Omega Nebula. { 'swän 'neb·yə·lə }

sweat cooling   A technique for cooling combustion chambers or aerodynamically heated surfaces by forcing a coolant through a porous wall, resulting in film cooling at the interface. Also known as transpiration cooling. { 'swet ˌkül·iŋ }

sweepback   **1.** The backward slant of a leading or trailing edge of an airfoil. **2.** The amount of this slant, expressed as the angle between a line perpendicular to the plane of symmetry and a reference line in the airfoil. { 'swēpˌbak }

swell diameter   In a body of revolution having an ogival portion, such as a projectile, the swell diameter is in the diameter of the maximum transverse section of the geometrical ogive. { 'swel dīˌam·əd·ər }

sweptback wing   An airplane wing on which both the leading and trailing edges have sweepback, the trailing edge forming an acute angle with the longitudinal axis of the airplane aft of the root. Also known as swept wing. { 'swep!bak ˌwiŋ }

swept wing   See sweptback wing. { 'swept ˌwiŋ }

swing-around trajectory   A planetary round-trip trajectory which requires minimal propulsion at the destination planet, but instead uses the planet's gravitational field to effect the bulk of the necessary orbit change to return to earth. { 'swiŋ ə!raùnd trə'jek·trē }

swing-by   See flyby. { 'swiŋˌbī }

swing-wing aircraft   An aircraft whose wings fold back along the fuselage at high flight speeds. { 'swiŋ ˌwiŋ 'erˌkraft }

Swordfish   See Dorado. { 'sórdˌfish }

symbiotic nova   See novalike symbiotic. { ˌsim·bē'äd·ik 'nō·və }

symbiotic objects   Stars whose spectra have characteristics of two disparate spectral classes. { ˌsim·bē'äd·ik 'äbˌjeks }

symbiotic star   A stellar object whose optical spectrum displays features indicative of two very different stellar regimes: a stellar spectrum whose flux distribution and absorption lines suggest the presence of a cool star, and emission lines which can be formed only in a much hotter medium. { ˌsim·bē'äd·ik 'stär }

synchrone   The geometrical locus of the dust grains ejected from the nucleus of a comet at the same time and having any value of beta. { 'siŋˌkrōn }

synchronous orbit   **1.** An orbit in which a satellite makes a limited number of equatorial

synchronous rotation

crossing points which are then repeated in synchronism with some defined reference (usually earth or sun). **2.** Commonly, the equatorial, circular, 24-hour case in which the satellite appears to hover over a specific point of the earth. { 'siŋ·krə·nəs 'ȯr·bət }

synchronous rotation   The rotation of a planet or satellite whose period is equal to its orbital period. { 'siŋ·krə·nəs rō'tā·shən }

synchronous satellite   *See* geostationary satellite. { 'siŋ·krə·nəs 'sad·əl͵īt }

syndyne   The geometrical locus of the dust grains ejected from the nucleus of a comet continuously and having a particular value of beta. { 'sin͵dīn }

synergic curve   A curve plotted for the ascent of a rocket, space-air vehicle, or space vehicle, calculated to give optimum fuel economy and optimum velocity. { sə'nər·jik 'kərv }

synodic   Referring to conjunction of celestial bodies. { sə'näd·ik }

synodic month   A month based on the moon's phases. { sə'näd·ik 'mənth }

synodic period   The time period between two successive astronomical conjunctions of the same celestial objects. { sə'näd·ik 'pir·ē·əd }

syzygy   **1.** One of the two points in a celestial object's orbit where it is in conjunction with or opposition to the sun. **2.** Those points in the moon's orbit where the moon, earth, and sun are in a straight line. { 'siz·ə·jē }

T

tactical air-direction center An air operations installation under the overall control of the tactical air-control center, from which aircraft and air warning service functions of tactical air operations in an area of responsibility are directed. { 'tak·tə·kəl !er di·rek·shən ·sen·tər }

tactical air force An air force charged with carrying out tactical air operations in coordination with ground or naval forces. { 'tak·tə·kəl 'er ·fórs }

tactical airlift That airlift which provides the immediate and responsive air movement and delivery of combat troops and supplies directly into objective areas through air landing, extraction, airdrop, or other delivery techniques; and the air logistic support of all theater forces, including those engaged in combat operations, to meet specific theater objectives and requirements. { 'tak·tə·kəl 'er·lift }

tactical air observer An officer trained as an air observer whose function is to observe from airborne aircraft and report on movement and disposition of friendly and enemy forces, on terrain and weather and hydrography, and to execute other missions as directed. { 'tak·tə·kəl 'er əb·zər·vər }

tactical air operations An air operation involving the employment of air power in coordination with ground or naval forces to gain and maintain air superiority, to prevent movement of enemy forces into and within the objective area and to seek out and destroy these forces and their supporting installations, and to join with ground or naval forces in operations within the objective area in order to assist directly in attainment of their immediate objective. { 'tak·tə·kəl 'er ·äp·ə·rā· shənz }

tactical air reconnaissance The use of air vehicles to obtain information concerning terrain, weather, and the disposition, composition, movement, installations, lines of communications, and electronic and communication emissions of enemy forces. { 'tak·tə·kəl 'er ri·kän·ə·səns }

tactical air support Air operations carried out in coordination with surface forces which directly assist the land or naval battle. { 'tak·tə·kəl 'er sə·pórt }

tactical air transport The use of air transport in direct support of airborne assaults, carriage of air-transported forces, tactical air supply, evacuation of casualties from forward airdromes, and clandestine operations. { 'tak·tə·kəl 'er 'tranz·pórt }

tactical transport aircraft Aircraft designed primarily for carrying personnel or cargo over short or medium distances. { 'tak·tə·kəl 'tranz·pórt !er·kraft }

tail **1.** The rear part of a body, as of an aircraft or a rocket. **2.** The tail surfaces of an aircraft or a rocket. **3.** The part of a comet that extends from the coma in a direction opposite to the sun; it consists of dust and gas that have been blown away from the coma by the solar wind and the sun's radiation pressure. { tāl }

tail assembly *See* empennage. { 'tāl ə‚sem·blē }

tail fin A fin at the rear of a rocket or other body. { 'tāl ‚fin }

tail surface A stabilizing or control surface in the tail of an aircraft or missile. { 'tāl ‚sər·fəs }

takeoff Ascent of an aircraft or rocket at any angle, as the action of a rocket vehicle departing from its launch pad or the action of an aircraft as it becomes airborne. { 'tāk‚óf }

takeoff assist 1. The extra thrust given to an airplane or missile during takeoff through the use of a rocket motor or other device. 2. The device used in such a takeoff. { 'tāk‚óf ə‚sist }

takeoff weight The weight of an aircraft or rocket vehicle ready for takeoff, including the weight of the vehicle, the fuel, and the payload. { 'tāk‚óf ‚wāt }

tandem The fore and aft configuration used in boosted missiles, long-range ballistic missiles, and satellite vehicles; stages are stacked together in series and are discarded at burnout of the propellant for each stage. { 'tan·dəm }

taper An airfoil feature in which either the thickness or the chord length or both decrease from the root to the tip. { 'tā·pər }

taper-in-thickness ratio A gradual change in the thickness ratio along the wing span with the chord remaining constant. { ˈtā·pər in ˈthik·nəs ‚rā·shō }

Tarantula *See* Loop Nebula. { tə'ran·chə·lə }

target acquisition The process of optically, manually, mechanically, or electronically orienting a tracking system in direction and range to lock on a target. { 'tär·gət ‚ak·wə'zish·ən }

target approach point In air transport operations, a navigational checkpoint over which the final turn-in to the drop zone-landing zone is made. { 'tär·gət ə'prōch ‚póint }

target drone A pilotless aircraft controlled by radio from the ground or from a mother ship and used exclusively as a target for antiaircraft weapons. { 'tär·gət ‚drōn }

target pattern The flight path of aircraft during the attack phase. { 'tär·gət ‚pad·ərn }

T association An association that includes many T Tauri stars. { 'tē ə‚sō·sē‚ā·shən }

Taurid meteor A meteor shower occurring from about October 26 to November 16 in the Northern Hemisphere, with the maximum occurring about the first week in November; the radiant lies in the constellation Taurus. { 'tór·əd 'mēd·ē·ər }

Taurus A northern constellation; right ascension 4 hours, declination 15° north; it includes the star Aldebaran, useful in navigation. Also known as Bull. { 'tór·əs }

Taurus A A strong, discrete radio source in the constellation Taurus, associated with the Crab Nebula. { 'tór·əs 'ā }

Taurus cluster A cluster of stars observed in the region of the constellation Taurus; it is about 130 light-years (1.23×10^{18} meters) from the sun, and 58 light-years (5.49×10^{17} meters) in diameter. { 'tór·əs 'kləs·tər }

Taurus dark cloud   A large, relative nearby aggregate of dust and gas in which star formation is taking place. { 'tȯr·əs 'därk 'klaùd }

teardrop balloon   A sounding balloon which, when operationally inflated, resembles an inverted teardrop; this shape was determined primarily by aerodynamic considerations of the problem of obtaining maximum stable rates of a balloon ascension. { 'tir‚dräp bə'lün }

Telescope   See Telescopium. { 'tel·ə‚skōp }

telescopic comet   A comet in which only the coma is observed. { ¦tel·ə¦skäp·ik 'käm·ət }

Telescopium   A constellation, right ascension 19 hours, declination 50° south. Also known as Telescope. { ‚tel·ə'skō·pē·əm }

Telesto   A small, irregularly shaped satellite of Saturn that librates about the trailing lagrangian point of Tethys's orbit. { te'les·tō }

terminator   The line of demarcation between the dark and light portions of the moon or planets. { 'tər·mə‚nād·ər }

terra   A bright upland or mountainous region on the surface of the moon, characterized by a lighter color than that of a mare, a relatively high albedo, and a rough texture formed by large intersecting or overlapping craters. { 'ter·ə }

terrestrial planet   One of the four small planets near the sun (Earth, Mercury, Venus, and Mars). { tə'res·trē·əl 'plan·ət }

test bed   A base, mount, or frame within or upon which a piece of equipment, especially an engine, is secured for testing. { 'test‚bed }

test chamber   The test section of a wind tunnel. { 'test ‚chām·bər }

test firing   The firing of a rocket engine, either live or static, with the purpose of making controlled observations of the engine or of an engine component. { 'test ‚fīr·iŋ }

test flight   A flight to make controlled observations of the operation or performance of an aircraft or a rocket, or of a component of an aircraft or rocket. { 'test ‚flīt }

test section   The section of a wind tunnel where objects are tested to determine their aerodynamic characteristics. { 'test ‚sek·shən }

test stand   A stationary platform or table, together with any testing apparatus attached thereto, for testing or proving engines and instruments. { 'test ‚stand }

Tethys   A satellite of the planet Saturn having a diameter of about 780 miles (1300 kilometers). { 'tē·thəs }

Thalassa   A satellite of Neptune orbiting at a mean distance of 31,000 miles (50,000 kilometers) with a period of 7.5 hours, and with a diameter of about 50 miles (80 kilometers). { thə'las·ə }

Thebe   A small satellite of Jupiter, having an orbital radius of 137,900 miles (221,900 kilometers), and a radius of 28-34 miles (48-55 kilometers). Also known as Jupiter XIV. { 'thē·bē }

Themis   An asteroid with a diameter of roughly 135 miles (225 kilometers), mean dis-

tance from the sun of 3.138 astronomical units, and C-type surface composition.
{ 'thē·məs }

thermal barrier A limit to the speed of airplanes and rockets in the atmosphere imposed by heat from friction between the aircraft and the air, which weakens and eventually melts the surface of the aircraft. Also known as heat barrier. { 'thər·məl 'bar·ē·ər }

thermal phase See gradual phase. { 'thər·məl ‚fāz }

thermal time scale See Kelvin time scale. { 'thər·məl 'tīm ‚skāl }

thermojet Air-duct-type engine in which air is scooped up from the surrounding atmosphere, compressed, heated by combustion, and then expanded and discharged at high velocity. { 'thər·mə‚jet }

thickness ratio The ratio of the maximum thickness of an airfoil section to the length of its chord. { 'thik·nəs ‚rā·shō }

Thisbe An asteroid with a diameter of about 120 miles (200 kilometers), mean distance from the sun of 2.768 astronomical units, and C-type surface composition. { 'thiz·bē }

three-alpha process A nuclear reaction in which three helium-4 nuclei (alpha particles) combine to form a carbon-12 nucleus, with the emission of a gamma ray; it converts helium into carbon in red giants. Also known as Salpeter process; triple-alpha process. { 'thrē ¦al·fə 'prä‚səs }

three-kiloparsec arm A region approximately 3 kiloparsecs from the galactic center that displays strong absorption in the 21-centimeter line of atomic hydrogen. { 'thrē ¦kil·ō¦pär‚sek 'ärm }

throat velocity See critical velocity. { 'thrōt və‚läs·əd·ē }

throttling The varying of the thrust of a rocket engine during powered flight. { 'thräd·əl·iŋ }

thrust augmentation The increasing of the thrust of an engine or power plant, especially of a jet engine and usually for a short period of time, over the thrust normally developed. { 'thrəst ‚óg·mən'tā·shən }

thrust augmenter Any contrivance used for thrust augmentation, as a venturi used in a rocket. { 'thrəst 'óg‚men·tər }

thrust axis A line or axis through an aircraft or a rocket, along which the thrust acts; an axis through the longitudinal center of a jet or rocket engine, along which the thrust of the engine acts. Also known as axis of thrust; center of thrust. { 'thrəst ‚ak·səs }

thrust coefficient See nozzle thrust coefficient. { 'thrəst ‚kō·i‚fish·ənt }

thruster A control jet employed in spacecraft; an example would be one utilizing hydrogen peroxide. { 'thrəs·tər }

thrust horsepower **1.** The force-velocity equivalent of the thrust developed by a jet or rocket engine. **2.** The thrust of an engine-propeller combination expressed in horsepower; it differs from the shaft horsepower of the engine by the amount the propeller efficiency varies from 100%. { 'thrəst 'hórs‚paù·ər }

thrust output   The net thrust delivered by a jet engine, rocket engine, or rocket motor. { 'thrəst 'aut,put }

thrust-pound   A unit of measurement for the thrust produced by a jet engine or rocket. { 'thrəst 'paund }

thrust power   The power usefully expended on thrust, equal to the thrust (or net thrust) times airspeed. { 'thrəst ,paú·ər }

thrust reverser   A device or apparatus for reversing thrust, especially of a jet engine. { 'thrəst ri'vər·sər }

thrust section   A section in a rocket vehicle that houses or incorporates the combustion chamber or chambers and nozzles. { 'thrəst ,sek·shən }

thrust terminator   A device for ending the thrust in a rocket engine, either through propellant cutoff (in the case of a liquid) or through diverting the flow of gases from the nozzle. { 'thrəst ,tər·mə,nād·ər }

thrust-weight ratio   A quantity used to evaluate engine performance, obtained by dividing the thrust output by the engine weight less fuel. { 'thrəst 'wāt ,rā·shō }

Thuban   A fourth-magnitude star of spectral class AO in the constellation Draco that was near the north celestial pole around 3000 B.C.; the star Alpha Draconis. { 'thü,ban }

Thule group   An accumulation of asteroids whose sidereal period of revolution is in the ratio 3/4 with that of Jupiter. { 'tü·lē ,grüp }

tidal radius   The distance from the center of a planet in formation at which the planet's gravitational attraction for nearby gas equals that of the Sun. { 'tīd·əl 'rād·ē·əs }

tilt   The inclination of an aircraft, winged missile, or the like from the horizontal, measured by reference to the lateral axis or to the longitudinal axis. { tilt }

tilt rotor   An assembly of rapidly rotating blades on a vertical takeoff and landing aircraft, whose plane of rotation can be continuously varied from the horizontal to the vertical, permitting performance as helicopter blades or as propeller blades. { 'tilt ,rōd·ər }

time diagram   A diagram in which the celestial equator appears as a circle, and celestial meridians and hour circles as radial lines; used to facilitate solution of time problems and other problems involving arcs of the celestial equator or angles at the pole, by indicating relations between various quantities involved; conventionally, the relationships are given as viewed from a point over the South Pole, in a westward direction or counterclockwise. Also known as diagram on the plane of the celestial equator; diagram on the plane of the equinoctial. { 'tīm ,dī·ə,gram }

time-distance graph   A graph used to determine the ground distance for air-route legs of a specified time interval; time-distance relationships are often simplified by considering air, wind, and ground distances for flight legs of 1-hour duration. { 'tīm 'dis·təns ,graf }

time front   A locus of points representing the maximum ground distances from a departure point that can be covered by an aircraft in a prescribed time interval. Also known as hour-out line; time curve. { 'tīm ,frənt }

time meridian   Any meridian used as a reference for reckoning time, particularly a zone or standard meridian. { 'tīm mə,rid·ē·ən }

time separation The time interval between adjacent aircraft flying approximately the same path. { 'tīm ˌsep·ə͵rā·shən }

time zone To avoid the inconvenience of the continuous change of mean solar time with longitude, the earth is divided into 24 time zones, each about 15° wide and centered on standard longitudes, 0°, 15°, 30°, and so on; within each zone the time kept is the mean solar time of the standard meridian. { 'tīm ͵zōn }

Tiros satellite Television infrared observation satellite; a meteorological satellite that takes television pictures of cloud cover, using radiation sensors and cameras; it stores and transmits this information on ground command. { 'tī͵rōs 'sad·əl͵īt }

Titan The largest satellite of Saturn, with a diameter estimated to be about 3600 miles (5800 kilometers). { 'tīt·ən }

Titania A satellite of Uranus, with a diameter estimated to be 990 miles (1600 kilometers). { tī'tā·nē·ə }

Titius-Bode law See Bode's law. { 'tēt·sē·əs 'bōd·ə ͵lȯ }

TLP See transient lunar phenomena.

topside sounder A satellite designed to measure ion concentration in the ionosphere from above the ionosphere. { 'täp͵sīd ⸗saún·dər }

Toro A small asteroid with a diameter of about 3.6 miles (6 kilometers), whose orbit, with semimajor axis of 1.368 astronomical units and eccentricity of 0.44, oscillates with that of Venus; it is about 0.13 astronomical unit from Earth at closest approach. { 'tȯr·ō }

total eclipse An eclipse that obscures the entire surface of the moon or sun. { 'tōd·əl i'klips }

total impulse The product of the thrust and the time over which the thrust is produced, expressed in pounds (force)-seconds; used especially in reference to a rocket motor or a rocket engine. { 'tōd·əl 'im͵pəls }

totality 1. The portion of a total eclipse of the sun during which the sun is entirely covered by the moon at a specified location on the earth's surface. 2. The portion of a total eclipse of the moon or other body during which the eclipsed body is entirely within the umbra of the eclipsing body. { tō'tal·ad·ē }

total lift The upward force produced by the gas in a balloon; it is equal to the sum of the free lift, the weight of the balloon, and the weight of auxiliary equipment carried by the balloon. { 'tōd·əl 'lift }

Toucan See Tucana. { 'tü͵kan }

tower telescope A telescope, usually of long focal length, that is situated underneath a solar tower to study the sun. { 'taú·ər ⸗tel·ə͵skōp }

track The actual line of movement of an aircraft or a rocket over the surface of the earth; it is the projection of the history of the flight path on the surface. Also known as flight track. { trak }

track made good The actual path of an aircraft over the surface of the earth, or its graphic representation. { 'trak ͵mād 'gúd }

traffic pattern The traffic flow that is prescribed for aircraft landing at, taxiing on, and taking off from an airport; the usual components of a traffic pattern are upwind leg, crosswind leg, downwind leg, base leg, and final approach. { 'traf·ik ˌpad·ərn }

trail   A luminous trace left in the sky by the passage of a large meteor. { trāl }

trail angle   The angle at an aircraft between the vertical and the line of sight to an object over which the aircraft has passed. { 'trāl ˌaŋ·gəl }

trail formation   Aircraft flying singly or in elements in such manner that each aircraft or element is in line behind the preceding aircraft or element. { 'trāl fȯrˌmā·shən }

trailing edge   The rear section of a multipiece airfoil, usually that portion aft of the rear spar. { 'trāl·iŋ 'ej }

trailing-edge tab   One of the devices on the aircraft elevator that reduce or eliminate hinge movements required to deflect the elevator during flight. { 'trāl·iŋ ᶫej ˌtab }

train   The bright tail of a comet or meteor. { trān }

transfer ellipse   *See* transfer orbit. { 'tranz·fər iˌlips }

transfer orbit   In interplanetary travel, an elliptical trajectory tangent to the orbits of both the departure planet and the target planet. Also known as transfer ellipse. { 'tranz·fər ˌȯr·bət }

transient lunar phenomena   Local obscurations and reddish glows that are sometimes observed in certain areas of the moon. Abbreviated TLP. { 'tranch·ənt 'lü·nər fə'näm·ə·nä }

transient x-ray source   *See* x-ray nova. { 'tranch·ənt 'eksˌrā ˌsȯrs }

transit   **1.** A celestial body's movement across the meridian of a place. Also known as meridian transit. **2.** Passage of a smaller celestial body across a larger one. **3.** Passage of a satellite's shadow across the disk of its primary. { 'trans·ət }

transition altitude   The altitude in the vicinity of an aerodrome at or below which the vertical position of an aircraft is controlled by reference to true altitude. { tran'zish·ən 'al·təˌtüd }

transition flow   A flow of fluid about an airfoil that is changing from laminar flow to turbulent flow. { tran'zish·ən ˌflō }

transition region   A layer of the solar atmosphere only a few hundred miles thick between the chromosphere and the corona across which the temperature rises rapidly from a few times 10^4 K to the order of 10^6 K. { tran'zish·ən ˌrē·jən }

translunar   Beyond the orbit of the moon. { tran'slü·nər }

transonic flight   Flight of vehicles at speeds near the speed of sound (660 miles per hour or 1060 kilometers per hour, at 35,000 feet or 10,700 meters altitude), characterized by great increase in drag, decrease in lift at any altitude, and abrupt changes in the moments acting on the aircraft; the vehicle may shake or buffet. { tran'sän·ik 'flīt }

transpiration cooling   *See* sweat cooling. { ˌtranz·pə'rā·shən 'kül·iŋ }

trap   That part of a rocket motor that keeps the propellant grain in place. { trap }

Trapezium

Trapezium   Four very hot stars that appear to the eye as a single star in the Great Nebula of Orion; the star symbol is M42. { trə'pē·zē·əm }

Triangle   See Triangulum. { 'trī‚aŋ·gəl }

Triangulum   A northern constellation, right ascension 2 hours, declination 30°N. Also known as Triangle. { trī'aŋ·gyə·ləm }

Triangulum Australe   A southern constellation, right ascension 16 hours, declination 65°S. Also known as Southern Triangle. { trī'aŋ·gyə·ləm ȯ'strä·lē }

Triangulum Nebula   A nebula that is part of a small cluster of galaxies known as the Local Group; the nebula is labeled M33. { trī'aŋ·gyə·ləm 'neb·yə·lə }

tricycle landing gear   A landing-gear arrangement that places the nose gear well forward of the center of gravity on the fuselage and the two main gears slightly aft of the center of gravity, with sufficient distance between them to provide stability against rolling over during a yawed landing in a crosswind, or during ground maneuvers. { 'trī·sik·əl 'land·iŋ ‚gir }

Trifid nebula   An emission nebula in Sagittarius that consists mostly of hydrogen ionized by hot, young stars, and displays dark lanes formed by dust. { 'trī‚fid 'neb·yə·lə }

trigonometric parallax   A parallax that may be determined for the nearest stars (less than 300 light-years or 2.84 × 10¹⁸ m) by a direct method utilizing trigonometry. { ⸽trig·ə·nə⸽me·trik 'par·ə‚laks }

trim   The orientation of an aircraft relative to the airstream, as indicated by the amount of control pressure required to maintain a given flight performance. { trim }

triple-alpha process   See three-alpha process. { 'trip·əl ⸽al·fə ‚prä·səs }

triple-mode Cepheid   A bent Cepheid that displays three nearly identical pulsation periods. { 'trip·əl ⸽mōd 'sef·ē·əd }

Triton   The largest satellite of Neptune, with a diameter of about 1681 miles (2705 kilometers), orbiting at a mean distance of 220,500 miles (354,800 kilometers) with a period of 5 days 21.0 hours. { 'trīt·ən }

Trojan planet   One of a group of asteroids whose periods of revolution are about equal to that of Jupiter, or about 12 years; these bodies move close to one or the other of two positions called Lagrangian points, 60° ahead of or 60° behind Jupiter; the asteroids near these positions are known as Greeks and Pure Trojans respectively. { 'trō·jən 'plan·ət }

tropical month   The average period of the revolution of the moon about the earth with respect to the vernal equinox, a period of 27 days 7 hours 43 minutes 4.7 seconds, or approximately 27¹/₃ days. { 'träp·ə·kəl 'mənth }

tropical year   A unit of time equal to the period of one revolution of the earth about the sun measured between successive vernal equinoxes; it is 365.2422 mean solar days or 365 days 5 hours 48 minutes 46 seconds. Also known as astronomical year. { 'träp·ə·kəl 'yir }

Tropic of Cancer   A small circle on the celestial sphere connecting points with declination 23.45° north of the celestial equator, the northernmost declination of the sun. { 'träp·ik əv 'kan·sər }

Tropic of Capricorn   A small circle on the celestial sphere connecting points with declination 23.45° south of the celestial equator, the southernmost declination of the sun. { 'träp·ik əv 'kap·ri,kȯrn }

true airspeed   The actual speed of an aircraft relative to the air through which it flies, that is, the calibrated airspeed corrected for temperature, density, or compressibility. { 'trü 'er,spēd }

true-airspeed indicator   An instrument for measuring true airspeed. Also known as true-airspeed meter. { 'trü 'er,spēd ,in·də,kād·ər }

true anomaly   See anomaly. { 'trü ə'näm·ə·lē }

true place   The position of a star on the celestial sphere as it would be observed from the center of the sun, referred to the celestial equator and celestial equinox at the moment of observation. { 'trü 'plās }

true solar day   See apparent solar day. { 'trü 'sō·lər 'dā }

true sun   See apparent sun. { 'trü 'sən }

T Tauri star   A star, with mass from 0.5 to 2.5 solar masses, in an early stage of formation at which interaction with its associated nebulosity, as well as possible internal instabilities, make it variable in luminosity and render its spectrum very peculiar. Also known as nebular variable. { 'tē 'tȯr·ē ,stär }

tube core   One type of sandwich configuration used in structural materials in aircraft; aluminum, steel, and titanium have been used for face materials with cores of wood, rubber, plastics, steel, and aluminum in the form of tubes. { 'tüb ,kȯr }

Tucana   A constellation in the southern hemisphere; right ascension 23 hours, declination 60° south. Also known as Toucan. { tü'kä·nə }

Tully-Fisher relation   A relation between the rotational velocity of a galaxy, as reflected in the width of the 21-centimeter line, and the intrinsic luminosity of the galaxy. { ¦təl·ē 'fish·ər ri,lā·shən }

tumbling   An attitude situation in which the vehicle continues on its flight, but turns end over end about its center of mass. { 'təm·bliŋ }

turbidity   The formation of disks centered on stars in long-exposure photographs as a result of light scattering by grains in the emulsion. { tər'bid·əd·ē }

turbofan   An air-breathing jet engine in which additional propulsive thrust is gained by extending a portion of the compressor or turbine blades outside the inner engine case. { 'tər·bō,fan }

turbojet   A jet engine incorporating a turbine-driven air compressor to take in and compress the air for the combustion of fuel (or for heating by a nuclear reactor), the gases of combustion (or the heated air) being used both to rotate the turbine and to create a thrust-producing jet. { 'tər·bō,jet }

turboprop   A gas turbine power plant that produces shaft power to drive aircraft propellers. { 'tər·bō,präp }

turboramjet   An aircraft engine that is a hybrid of a turbofan and a ramjet; operates as a ramjet for efficient propulsion at very high supersonic cruise speeds, or as a turbofan for relatively efficient propulsion at low flight speeds. { ¦tər·bō'ram,jet }

turning error   See northerly turning error. { 'tərn·iŋ ,er·ər }

turnoff mass   The mass of those stars in a cluster that are at the turnoff point. { 'tərn,òf ,mas }

turnoff point   The point on a Hertzsprung-Russell diagram of a star cluster at which stars leave the main sequence and move toward the giant branch. { 'tərn,òf ,pòint }

twilight   An intermediate period of illumination of the sky before sunrise and after sunset; the three forms are civil, nautical, and astronomical. { 'twī,līt }

twilight correction   In the interpretation of the records of sunshine recorders, the difference between the time of sunrise and the time at which a record of sunshine first began to be made by the sunshine recorder; and conversely at sunset; this correction is added only when the horizon is clear during the period. { 'twī,līt kə,rek·shən }

twilight zone   That zone of the earth or other planet in twilight at any time. { 'twī ,līt ,zōn }

twinkling stars   Rapid fluctuations of the brightness and size of the images of stars caused by turbulence in the earth's atmosphere. { 'twink·liŋ 'stärz }

twin ring structures   Consanguineous ring structures whose component craters are of the same size, as well as being similar in form. { 'twin 'riŋ ,strək·chərz }

two-position propeller   An airplane propeller whose blades are limited to two angles, one for take off and climb and the other for cruising. { 'tü ¦pə¦zish·ən prə'pel·ər }

Tycho   A crater on the near side of the moon. { 'tī·kō }

Tychonic system   A theory of the planetary motion proposed by the astronomer Tycho Brahe in which the earth is stationary, with the sun and moon revolving about it but all the other planets revolving about the sun. { tī'kän·ik ,sis·təm }

Tycho's Nova   A supernova that appeared in the constellation Cassiopeia in 1572; the star B Cassiopeiae. Also known as Tycho's star. { 'tī·kōz 'nō·və }

Tycho's star   See Tycho's Nova. { 'tī·kōz 'stär }

Type II Cepheids   See W Virginis stars. { 'tīp ¦tü 'sef·ē·ədz }

type I supernova   A member of a class of supernovae which attain a maximum absolute magnitude of at least 16, have similar light curves characterized by a rapid rise and rapid decline, and have spectra formed of extremely broad, overlapping bright lines. { 'tīp ¦wən ¦sü·pər'nō·və }

type II supernova   A member of a class of supernovae whose individual light curves vary considerably, but which in general show a weaker maximum and slower decline than type I supernovae, with marked periods of constant brightness during the decrease, and whose spectra are continuous until about a month after maximum when broad emission lines develop. { 'tīp ¦tü ¦sü·pər'nō·və }

U

UBV photometry A system of three-color photometry used to obtain specific stellar magnitudes; the system is based on the comparison of stars' magnitudes with a standard sequence of about 400 stars. { ¦yü¦bē¦vē fə'täm·ə·trē }

UBV system A system of stellar magnitudes in which an object's apparent magnitude is measured at three wavelengths, labeled U, at 360 nanometers; B, at 420 nanometers; and V, at 540 nanometers; and is characterized by the color indices B − V and U − B, which are both defined to be 0 for a star of spectral type A0. Also known as Johnson-Morgan system. { ¦yü¦bē¦vē ˌsis·təm }

U Cephei A binary star; in this double-star eclipsing system, one component has reached its Roche limit (a dynamical barrier beyond which the size of neither star can expand) while the other is distinctly smaller than this limit. { 'yü 'sef·ē¸ī }

U Geminorum stars A class of variable stars known as dwarf novae; their light curves resemble those of novae, with range brightness variations of about 4 magnitudes; examples are U Gemini and SS Cygni. Also known as SS Cygni stars. { 'yü ˌjem·ə'nȯr·əm ˌstärz }

ullage rocket A small rocket used in space to impart an acceleration to a tank system to ensure that the liquid propellants collect in the tank in such a manner as to flow properly into the pumps or thrust chamber. { 'əl·ij ˌräk·ət }

ultimate lines Special spectral lines that can be used to indicate the existence of an element in the sun or other star. { 'əl·tə·mət 'līnz }

ultralight aircraft An extremely lightweight, single-seat aircraft with low flight speed, power, and fuel capacity, used for sport or recreation. { 'əl·trəˌlīt 'erˌkraft }

ultraviolet astronomy Astronomical investigations utilizing observations carried out in the spectral region from approximately 350 to 90 nanometers. { ¦əl·trə'vī·lət ə'strän·ə·mē }

ultraviolet-bright star A star that is brighter than stars on the horizontal branch and bluer than stars on the giant branch. { ¦əl·trə'vī·lət 'brīt 'stär }

ultraviolet star A very hot star that is evolving toward the white dwarf stage; usually the central star of a planetary nebula. { ¦əl·trə'vī·lət 'stär }

umbilical connections Electrical and mechanical connections to a launch vehicle prior to lift off; the umbilical tower adjacent to the vehicle on the launch pad supports these connections which supply electrical power, control signals, data links, propellant loading, high pressure gas transfer, and air conditioning. { əm'bil·ə·kəl kə'nek·shənz }

umbilical cord

umbilical cord   Any of the servicing electrical or fluid lines between the ground or a tower and an uprighted rocket vehicle before the launch. Also known as umbilical. { əm'bil·ə·kəl ˌkȯrd }

umbilical tower   A vertical structure supporting the umbilical cords running into a rocket in launching position. { əm'bil·ə·kəl 'taú·ər }

umbra   The dark, central region of a sunspot. { 'əm·brə }

Umbriel   A satellite of Uranus orbiting at a mean distance of 165,300 miles (266,000 kilometers) with a period of 4.144 days, and with a diameter of about 740 miles (1190 kilometers). { 'əm·brē·əl }

undercarriage   The landing gear assembly for an aircraft. { 'ən·dərˌkar·ij }

universal time   See Greenwich mean time. { ˈyü·nəˌvər·səl 'tīm }

universal time 0   The uncorrected time of the earth's rotation as measured by the transit of stars across the observer's meridian. Abbreviated UT 0. { ˈyü·nəˌvər·səl ˈtīm 'zirˌō }

universal time 1   Universal time 0 corrected for polar motion; it is the true angular rotation. Abbreviated UT 1. { ˈyü·nəˌvər·səl ˈtīm 'wən }

universal time 2   Universal time 1 corrected for seasonal variations in the earth's rotation. Abbreviated UT 2. { ˈyü·nəˌvər·səl ˈtīm 'tü }

universal time coordinated   The coordinated time kept by a uniformly running clock, approximating the measure UT 2. Abbreviated UTC. { ˈyü·nəˌvər·səl ˈtīm kō'ȯrdˌənˌād·əd }

universe   The totality of astronomical things, events, relations, and energies capable of being described objectively. { 'yü·nəˌvərs }

upper culmination   See upper transit. { 'əp·ər ˌkəl·mə'nā·shən }

upper limb   That half of the outer edge of a celestial body having the greatest altitude. { 'əp·ər 'lim }

upper transit   The movement of a celestial body across a celestial meridian's upper branch. Also known as superior transit; upper culmination. { 'əp·ər 'trans·ət }

uranography   The science of mapping stars, groups of stars, and star clusters. { ˌyùr·ə'näg·rə·fē }

uranometry   The science of the measurement of the celestial sphere and celestial bodies. { ˌyùr·ə'näm·ə·trē }

Uranus   A planet, seventh in the order of distance from the sun; it has five known satellites, and its equatorial diameter is about four times that of the earth. { 'yùr·ə·nəs or yú'rā·nəs }

Urca process   A series of nuclear reactions, chiefly among the iron group of elements, that are postulated as a cause of stellar collapse, due to the energy lost to neutrinos that are rapidly formed in the reactions. { 'ər·kə ˌprä·ses }

Ursa Major   A northern constellation, right ascension 11 hours, declination 50°N; it contains a group of seven stars known as the Big Dipper. { 'ər·sə 'mā·jər }

Ursa Major cluster **1.** A group of about 126 stars, including 5 stars of the constellation Ursa Major; the sun is passing through this cluster which occupies a spherical space of about 450 light-years in diameter. **2.** A cluster of galaxies in the constellation Ursa Major having a redshift of about 0.051. { 'ər·sə 'mā·jər ˌkləs·tər }

Ursa Minor A northern constellation, right ascension 15 hours, declination 70°N; its brightest star, Polaris, is almost at the north celestial pole; seven of the eight stars form a dipper ouline. Also known as Little Bear; Little Dipper. { 'ər·sə 'mī·nər }

Ursa Minor system A dwarf elliptical galaxy in the Local Group, about 2.2 × 10⁵ light-years (1.3 × 10¹⁸ miles or 2.1 × 10¹⁸ kilometers) away. { 'ər·sə 'mī·nər ˌsis·təm }

ursids A shower of meteors occurring about December 22 from a radiant in the constellation Ursa Minor. { 'ər·sədz }

U Sagittae An eclipsing binary star in which one component has attained its Roche limit, while its mate is distinctly smaller than this limit. { 'yü 'saj·əˌtē }

UT 0 See universal time 0.

UT 1 See universal time 1.

UT 2 See universal time 2.

UTC See universal time coordinated.

utilization rate The amount of flying time produced in a specific period expressed in hours per period per aircraft. Also known as flying hour rate. { ˌyüd·əl·ə'zā·shən ˌrāt }

uvby system A four-color stellar magnitude system based on measurements in the ultraviolet, violet, blue, and yellow regions. Also known as Strömgren four-color index. { 'yüv·bē ˌsis·təm }

UV Ceti stars A class of stars that have brief outbursts of energy over their surface areas; they may have an increase of about 1 magnitude for periods of 1 hour; the type star is UV Ceti. Also known as flare stars. { ˌyü¦vē 'sed·ē ˌstärz }

V

vane A device that projects ahead of an aircraft to sense gusts or other actions of the air so as to create impulses or signals that are transmitted to the control system to stabilize the aircraft. { vān }

variable-area exhaust nozzle On a jet engine, an exhaust nozzle of which the exhaust exit opening can be varied in area by means of some mechanical device, permitting variation in the jet velocity. { 'ver·ē·ə·bəl ¦er·ē·ə ig'zȯst ˌnäz·əl }

variable-cycle engine A type of gas turbine jet engine whose cycle parameters, such as pressure ratio, temperature, gas flow paths, and air-handling characteristics, can be varied between those of a turbojet and a turbofan, enabling it to combine the advantages of both. { 'ver·ē·ə·bəl ¦sī·kəl 'en·jən }

variable geometry aircraft Aircraft with variable profile geometry, such as variable sweep wings. { 'ver·ē·ə·bəl jē¦äm·ə·trē 'er‚kraft }

variable nebula A nebula whose shape and brightness vary; an example is in the constellation Monoceros. { 'ver·ē·ə·bəl 'neb·yə·lə }

variable star A star that has a detectable change in its intensity which is often accompanied by other physical changes; changes in brightness may be a few thousandths of a magnitude to 20 magnitudes or even more. { 'ver·ē·ə·bəl 'stär }

variational inequality An inequality in the moon's motion, due mainly to the tangential component of the sun's attraction. { ˌver·ē'ā·shən·əl ˌin·i'kwäl·əd·ē }

vector steering A steering method for rockets and spacecraft wherein one or more thrust chambers are gimbal-mounted so that the direction of the thrust force (thrust vector) may be tilted in relation to the center of gravity of the vehicle to produce a turning movement. { 'vek·tər ˌstir·iŋ }

Vega One of the brightest stars, apparent magnitude 0.1; it is a main sequence star of spectral type A0, distance is 8 parsecs, and it is 40 times brighter than the sun. Also known as α Lyrae. { 'vā·gə }

vehicle 1. A structure, machine, or device, such as an aircraft or rocket, designed to carry a burden through air or space. 2. More restrictively, a rocket vehicle. { 've·ə·kəl }

vehicle control system A system, incorporating control surfaces or other devices, which adjusts and maintains the altitude and heading, and sometimes speed, of a vehicle in accordance with signals received from a guidance system. Also known as flight control system. { 've·ə·kəl kən'trōl ˌsis·təm }

vehicle mass ratio

vehicle mass ratio   The ratio of the final mass of a vehicle after all propellant has been used, to the initial mass. { 've·ə·kəl 'mas 'rā·shō }

Veil Nebula   See Cygnus loop. { 'vāl 'neb·yə·lə }

Vela   A southern constellation, right ascension 9 hours, declination 50°S. Also known as Sail. { 've̅·lə }

Vela pulsar   A pulsar with a period of 80 milliseconds, about 1500 light-years (1.4 × 10¹⁹ meters) away in the constellation Vela, whose variation has been detected at radio, gamma-ray, and optical wavelengths; probably associated with the Vela supernova remnant. { 've̅·lə·'pəl,sär }

Vela supernova remnant   A gaseous nebula that is the result of a supernova whose light reached Earth about 10,000 years ago. { 've̅·lə ˈsü·pər'nō·və ,rem·nənt }

Vela X   A compact, nonthermal radio source associated with the Vela pulsar but displaced from it by about 0.7°. { 've̅·lə 'eks }

Vela X-1   A pulsing, eclipsing x-ray source in the constellation Vela that is a particularly intense emitter of hard x-rays. { 've̅·lə ,eks'wən }

Vela X-2   The pulsed x-ray emission associated with the Vela pulsar. { 've̅·lə ,eks'tü }

velocity curve   A graphical representation of the line-of-sight velocity (versus time) of a star or components of a spectroscopic binary system. { və'läs·əd·ē ,kərv }

velocity-distance relation   The relation wherein all the exterior galaxies are moving away from the galaxy that the sun is part of, with velocities that are greater with increasing distance of the galaxy. { və'läs·əd·ē 'dis·təns ri,lā·shən }

velocity-of-light cylinder   A cylinder whose axis is the axis of rotation of a neutron star and whose radius is such that the velocity of a plasma rotating with the neutron star would equal the velocity of light at the surface of the cylinder. Also known as light cylinder. { vəˈläs·əd·ē əv ˈlīt 'sil·ən·dər }

velocity-of-light radius   The radius of the velocity-of-light cylinder. Also known as light radius. { vəˈläs·əd·ē əv ˈlīt 'rād·ē·əs }

Venus   The planet second in distance from the sun; the linear diameter, about 7500 miles (12,200 kilometers), includes the top of a cloud layer; the diameter of the solid globe is about 30 miles (50 kilometers) less; the mass is about 0.815 (earth = 1). { 've̅·nəs }

Venus probe   A probe for exploring and reporting on conditions on or about the planet Venus, such as Pioneer and Mariner probes of the United States, and Venera probes of the Soviet Union. { 've̅·nəs 'prōb }

vernal equinox   The sun's position on the celestial sphere about March 21; at this time the sun's path on the ecliptic crosses the celestial equator. Also known as first point of Aries; March equinox; spring equinox. { 'vərn·əl 'ē·kwə,näks }

vernier engine   A rocket engine of small thrust used primarily to obtain a fine adjustment in the velocity and trajectory of a rocket vehicle just after the thrust cutoff of the last sustainer engine, and used secondarily to add thrust to a booster or sustainer engine. Also known as vernier rocket. { 'vər·nē·ər 'en·jən }

vernier rocket   See vernier engine. { 'vər·nē·ər 'räk·ət }

vertex 1. The highest point that a celestial body attains. 2. On a great circle, that point that is closest to a pole. { 'vər,teks }

vertical circle A great circle of the celestial sphere, through the zenith and nadir of the celestial sphere; vertical circles are perpendicular to the horizon. { 'vərd·ə·kəl 'sər·kəl }

vertical gyro A two-degree-of-freedom gyro with provision for maintaining its spin axis vertical; output signals are produced by gimbal angular displacements which correspond to components of the angular displacements of the base about two orthogonal axes; used in aircraft to measure both bank angle and pitch attitude. { 'vərd·ə·kəl 'jī·rō }

vertical or short takeoff and landing aircraft See V/STOL aircraft. { 'vərd·ə·kəl òr ¦shòrt ¦tāk,òf and ¦land·iŋ 'er,kraft }

vertical separation A specified vertical distance measured in terms of space between aircraft in flight at different altitudes or flight levels. { 'vərd·ə·kəl ,sep·ə'rā·shən }

vertical speed indicator See rate-of-climb indicator. { 'vərd·ə·kəl ¦spēd ,in·də,kād·ər }

vertical tail A part of the tail assembly of an aircraft; consists of a fin (a symmetrical airfoil in line with the center line of the fuselage) fixed to the fuselage or body and a rudder which is movable by the pilot. { 'vərd·ə·kəl 'tāl }

vertical takeoff and landing A flight technique in which an aircraft rises directly into the air and settles vertically onto the ground. Abbreviated VTOL. { 'vərd·ə·kəl 'tāk,òf ən 'land·iŋ }

Vesta The third-largest asteroid with a diameter of about 300 miles (500 kilometers), mean distance from the sun of 2.362 astronomical units, and a unique surface composition resembling basaltic, achondritic meteorites. { 'ves·tə }

VFR See visual flight rules.

VFR between layers A flight condition wherein an aircraft is operated under modified visual flight rules while in flight between two layers of clouds or obscuring phenomena, each of which constitutes a ceiling. { ,vē,ef'är bi,twēn 'lā·ərz }

VFR on top A flight condition wherein an aircraft is operated under modified visual flight rules while in flight above a layer of clouds or an obscuring phenomenon sufficient to constitute a ceiling. { ,vē,ef'är òn 'täp }

VFR terminal minimums A set of operational weather limits at an airport, that is, the minimum conditions of ceiling and visibility under which visual flight rules may be used. { ,vē,ef'är 'tər·mən·əl 'min·ə·məmz }

violet layer A layer of particles in the upper Martian atmosphere that scatter and absorb electromagnetic radiation at shorter wavelengths, making the atmosphere opaque to blue, violet, and ultraviolet light. { 'vī·ə·lət ,lā·ər }

Virgo A constellation, right ascension 13 hours, declination 0°. Also known as Virgin. { 'vər·gō }

Virgo A A radio galaxy; it is associated with the galaxy M 87 (NGC 4486). { 'vər·gō 'ā }

Virgo cluster A cluster of galaxies which is the nearest to the galaxy that includes the

Virgo X-1

sun; the cluster is centered in the constellation Virgo and is about 1.6×10^7 light-years $(1.51 \times 10^{23}$ m) from earth. { 'vər·gō ˌkläs·tər }

Virgo X-1   An x-ray source that is identical with Virgo A. { 'vər·gō ˌeks'wən }

Virgo supercluster   See Local supercluster. { 'vər·gō 'sü·pərˌkläs·tər }

virial-theorem mass   The mass of a cluster of stars or galaxies calculated from the observed mean-square velocity of the objects and application of the virial theorem. { ˌvir·ē·əl 'thir·əm ˌmas }

visible horizon   That line where earth and sky appear to meet, and the projection of this line upon the celestial sphere. { 'viz·ə·bəl hə'rīz·ən }

visual binaries   Binary stars that to the naked eye seem to be single stars, but when viewed through the telescope, are separated into pairs. Also known as visual doubles. { 'vizh·ə·wəl 'bīˌner·ēz }

visual doubles   See visual binaries. { 'vizh·ə·wəl 'dəb·əlz }

visual flight   An aircraft flight occurring under conditions which allow navigation by visual reference to the earth's surface at a safe altitude and with sufficient horizontal visibility, and operating under visual flight rules. Also known as VFR flight. { 'vizh·ə·wəl 'flīt }

visual flight rules   A set of regulations set down by the U.S. Civil Aeronautics Board (in Civil Air Regulations) to govern the operational control of aircraft during visual flight. Abbreviated VFR. { 'vizh·ə·wəl 'flīt ˌrülz }

visual magnitude   A celestial body's magnitude as seen by the eye of the observer. { 'vizh·ə·wəl 'mag·nəˌtüd }

Vogt-Russell theorem   A theorem that states that if the pressure, opacity, and rate of energy generation in a star depend only on the local values of temperature, density, and chemical composition, then the star's structure is uniquely determined by its mass and chemical composition. Also known as Russell-Vogt theorem. { 'fōkt 'rəs·əl ˌthir·əm }

Volan   A southern constellation, right ascension 8 hours, declination 70°S. Also known as Flying Fish; Pisces Volan. { 'vōˌlan }

volcanic theory   A theory which holds that most features of the moon's surface were formed by volcanic eruptions, lava flows, and subsidences when lunar rocks were plastic. Also known as igneous theory; plutonic theory. { väl'kan·ik 'thē·ə·rē }

vortex generator   Any of the small, upright vanes that are attached to aircraft surfaces to inhibit boundary-layer separation and thereby reduce drag. { 'vȯrˌteks ˌjen·əˌrād·ər }

V/STOL aircraft   An aircraft that can take off vertically or by a short running. Abbreviation for vertical or short takeoff and landing. { 'vēˌstȯl ˌerˌkraft }

VTOL   See vertical takeoff and landing.

VTOL aircraft   A heavier-than-air craft that can take off and land vertically. Abbreviation for vertical takeoff and landing. { 'vēˌtȯl ˌerˌkraft }

Vulcan   A hypothetical planet that was supposed to have an orbit within the orbit of

Mercury; its existence was considered about 1859 and in the next few years, but it is generally considered by present-day astronomers to be nonexistent. { 'vəl·kən }

Vulpecula   A northern constellation, right ascension 20 hours, declination 25°N. Also known as Little Fox. { ˌvəl'pek·yə·lə }

VV Cephei stars   A class of long-period eclipsing binary stars, with M supergiant primaries, a blue (usually B) supergiant or giant secondaries, and small variations in light. { ˈvēˈvē 'sef·ē·ī ˌstärz }

W

waning moon   The moon between full and new when its visible part is decreasing. { 'wān·iŋ 'mün }

Warrior   *See* Orion. { 'wär·ē·ər }

wash   The stream of air or other fluid sent backward by a jet engine or a propeller. { wäsh }

Water Bearer   *See* Aquarius. { 'wȯd·ər 'ber·ər }

Water Monster   *See* Hydra. { 'wȯd·ər ‚män·stər }

Water Snake   *See* Hydrus. { 'wȯd·ər ‚snāk }

water tunnel   A device similar to a wind tunnel, but using water as the working fluid instead of air or other gas. { 'wȯd·ər ‚tən·əl }

waxing moon   The moon between new and full, when its visible part is increasing. { 'waks·iŋ 'mün }

weak-line T Tauri star   A T Tauri star that lacks strong emission lines in its optical spectrum, and lacks both strong stellar winds and a circumstellar accretion disk. Also known as naked T Tauri star; weak T Tauri star. { ¦wēk ‚līn ¦tē 'tȯr·ē ‚stär }

weak T Tauri star   *See* weak-line T Tauri star. { ¦wēk ¦tē 'tȯr·ē ‚stär }

weathercocking   The aerodynamic action causing alignment of the longitudinal axis of a rocket with the relative wind after launch. Also known as weather vaning. { 'weth·ər‚käk·iŋ }

weathercock stability   *See* directional stability. { 'weth·ər‚käk stə'bil·əd·ē }

weather vaning   *See* weathercocking. { 'weth·ər ‚vān·iŋ }

week   A time period of 7 days which has been accepted from ancient Babylon; the 7 days of the week were first given names of the seven celestial bodies: the sun, moon, and five visible planets. { wēk }

weight and balance sheet   A sheet which records the distribution of weight in an aircraft and shows the center of gravity of an aircraft at takeoff and landing. { ¦wat ən ¦bal·əns ‚shēt }

Weizsaecker's theory   A theory of the origin of the solar system; it hypothesizes primeval turbulent eddies which become permanent and self-gravitating; Weizsaecker does not discuss the origin of the gas clouds. { 'vīt‚sek·ərz ‚thē·ə·rē }

west point That point on the celestial sphere that is due west of observer; at this point the celestial equator crosses the horizon. { 'west 'póint }

wet emplacement A launch emplacement that provides a deluge of water for cooling the flame bucket, the rocket engines, and other equipment during the launch of a missile. { 'wet im'plās·mənt }

Whale See Cetus. { wāl }

Whirlpool galaxy A spiral galaxy of type Sc (open spiral structure), seen face on, in the constellation Canes Venatici. { 'wərl₁pül ₁gal·ik·sē }

white dwarf star An intrinsically faint star of very small radius and high density; the mass is about 0.6 that of the sun and the average radius is about 5000 miles (8000 kilometers); it is one final stage of stellar evolution with thermonuclear energy sources extinct. { 'wīt ¦dwȯrf 'stär }

whole range point The point vertically below an aircraft at the moment of impact of a bomb released from that aircraft, assuming that the aircraft's velocity has remained unchanged. { 'hōl 'rānj ₁póint }

Wilson-Bappu effect A linear relation between the absolute magnitudes of late-type stars and the width of the K_2 emission core in the resonance line of ionized calcium (CaII) at a wavelength of 3933 nanometers. { 'wil·sən 'bä·pü i₁fekt }

Wilson effect An effect in which the penumbra of a sunspot appears narrower in the direction toward the sun's center than in the direction toward the sun's limb. { 'wil·sən i₁fekt }

window An interval of time during which conditions are favorable for launching a spacecraft on a specific mission. { 'win·dō }

wind triangle A vector diagram showing the effect of the wind on the flight of an aircraft; it is composed of the wind direction and wind speed vector, the true heading and true airspeed vector, and the resultant track and ground speed vector. { 'wīn 'trī₁aŋ·gəl }

wind-tunnel balance A device or apparatus that measures the aerodynamic forces and moments acting upon a body tested in a wind tunnel. { 'win ₁tən·əl ₁bal·əns }

wing 1. A major airfoil. 2. An airfoil on the side of an airplane's fuselage or cockpit, paired off by one on the other side, the two providing the principal lift for the airplane. { wiŋ }

wing assembly An aeronautical structure designed to maintain a guided missile in stable flight; it consists of all panels, sections, fastening devices, chords, spars, plumbing accessories, and electrical components necessary for a complete wing assembly. { 'wiŋ ə₁sem·blē }

wing axis The locus of the aerodynamic centers of all the wing sections of an airplane. { 'wiŋ ₁ak·səs }

Winged Horse See Pegasus. { 'wiŋd 'hȯrs }

winglet A small, nearly vertical surface mounted at the tip of an aircraft wing to decrease drag resistance. { 'wiŋ·lət }

wing loading A measure of the load carried by an airplane wing per unit of wing area;

commonly used units are pounds per square foot and kilograms per square meter. { 'wiŋ ˌlōd·iŋ }

wing panel   That portion of a multipiece wing section that usually lies between the front and rear spars; it may be designed to include either the leading edge or the trailing edge as an integral part, but never both, and excludes control surfaces. { 'wiŋ ˌpan·əl }

wing profile   The outline of a wing section. { 'wiŋ ¦prō·fīl }

wing rib   A chordwise member of the wing structure of an airplane, used to give the wing section its form and to transmit the load from the fabric to the spars. { 'wiŋ ˌrib }

wing section   See airfoil profile. { 'wiŋ ˌsek·shən }

wing structure   In an aircraft, the combination of outside fairing panels that provide the aerodynamic lifting surfaces and the inside supporting members that transmit the lifting force to the fuselage; the primary load-carrying portion of a wing is a box beam (the prime box) made up usually of two or more vertical webs, plus a major portion of the upper and lower skins of the wing, which serve as chords of the beam. { 'wiŋ ˌstrək·chər }

wing-tip rake   The shape of the wing when the tip edge is straight in plan but not parallel to the plane of symmetry; the amount of rake is measured by the acute angle between the straight portion of the wing tip and the plane of symmetry; the rake is positive when the trailing edge is longer than the leading edge. { 'wiŋ ¦tip ˌrāk }

winter   The period from the winter solstice, about December 22, to the vernal equinox, about March 21; popularly and for most meteorological purposes, winter is taken to include December, January, and February in the Northern Hemisphere, and June, July, and August in the Southern Hemisphere. { 'win·tər }

winter solstice   1. The sun's position on the ecliptic (about December 22). Also known as first point of Capricorn. 2. The date (December 22) when the greatest southern declination of the sun occurs. { 'win·tər 'säl·stəs }

Wolf-Lundmark-Melotte galaxy   A dwarf irregular galaxy that is about 1.3 to 1.8 megaparsecs distant and is probably a member of the Local Group. { 'vȯlf 'lünd ˌmärk mə'lät ˌgal·ik·sē }

Wolf number   See relative sunspot number. { 'vȯlf ˌnəm·bər }

Wolf-Rayet nebula   A bright ring-shaped nebula that is radiatively ionized by a central Wolf-Rayet star. Also known as Wolf-Rayet ring. { ¦vȯlf rī¦ā ˌneb·yə·lə }

Wolf-Rayet ring   See Wolf-Rayet nebula. { ¦vȯlf rī¦ā ˌriŋ }

Wolf-Rayet star   A member of a class of very hot stars (100,000-35,000 K) which characteristically show broad bright emission lines in their spectra; luminosities are high, probably in the range 10^4-10^5 times that of the sun; these stars are probably very young and represent an early short-lived stage in stellar evolution. { ¦vȯlf rī¦ā ˌstär }

Wolf 359   A star of absolute magnitude 16.6; it is 7.7 light-years from the sun and is a variable flare star, which may emit bursts of light and even radio noise. { wu̇lf ¦thrē ¦fif·tē'nīn }

Wolf-Wolfer number   See relative sunspot number. { 'vȯlf 'vu̇l·fər ˌnəm·bər }

Workshop

Workshop *See* Sculptor. { 'wərk‚shäp }

world calendar A proposed calendar in which the present 12 months are retained but the days are divided into four equal quarters; January, April, July, and October begin on Sunday and have 31 days, the other months have 30 days, so that there are 364 days with the 365th day following December 30 in no month; leap-year days would follow June 30. { 'wərld 'kal·ən·dər }

Wright's phenomenon The phenomenon that the diameter of Mars appears greater when viewed from earth in ultraviolet light than when viewed in infrared light. { 'rīts fa‚nam·ə‚nän }

wrinkle ridge A prominent, well-defined, often sinuous ridge on a lunar mare, with gently sloping sides and a height of generally less than 500 feet (150 meters). { 'riŋ·kəl ‚rij }

W stars Stars of the W spectral class; their spectra contain an abundance of highly ionized elements such as He, C, N, and O, and they are intensely hot with surface temperatures of about 50,000 to 100,000 K. { 'dəb·əl·yü ‚stärz }

W Ursae Majoris stars Eclipsing variable stars whose brightness is continuously varying in periods of a few hours; they are composed of two close stars that have a common gaseous envelope. { ¦dəb·əl·yü 'ər‚sī mə'jör·əs ‚stärz }

W Virginis stars Periodic variable stars with periods of about 10 to 30 days; they exhibit two surges of activity from the same star so that there is a doubling of their spectral lines. Also known as type II Cepheids. { ¦dəb·əl·yü vər'jin·əs ‚stärz }

X

x-ray astronomy   The study of x-rays mainly from sources outside the solar system; it includes the study of novae and supernovae in the Milky Way Galaxy, together with extragalactic radio sources. { 'eks₁rā ə'strän·ə·mē }

x-ray background   Diffuse, almost isotropic x-radiation from beyond the solar system, believed to be the summed contribution of many unresolved sources. { 'eks ₁rā 'bak₁graund }

x-ray binary   An x-ray source that is a member of a binary system. { 'eks₁rā 'bī₁ner·ē }

x-ray burster   One of a class of celestial x-ray sources which produce bursts of x-rays in the 1-20-kiloelectronvolt range and which are characterized by rise times of less than a few seconds and decay times of a few seconds to a few minutes; the peak luminosity is of the order of 10^{38} ergs per second (10^{31} watts) and the sources have an average equivalent temperature of 10^8 K. { 'eks₁rā 'bər·stər }

x-ray cluster   A cluster of galaxies that is pervaded by a diffuse medium that emits x-rays. { 'eks₁rā ₁kləs·tər }

x-ray nebulae   The remnant of an ancient supernova that has been identified as a source of x-rays; an example is the Crab Nebula. { 'eks₁rā 'neb·yə₁lī }

x-ray nova   An x-ray source which appears suddenly in the sky, dramatically increases in intensity over a few days, and then decays away with a lifetime of several months. Also known as transient x-ray source. { 'eks₁rā 'nō·və }

x-ray star   A source of x-rays from outside the solar system; examples are the point x-ray sources Scorpius X-1, Cygnus X-2, and the Crab x-ray source. { 'eks₁rā ₁stär }

Y

Yarkovsky effect The effect of a small particle's rotation on its orbit about the sun, due to anisotropic reradiation. { yär′käf·skē i‚fekt }

yaw angle *See* angle of yaw. { ′yȯ ‚aŋ·gəl }

yaw damper A control system or device that reduces the yaw of an aircraft, guided missile, or the like. { ′yȯ ‚dam·pər }

yaw indicator A device that measures the angular direction of the airflow relative to the longitudinal vertical plane of the aircraft; this may be accomplished by a balanced vane or by a differential pressure sensor that aligns the detector to the airflow, and in so doing transmits the measured angle between the normal axis and the detector as the yaw angle. { ′yȯ ‚in·də‚kād·ər }

year Any of several units of time based on the revolution of the earth about the sun; the tropical year to which the calendar is adjusted is the period required for the sun's longitude to increase 360°; it is about 365.24220 mean solar days. Abbreviated yr. { yir }

Yerkes system *See* MK system. { ′yər·kēz ‚sis·təm }

ylem The primordial matter which according to the big bang theory existed just prior to the formation of the chemical elements. { ′ī·ləm }

yr *See* year.

Z

Z cam A representative type of variable star; it is eruptive with a cycle of about 10-600 days; magnitude ranges from 2 to 6. { 'zē ˌkam }

Z Camelopardalis stars A class of dwarf novae which exhibit unpredictable, and sometimes very protracted, pauses in the decline from maximum to minimum brightness. { 'zē kəˌmel·ə'pärd·əl·əs ˌstärz }

zenith That point of the celestial sphere vertically overhead. { 'zē·nəth }

zenithal hourly rate The number of meteors in a meteor shower which would be observed per hour if the radiant of the meteor shower were overhead and there were no moonlight. { 'zē·nə·thəl 'aúr·lē 'rāt }

zenith angle The angle between the direction to the zenith and the direction of a light ray. { 'zē·nəth ˌaŋ·gəl }

zenith distance Angular distance from the zenith; the arc of a vertical circle between the zenith and a point on the celestial sphere, measured from the zenith through 90°, for bodies above the horizon. Also known as co-altitude. { 'zē·nəth ˌdis·təns }

zenocentric coordinates Coordinates that indicate the position of a point on the surface of Jupiter, determined by the direction of a line joining the center of Jupiter to the point. { ˌzēn·əˈsen·trik kō'órd·ən·əts }

zenographic coordinates Coordinates that indicate the position of a point on the surface of Jupiter, determined by the direction of a line perpendicular to the mean surface at the point. { ˌzēn·əˈgraf·ik kō'órd·ən·əts }

zero-age main sequence The position on the Hertzsprung-Russell diagram of a star that has just reached the main sequence, when it has reached hydrostatic equilibrium and thermonuclear reactions have begun in its core, but these reactions have not had time to produce an appreciable change in composition. { 'zir·ō ¦āj 'mān 'sē·kwəns }

zero length In rocket launchers, zero length indicates that the launcher is designed to hold the rocket in position for launching but not to give it guidance. { 'zir·ō 'leŋkth }

zero-lift angle The angle of attack of an airfoil when its lift is zero. { 'zir·ō ¦lift 'aŋ·gəl }

zero-lift chord A chord taken through the trailing edge of an airfoil in the direction of the relative wind when the airfoil is at zero-lift angle of attack. { 'zir·ō ¦lift 'kórd }

ζ Aurigae star A binary system with a supergiant primary in spectral class K and a main-sequence secondary. { 'zād·ə 'ȯr·ə‚gē ‚stär }

ζ Geminorum stars A subgroup of classical Cepheid variable stars whose variation of magnitude with time for one complete cycle produces a quasi-bell-shaped curve. { 'zād·ə ‚jem·ə'nȯr·əm ‚stärz }

Zodiac A band of the sky extending 8° on each side of the ecliptic, within which the moon and principal planets remain. { 'zō·dē‚ak }

zodiacal constellations The constellations Aries, Taurus, Gemini, Cancer, Leo, Virgo, Libra, Scorpio, Sagittarius, Capricorn, Aquarius, and Pisces which are assigned to 12 equal portions of the zodiac. { zō'dī·ə·kəl ‚kän·stə'lā·shənz }

zodiacal counterglow *See* gegenschein. { zō'dī·ə·kəl 'kaůnt·ər‚glō }

zone meridian The meridian used for reckoning zone time; this is generally the nearest meridian whose longitude is exactly divisible by 15°. { 'zōn mə'rid·ē·ən }

zone noon Twelve o'clock zone time, or the instant the mean sun is over the upper branch of the zone meridian. { 'zōn 'nün }

zone of avoidance An irregularly shaped area in the Milky Way Galaxy in which no extragalactic nebulae are observed because of the presence of interstellar matter. { 'zōn əv ə'vȯid·əns }

zone time The local mean time of a reference or zone meridian whose time is kept throughout a designated zone; the zone meridian is usually the nearest meridian whose longitude is exactly divisible by 15°. { 'zōn 'tīm }

Z time *See* Greenwich mean time. { 'zē ‚tīm }

Zulu time *See* Greenwich mean time. { 'zü·lü ‚tīm }

Zurich number *See* relative sunspot number. { 'zůr·ik ‚nəm·bər }

Zwicky dark matter Matter of unknown nature that is postulated to exist outside the visible parts of galaxies or between galaxies in order to account for the radial velocity dispersion of galaxies in clusters. { ¦zwik·ē 'därk ‚mad·ər }

ZZ Ceti stars A small class of variable-luminosity white dwarfs with small amplitude oscillations having periods of 10-100 seconds and effective temperatures of 10,000-14,000 K (18,000-25,000°F). { ¦zē¦zē 'sed·ē ‚stärz }

Appendix

Equivalents of commonly used units for the U.S. Customary System and the metric system

1 inch = 2.5 centimeters (25 millimeters)
1 foot = 0.3 meter (30 centimeters)
1 yard = 0.9 meter
1 mile = 1.6 kilometers

1 centimeter = 0.4 inch
1 meter = 3.3 feet
1 meter = 1.1 yards
1 kilometer = 0.6 mile

1 inch = 0.08 foot
1 foot = 0.3 yard (12 inches)
1 yard = 3 feet (36 inches)
1 mile = 5280 feet (1760 yards)

1 acre = 0.4 hectare
1 acre = 4047 square meters

1 hectare = 2.47 acres
1 square meter = 0.0002 acre

1 gallon = 3.8 liters
1 fluid ounce = 29.6 milliliters
32 fluid ounces = 946.4 milliliters

1 liter = 0.26 gallon
1 milliliter = 0.03 fluid ounce
1 liter = 1.1 quarts (0.3 gallon)

1 quart = 0.25 gallon (32 ounces; 2 pints)
1 pint = 0.125 gallon (16 ounces)
1 gallon = 4 quarts (8 pints)

1 quart = 0.9 liter
1 ounce = 28.4 grams
1 pound = 0.5 kilogram
1 ton = 907.18 kilograms

750 milliliters = 25.36 fluid ounces
1 gram = 0.04 ounce
1 kilogram = 2.2 pounds
1 kilogram = 1.1×10^{-3} ton

1 ounce = 0.6 pound
1 pound = 16 ounces
1 ton = 2000 pounds

$°F = (1.8 \times °C) + 32$

$°C = (°F - 32) \div 1.8$

Appendix

Conversion factors for the U.S. Customary System, metric system, and International System

A. UNITS OF LENGTH

Units	cm	m	in	ft	yd	mi
1 cm	= 1	0.01*	0.39	0.033	0.01	6.21×10^{-6}
1 m	= 100.	1	39.37	3.28	1.09	6.21×10^{-4}
1 in	= 2.54	0.03	1	0.08...	0.03...	1.58×10^{-5}
1 ft	= 30.48	0.30	12.	1	0.33...	$1.89... \times 10^{-4}$
1 yd	= 91.44	0.91	36.	3.	1	$5.68... \times 10^{-4}$
1 mile	= 1.61×10^{5}	1.61×10^{3}	6.34×10^{4}	5280.	1760.	1

B. UNITS OF AREA

Units	cm²	m²	in²	ft²	yd²	mi²
1 cm²	= 1	10^{-4}	0.16	1.08×10^{-3}	1.20×10^{-4}	3.86×10^{-11}
1 m²	= 10^{4}	1	1550.00	10.76	1.30	3.86×10^{-7}
1 in²	= 6.45	6.45×10^{-4}	1	$6.94 \times 10^{-3}...$	7.72×10^{-4}	2.49×10^{-10}
1 ft²	= 929.03	0.09	1.44	1	0.11...	3.59×10^{-8}
1 yd²	= 8361.27	0.84	1296.	9.	1	3.23×10^{-7}
1 mi²	= 2.59×10^{10}	2.59×10^{6}	4.01×10^{9}	2.79×10^{7}	3.10×10^{6}	1

C. UNITS OF VOLUME

Units	m³	cm³	liter	in³	ft³	qt	gal
1 m³	= 1	10^6	10^3	6.10×10^4	35.31	1.057×10^3	264.17
1 cm³	= 10^{-6}	1	10^{-3}	0.061	3.53×10^{-5}	1.057×10^{-3}	2.64×10^{-4}
1 liter	= 10^{-3}	1000.	1	61.02374	0.03531467	1.056688	0.26
1 in³	= 1.64×10^{-5}	16.39	0.02	1	5.79×10^{-4}	0.02	4.33×10^{-3}
1 ft³	= 2.83×10^{-2}	28316.85	28.32	1728.	1	2.99	7.48
1 qt	= 9.46×10^{-4}	946.35	0.95	57.75	0.03	1	0.25
1 gal (U.S.)	= 3.79×10^{-3}	3785.41	3.79	231.	0.13	4.	1

D. UNITS OF MASS

Units	g	kg	oz	lb	metric ton	ton
1 g	= 1	10^{-3}	0.04	2.20×10^{-3}	10^{-6}	1.10×10^{-6}
1 kg	= 1000.	1	35.27	2.20	10^{-3}	1.10×10^{-3}
1 oz (avdp)	= 28.35	0.028	1	0.06	2.83×10^{-5}	$5. \times 10^{-4}$
1 lb (avdp)	= 453.59	0.45	16.	1	4.54×10^{-4}	0.0005
1 metric ton	= 10^6	1000.	35273.96	2204.62	1	1.10
1 ton	= 907184.7	907.18	32000.	2000.	0.91	1

Appendix

Conversion factors for the U.S. Customary System, metric system, and International System (cont.)

E. UNITS OF DENSITY

Units	$g \cdot cm^{-3}$	$g \cdot L^{-1}, kg \cdot m^{-3}$	$oz \cdot in^{-3}$	$lb \cdot in^{-3}$	$lb \cdot ft^{-3}$	$lb \cdot gal^{-1}$
1 $g \cdot cm^{-3}$	$= 1$	1000.	0.58	0.036	62.43	8.35
1 $g \cdot L^{-1}, kg \cdot m^{-3}$	$= 10^{-3}$	1	5.78×10^{-4}	3.61×10^{-5}	0.06	8.35×10^{-3}
1 $oz \cdot in^{-3}$	$= 1.729994$	1730	1	0.06	108.	14.44
1 $lb \cdot in^{-3}$	$= 27.68$	27679.91	16.	1	1728.	231.
1 $lb \cdot ft^{-3}$	$= 0.02$	16.02	9.26×10^{-3}	5.79×10^{-4}	1	0.13
1 $lb \cdot gal^{-1}$	$= 0.12$	119.83	4.75×10^{-3}	4.33×10^{-3}	7.48	1

F. UNITS OF PRESSURE

Units	$Pa, N \cdot m^{-2}$	$dyn \cdot cm^{-2}$	bar	atm	$kg (wt) \cdot cm^{-2}$	mmHg (torr)	in Hg	$lb (wt) \cdot in^{-2}$
1 Pa, 1 $N \cdot m^{-2}$	$= 1$	10	10^{-5}	9.87×10^{-6}	1.02×10^{-5}	7.50×10^{-3}	2.95×10^{-4}	1.45×10^{-4}
1 $dyn \cdot cm^{-2}$	$= 0.1$	1	10^{-6}	9.87×10^{-7}	1.02×10^{-6}	7.50×10^{-4}	2.95×10^{-5}	1.45×10^{-5}
1 bar	$= 10^5$	10^6	1	0.99	1.02	750.06	29.53	14.50
1 atm	$= 101325.0$	1013250.	1.01	1	1.03	760.	29.92	14.70
1 $kg (wt) \cdot cm^{-2}$	$= 98066.5$	980665.	0.98	0.97	1	735.56	28.96	14.22
1 mmHg (torr)	$= 133.32$	1333.22	1.33×10^{-3}	1.32×10^{-3}	1.36×10^{-3}	1	0.04	0.02
1 in Hg	$= 3386.39$	33863.88	0.03	0.03	0.03	25.4	1	0.49
1 $lb (wt) \cdot in^{-2}$	$= 6894.76$	68947.57	0.07	0.07	0.07	51.71	2.04	1

G. UNITS OF ENERGY

Units	g mass	J	int J	cal	cal_{IT}	Btu_{IT}	kWh	hp h	ft-lb (wt)	cu ft-lb (wt) in²	liter-atm
1 g mass	$=1$	8.99×10^{13}	8.99×10^{13}	2.15×10^{13}	2.15×10^{13}	8.52×10^{10}	2.50×10^{7}	3.35×10^{7}	6.63×10^{13}	4.60×10^{11}	8.87×10^{11}
1 J	$=1.11 \times 10^{-14}$	1	1.00	0.24	0.24	9.48×10^{-4}	$2.78... \times 10^{-7}$	3.73×10^{-7}	0.74	5.12×10^{-3}	9.87×10^{-3}
1 int J	$=1.11 \times 10^{-14}$	1.00	1	0.24	0.24	9.48×10^{-4}	2.78×10^{-7}	3.73×10^{-7}	0.74	5.12×10^{-3}	9.87×10^{-3}
1 cal	$=4.66 \times 10^{-14}$	4.18	4.18	1	1.00	3.97×10^{-3}	$1.16... \times 10^{-6}$	1.56×10^{-6}	3.09	2.14×10^{-2}	0.04
1 cal_{IT}	$=4.66 \times 10^{-14}$	4.19	4.19	1.00	1	3.97×10^{-3}	1.16×10^{-6}	1.56×10^{-6}	3.09	2.14×10^{-2}	0.04
1 Btu_{IT}	$=1.17 \times 10^{-11}$	1055.06	1054.88	252.16	252	1	2.93×10^{-4}	3.93×10^{-4}	778.17	5.40	10.41
1 kWh	$=4.01 \times 10^{-8}$	3600000.	3599406.	860420.7	859845.2	3412.14	1	1.34	2655224.	18439.06	35529.24
1 hp h	$=2.99 \times 10^{-8}$	2684519.	2684077.	641615.6	641186.5	2544.33	0.75	1	1980000.	13750.	26494.15
1 ft-lb (wt)	$=1.51 \times 10^{-14}$	1.36	1.36	0.32	0.32	1.29×10^{-3}	3.77×10^{-7}	$5.05... \times 10^{-7}$	1	$6.94... \times 10^{-3}$	0.01
1 cu ft-lb (wt) in²	$=2.17 \times 10^{-12}$	195.24	195.21	46.66	46.63	0.19	5.42×10^{-5}	$7.27... \times 10^{-5}$	144.	1	1.93
1 liter-atm	$=1.13 \times 10^{-12}$	101.33	101.31	24.22	24.20	0.10	2.81×10^{-5}	3.77×10^{-5}	74.73	0.52	1

Appendix

Total solar eclipses, 1991–2013*

Date	Maximum duration of totality	Location
July 11, 1991	6 m 54 s	Hawaii, Mexico, Central America, South America
June 30, 1992	5 m 20 s	Uruguay, Atlantic Ocean
Nov. 3, 1994	4 m 24 s	South America, South Atlantic Ocean
Oct. 24, 1995	2 m 10 s	India, southeastern Asia, Borneo, Pacific Ocean
Mar. 9, 1997	2 m 50 s	Siberia
Feb. 26, 1998	4 m 08 s	Pacific Ocean, north of South America, Caribbean islands, Atlantic Ocean
Aug. 11, 1999	2 m 23 s	Atlantic Ocean, Europe, southwestern Asia, India
June 21, 2001	4 m 56 s	Atlantic Ocean, South Africa, Madagascar
Dec. 4, 2002	2 m 04 s	South Africa, Indian Ocean, Australia
Nov. 23, 2003	1 m 57 s	Antarctica
Apr. 8, 2005	0 m 42 s[†]	Pacific Ocean
Mar. 29, 2006	4 m 07 s	Atlantic Ocean, Africa, Turkey, Central Asia
Aug. 1, 2008	2 m 27 s	Northern Canada, Greenland, Siberia, China
July 22, 2009	6 m 40 s	India, China, Pacific Ocean
July 11, 2010	5 m 20 s	Pacific Ocean, south of South America
Nov. 13, 2012	4 m 02 s	Australia, Pacific Ocean
Nov. 3, 2013	1 m 40 s[†]	Atlantic Ocean, Africa

*Compiled by Jean Meeus.
[†]These eclipses are annular-total; that is, they are total only near the middle of their central line.

Lunar eclipses in the umbra, 1993–2013

Date	Magnitude	Date	Magnitude
June 4, 1993	1.56	May 4, 2004	1.31
Nov. 29, 1993	1.09	Oct. 28, 2004	1.31
May 25, 1994	0.25	Oct. 17, 2005	0.07
Apr. 15, 1995	0.12	Sept. 7, 2006	0.19
Apr. 4, 1996	1.38	Mar. 3, 2007	1.24
Sept. 27, 1996	1.24	Aug. 28, 2007	1.48
Mar. 24, 1997	0.92	Feb. 21, 2008	1.11
Sept. 16, 1997	1.20	Aug. 16, 2008	0.81
July 28, 1999	0.40	Dec. 31, 2009	0.08
Jan. 21, 2000	1.33	June 26, 2010	0.54
July 16, 2000	1.77	Dec. 21, 2010	1.26
Jan. 9, 2001	1.19	June 15, 2011	1.70
July 5, 2001	0.50	Dec. 10, 2011	1.11
May 16, 2003	1.13	June 4, 2012	0.37
Nov. 9, 2003	1.02	Apr. 25, 2013	0.02

Physical elements of the planets

Planet	Equatorial radius, r_e (Earth = 1)	mi	km	Ellipticity	Volume (Earth = 1)	Mass (Earth = 1)	Density, g/cm³	Escape velocity mi/s	km/s	Rotation period	Inclination of axis
Mercury	0.38	1515	2439	0.000	0.055	0.053	5.6	2.6	4.2	58.65d	2
Venus	0.95	3760	6051	0.000	0.87	0.815	5.2	6.4	10.3	243d	177.3
Earth	1.00	3963	6378	0.0034	1.00	1.000	5.52	7.0	11.2	23h56m22.7s	23.45
Mars	0.53	2110	3395	0.006	0.150	0.107	3.95	3.1	5.0	24h37m22.6s	23.98
Jupiter	11.21	44423	71492	0.064	1408.	317.93	1.33	37.0	59.5	9h50m30s	3.1
Saturn	9.45	37449	60268	0.098	844.	95.18	0.69	22.1	35.6	10h14m	26.73
Uranus	4.01	15882	25559	0.023	64.	14.53	1.20	13.2	21.2	17h54m	97.9
Neptune	3.89	15410	24800	0.020	59.	17.07	1.64	14.7	23.3	17h48m	29.6
Pluto	0.18	715	1150	?	0.006	0.002	2.0	0.7	1.1	6.39d	122.5

Elements of planetary orbits

Planet	Mean distance (semimajor axis) AU	10⁶ mi	10⁶ km	Sidereal period of revolution Years	Days	Synodic period, days	Mean velocity mi/s	km/s	Eccentricity	Inclination
Mercury	0.387	36.0	57.9	0.241	87.97	115.88	29.76	47.89	0.206	7°00'
Venus	0.723	67.2	108.2	0.615	224.70	583.92	21.77	35.03	0.007	3°24'
Earth	1.000	93.0	149.6	1.000	365.26		18.51	29.79	0.017	0°00'
Mars	1.524	141.7	227.9	1.881	686.98	779.94	14.99	24.13	0.093	1°51'
Jupiter	5.203	483.6	778.3	11.862	4332.71	398.88	8.12	13.06	0.048	1°18'
Saturn	9.539	886.7	1427.	29.458	10759.	378.09	5.99	9.64	0.056	2°30'
Uranus	19.19	1784.	2871.	84.014	30685.	369.66	4.23	6.81	0.046	0°46'
Neptune	30.06	2794.	4497.	164.79	60189.	367.49	3.37	5.43	0.010	1°46'
Pluto	39.53	3674.	5913.	248.5	90800.	366.73	2.95	4.74	0.248	17°09'

Appendix

Satellites of the planets

Satellite		Mean distance from center of planet		Sidereal period, days	Diameter	
		10^3 mi	10^3 km		mi	km
EARTH						
	Moon	238.9	384.4	27.322	2,160	3,470
MARS						
	Phobos	5.8	9.35	0.326	12 × 14 × 17	19 × 22 × 27
	Deimos	14.6	23.5	1.251	7 × 8 × 9	11 × 12 × 15
JUPITER						
XVI	Metis	80	128	0.294	~25	~40
XV	Adrastea	80	129	0.297	~16	~25
V	Amalthea	112	180	0.498	106	170
XIV	Thebe	138	222	0.674	~62	~100
I	Io	262	422	1.769	2,256	3,630
II	Europa	417	671	3.551	1,951	3,140
III	Garymede	665	1,070	7.155	3,269	5,260
IV	Callisto	1,171	1,885	16.689	2,983	4,800
XIII	Leda	6,903	11,110	240	~9	~15
VI	Himalia	7,127	11,470	251	115	185
X	Lysithea	7,276	11,710	260	~22	~35
VII	Elara	7,295	11,740	260	47	75
XII	Ananke	13,173	21,200	631	~19	~30
XI	Carme	13,888	22,350	692	~25	~40
VIII	Pasiphae	14,497	23,350	735	~31	~50
IX	Sinope	14,522	23,370	758	~22	~35
SATURN						
XVIII	Pan	83	134	0.576	12	20
XV	Atlas	85	137	0.601	19	30
XVI	Prometheus	86	139	0.613	62	100
XVII	Pandora	88	142	0.628	56	90
X	Janus	94	151	0.695	118	190
XI	Epimetheus	94	151	0.695	75	120
I	Mimas	116	187	0.942	242	390
II	Enceladus	148	238	1.370	311	500
III	Tethys	183	295	1.888	659	1,060
XIII	Telesto	183	295	1.888	16	25
XIV	Calypso	183	295	1.888	16	25
IV	Dione	235	378	2.737	696	1,120
XII	Electra	235	378	2.737	19	30
V	Rhea	327	526	4.517	951	1,530
VI	Titan	759	1,221	15.945	3,604	5,800
VII	Hyperion	920	1,481	21.276	186	300
VIII	Iapetus	2,213	3,561	79.331	907	1,460
IX	Phoebe	8,053	12,960	550.5	137	220

Satellites of the planets (cont.)

Satellite	Mean distance from center of planet 10^3 mi	10^3 km	Sidereal period, days	Diameter mi	km
URANUS					
Cordelia	30.9	49.7	0.34	25	40
Ophelia	33.4	53.8	0.38	31	50
Bianca	36.8	59.2	0.44	31	50
Cressida	38.4	61.8	0.46	37	60
Desdemona	39.0	62.7	0.48	37	60
Juliet	40.1	64.6	0.50	50	80
Portia	41.1	66.1	0.51	50	80
Rosalind	43.4	69.9	0.56	37	60
Belinda	46.8	75.3	0.63	37	60
Puck	53.5	86.0	0.76	106	170
Miranda	80.8	130	1.41	302	486
Ariel	119	191	2.52	721	1,160
Umbriel	165	266	4.14	739	1,190
Titania	271	436	8.71	1,000	1,610
Oberon	362	583	13.5	963	1,550
NEPTUNE					
Naiad	29.9	48.0	0.30	34 ± 10	54 ± 16
Thalassa	31.1	50.0	0.31	50 ± 10	80 ± 16
Despina	32.6	52.5	0.33	112 ± 12	180 ± 20
Galatea	38.5	62.0	0.43	93 ± 19	150 ± 30
Larissa	45.7	73.6	0.55	118 ± 12	190 ± 20
Proteus	73.1	117.6	1.12	249 ± 12	400 ± 20
Triton	220.5	354.8	5.88	$1,681 \pm 4$	$2,705 \pm 6$
Nereid	3,425.9	5,513.4	360.13	211 ± 31	340 ± 50
PLUTO					
Charon	12.2	19.6	6.387	735 ± 18	$1,185 \pm 28$

Appendix

Noteworthy asteroids

Size rank	Number and name		Spectral type	Diameter, mi (km)	Spin period, h	Orbital elements		
						a, AU	e	i, degrees
1	1	Ceres	G (C-like)	578 (930)	9.1	2.77	0.08	10.6
2	2	Pallas	B (C-like)	343 (552)	7.8	2.77	0.23	34.8
3	4	Vesta	Achondrite	324 (521)	5.3	2.36	0.09	7.1
4	10	Hygiea	C	260 (419)	17.5	3.14	0.12	3.8
5	704	Interamnia	F (C-like)	203 (327)	8.7	3.06	0.15	17.3
6	511	Davida	C	200 (322)	5.2	3.18	0.17	15.9
7	52	Europa	C	183 (295)	5.6	3.09	0.11	7.5
8	87	Sylvia	P	172 (277)	5.2	3.48	0.09	10.9
9	65	Cybele	P	167 (269)	6.1	3.43	0.11	3.6
10	15	Eunomia	S	161 (259)	6.1	2.64	0.19	11.8
11	16	Psyche	M	155 (249)	4.2	2.92	0.14	3.1
12	31	Euphrosyne	B (C-like)	154 (248)	5.5	3.15	0.23	26.3
13	451	Patientia	B (C-like)	153 (247)	9.7	3.06	0.07	15.2
14	3	Juno	S	150 (242)	7.2	2.67	0.25	13.0
15	324	Bamberga	C	149 (240)	29.4	2.68	0.34	11.2
16	13	Egeria	G (C-like)	139 (224)	7.0	2.58	0.09	16.5
17	45	Eugenia	F (C-like)	139 (223)	5.7	2.72	0.08	6.6
18	624	Hektor	D	186 × 93 (300 × 150)	6.9	5.15	0.03	18.3

19	532	Herculina	S	137 (220)	9.4	2.77	0.17	16.3
20	107	Camilla	C	137 (220)	4.9	3.49	0.07	10.0
21	423	Diotima	P?	135 (217)	4.6	3.07	0.03	11.2
22	121	Hermione	C	135 (217)	8.9	3.46	0.14	7.6
23	19	Fortuna	C	130 (210)	7.5	2.44	0.16	1.6
24	24	Themis	C	129 (207)	8.4	3.13	0.13	0.8
25	7	Iris	S	127 (204)	7.1	2.39	0.23	5.5
26	6	Hebe	S	126 (202)	7.3	2.42	0.20	14.8
27	702	Alauda	C	126 (202)	8.4	3.19	0.03	20.5
28	88	Thisbe	C	124 (200)	6.0	2.77	0.16	5.2

Other interesting asteroids

41	Daphne	C	116 (187)	6.0	2.77	0.27	15.8
44	Nysa	Aubrite?	42 (68)	6.4	2.42	0.15	3.7
165	Loreley	C	99 (160)	6.?	3.14	0.07	11.2
216	Kleopatra	M	87 (140)	5.4	2.79	0.25	13.2
243	Ida	S	20 (32)	4.6	2.86	0.04	1.1
250	Bettina	M	53 (86)	5.1	3.14	0.14	12.9
349	Dembowska	Achondrite?	90 (145)	4.7	2.93	0.09	8.3
433	Eros	Chon./S?	22 × 7	5.3	1.46	0.22	10.8
			(36 × 12)				
747	Winchester	P	116 (186)	9.4	3.00	0.34	18.2
951	Gaspra	S	7.6 (12)	7.0	2.21	0.17	4.1
1566	Icarus	Chon.?	1 (2)	2.3	1.08	0.83	22.9
1620	Geographos	S	1.3 (2.1)	5.2	1.24	0.33	13.3
4179	Toutatis	S	~2 (4)	Tumbling?	2.51	0.64	0.5

Major meteor showers

Shower	Duration	Approx. date of maximum	Approx. radiant coordinates, degrees		Meteoroid orbital speed		Strength*	Suggested parent body	Notes
			Right ascension	Declination	mi/s	km/s			
Quadrantids	Jan. 1–6	Jan. 3	230	+49	27	42	M	—	Sharp maximum
Lyrids	Apr. 20–23	Apr. 22	271	+34	30	48	M–W	1861 I	Good in 1982
π Puppids	Apr. 16–25	Apr. 23	110	−45	—	—	W–M	Grigg-Skjellerup	Highly variable
η Aquarids	Apr. 21 – May 12	May 4	336	−2	40	64	M	Halley	Second peak May 6
Arietids	May 29 –June 19	June 7	44	+23	24	39	S	—	Daytime shower
ζ Perseids	June 1–17	June 7	62	+23	18	29	S	—	Daytime shower
β Taurids	June 24 – July 6	June 29	86	+19	20	32	S	Encke	Daytime shower
S. δ Aquarids	July 21 – Aug. 25	July 30	333	−16	27	43	M	—	Primary radiant
S. ι Aquarids	July 15 – Aug. 25	Aug. 6	333	−15	19	31	W	—	Primary radiant
Perseids	July 23 – Aug. 23	Aug. 12	46	+57	37	60	S	1862 III	Best-known shower
Orionids	Oct. 2 – Nov. 7	Oct. 21	94	+16	41	66	M	Halley	Trains common
S. Taurids	Sept. 15 – Nov. 26	Nov. 3	50	+14	17	27	M	Encke	Known fireball producer
Leonids	Nov. 14–20	Nov. 17	152	+22	45	72	W–S	1866 I	Next peak due 1999?
Puppids-Velids	Nov. 27 – Jan.	Dec. 9	135	−48	—	—	M	2102 Tantalus?	Many radiants in region
Geminids	Dec. 4–16	Dec. 13	112	+32	23	36	S	3200 Phaethon	Many bright meteors

*Estimate of relative meteor hourly rate for visual observers: S = strong (sometimes above 30 per hour at peak); M = moderate (10 to 30 per hour at peak); W = weak (5 to 10 per hour at peak).

Minor meteor showers*

Shower	Duration	Approx. date of maximum	Approx. radiant coordinates, degrees		Meteoroid orbital speed		Suggested parent body	Notes
			Right ascension	Declination	mi/s	km/s		
Coma Berenicids	Dec. 12 – Jan. 23	Jan. 17	186	+20	40	65	1913 I	Uncertain radiant position
α Centaurids	Jan. 28 – Feb. 23	Feb. 8	209	−59	—	—	—	Colors in bright meteors
δ Leonids	Feb. 5 – Mar. 19	Feb. 26	159	+19	14	23	—	Slow, bright meteors
Virginids	Feb. 3 – Apr. 15	Mar. 13?	186	+00	21	35	—	Other radiants in region
δ Normids	Feb. 25 – Mar. 22	Mar. 14	245	−49	—	—	—	Sharp maximum
δ Pavonids	Mar. 11 – Apr. 16	Apr. 6	305	−63	—	—	Grigg-Mellish	Rich in bright meteors
σ Leonids	Mar. 21 – May 13	Apr. 17	195	−05	12	20	—	Slow, bright meteors
α Scorpids	Apr. 11 – May 12	May 3	240	−22	21	35	—	Other radiants in region
τ Herculids	May 19 – June 14	June 3	228	+39	9	15	—	Very slow meteors
Ophiuchids	May 19 – July	June 10	270	−23	—	—	—	One of many in region
Corvids	June 25–30	June 26	192	−19	6	11	—	Very low speed
June Draconids	June 5 – July 19?	June 28	219	+49	8	14	Pons-Winnecke	Maximum only 1916
Capricornids	July – Aug.	July 8	311	−15	—	—	—	May be multiple
Picis-Australids	July 15 – Aug. 20	July 31	340	−30	—	—	—	Poorly known
α Capricornids	July 15 – Aug. 25	Aug. 2	307	−10	14	23	—	Bright meteors
N. δ Aquarids	July 14 – Aug. 25	Aug. 12	327	−06	26	42	1948 n	Secondary radiant
κ Cygnids	Aug. 9 – Oct. 6	Aug. 18	286	+59	15	25	—	Bursts of activity
N. ι Aquarids	July 15 – Sept. 20	Aug. 20	327	−06	19	31	—	Secondary radiant
S. Piscids	Aug. 31 – Nov. 2	Sept. 20	6	+00	16	26	—	Primary radiant
Andromedids	Sept. 25 – Nov. 12	Oct. 3	20	+34	11	18	—	"Annual" version
October Draconids	Oct. 10	Oct. 10	262	+54	14	23	Giacobini-Zinner	Can be spectacular
N. Piscids	Sept. 25 – Oct. 19	Oct. 12	26	+14	18	29	—	Secondary radiant
Leo Minorids	Oct. 22–24	Oct. 24	162	+37	38	62	1739	Probable comet association
μ Pegasids	Oct. 29 – Nov. 12	Nov. 12	335	+21	7	11	1819 IV	Probable comet association
Andromedids	Nov. 25	Nov. 25	25	+44	10	17	Biela	Once only, 1885
Phoenicids	Dec. 5	Dec. 5	15	−50	—	—	—	Once only, 1956
Ursids	Dec. 17–24	Dec. 22	217	+76	20	33	—	Good in 1986

*Peak strength for visual observers usually less than 5 per hour.

Appendix

The constellations*

Latin name	Genitive	Abbreviation	English translation
Andromeda	Andromedae	And	Andromeda[†]
Antlia	Antliae	Ant	Pump
Apus	Apodis	Aps	Bird of Paradise
Aquarius	Aquarii	Aqr	Water Bearer
Aquila	Aquilae	Aqi	Eagle
Ara	Arae	Ara	Altar
Aries	Arietis	Ari	Ram
Auriga	Aurigae	Aur	Charioteer
Boötes	Boötis	Boo	Herdsman
Caelum	Caeli	Cae	Chisel
Camelopardalis	Camelopardalis	Cam	Giraffe
Cancer	Cancri	Cnc	Crab
Canes Venatici	Canum Venaticorum	CVn	Hunting Dogs
Canis Major	Canis Majoris	CMa	Big Dog
Canis Minor	Canis Minoris	CMi	Little Dog
Capricornus	Capricorni	Cap	Goat
Carina	Carinae	Car	Ship's Keel
Cassiopeia	Cassiopeiae	Cas	Cassiopeia[†]
Centaurus	Centauri	Cen	Centaur[†]
Cepheus	Cephei	Cep	Cepheus[†]
Cetus	Ceti	Cet	Whale
Chamaeleon	Chamaeleonis	Cha	Chameleon
Circinus	Circini	Cir	Compass
Columba	Columbae	Col	Dove
Coma Berenices	Comae Berenices	Com	Berenice's Hair[†]
Corona Australis	Coronae Australis	CrA	Southern Crown
Corona Borealis	Coronae Borealis	CrB	Northern Crown
Corvus	Corvi	Crv	Crow
Crater	Crateris	Crt	Cup
Crux	Crucis	Cru	Southern Cross
Cygnus	Cygni	Gyg	Swan
Delphinus	Delphini	Del	Dolphin
Dorado	Doradus	Dor	Swordfish
Draco	Draconis	Dra	Dragon
Equuleus	Equulei	Equ	Little Horse
Eridanus	Eridani	Eri	River Eridanus[†]
Fornax	Fornacis	For	Furnace
Gemini	Geminorum	Gem	Twins
Grus	Gruis	Gru	Crane
Hercules	Herculis	Her	Hercules[†]
Horologium	Horologii	Hor	Clock
Hydra	Hydrae	Hya	Hydra[†] (water monster)
Hydrus	Hydri	Hyi	Sea Serpent
Indus	Indi	Ind	Indian
Lacerta	Lacertae	Lac	Lizard
Leo	Leonis	Leo	Lion
Leo Minor	Leonis Minoris	LMi	Little Lion
Lepus	Leporis	Lep	Hare
Libra	Librae	Lib	Scales
Lupus	Lupi	Lup	Wolf
Lynx	Lyncis	Lyn	Lynx
Lyra	Lyrae	Lyr	Harp

*After J. M. Pasachoff, *Contemporary Astronomy*, 4th ed., 1989.
†Proper names.

The constellations (cont.)*

Latin name	Genitive	Abbreviation	English translation
Mensa	Mensae	Men	Table (mountain)
Microscopium	Microscopii	Mic	Microscope
Monoceros	Monocerotis	Mon	Unicorn
Musca	Muscae	Mus	Fly
Norma	Normae	Nor	Level (square)
Octans	Octantis	Oct	Octant
Ophiuchus	Ophiuchi	Oph	Ophiuchus† (serpent bearer)
Orion	Orionis	Ori	Orion†
Pavo	Pavonis	Pav	Peacock
Pegasus	Pegasi	Peg	Pegasus† (winged horse)
Perseus	Persei	Per	Perseus†
Phoenix	Phoenicis	Phe	Phoenix
Pictor	Pictoris	Pic	Easel
Pisces	Piscium	Psc	Fish
Piscis Austrinus	Piscis Austrini	PsA	Southern Fish
Puppis	Puppis	Pup	Ship's Stern
Pyxis	Pyxidis	Pyx	Ship's Compass
Reticulum	Reticuli	Ret	Net
Sagitta	Sagittae	Sge	Arrow
Sagittarius	Sagittarii	Sgr	Archer
Scorpius	Scorpii	Sco	Scorpion
Sculptor	Sculptoris	Sci	Sculptor
Scutum	Scuti	Sct	Shield
Serpens	Serpentis	Ser	Serpent
Sextans	Sextantis	Sex	Sextant
Taurus	Tauri	Tau	Bull
Telescopium	Telescopii	Tel	Telescope
Triangulum	Trianguli	Tri	Triangle
Triangulum Australe	Trianguli Australis	TrA	Southern Triangle
Tucana	Tucanae	Tuc	Toucan
Ursa Major	Ursae Majoris	UMa	Big Bear
Ursa Minor	Ursae Minoris	UMi	Little Bear
Vela	Velorum	Vel	Ship's Sails
Virgo	Virginis	Vir	Virgin
Volans	Volantis	Vol	Flying Fish
Vulpecula	Vulpeculae	Vul	Little Fox

*After J. M. Pasachoff, *Contemporary Astronomy*, 4th ed., 1989.
†Proper names.

The 26 nearest stars

Name	Parallax, seconds of arc	Distance. light-years	Annual proper motion, seconds of arc	Radial velocity, km/s (mi/s)	Transverse velocity, km/s (mi/s)	Apparent magnitude and spectrum	Absolute magnitude*
Sun						−26.7 G2	+ 4.8
α Centauri	.760	4.3	3.68	−25 (−16)	23 (14)	+ 0.3 G2(1.7 K5)	4.7(6.1)
Barnard's star	.545	6.0	10.30	−108 (−67)	90 (56)	9.5 M5	13.2
Wolf 359	.421	7.7	4.84	+13 (+8)	54 (34)	13.5 M6e, v	16.6
Luyten 726−8	.410	7.9	3.35	+29 (+18)	38 (24)	12.5 M6e(13.0 M6e)v	15.6(16.1)
Lalande 21185	.398	8.2	4.78	−86 (−53)	57 (35)	7.5 M2	10.5
Sirius	.375	8.7	1.32	−8 (−5)	16 (10)	− 1.5 A0(8.7 DA)	1.4(11.6)
Ross 154	.351	9.3	0.67	−4 (−2)	9 (6)	10.6 M5e	13.3
Ross 248	.316	10.3	1.58	−81 (−50)	23 (14)	12.2 M6e	14.7
ε Eri	.303	10.8	0.97	+15 (+9)	15 (9)	3.8 K2	6.2
Ross 128	.298	10.9	1.40	−13 (−8)	22 (14)	11.1 M5	13.5
61 Cyg	.293	11.1	5.22	−64 (−40)	84 (52)	5.6 K6(6.3 M0)	7.9(8.6)
Luyten 789−6	.292	11.2	3.27	−60 (−37)	53 (33)	12.2 M6	14.5
Procyon	.288	11.3	1.25	−3 (−2)	20 (12)	0.5 F5(10.8 DA?)	2.8(13.1)
ε Indi	.285	11.4	4.67	−40 (−25)	77 (48)	4.7 K5	7.0
Σ 2398	.280	11.6	2.29	+1 (+1)	38 (24)	8.9 M4(9.7 M4)	11.1(11.9)
Groombr. 34	.278	11.7	2.91	+14 (+9)	49 (30)	8.1 M2e(10.9 M4e), v	10.3(13.1)
τ Cet	.275	11.8	1.92	−16 (−10)	33 (21)	3.6 G4	5.8
Lacaille 9352	.273	11.9	6.87	+10 (+6)	118 (73)	7.2 M2	9.4
+5° 1668	.263	12.4	3.73	+26 (+16)	67 (42)	9.8 M4	12.0
Lacaille 8760	.255	12.8	3.46	+23 (+14)	64 (40)	6.6 M1	8.6
Kapetyn's star	.251	13.0	8.79	+242 (+150)	166 (103)	9.2 M0	11.2
Ross 614	.251	13.1	0.97	+24 (+15)	18 (11)	11.1 M5e(14.8)	13.1(16.8)
Kruger 60	.249	13.1	0.87	−24 (−15)	16 (10)	9.9 M4(11.4 M5e)	11.9(13.4)
−12° 4523	.244	13.4	1.24	−13 (−8)	24 (15)	10.0 M5	11.9
vMa 2	.236	13.8	2.98	+70 (+43)	59 (37)	12.3 DG	14.2

*Parentheses indicate uncertain value.

The 26 brightest stars*

Star	Name	Spectrum	Absolute visual magnitude, M_v	Visual brightness, V	Color index, B–V	Remarks
Sun		G2 V	+4.8	−26.72	+0.65	
α CMa	Sirius	A1 V	+1.4	−1.43	0.00	
α Car	Canopus	F0 Ia	−4.5	−0.73	+0.15	Double
α Cen		G2 V	+4.7	−0.27	+0.66	
α Boo	Arcturus	K2 IIIp	−0.1	−0.06	+1.23	
α Lyr	Vega	A0 V	+0.5	+0.04	0.00	
α Aur	Capella	G0 IIIp	−0.6	+0.09	+0.80	Spectroscopic binary, double
β Ori	Rigel	B8 Ia	−7	+0.15	−0.04	Double
α CMi	Procyon	F5 IV-V	+2.7	+0.37	+0.41	
α Eri	Achernar	B3 V	−2	+0.53	−0.16	
β Cen		B0.5 V	−4	+0.66	−0.21	Double
α Ori	Betelgeuse	M2 Iab	−5	+0.7	+1.87	Variable
α Aql	Altair	A7 IV-V	+2.2	+0.80	+0.22	Variable, double
α Tau	Aldebaran	K5 III	−0.7	+0.85	+1.52	Double
α Cru		B0.5 V	−4	+0.87	−0.24	Double, variable
α Sco	Antares	M1 Ib	−3	+0.98	+1.80	Spectroscopic binary
α Vir	Spica	B1 V	−3	+1.00	−0.23	
α PsA	Fomalhaut	A3 V	+1.9	+1.16	+0.09	
β Gem	Pollux	K0 III	+1.0	+1.16	+1.01	
α Cyg	Deneb	A2 Ia	−7	+1.26	+0.09	
β Cru		B0.5 IV	−4	+1.31	−0.23	
α Leo	Regulus	B7 V	−0.7	+1.36	−0.11	Double
ε CMa	Adhara	B2 II	−5	+1.49	−0.17	
α Gem	Castor	A0	+0.9	+1.59	+0.05	Double, spectroscopic binary
λ Sco	Shaula	B2 IV	−3	+1.62	−0.23	
γ Ori	Bellatrix	B2 III	−4	+1.64	−0.23	

*Colors and magnitudes are photoelectric, V being the equivalent of a visual brightness and B–V a blue minus visual color index. The absolute visual magnitudes M_v are based on measured parallaxes; when only one significant figure is given, however, they are only estimates.

Appendix

		Distance,	Solar
Name	Type	10^6 light-years	luminosities

Members of the Local Group of galaxies, ordered from brightest to faintest

Name	Type	Distance, 10^6 light-years	Solar luminosities
1. M31 = Andromeda	Spiral	2.5	3×10^{10}
2. Milky Way Galaxy	Spiral	—	2×10^{10}
3. M33 = Triangulum	Spiral	2.7	6×10^{9}
4. Large Magellanic Cloud	Irregular	0.16	3×10^{9}
5. Small Magellanic Cloud	Irregular	0.19	7×10^{8}
6. IC 10	Irregular	2.	5×10^{8}
7. NGC 3109*	Irregular	4.1	3×10^{8}
8. NGC 205	Elliptical	2.5	3×10^{8}
9. M32	Elliptical	2.5	2×10^{8}
10. NGC 6822	Irregular	1.7	2×10^{8}
11. WLM	Irregular	3.1	2×10^{8}
12. NGC 404*	Elliptical	8.	2×10^{8}
13. NGC 185	Elliptical	2.1	2×10^{8}
14. Leo A*	Irregular	7.	2×10^{8}
15. NGC 147	Elliptical	2.0	1×10^{8}
16. IC 5152	Irregular	3.	1×10^{8}
17. IC 1613	Irregular	2.5	1×10^{8}
18. Pegasus*	Irregular	6.	1×10^{7}
19. Sextans A*	Dwarf irregular	4.	8×10^{7}
20. Sextans B*	Dwarf irregular	4.	5×10^{7}
21. DDO 210	Dwarf irregular	2.	3×10^{7}
22. 1001-27*	Dwarf irregular	4.	1×10^{7}
23. Fomax	Dwarf spheroidal	0.46	7×10^{6}
24. DDO 187*	Dwarf irregular	7.	7×10^{6}
25. DDO 155 = GR8*	Dwarf irregular	5.	4×10^{6}
26. Sculptor	Dwarf spheroidal	0.27	4×10^{6}
27. Andromeda III	Dwarf spheroidal	2.3	3×10^{6}
28. Andromeda I	Dwarf spheroidal	2.	2×10^{6}
29. Andromeda II	Dwarf spheroidal	1.9	2×10^{6}
30. SAGDIG	Dwarf irregular	2.	2×10^{6}
31. Phoenix	Dwarf irregular	1.4	2×10^{6}
32. Leo I	Dwarf spheroidal	0.88	1×10^{6}
33. Leo II	Dwarf spheroidal	0.75	8×10^{5}
34. Tucana	Dwarf irregular	3.	6×10^{5}
35. Andromeda IV	Dwarf spheroidal	2.	6×10^{5}
36. LGS 3	Dwarf irregular	2.	5×10^{5}
37. Sextans	Dwarf spheroidal	0.27	5×10^{5}
38. Draco	Dwarf spheroidal	0.24	4×10^{5}
39. Ursa Minor	Dwarf spheroidal	0.21	3×10^{5}
40. Carina	Dwarf spheroidal	0.28	2×10^{5}
41. 1010-01	Dwarf spheroidal	?	
42. Capricornus	Dwarf spheroidal	?	

*Doubtful members.

Large optical telescopes

Some of the world's largest reflecting telescopes

Mirror diameter		Observatory	Year completed
Meters	Inches		
6.0	236	Special Astrophysical Observatory, Zelenchukskaya, Caucasus, Russia	1976
5.1	200	California Institute of Technology/Palomar Observatory, Palomar Mountain, California	1950
4.2	165	William Herschel Telescope, La Palma, Canary Islands	1987
4.0	158	Kitt Peak National Observatory, Arizona	1973
4.0	158	Cerro Tololo Inter-American Observatory, Chile	1976
3.9	153	Anglo-Australian Telescope, Siding Spring Observatory, Australia	1975
3.8	150	United Kingdom Infrared Telescope, Mauna Kea Observatory, Hawaii	1978
3.6	144	Canada-France-Hawaii Telescope, Mauna Kea Observatory, Hawaii	1979
3.6	142	Cerro La Silla European Southern Observatory, Chile	1976
3.6	141	New Technology Telescope, European Southern Observatory, Chile	1989
3.5	138	Calar Alto Observatory, Calar Alto, Spain	1984
3.5	138	Astrophysics Research Consortium, Apache Point, New Mexico	1993
3.5	138	Wisconsin-Indiana-Yale-NOAO (WIYN), Kitt Peak, Arizona	1994
3.2	126	NASA Infrared Telescope, Mauna Kea Observatory, Hawaii	1979
3.0	120	Lick Observatory, Mount Hamilton, California	1959
2.7	107	McDonald Observatory, Fort Davis, Texas	1968
2.6	102	Crimean Astrophysical Observatory, Ukraine	1960
2.6	102	Byurakan Observatory, Yerevan, Armenia	1976
2.56	101	Nordic Optical Telescope, La Palma, Canary Islands	1989
2.5	100	Mount Wilson and Las Campanas, Mount Wilson, California	1917
2.5	100	Cerro Las Campanas, Carnegie Southern Observatory, Chile	1976
2.5	96	Isaac Newton Telescope, La Palma, Canary Islands	1984
2.4	94	University of Michigan–Dartmouth College–Massachusetts Institute of Technology, Kitt Peak, Arizona	1986
2.4	94	Hubble Space Telescope, Low Earth orbit	1990
36 × 1.8	6 × 72	Keck Telescope, Mauna Kea, Hawaii	1993
6 × 1.8	6 × 71	Multi-Mirror Telescope, Mount Hopkins, Arizona	1979

Appendix

Large optical telescopes (cont.)

Mirror diameter		Observatory	Year completed
Meters	Inches		
		World's largest refracting telescopes	
1.02	40	Yerkes Observatory, Williams Bay, Wisconsin	1897
0.91	36	Lick Observatory, Mount Hamilton, California	1888
0.83	33	Observatoire de Paris, Meudon, France	1893
0.80	32	Astrophysikalisches Observatory, Potsdam, Germany	1899
0.76	30	Allegheny Observatory, Pittsburgh, Pennsylvania	1914

Largest Schmidt telescopes

Telescope or institution	Location	Diameter		Focal ratio	Date completed
		Corrector plate, in. (m)	Spherical mirror, in. (m)		
Karl Schwarzschild Observatory	Tautenberg, Germany	53 (1.3)*	79 (2.0)	f/2	1960
Oschin Telescope, Palomar Observatory	Palomar Mountain, California	48 (1.2)	72 (1.8)	f/2.5	1948, 1987
United Kingdom Schmidt, Anglo-Australian Observatory	Warrumbungle National Park, N.S.W., Australia	48 (1.2)	72 (1.8)	f/2.5	1973
Tokyo Astronomical Observatory	Kiso Mountains, Japan	41 (1.1)	60 (1.5)	f/3.1	1975
European Southern Observatory Schmidt	La Silla, Chile	39 (1.0)	64 (1.6)	f/3	1972

*Removable.

Large radio telescopes

Institution	Location	Size of reflector, ft (m)
Radio telescopes for meter and centimeter wavelengths		
Fully steerable paraboloids		
Max Planck Institut für Radioastronomie	Effelsberg, Germany	330 (100)
Nuffield Radio Astronomy Laboratory	Jodrell Bank, England	250 (76)
CSIRO	Parkes, N.S.W., Australia	211 (64)
Jet Propulsion Laboratory	Goldstone, California	211 (64)
Algonquin Radio Observatory	Lake Traverse, Ontario	152 (46)
National Radio Astronomy Observatory	Green Bank, West Virginia	142 (43)
California Institute of Technology	Big Pine, California	132 (40)
Haystack Observatory	Westford, Massachusetts	122 (37)
Crimean Astrophysical Observatory	Crimea	73 (22)
Limited-tracking transit telescopes		
Special Astrophysical Observatory	Crimea	33 × 6221 (10 × 1885)
Tata Institute	Ootacamund, India	99 × 1746 (30 × 529)
National Astronomy and Ionosphere Center	Arecibo, Puerto Rico	1007 (305)
Observatory of Paris	Nancy, France	132 × 660 (40 × 200)
Radio telescopes for millimeter wavelengths		
Nobeyama Radio Observatory*	Nobeyama, Japan	148 (45)
Institut de Radio Astronomie Millimetrique	Pico de Veleta, Spain	99 (30)
Onsala Observatory	Gothenburg, Sweden	66 (20)
University of Massachusetts	Amherst, Massachusetts	46 (14)
National Radio Astronomy Observatory	Kitt Peak, Arizona	40 (12)
California Institute of Technology†	Big Pine, California	33 (10)
University of Texas	Fort Davis, Texas	16 (5)
University of California‡	Hat Creek, California	13 (4)

*Also five-element millimeter-wave interferometer.
†Also three-element millimeter-wave interferometer.
‡Four-element millimeter-wave interferometer.

Appendix

Some telescopes for submillimeter astronomy

Name	Location	Elevation, ft (m)	Diameter, ft (m)
Kuiper Airborne Observatory (KAO)	Suborbital	45,000 (13,700)	3.0 (0.9)
Cologne 3-m Telescope	Gornergrat, near Zermatt, Switzerland	10,285 (3,135)	9.8 (3.0)
Caltech Submillimeter Observatory (CSO)	Mauna Kea, Hawaii	13,360 (4,072)	34.1 (10.4)
Swedish-ESO Submillimeter Telescope (SEST)	La Silla, Chile	7,850 (2,400)	49.2 (15.0)
James Clerk Maxwell Telescope (JCMT)	Mauna Kea, Hawaii	13,425 (4,092)	49.2 (15.0)
Max-Planck-Institute for Radioastronomie/ University of Arizona 10-m Submillimeter Telescope	Mount Graham, Arizona	10,466 (3,190)	32.8 (10.0)